HOW REVOLUTIONARY
WERE THE BOURGEOIS REVOLUTIONS?

Abridged

Francisco Goya, *What Courage!* from *The Disasters of War* (1810–1815)

HOW REVOLUTIONARY
WERE THE BOURGEOIS REVOLUTIONS?

Abridged

NEIL DAVIDSON

Haymarket Books
Chicago, Illinois

© 2017 Neil Davidson

Published in 2017 by Haymarket Books
PO Box 180165
Chicago, IL 60618
www.haymarketbooks.org
773-583-7884

ISBN: 978-1-60846-731-0

Trade distribution:
In the US, Consortium Book Sales and Distribution, www.cbsd.com
In Canada, Publishers Group Canada, www.pgcbooks.ca
In the UK, Turnaround Publisher Services, www.turnaround-uk.com
All other countries, Publishers Group Worldwide, www.pgw.com

Cover image of *La Liberté guidant le peuple*, 1830, by Eugène Delacroix.

Published with the generous support of Lannan Foundation and the Wallace Action Fund.

Printed in Canada with union labor.

Library of Congress cataloging-in-publication data is available.

10 9 8 7 6 5 4 3 2 1

RECYCLED
Paper made from
recycled material
FSC® C103567

CONTENTS

A Note on the Reproductions   vii

Preface to the Abridged 2017 Edition   xi

Preface to the 2012 Edition   xv

1. Between Two Social Revolutions   1

2. Preconditions for an Era of Bourgeois Revolution   21

3. Patterns of Consummation   90

Epilogue: Reflections in a Scottish Cemetery   147

Notes   173

Bibliography   193

Index   215

A NOTE ON THE REPRODUCTIONS

W hat image first comes to mind when we think about the bourgeois revolutions? Most commonly we think of France and the people in the act of insurgency; storming the Bastille, perhaps, or mounting a barricade on the streets of Paris. The painting that captures the latter image more effectively than any other is Eugene Delacroix's *Liberty Guiding the People* (1830–31), a detail from which is featured on the front cover. Eric Hobsbawm has written of "the romantic vision of revolution and the romantic style of being a revolutionary" that it embodies: "Here saturnine young men in beards and top hats, shirtsleeved workers, tribunes of the people in flowing locks under sombrero-like hats, surrounded by tricolors and Phrygian bonnets, re-create the Revolution of 1793—not the moderate one of 1789, but the glory of the Year II—raising its barricades in every city of the continent."[1] The original title of the painting was *The 28th July: Liberty Leading the People* and it refers to an actual event that took place on that date during the French revolution of 1830, namely the last attempt by insurgents to overcome the Swiss Guards at Pont d'Arcole. It is a mythical rendering: Liberty herself is shown both as a woman of the people she is guiding over the barricades and as the embodiment of a number of abstract revolutionary virtues: courage, audacity, leadership. Above all she is a representation of Marianne, since 1792 the symbol of the Great Revolution, the republic, and France itself. Could Liberty have been portrayed in any other way than as a half-mythical goddess? Certainly no other women are portrayed on the barricades, although we know that they participated in the revolution.[2] Of the four male figures Delacroix depicts in detail, only one is a bourgeois, identifiable by his top hat, waistcoat, and cravat—an armed participant to be sure, but a minority next to the sword- and musket-brandishing plebeians. Delacroix enshrined the heroic conception of the bourgeois revolution at precisely the moment when the process began to overlap with the formative stages of the working-class struggle. Are the revolutionary masses overspilling their barricade here also overstepping the boundaries of bourgeois order?[3] The people, after all, are charging toward the likely viewer of the

1830s; the bourgeois habituè of the gallery who would have contemplated the painting from the perspective of the forces of counterrevolution, which may explain its relative unpopularity when first exhibited. But this is not the only ambiguity. Liberty appears to be trampling on the people as much as leading them, which may be suggestive of Delacroix's own ambivalence toward the revolution.

If Delacroix's painting hints at one of the fracture lines of the bourgeois revolution, an earlier work, from the period of the first French Revolution of 1789–1815, portrays another, darker one. The illustration facing the title page is Francisco Goya's *What Courage!* The engraving was seventh in a sequence of eighty-five collectively known as *The Disasters of War*. The artist produced these in the years leading up to 1820, but they were only published for the first time in 1863, thirty-five years after his death. Like Liberty, his subject fights on a pile of corpses, but this is virtually the only point of comparison with Delacroix's work. Goya certainly depicts a woman; she is not a mythical figure, however, but a historical one called Agustina Zaragoza Domenech, known as Agustina of Aragon for her part in the defense of the regional capital of Zaragoza in 1808. Goya emphasizes not glory but tragedy. Unlike the Scottish painter David Wilkie's saccharine version of the same episode, *The Defence of Saragoça* (1828), Goya does not show us Agustina's face, which is turned toward the enemy, but her back; a solitary figure lighting the fuse of a cannon in a landscape made desolate by war. And who is the enemy? The irony, of course, is that she is defending the city against the French. At home, the Napoleonic armies were the mainstay of an imperial dictatorship; abroad, they imposed the bourgeois revolution from above on the point of their bayonets. But in Spain at least, they were welcomed only by a relatively wealthy, politically liberal minority of the population; the majority rose against the invaders and their local supporters under the banner of church and king. *The Disasters of War* shows other aspects of the people than those celebrated by Delacroix: ignorant, bestial, in thrall to superstition—the best that can be said is that the French had provoked them with atrocities even more savage than those committed in response. But this is not all they show. No genuinely popular rising—as this one was—can ever be entirely reactionary. *What Courage!* is not alone among *The Disasters of War* in portraying the heroism of the Spanish resistance; and most of the others also feature women— Agustina's anonymous sisters. But even the titles convey the ambiguity of Goya's position: *The Women Inspire Courage* proclaims one, *And They Are Like Wild Beasts* shudders another.[4]

Despite the very different national contexts from which they sprang, both Delacroix's painting and Goya's engravings are recognizably part of a common bourgeois culture, which in these decades approached the summit of its greatness, and which can still speak to us today. The greatness of bourgeois art did not cease at this point, of course, but it did cease to be directly expressive or representative of the bourgeois worldview. The emergence of the modernist avant-garde in the second half of the nineteenth century may be an inescapable corollary of the consolidation of the bourgeoisie as an actual rather than a potential ruling class, in that its conditions of existence are no longer possible to directly express or represent.[5] *Liberty Guiding the People* shows a climactic moment of a successful bourgeois revolution from below, whose self-image a sympathetic if somewhat ambivalent artist was able to encapsulate successfully in the immediate aftermath of victory. *What Courage!* depicts a similarly heroic moment, but one that involved the defeat of an unwanted bourgeois revolution from above and outside, captured by an artist torn between his national pride and his Enlightenment principles in a period of reaction during which they appeared to be irreconcilable.[6] Yet, despite what appears to be an almost polar opposition, the revolution of *Liberty Guiding the People* and the counterrevolution of *The Disasters of War* share one theme in common, which is suspicion of the bourgeoisie. In the case of the French, where a working class had begun to emerge as an independent social force, it is the beginning of a doubt about bourgeois intentions, the dawning realization that the rhetoric of national unity concealed irreconcilable class divisions. In the case of Spain, where the working class had barely begun the process of formation, it is an already firm conviction that the bourgeoisie not only had different economic interests from the popular majority—"A liberal is a man with a carriage," as the saying went—but was also prepared to advance them by betraying the nation to foreign invaders. In the former the bourgeoisie are regarded as being insufficiently opposed to the institution of monarchy; in the latter, of being insufficiently respectful of it. The ambivalence of the bourgeoisie toward the revolutions that bear its name and the contradictions of the bourgeoisie as a revolutionary class, which that relationship reveals, are themes that both these paintings explore in different ways: they are also the subject of this book.

Preface to the
Abridged 2017 Edition

The original edition of *How Revolutionary Were the Bourgeois Revolutions?* grew out of another book. In 2003, for the first time since it was established in 1969, the Isaac and Tamara Deutscher Memorial Prize Committee failed to agree on which contender for the prize should receive it. As a result it was jointly awarded to Benno Teschke for *The Myth of 1648* and to me for *Discovering the Scottish Revolution*. As my book was an attempt to establish the hitherto unidentified Scottish bourgeois revolution, it necessarily contained some general reflections on the nature of bourgeois revolutions. Nevertheless, these remarks were highly compressed and dispersed throughout the text to the sections where they seemed most relevant.[1] They lacked depth and focus compared with, for example, the extensive theoretical considerations that open two previous historical works to have been awarded the prize: Geoffrey de Ste. Croix's *The Class Struggle in the Ancient Greek World* (1981) and James Holstun's *Ehud's Dagger* (2000).[2] I would not necessarily have devoted further time to thinking about bourgeois revolutions except that the question of their existence was the one area where my book overlapped with Teschke's. Consequently, the subject provided us with a common theme for our presentations at the prize lecture—which was effectively a debate—on October 9, 2004. The editorial board of *Historical Materialism*, at whose conference the lecture took place, agreed to publish my contribution, even though its content ranged far wider than my remarks on the day and its excessive length required that it be spread over two issues.[3] Having begun to think in a more systematic way about the subject, I planned to develop the published lecture into a book, but competing priorities prevented me from doing anything serious toward this goal for several years. When Anthony Arnove contacted me in 2008 on behalf of Haymarket Books, having heard that I was engaged in writing such a work and offering to publish it, I immediately accepted with the usual overoptimistic promises about when the text was likely to be delivered. Several missed deadlines later, the book was finally published in 2012.

My original conception of the book involved a tripartite structure: a first section was to have traced the development of the theory of bourgeois revolution, including the emergence of the distinct theory of proletarian revolution, against the backdrop of the actual history that the different versions of these theories were intended to explain or influence; a second was to have synthesized this discussion to present a general theory of revolution; and a third was to have revisited the historical trajectory overviewed in part one, but now foregrounding the actual events themselves. In other words, this third section would have been the actual history of the bourgeois revolutions. In the end, this plan was simply impossible to achieve as a single project. I therefore narrowed—if that word does not seem too absurd in relation to a work of this size—to the first two sections, so that it became essentially an exercise in the history of ideas, in this case the idea of bourgeois revolution. That history is of course inseparable from the events during which the idea emerged. I try to show how social change enabled certain theoretical positions that had hitherto been literally "unthinkable" to emerge, and establish the mediations between historical process, direct experience, and theoretical production on a basis that can be defended. A detailed history of the bourgeois revolutions is no doubt still required; but it is not a prerequisite for understanding how they have been theorized.

The formidable challenge presented by the book's length led to requests to Haymarket Books from readers, or perhaps potential readers, for a shorter, more accessible version. This abridged version is not, however, simply a condensed version of the original book. Editing the entire text down by two thirds would only have been possible by excising most of the extensive quotations from the thinkers I discuss; but demonstrating that they held certain positions and not others required presenting what they had actually written. Rather than do this, I have instead extracted Part Four ("The Specificity of the Bourgeois Revolutions"), in which I attempt to present a synthesis based on the preceding historical discussion, but which does not depend on it. The reader is not required to know, for example, the extent to which Locke retreated from the positions earlier established by Harrington toward a cyclical theory of revolution in the 1680s, or the extent to which Lenin came to agree with Trotsky's version of the permanent revolution strategy in 1917, to understand the argument.

Leaving aside the introductory material, this abridgement therefore presents a general theory of revolution, distinguishing first between political and social revolutions and then different types of social revolution ("feudal," bourgeois, and socialist), before establishing the preconditions for the era of bourgeois revolution and the outcomes that would allow us to say when both individual instances of bourgeois revolution and "the" bourgeois revolution as a whole had been consummated. Chapter 1 establishes the structural relationship between revolution, class struggle, and the transition from one mode of production to another. Chapter 2 situates bourgeois revolutions within this general framework, and chapter 3 concludes the discussion with an interpretive essay on the history of the bourgeois revolution, both as a series of national transformations and as a cumulative global process. In an epilogue, I take two monuments situated in Edinburgh and inspired by important moments in the overall history of the bourgeois revolution as the starting point for some concluding reflections on its meaning today.

It might be helpful here to briefly set out my conception of the bourgeois revolution (discussed in chapter 19 of the original book). This is usually referred to as a "consequentialist" one. I make no claims for originality in this respect: the concept, if not the actual term, can be found in the work of several classical Marxists, above all Engels, Lenin, Lukács, and Gramsci, and in that of later Marxists, notably Isaac Deutscher, Christopher Hill, Geoff Ely, and Alex Callinicos. The term *consequentialism* was originally one associated with moral philosophy and for that reason not perhaps the happiest to use in this context, although it flows more readily off the tongue than *outcome-ism*, which might nevertheless be more exact. In any event, and as both words suggest, it means that individual bourgeois revolutions, early or late, can be identified, not by the structural forms that they took, nor by the social forces that brought them about, but by their consequences, their outcomes. Decisive among these consequences is the transformation of the state into one that—depending on where in the overall cycle a particular bourgeois revolution took place—either initiates or consolidates the period of capitalist dominance. This definition does not commit us to a position that holds that the bourgeoisie has *never* been a revolutionary class; only that they are not required to be for the theory of bourgeois revolution to be coherent. In fact, I am concerned to defend the historical role of the bourgeoisie where it has been revolutionary, against claims by revisionists of various sorts that it has never been so.

Finally, some sections from the original preface have been removed, although none relevant to the core argument.[4] The text is otherwise untouched except for the correction of factual errors, several of which were helpfully identified by my critics. I have responded to some of these critics in relation to their substantive objections and will respond to others in due course.[5] Any developments to my position will appear in new work, clearly identified as such, and not in surreptitious revisions. For the moment, however, I hope that this presentation of my core argument will provide readers with a useful entry point into the debate and provide some sense of how revolutionary the bourgeois revolutions were.

Neil Davidson
West Calder
West Lothian
Scotland
October 2016

PREFACE TO THE 2012 EDITION

I t should have come as no surprise that the years of neoliberal ascendancy saw Marxism attacked by the ideologues of a triumphalist bourgeoisie. What is surprising is that these attacks were often given theoretical support by Marxists themselves. Perhaps no other concept in historical materialism came under quite such sustained friendly fire as that of "bourgeois revolution," usually on the grounds that the version associated with Stalinism was the only one possible and that intellectual credibility therefore required it to be abandoned. Although the intention of these internal critics was to strengthen Marxism by discarding what they saw as an unnecessary and misleading foreign implantation, their arguments effectively converged with those of earlier anti-Marxists, who more accurately understood what was at stake: the integrity of historical materialism as a coherent intellectual tradition. The title of this book therefore reflects a widespread belief on the left that the bourgeois revolutions—or perhaps we should now describe them as the Events Formerly Known as the Bourgeois Revolutions—were far less significant than had previously been believed. To ask *how* revolutionary these revolutions were is therefore to ask *what type* of revolutions they were. In effect, the current consensus has downgraded them from social to political revolutions and it is precisely this reclassification that I want to challenge in what follows. Why? The relevance of this particular Marxist concept, which is concerned with historical events, may not be as immediately obvious as those dealing with, for example, economic crises, which, as we have recently been reminded, are still an inescapable feature of the contemporary world and will remain so as long as capitalism persists. Nevertheless, there are four major reasons why bourgeois revolutions should retain a claim to our attention.

First, this is not simply a question of history. Although it will no doubt astonish future generations, one of the persistent problems of the left for much of the twentieth century was an inability to distinguish between bourgeois and proletarian revolutions. The Third World revolutionary movements that followed the Second World War were rightly supported by most socialists on grounds of national self-determination. Doing so did not, however, have to involve claiming that the new regimes were socialist in any sense. How, for example, do we understand the social content of the Chinese Revolution of 1949? Was it a proletarian revolution that—although not involving any actual proletarians—led to the creation of a worker's state transitional to socialism? Or was it, as will be argued here, a modern form of bourgeois revolution that led to the formation of a state capitalist regime, whose managers have—without any counterrevolution taking place—now adopted one of the most extreme versions of neoliberalism? In other words, how one defines bourgeois revolution and capitalism impacts in fundamental ways how one defines proletarian revolution and socialism.

Second, if the theory of bourgeois revolution does illuminate the process by which capitalism in all its myriad forms came to dominate the world, certain political conclusions follow. Above all, the capitalist system, which its current beneficiaries present as having evolved peaceably by virtue of its congruence with human nature, was in fact imposed during centuries of revolutionary violence exercised by, or on behalf of, their predecessors. The political implications of this conclusion are twofold. On the one hand, it means that the claims that are regularly made about why revolutions should be avoided are clearly untrue. "If we ourselves are the product of a supremely successful revolution," writes Terry Eagleton, "then this in itself is an answer to the conservative charge that all revolutions end up failing, or reverting to how things were before, or making things a thousand times worse, or eating up their own children."[1] On the other hand, if the capitalist system did indeed come to dominate the world through revolution, this does rather raise the issue of why those who wish to see socialism replace it should not also avail themselves of the revolutionary option. The answer that supporters of capitalism usually give to this question is that it has created democracy, which renders any contemporary recourse to revolution illegitimate, except perhaps in regions where democracy is restricted or nonexistent. Neither point is defensible. If we take bourgeois democracy to involve, at a minimum, a representative government elected by the adult population, in which votes have equal weight and can be exercised without intimidation by the state, then it is a relatively recent development in the history of capitalism, long postdating the bourgeois revolutions in the West. Indeed, far from being intrinsic to bourgeois society, representative democracy has largely been introduced by pressure from the working class, often involving the threat of revolution, and extended by pressure from the oppressed.[2] Nor have capitalism and democracy been compatible since. As the author of one recent and by no means wholly critical study remarks, in unnecessarily tentative tones: "Capitalism's history suggests that democracy and capitalism might be decoupled because they generate values that are often in conflict."[3] If we review the counterreformist activities supported and in some cases initiated by the United States in the territories nearest to it, and restrict our considerations to elected leaders whose names start with the first letter of the alphabet, then the fates of Allende in Chile, Árbenz in Guatemala, and Aristide in Haiti should dispel any notion that democratic choices will be respected where they are contrary to the interests of capitalist power.

Third, regardless of whether we call them bourgeois revolutions or not, the meaning of the events previously described in this way will remain contested until, as Gracchus Babeuf put it in the context of the French Revolution, they are overtaken by another revolution, which is greater, more solemn, and final. In other words, unless the socialist revolution is successfully achieved, neither the French nor any other bourgeois revolution will ever be truly "over," but will always be open to rediscovery, reinterpretation—and misappropriation. The most obvious example of this is not France in relation to the revolution of 1789, but the United States in relation to the revolution of 1776. "People want to know what Thomas Jefferson would think of affirmative action, or how George Washington would regard the invasion of Iraq," writes historian Gordon Wood: "Americans seem to have a special need for these authentic historical figures in the here and now."[4] In the case of the Tea Party, the right-wing populist movement that emerged in 2009 in the wake of Barack Obama's election as president, the issue is not so much what Jefferson or Washington would have thought of contemporary events—since Tea Party supporters claim to know precisely what they would have thought—but rather the way in which the revolution is treated as an event outside of history, whose function is to provide the founding principles for an eternal struggle between "tyranny," understood as the activities of the state in relation to welfare and redistribution, and "liberty," understood as individual freedom from constraint, above all in relation to the accumulation of capital. In this respect, as Jill Lepore writes, "nothing trumps the Revolution." She continues, "From the start, the Tea Party's chief political asset was its name: the echo of the Revolution conferred upon a scattered, diffuse, and confused movement a degree of legitimacy and the appearance, almost, of coherence. Aside from the name and the costume, the Tea Party offered an analogy: rejecting the bailout is like dumping the tea; health care reform is like the Tea Act; our struggle is like theirs."[5]

The Tea Party attempt to claim the American Revolution is, in short, a perfect example of what Walter Benjamin warned against in 1940: "The only historian capable of fanning the spark of hope in the past is the one who is firmly convinced that *even the dead* will not be safe from the enemy if he is victorious. And this enemy has never ceased to be victorious."[6] This notoriously cryptic passage can be interpreted in several ways, but what Benjamin seems to mean is something close to the party slogan George Orwell has O'Brien make Winston Smith repeat in *Nineteen Eighty-Four*: "Who controls the past controls the future: who controls the present controls the past."[7] The past can be changed to suit the needs of the ruling class and only the victory of socialism will ensure that it remains safe. Benjamin could not perhaps have imagined how the fallen patriots of Lexington and Concord would be called from their graves to justify the goals of the Tea Party—nor, for that matter, could he have foreseen how the struggle to separate church and state in postrevolutionary France would today be turned into a justification for oppressing female Muslims by denying them the right to wear the hijab or burka. But the project of claiming particular figures or moments from the historical past for contemporary politics is neither new, nor confined to the United States, nor yet exclusive to the right. Indeed, right-wing appropriation of the American case is possible only because—as I argue in chapter 4—it was the least decisive and most ambiguous of all those generally thought to comprise the "classical" bourgeois revolutions. In relation to the Dutch, English, and French cases, it is the liberal and socialist left that has been the most active in identifying continuities between themselves and participants in these revolutions. The problem here is that the project of "fanning the spark of hope in the past" is not served by the left simply engaging in the same type of distortions as the right but from the opposite perspective. In most respects the revolutionaries of 1776 are as distant from modern socialists in their beliefs, aims, and values as they are from Sarah Palin and her supporters. The bourgeois revolutions are of historical importance regardless of whether individual episodes and participants constitute part of the socialist tradition or not.

Fourth, despite their opposition to Marxist conceptions of the bourgeois revolutions as historical phenomena, bourgeois commentators have recently begun to use their own interpretation of the term. There is what can be called a weak version of the bourgeois revolution thesis associated with developmental economics, which focus on what Daron Acemoglu and James Robinson call "inclusive political revolutions," starting with the English Revolution of 1688:

> The Glorious Revolution was a radical change, and it led to what perhaps turned out to be the most important political revolution of the past two millennia. The French Revolution was even more radical, with its chaos and excessive violence and the ascent of Napoleon Bonaparte, but it did not re-create the *ancien régime*. Three factors greatly facilitated the emergence of more inclusive political institutions following the Glorious Revolution and the French Revolution. The first was new merchants and businessmen wishing to unleash the power of creative destruction from which they themselves would benefit; these new men were among the key members of the revolutionary coalitions and did not wish to see the development of yet another set of extractive institutions that would again prey on them. . . . The second was the nature of the broad coalition that had formed in both cases. . . . The third factor relates to the history of English and French political intuitions. They created a background against which new, more inclusive regimes could develop.[8]

For these authors, without the involvement of actual capitalists, the construction of coalitions, and the preexistence of institutions, the capacity of any revolution to make fundamental change is in doubt:

> History . . . is littered with examples of reform movements that succumbed to the iron law of oligarchy and replaced one set of extractive institutions with even more pernicious ones. . . . England in 1688, France in 1789, and Japan during the Meiji Restoration of 1868 started the process of forging inclusive political institutions with a political revolution. But such political revolutions generally create much destruction

and hardship, and their success is far from certain. The Bolshevik revolution advertised its aim as replacing the exploitative system of tsarist Russia with a more just and efficient one that would bring freedom and prosperity to millions of Russians. Alas, the outcome was the opposite, and much more repressive and extractive institutions replaced those the Bolsheviks overthrew.[9]

More commonly, however, the *only* type of social revolutions that bourgeois ideology recognized before 1989 were the so-called communist revolutions, since these supposedly involved a break with the evolutionary development of capitalism and the imposition of a different type of economy. Following the Eastern European revolutions of that year an additional type was identified: those that undid the original revolutions and allowed the economies to revert to capitalism. It was in the context of these events that the bourgeoisie reappropriated both the concept of bourgeois revolution and its link with capitalism, but in a way opposed to any Marxist conception. There were precursors to this semantic shift before 1989, notably in Britain among the supporters of Margaret Thatcher. One of her court historians, Norman Stone, wrote in 1988:

> Why were the English unique? According to Alan Macfarlane, the best writer on these matters, they were exceptional even in Anglo-Saxon times. . . . Other viewers disagree, claiming that the English difference really occurred in the mid-17th century when there was "a bourgeois revolution." If this is true, then most of continental Europe did not experience this until a century later, with events such as the French revolution. But I am tempted to ask: what English bourgeois revolution? In many respects we have never had one. . . . England's institutions still get in the way of successful capitalism and enterprise, though there are many signs that this is now changing.

Stone assessed the actions of the Thatcher regime as "a start towards that bourgeois revolution that, in my opinion, never really occurred in this country and if Margaret Thatcher goes down in history as the natural complement of Oliver Cromwell—good." Stone was of course less concerned with "bourgeois revolution" as an assault on a feudal aristocracy, but on the socialist working class, or more precisely, the organized labor movement and the postwar welfare state—"measures of socialism" welded to "this semi-modernized feudal structure."[10] The concept of "bourgeois revolution" has therefore been reincorporated into the discourse of bourgeois ideology, but only by reversing the original meaning. For in this version the bourgeois revolution was not conducted against precapitalist fetters preventing the capitalist system from achieving full dominance, but against attempts to impose constraints on that system, whether these were effective trade unions, universal welfare provisions, and state ownership in the West, the supposedly "postcapitalist" alternative represented by the Stalinist regimes in the East, or radical nationalist regimes insufficiently subservient to the dominant imperialist powers in the Global South.

The eventual overthrow of the Stalinist regimes prompted more widespread use of the term "bourgeois revolution" and it has been used since to describe any movement for the removal of a regime to which Western powers are opposed, as in the cases of the so-called color revolutions in the former Soviet republics. One Ukrainian writer and intellectual, Olexander Invanets, was reported on the BBC as describing the demonstrations in Kiev during December 2004, which forced a rerun of the presidential elections, as "a Ukrainian bourgeois revolution."[11] And similar terminology has subsequently been applied in the Global South: the victory of the Thai People's Alliance for Democracy ("the yellow shirts") in forcing the resignation of Prime Minister Thaksin Shinawatra in 2006 was described as "the bourgeois revolution" of "the democracy-hating middle class."[12] However, *bourgeois revolution* has not only reentered the language of the bourgeois media as a description but also as a program. While cheerleading for the Gulf War of 2003, Christopher Hitchens claimed that the United States was waging a bourgeois revolution that would eventually encompass all of the Middle East. Whereas "in 1989 the communist world was convulsed by a revolution from below," the Iraqis would have to be rescued from their regime by a "revolution from above" delivered by "American intervention."[13] This is a theme to which Hitchens has repeatedly returned in his journalism: "What is happening in today's Iraq is something more like a social and political revolution than a military occupation. It's a revolution from above, but in some ways no less radical for that."[14] He takes the example of US involvement in Germany after the Second World War as his model, arguing that this, rather than the more limited changes imposed on Japan, "would be more like a revolution from above or what colonial idealists used to call 'the civilizing mission': everything from the education system to the roads."[15] Hitchens has the audacity to invoke heroes of the revolution that created the United States of America to justify contemporary American imperialism: "That old radical Thomas Paine was forever at Jefferson's elbow, urging that the United States become a superpower for democracy."[16] And if the motives of the leaders of the contemporary United States are not entirely free of self-interest, neither were those of their revolutionary predecessors: "The Union under Lincoln wasn't wholeheartedly against slavery."[17] Finally, in an unparalleled feat of insolence, Hitchens summons up one of the greatest fighters for black liberation to support his case for the invasion of Iraq: "As Frederick Douglass once phrased it, those who want liberty without a fight are asking for the beauty of the ocean without the roar of the storm."[18] Douglass's remarks do of course have relevance for Afghanistan and Iraq, but not quite in the way Hitchens imagines. In his speech on West Indian emancipation, Douglass recalled "the revolution— the wondrous transformation which took place in the British West Indies, twenty-three years ago," and quoted the Irish revolutionary Daniel O'Connell: "Who would be free, themselves must strike the blow." In other words, it is the emergence of anticolonial struggle in the Caribbean and Ireland that forms the context for the famous peroration that Hitchens so woefully abuses:

> If there is no struggle, there is no progress. Those who profess to favor freedom and yet deprecate agitation are men who want crops without ploughing up the ground, they want rain without thunder and lightning. They want the ocean without the awful

roar of its many waters. The struggle may be a moral one, or it may be a physical one, and it may be both moral and physical, but it must be a struggle. Power concedes nothing without a demand. It never did and it never will.[19]

We have recently heard the awful roaring of the waters again, in the demonstrations, risings, and strikes that began to sweep across North Africa and the Middle East in January 2011. The Arab Spring, the first great revolutionary movement of the twenty-first century, has disposed of liberal interventionist claims that the invasions of Afghanistan and Iraq, the so-called revolutions from above, were necessary because the Arab masses were incapable of liberating themselves. Attempts are of course under way to recuperate these revolutions even while they are still unfolding: the NATO intervention in Libya is one aspect of this, but another, more relevant to our subject, is the claim that they are essentially bourgeois, the work of respectable middle-class professionals organized through Facebook and Twitter. The new Arab revolution is still in motion: It has the potential to become a socialist revolution; it may end as a political revolution. What it is not, and will not become, is a bourgeois revolution. One of my aims in what follows is to demonstrate why this is so.

Neil Davidson
West Calder
West Lothian
Scotland
March 2012

1
BETWEEN TWO
SOCIAL REVOLUTIONS

The concept of bourgeois revolution is a specific application of the materialist conception of history that provides an explanation for the consolidation, extension, and ultimate domination of society by capitalism. In doing so, it links together events otherwise distant from each other in terms of time, space, and form. There are alternative explanations for these events, most of which would make no conceivable connection between, for example, the sixteenth-century wars of religion and the twentieth-century wars of national liberation; but these explanations also involve theories. It was no Marxist but Frederick von Hayek, a supporter of one of these alternatives (the Marginalist variant of neoclassical economics) and a virulent opponent of historical materialism, who wrote:

> The idea that you can trace the causal connections of any events without employing a theory, or that a theory will emerge automatically from the accumulation of a sufficient amount of facts, is of course sheer illusion. The complexity of social events in particular is such that, without the tools of analysis which a systematic theory provides, one is almost bound to interpret them; and those who eschew the conscious use of an explicit and tested logical argument usually merely become the victims of the popular beliefs of their time.[1]

Any theory is of course open to misuse. Perez Zagorin has argued, with specific reference to our subject: "Marxist historical scholarship has too often had to impose a mutilating pressure on the facts and in the face of recalcitrant evidence to resort to excessively ingenious methods of interpretation, which causes its procedures to resemble the addition of epicycles to the Ptolemaic hypothesis in order to 'save the phenomena.'"[2] In effect he claims that, in this respect at least, Marxists respond to the threat of empirical refutation by resorting to auxiliary hypotheses in order to protect the inner core of the concept, the type of procedure that the philosopher of science Imre Lakatos once identified as characteristic of a "degenerating research programme."[3] Like every other historical concept, that of bourgeois revolution must ultimately be assessed on the basis of whether or not it makes the past more comprehensible to us, in ways that are compatible with the available evidence. MacIntyre once outlined the tasks that any successful social theory must accomplish. How, he asked, did Charles Darwin demonstrate the validity of "evolution by natural selection"?

> Darwin states his own thesis [in *The Origin of Species*] with remarkable brevity. He then takes hard case after hard case and shows how in fact all can be fitted into the evolutionary picture. How many hard cases does he need to dispose of before his case is established? Clearly there is no simple answer, but at a certain point conviction becomes overwhelming. Equally historical materialism is established by showing the amount of history that is made intelligible by it; and once again there is no hard and fast rule as to the point at which such a view becomes plausible.[4]

A defensible concept of bourgeois revolution must also be able to explain "hard cases" in a way that makes history "intelligible," without adjusting the concept to fit the evidence or misrepresenting the evidence to fit the concept. Henryk Grossman once wrote that Marx was attempting to understand social phenomena, not by focusing on their "superficial attributes . . . at any given moment or period," but "in their successive transformations, and thus to discover their essence."[5] What is the essence of a bourgeois revolution? Or, to put it more prosaically, how would we recognize that one has taken place?

The general method of Political Economy described by Marx in the *Grundrisse* as "obviously . . . scientifically correct" begins with an abstract conception, proceeds by moving back and forth between it and concrete examples in a process that deepens the original concept and eventually arrives at a view of the concrete as "a rich totality of many determinations and relations."[6] The usefulness of this approach is not, however, restricted to Political Economy or, as in Marx's case, its critique. MacIntyre once suggested an example in relation to one of the most famous claims by Marx and Engels: "The history of all hitherto existing history is the history of class struggles."[7] As MacIntyre writes, this "is not a generalisation built up from instances, so much as a framework without which we should not be able to identify our instances; yet also a framework which could not be elaborated without detailed empirical study."[8] But formulating a concept ("elaborating a framework" in MacIntyre's terms) is only possible through abstracting from the essential qualities present in a range of cases. The difficulty in relation to bourgeois revolutions is precisely that there is no agreement about what the essential qualities of the concept are. Domenico Losurdo, for example, has written that, as a category, bourgeois revolution "is at once too narrow and too broad":

> As regards the first aspect, it is difficult to subsume under the same category of bourgeois revolution the Glorious Revolution and the parliamentary revolt that preceded the upheavals that began in France in 1789, not to mention the struggles against monarchical absolutism, explicitly led by the liberal nobility, which developed in Switzerland and other countries. On the other hand, the category of bourgeois revolution is too broad: it subsumes both the American Revolution that sealed the advent of a racial state and the French Revolution and San Domingo Revolution, which involved complete emancipation of black slaves.[9]

One solution might be to adopt the more specific procedure Marx outlined in the "Preface" to the first edition of *Capital*, Volume 1:

> The physicist either observes physical phenomena where they occur in their most typical form and most free from disturbing influence, or, wherever possible, he makes experiments under conditions that assure the occurrence of the phenomenon in its normality. In this work I have to examine the capitalist mode of production, and the conditions of production and exchange corresponding to that mode. Up to the present time, their classic ground is England. That is the reason why England is used as the chief illustration in the development of my theoretical ideas.[10]

In other words, we should select the "classic" case where the fundamental characteristics of the concept are most fully developed. In one sense this is exactly what Marx and Engels did in relation to bourgeois revolutions. In a note to the *Manifesto of the Communist Party* added in 1888, forty years after it was first published, Engels wrote: "Generally speaking, for the economic development of the bourgeoisie, England is taken here as the typical country; for its political development, France."[11] Three years earlier he had explained the centrality of the French experience to historical materialism in greater detail:

> France is the land where, more than anywhere else, historical class struggles were each time fought out to a decision and where, consequently, the changing political forms within which they move and in which their results are condensed have been stamped in the sharpest outlines. The focus of feudalism in the Middle Ages, the model country of unified estate monarchy since the Renaissance, France demolished feudalism in the Great Revolution and established the unalloyed rule of the bourgeoisie in a classical purity unequalled by any other European land. And the struggle of the rising proletariat against the ruling bourgeoisie manifested itself here in an acute form unknown elsewhere.[12]

Eric Hobsbawm developed Engels's point by setting out a detailed case for the "typical" status of the Great French Revolution. By 1794, he wrote:

> The main shape of French and all subsequent bourgeois-revolutionary politics were now clearly visible. This dramatic dialectical dance was to dominate the future generations. Time and time again we shall see the moderate middle-class reformers mobilizing the masses against die-hard resistance or counter-revolution. We shall see the masses pushing beyond the moderates' aims to their own social revolutions, and the moderates in turn splitting into a conservative group henceforth making common cause with the reactionaries, and a left wing group determined to pursue the rest of the as yet unachieved moderate aims with the help of the masses, even at the risk of losing control over them.

Hobsbawm does note that "in most subsequent bourgeois revolutions the moderate liberals were to pull back, or to transfer into the conservative camp, at a very early stage," which already introduces a distinction between the French Revolution and those which followed it.[13] More problematic is the fact that the process Hobsbawm describes is not in fact characteristic of most subsequent bourgeois revolutions: France in 1830, certainly; Germany in 1848, perhaps (although it failed); but beyond them?

The key problem, however, is the procedure outlined by Marx and Engels. It is certainly appropriate when discussing the capitalist mode of production, which by definition has certain indispensable characteristics, such as generalized commodity production or the self-expansion of capital. It would be equally appropriate in a discussion of any other embodiment of a structured social relationship, like the absolutist state ("unified estate monarchy"), in relation to which France before 1789 can, as Engels says, be treated as the "classic" case. But the bourgeois revolution is not the embodiment of a structured relationship, like those of wage labor to capital or of peasants to the tax collector; it is the enactment of a process. Consequently, to treat the characteristics of the French case as the highest level of bourgeois revolutionary development is to imply that countries that do not display these characteristics have either undergone an incomplete experience or failed to undergo the experience at all, with all the political and theoretical confusions that follow.

Perhaps another revolution might be more suitable as a "classic" case then? Tony Cliff wrote: "The 'Bismarckian' path was not the exception for the bourgeoisie, but the rule, the exception was the French revolution."[14] Geoff Eley similarly argued that the German experience, in avoiding the "volatile scenario of the English and French Revolutions," is actually a better model than them: "In some ways—the sharpness of the rupture with the past, the definitive character of the legal settlement, the commanding strength of capital in the new national economy—German Unification was more specifically 'bourgeois' in its content and more resoundingly 'bourgeois' in its effects than either the English or the French Revolutions had been, precisely because significant popular interventions failed to occur."[15] But is Otto von Bismarck any more of a representative figure than Maximilien Robespierre? In fact, the German experience of territorial expansion by military conquest at the hands of an internally transformed absolutist state has close parallels only with the contemporary events of the Italian Risorgimento, although more distant comparisons can be found in the American Civil War and Canadian Confederation.

In response to these difficulties some Marxists have simply abandoned any attempt to establish a "classic" case. In 1968 Nicos Poulantzas wrote, "though the transition to feudalism throughout Western Europe presents common tendential characteristics, no paradigm case of the bourgeois revolution can be found."[16] In his 1976 lecture on the subject Perry Anderson similarly emphasized the difficulties involved in identifying a common set of constitutive elements for the bourgeois revolutions: "Here the exception was the rule—every one was a bastard birth."[17] As long as attempts to establish a definition depend on aspects of the bourgeois revolutions as a process, they are bound to end up with a series of national "peculiarities" that, as Anderson himself noted in a related context, lead "into the sands of an interminable nominalism."[18] In fact, the problem is irresolvable so long as we treat "bourgeois" as referring to the dominant agency and "revolution" as taking a particular form. A more useful approach is therefore to place the concept of bourgeois revolution on the terrain of what Andrew Abbott calls "turning point" analysis, in which "neither the beginning nor the end of the turning point can be defined until the whole turning point has passed, since it is the arrival and establishment of a new trajectory ... that defines the turning point itself." Consequently, "turning point analysis makes sense only after the fact."[19] To establish the nature of the turning point in relation to bourgeois revolutions we need temporarily to pull back from specific detail of their form and survey instead the general pattern of revolution in history.

POLITICAL REVOLUTIONS, SOCIAL REVOLUTIONS, AND VARIETIES OF CLASS STRUGGLE

I began this book by noting that, in one sense, the entire debate about the events conventionally known as bourgeois revolutions centered on whether they were political or social in character, and the distinction has recurred repeatedly throughout the subsequent pages. If we are to identify what is specific to bourgeois revolutions, then we need first to clarify the distinction, which has by no means received universal support. Steve Pinkus, for example, argues that it is not "useful" to distinguish between political and social revolutions, and that the former must be understood simply as "civil wars, rebellions, or coups d'état." In effect, Pinkus seems to believe that *all* genuine revolutions are social in nature:

> Revolutions must involve both a transformation of the socioeconomic orientation and of the political structures. That transformation must take place through a popular movement, and the transformation must involve a self-consciousness that a new era has begun. The distinction drawn in the literature between social and political revolutions, it seems to me, is normative as much as analytical. Scholars draw a bold line in the sand between social and political revolutions because they admire some revolutionary outcomes and disdain others. Analytical language has been used to disguise political preferences.[20]

There are certainly works where revolutions have been described as either political or social on the basis of political preference, but this book is not one of them. On the one hand, I "admire" the popular movements for greater democracy involved in the American War of Independence, although I regard it as a political revolution. On the other hand, the Meiji Restoration is scarcely the kind of event to inspire admiration in democrats, although I regard it as a social revolution and historically progressive in the sense that it brought an end to the tributary regime in Japan. The assertions that Pinkus himself makes about the character of social revolutions involve elements that are entirely arbitrary. I would be prepared to accept that they "must involve ... transformation of the socioeconomic orientation and of the political structures," but why "must" these transformations be achieved by a self-conscious popular movement?

In fact the distinction between political and social revolutions is perfectly valid, as is indicated by the way it has been used by writers from Harrington and Locke onward, even only in implicit ways. As we saw in chapter 8, the dominant position on the left between the Conspiracy of the Equals in 1795 and the Springtime of the Peoples in 1848 was that all previous revolutions, including the Great French Revolution, had been merely political revolutions; the social revolution had yet to occur and when it did it would be socialist in content. It was only while formulating the principles of historical materialism that Marx and Engels began to argue, from late in 1845, that the revolutions that had brought about the dominance of capital, and were still doing so, were also social: the bourgeois revolutions. Yet even within the later classical Marxist tradition there was by no means complete unanimity on this question.

In one passage from his great work, *History and Class Consciousness*, Lukács suggested that the French Revolution could be a bourgeois revolution *without* being a social revolution:

> A political revolution does no more than sanction a socio-economic situation that has been able to impose itself at least in part upon the economic reality. Such a revolution forcibly replaces the old legal order, now felt to be "unjust" by the new "right," "just" law. There is no radical reorganization of the social environment. (Thus conservative historians of the Great French Revolution emphasize that "social" conditions remained relatively unchanged during the period.) Social revolutions, however, are concerned precisely to change this environment.[21]

Leave aside, for the moment, the accuracy of any judgment that claims that the French Revolution failed to "change the social environment"; Lukács has effectively retreated here to the pre-Marxist position that only socialist revolutions are truly social, since they are not the culmination of previous socioeconomic changes, but the mechanism by which such changes are put into effect. The problem is that these transformative powers are not exclusive to socialist revolutions: the establishment of capitalism in Scotland followed the suppression of the last Jacobite Rebellion in 1746; to a still greater extent, the establishment of capitalism in Japan followed the Meiji Restoration of 1868. The implication of his argument are therefore that these bourgeois revolutions from above were more significant ("social") than the French bourgeois revolution from below—an extraordinary conclusion given the way in which Lukács elsewhere treats the French Revolution as an exemplar for all modern revolutions.

The identification of social revolutions only with those events that initiate a process of socioeconomic transformation has also been made—albeit from a completely different theoretical starting point—by Theda Skocpol:

> Social revolutions are rapid, basic transformations of a society's state and class structures; and they are accompanied and in part carried through by class-based revolts from below. Social revolutions are set apart from other sorts of conflicts and transformative processes above all by the combination of two coincidences: the coincidence of societal structural change with class upheaval and the coincidence of political with social transformation.... Political revolutions transform state structures but not social

structures, and they are not necessarily accomplished through class conflict. . . . What is unique to social revolution is that basic changes in social structure and in political structure occur together in a mutually reinforcing fashion. And these changes occur through intense sociopolitical conflicts in which class struggles play a key role.[22]

This is a good example of how writers can arrive at an inadequate model by arbitrarily isolating features from a handful of cases (a problem that also affects her critic Pinkus). Skocpol rightly argues that the French, Russian, and Chinese Revolutions were all social revolutions, a fact that is more significant in this context than their specific class character; but her definition also leads to other key modern revolutions being excluded from the category. She notes that the course of the English Revolution involved episodes "very similar indeed to the developments that would mark the trajectory of the French Revolution 150 years later":

Partly because of such similarities and partly because both Revolutions happened in countries that became capitalist, liberal democracies, the English and the French Revolutions are often labeled "bourgeois revolutions." Whatever the appropriateness of this label for either revolution, it should not blind us to the very important differences between them. Though the English Revolution was certainly a successful revolution, it was not a *social* revolution like the French. It was accomplished not through class struggle but through a civil war between segments of dominant landed class (with each side drawing support from all of the other classes and strata). And whereas the French Revolution markedly transformed class and social structures, the English revolution did not. Instead it revolutionized the political structure of England.[23]

The assumption here is that, in a social revolution, the relationship between state and socioeconomic transformation must be unidirectional from the former to the latter; but this leads to the conclusion that two societies that are essentially of the same type, have undergone very similar revolutionary experiences, and in both cases led to the transformation of the state—all of which Skocpol accepts with respect to England and France—must nevertheless be deemed to have undergone different types of revolution, simply because the extent of prior socioeconomic transformation was different in degree.

If the categories of political and social revolution are to be helpful in terms of historical understanding, then I think we have to narrow the scope of political revolutions so that they are not about transformation but control of the state and broaden the scope of social revolutions so that transformations of the state can be both an effect and a cause of socioeconomic transformation. Political revolutions therefore take place *within* a socioeconomic structure and social revolutions involve a *change from* one socioeconomic structure to another. Hal Draper has perhaps made the clearest distinction between these two types of revolution:

Political revolution . . . puts the emphasis on the changes in governmental leadership and forms, transformations in the superstructure. . . . If . . . social boundaries are burst by the change, then we have a different sort of revolution, which is of special importance to Marx's theory. . . . The outcome is a revolution involving the transference of political power to a new class; and this change in ruling class tends to entail a basic change in the social system (mode of production). It is this kind of revolution which is most properly called a *social* revolution.[24]

To this very helpful distinction Draper then adds what I regard as an unnecessary complication:

> If we decide to define social revolution as a basic transformation in the social system involving its class base, then it is apparent that such a sweeping change cannot be conceived as a mere act or event, but as a process more or less extended in time. . . . Moreover, it is clear that in some case in the past, social systems have changed basically, and classes have risen and fallen, in a secular movement of history which can be described as a social revolution—at least in historical retrospect, even though no one may have been aware that a revolution was going on.

Draper argues that "such a long-term or secular transformation in society, however achieved," has no widely accepted name leading him to the "desperate recourse of inventing one." His invention is "a *societal revolution*, meaning that it denotes a change from one type of society to another."[25] Some writers, like Joseph Choonara, have found this distinction meaningful, but I remain unconvinced.[26] By "societal" Draper seems to have been thinking of two processes. One is the specific case of the transition from slavery to feudalism, a process of which it could certainly be said, "no one may have been aware that a revolution was going on." If, however, we understand that social revolutions take different forms, I see no reason why this transition cannot also be accommodated under that rubric, without the need for desperate terminological recourse. The other process Draper seems to mean by "societal" is the more general one of transition from one mode of production to another. The extent to which these take place before, during, or after a revolution will vary depending on which type of social revolution and, in the case of the bourgeois revolution, which period in their development we are discussing. Again, the existing notion of transition is perfectly adequate to identify processes of long-term change with moments of social revolution at their core, without confusing matters by also describing the former as revolutions. As Eley writes of the bourgeois revolutions, we have in each case to distinguish "between two levels of determination and significance":

> Between the revolution as a specific crisis of the state, involving widespread popular mobilization and a reconstitution of political relationships, and on the other the deeper processes of structural change, involving the increasing predominance of the capitalist mode of production, the potential obsolescence of many existing practices and institutions, and the uneven transformation of social relations. How these two levels became articulated together in the revolutionary conjuncture of a 1789 or 1848—change at the level of the state, change in the social formation—is a matter for detailed historical investigation.[27]

A focus on fundamental change at the level of the state seems to be the best means of distinguishing between the process of modal transition and the moment of social revolution.

In summary then, we can say the following: Political revolutions are struggles within society for control of the state, involving factions of the existing ruling class, which leave fundamental social and economic structures intact. These revolutions have been relatively frequent in history and include: the Roman Civil Wars, which led to the abandonment of Republican rule for the Principate in 27 BCE; the victory of the Abbasid over the Umayyad dynasty in 750, which led to the opening up to all Muslims the elite offices of the Caliphate formerly held exclusively by Arabs; and the Eastern European Revolutions of 1989–91, which swept away the Stalinist regimes and began the transformation of Eastern state capitalism into an approximation of the Western trans-state model. Political revolutions may involve more or less popular participation, may result in more or less improvement in the condition of the majority, can introduce democracy where it has previously been absent; but ultimately the ruling class that was in control of the means of production at the beginning will remain so at the end (although individuals and political organizations may have been replaced on the way), and the classes that were exploited within the productive process at the beginning will also remain so at the end (although concessions may have been made by the winning faction to secure their acquiescence or participation).

The absence of fundamental social change associated with political revolutions means that there is far less distinction between them and processes of accelerated reform. Take, for example, the Great Reform Act of 1832 in Britain. For Mark Neocleous, "the fundamental issue" is this: "Was it a reform for the bourgeois class, *the completion of the bourgeois revolution*, or merely a hacking at the old aristocratic structure to avoid bourgeois power?"[28] In fact the surgery was neither as invasive nor as cosmetic as these alternatives suggest. The bourgeois revolutions in Britain had been completed by 1688–89 in England and by 1745–46 in Scotland: the Great Reform Act was a successful attempt by the industrial bourgeoisie to achieve the franchise for itself and thereby gain more direct access to an already-capitalist British state. If a revolution had actually taken place, as Edward Thompson believed was possible between February 1831 and May 1832, then British society might have been more thoroughly democratized than it in fact was, but—given that socialism was not on the agenda at this early date—such a revolution would still have remained within the realm of the political.[29]

Social revolutions, however, are not merely struggles for control of the state, but struggles to transform it, either in response to changes that have already taken place in the mode of production, or in order to bring such changes about. As Perry Anderson notes, "modes of production change when the forces and relations of production enter into decisive contradiction with one another": "The maturing of such a contradiction need involve no conscious class agency on either side, by exploiters and exploited—no set battle for the future of economy and society; although its subsequent unfolding, on the other hand, is likely to unleash relentless social struggles between opposing forces."[30] Only three epochal processes fall into the category of social revolution. At one extreme is the transition from slavery to feudalism. At the other extreme is the socialist revolution, to date a possibility rather than a reality, but which, if achieved, will begin the transition from capitalism to socialism. Between these two extremes lie the bourgeois revolutions and, as we shall see, their intermediacy is not simply chronological. As Alex Callinicos writes: "The balance between the role played by structural contradictions and conscious human agency in resolving organic crisis has shifted from the former to the latter in the course of the past 1,500 years. The transition from feudalism to capitalism occupies an intermediate position in this respect between the fall of the Roman Empire and the Russian Revolution."[31] The relationship between political and social revolutions is complex. Some political revolutions have social implications and all social revolutions have political implications. Some revolutions, taken by themselves, appear to be merely political revolutions, are in fact the opening or concluding episode of a more extended social revolution. In relation to the bourgeois revolution, the English Revolution of 1688 has this relationship to the revolution of 1640.[32] Reversing the chronological order of importance, the American Revolution of 1776 has this in relation to the Civil War of 1861–65. More importantly in the context of this discussion, some revolutions conclude as political revolutions because they fail as social revolutions. In relation to the socialist revolution, this is clearly the case with the German Revolution of 1918. A similar case could also be made for the Bolivian Revolution of 1952, the Portuguese Revolution of 1974–75 and indeed most of the so-called democratic revolutions to have taken place since, most recently in Indonesia (1998) and Serbia (2000); it is still unclear whether the revolutions of the Arab Spring (2011–?) will also be halted within the confines of the political. Finally, as the "turning point" analysis I referred to earlier would suggest, it is only after a revolutionary process has concluded that it is possible to say whether it has involved political or social revolution. As Jeffery Webber writes: "One way out of the quandaries of process and consequence that arise in defining revolution is to separate the notion of *revolutionary epoch* from *social revolution*. The concept of revolutionary epoch provides us with a way of understanding that revolutionary transformative change is possible but not predetermined in a certain period, stressing the uncertainty—and yet not wide openness—of alternative outcomes."[33]

Because social revolutions are so rare, it is difficult to make generalizations about their nature. It is not even possible to say that in every case social revolution involves the replacement of one ruling class with another, since in some cases the personnel of a former ruling class remained in place while their role in the social relations of production changed—where, for example, slave owners became feudal lords or feudal lords became capitalist landowners. As this suggests, not all social revolutions are brought about by the direct triumph of one class over another through the class struggle, for "the history of all hitherto existing society" has involved two different types of class struggle, "two different categories of historical process."[34] Claudio Katz has identified these as exemplifying, respectively: "The antagonism within a class system and that between class systems."[35]

The first type, "within a class system," is where the classes involved are exploiter and exploited. The issues here are relatively straightforward. Slave owners extract surplus value from slaves, feudal lords and tributary bureaucrats do the same to peasants, and capitalists do the same to workers. In each case the exploited class resists to the extent that material conditions allow, but it is not always possible for them to go beyond resistance to create a new society based on a different mode of production. Alvin Gouldner writes of the one "unspoken regularity" of the series of class struggles listed in the *Manifesto of the Communist Party*: "The slaves did not succeed the masters, the plebeians did not vanquish the patricians, the serfs did not overthrow the lords, and the journeymen did not triumph over the guild-masters. The lowliest class never came to power. Nor does it seem likely to now."[36] We need not accept this dismal conclusion; nevertheless, it is true that exploited classes do not always have the structural capacity to make a social revolution: slaves did not; the majority of peasants did not; the working class does, and in this respect— among several others—it is unique among the exploited classes in history.

The other type of class struggle, "between class systems," is where those involved are oppressor and oppressed. The issues here are considerably more complex. For one thing, while all exploited classes (slaves, peasants, workers) are oppressed, not all oppressed classes are exploited and they may even be exploiters themselves. The number of oppressed classes that have the capacity to remake society is as limited as the number of exploited classes with that capacity. Among oppressed classes it is the bourgeoisie that is unique. Anthony Giddens writes:

> The struggle between the feudal nobility and rising bourgeoisie, in fact, does not appear in the classification of conflicting classes which Marx offers.... Here the criterion for the identification of class conflict is obviously that of the "exploitative dependence" of one class upon the other in the dichotomous model; there is a direct conflict of interest having its source in the appropriation of surplus value by a nonproductive class. In the case of the nobility and the bourgeoisie, however, conflict of interest derives from the need of the latter to dissolve the social and economic relationships characteristic of the feudal order, and of the former to maintain them. Thus although the bourgeoisie is in one sense a "subordinate" class within post-feudal society, in an other sense it constitutes a "dominant" class, in terms of the exploitative relationship in which it stands with wage-labor.[37]

The class struggle can therefore be not only between exploiters and exploited but also between exploiter and exploiter: it can nevertheless still be the means of bringing about social revolution, provided that the modes of production represented by these classes are different and one is more "progressive," in the Marxist sense of involving the greater development of the productive forces. Louis Althusser described "the central contradiction of the French Revolution, and of bourgeois revolution in general," as being that it involved "a struggle for state power *between two equally exploitative classes*, feudal aristocracy and bourgeoisie."[38] The notion of "equality" is misleading here since, before the bourgeois revolution, the former class could rely on the state to act in its interests, and the latter could not, that is why revolutions were required; but both classes were certainly exploitative.

The class struggle in history has therefore taken multifaceted forms. It is a permanent feature of the relationship between exploiting and exploited classes, but can also occur between dominant and subordinate exploiting classes, or between existing and potential exploiting classes. And these different class struggles have taken place simultaneously, intertwining and overlapping. The precise combinations have been or (in the case of socialism) will be different in relation the case of each of the great social revolutions. What form did they take in those that came before and may yet come after the bourgeois revolutions?

FROM SLAVERY TO FEUDALISM, FROM CAPITALISM TO SOCIALISM

In parts of the north and far west of Europe, such as Scandinavia and Scotland, feudalism evolved spontaneously out of primitive communism and through the Asiatic mode, understood here as a general term for the transitional process through which all pre-capitalist class societies first evolved.[39] The rise of feudalism in the former territories of the Roman Empire in the West from the 470s therefore represents the first direct passage in history from one exploitative mode of production to another. But was there a "feudal revolution"? George Duby was perhaps the first writer to refer to one occurring around 1000 and in doing so invoked an explicit parallel with the bourgeois revolution.[40] The concept was taken up by other, mainly French historians, above all by Guy Bois.[41] However, despite the endorsement of distinguished names like these, it seems more accurate to treat the transition to feudalism as a whole *as* the feudal "revolution," since there was no seizure of power and members of the former slave-owning ruling class simply changed their roles and added to their ranks from those of the former "barbarian" tribal chiefs. The transition from slavery to feudalism on the former territories of the Roman Empire in the West was unintended in the sense that no one consciously set out to establish the latter system; it emerged through a series of pragmatic adaptations in the ways production and exploitation took place. The peasants had to try new methods of production since their own subsistence—or at least continued tenure—now depended on doing so in a way that it did not for slaves; their success in achieving greater productivity encouraged the slave-owners-cum-lords to orient still further toward non-slave agriculture: "Slavery became extinct against a background of almost continuous and increasingly more marked development of the forces of production."[42] Feudalism is an integrated system in which, unlike capitalism, the economic, the social, the political, and the ideological are not separable in either appearance or reality; it is not therefore that socioeconomic change preceded the formation of new political and ideological forms (the estates monarchy, the "three orders") that we now regard as characteristic of feudalism, so much as that these were consolidated and formalized between c. 700 and c. 1000.[43]

If the feudal "revolution" was a process of socioeconomic transition out of whose completion new political forms eventually emerged, then the socialist revolution will be a socio-political struggle for power whose completion will allow a new economic order to be constructed. The precondition for socialism is the development of the productive forces by capitalism. As Marx and Engels wrote early in their careers, "development of productive forces . . . is an absolutely necessary practical premise, because without it privation, *want* is merely made general, and with *want* the struggle for necessities would begin again, and all the old filthy business would necessarily be restored."[44] Because the working class is non-exploitative there is no prior development of an alternative socialist or communist mode of production. As Lukács noted:

> It would be a utopian fantasy to imagine that anything tending towards socialism could arise within capitalism apart from, on the one hand, the *objective economic premises that make it a possibility* which, however, can only be *transformed* in to the true elements of a socialist system of production after and in consequence of the collapse of capitalism; and, on the other hand, the development of the proletariat as a class. . . . But even the most highly developed capitalist concentration will still be qualitatively different, even economically, from a socialist system and can neither change into one "by itself" nor will be amenable to such change "through legal devices" within the framework of capitalist society.[45]

The process of transition therefore *begins* with the destruction of capitalist states and the substitution of transitional soviet "states that are not states"—but only as the prelude to their ultimate self-dissolution, as capitalist (and in some cases residual pre-capitalist) productive relations are replaced by socialist ones. In that sense the transition to socialism involves the withering away of both the market *and* the state: "The foundations of capitalist modes of production and with them their 'necessary natural laws' do not simply vanish when the proletariat seizes power or even as a result of the socialization, however thoroughgoing, of the means of production. But their elimination and replacement by a consciously organized socialist economics must not be thought of only as a lengthy process but as a consciously conducted, stubborn battle. Step by step the ground must be wrested from this 'necessity'."[46]

Socialist productive relations will potentially allow even greater growth of the productive forces than under capitalism, but would only do so on the basis of a democratic decision taken by inhabitants of the new society after careful consideration of the all the implications, not least those concerning the environment. But even if growth was desired, it is unlikely to be achieved immediately. Bukharin's account of the postrevolutionary economic collapse inevitably generalized too much from the Russian Revolution, given it was the only experience available to him, but even in more advanced countries there can be little doubt that a combination of physical destruction, deskilling, the dislocation of the factors of production and necessary redistribution into nonproductive consumption will initially lead to a temporary decline of the productive forces before they can be reconstituted on a higher basis.[47] Clearly we are at a disadvantage in discussing the details of the transition to socialism since, unlike the transition to feudalism, we are discussing a process that has still to occur: the precise characteristics of socialist society are still obscure to us and, although some interesting work has now been done on what a genuine socialist economy would involve, these necessarily have a speculative character.[48] The only socialist revolution to have sustained itself for years rather than months, the Russian Revolution of October 1917, was thrown into reverse by the triumph of the Stalinist counterrevolution by 1928 and the transition it initiated has still to be successfully resumed. Nevertheless, from that experience and those of the brief but illuminating moments in failed socialist revolutions both before (the Paris Commune) and after (Germany 1918–23, Spain 1936–37, Hungary 1956, Portugal 1974–75, Iran 1978–79, Poland 1980–81, Egypt 2011–?), it is possible to see how the working class can establish new democratic institutions that have taken over the running of the economy, society, and the state. And these have never ceased to emerge, the most recent being the Argentinean *piqueteros* and *asembleas* of the crisis of 2000–01.

The experience of the Russian Revolution highlights another important difference between these two social revolutions. The societies that were transformed on feudal lines occupied a relatively small region of Western and Central Europe. In its formative stages feudalism did not contain an inherent tendency toward expansion and therefore did not require a world or even continental system either for exploitation (the territorial acquisitions of the Crusaders in the Middle East were—to adopt a term associated with political Marxism—"opportunities" rather than "necessities") or for self-defense, since the great tributary states of the East were almost completely uninterested in these undeveloped formations, so obviously inferior to them in every respect except that of warfare, as they would eventually find to their cost. Feudalism had centuries to develop and expand outwards from its initial heartlands in what are now parts of France and Belgium; it was only in its later period of crisis that individual feudal states seriously sought to expand beyond Europe, most obviously in the irruption of the Hispanic states into the Americas. The socialist revolution, on the other hand, is necessarily a global event. As long as it remains isolated it remains susceptible to counterrevolution, either from without, as in most cases from the Paris Commune onward, or from within, as was the case in Russia. The latter point perhaps bears some elaboration. The threat to the Russian Revolution, which was eventually realized, was not simply the backwardness of the economy, but the fact that in the capitalist world system, the pressures of competitive accumulation would ultimately make themselves felt, to the point of determining what happened in Russian factories. Greater levels of economic development might enable a state to hold out from internal degeneration longer than Russia was able, but cannot ultimately protect against this process. That is why the international nature of the socialist revolution is a necessity, not a desirable but optional extra. Space has implications for time: the territorial extent of the socialist revolution exercises severe restraints over its temporality.

The final contrast lies between the different types of agency and their associated levels of consciousness. The exploited class on which the dominant slave mode of production was based was not responsible for overthrowing the slave owners. Indeed we know of only three major slave revolts in Roman history, two on Sicily during the second century BCE, and the most famous, that of Spartacus, on the Italian mainland during the first century BCE. Some other, smaller revolts have more recently come to light, but the fundamental picture remains unchanged. The absence of slave rebellion is at least partly the result of the extreme difficulty that the conditions of slavery posed, but it also worth considering what "success" might have meant. The leaders of the Sicilian slave revolts were intent on taking over existing institutions—including slavery—and establishing a Hellenistic kingdom on the Syrian Seleucid model. "The tragedy and moral of the whole episode is that no conceivable alternative existed."[49] Slaves dreamed, not of replacing slavery with a different system, but of escaping from it, either in order to return to the societies from which they had been captured (which were themselves in the process of transition to full-blown class societies) or by setting up their own communities outside of the Roman domains: even the Spartacists' final attempt on Rome seems to have been an effort to achieve this rather than to establish a new regime in Rome itself.[50] The class struggle in the Roman world was conducted between the free citizens, over an overwhelmingly passive slave population. But the inheritors were no more the peasants and plebeians of Ancient Rome than they were the slaves (although the slaves who obtained their freedom clearly benefited). Despite several important risings from early in the fifth century, the role of peasants was not principally as participants in open class struggle.

The new ruling class was in fact an alliance of the two forces that were actually responsible for ending the empire in the West: from within, the landowners who withdrew support for the state in opposition to its increasing demands for taxation; from without, the tribal chiefs and their retinues who led the barbarian invasions. The decline of slavery began toward the end of the second century, as the territorial limits of the empire were reached. In circumstances where new supplies of slaves could not simply be seized, the only way in which landowners could maintain numbers was by the more expensive business of physically reproducing the existing labor force—breeding new slaves, in other words. Similarly, if new territorial gains were excluded, the only mechanism through which landowners could expand their estates was by acquiring land from other, usually smaller landowners who would then be reduced in status. But the more land was acquired the greater the liability for tax, which landowners tried with increasing success to evade, thus reducing the resources available to the state. The main recipient of state funding was the army, engaged in increasingly futile attempts to repel the Germanic invasions—attempts whose lack of success provided an even greater incentive to tax evasion. Meanwhile the German invaders began to appear an attractive alternative to supporting a declining but increasingly acquisitive state apparatus. The triumph of the barbarians did not immediately lead to total transformation. Taxation continued, but without the need for a centralized army—since the new states raised armies from their own landowners and retainers—the main purpose for raising taxation no longer existed. Tax collection became increasingly fragmented: inessential for supporting monarchs, whose wealth derived from their own estates, it became principally used for securing support through gifts or bribes. Previously, members of the ruling class had sought to acquire land in order to gain access to control of the state apparatus, but now it became an end in itself. Simultaneously, from the reign of Augustus (27BCE–14AD), the freedom of the peasant-citizen began to be eroded as the state no longer permitted him to vote or required him to fight, with the restriction of the franchise to what were now openly called the *honestiores* ("upper classes") and the recruitment of armies by enlistment rather than as a duty of citizenship. Increasingly taxed to pay for the wars and the burgeoning bureaucracy, including that of the Church, peasants also inadvertently hastened the internal disintegration of the empire by placing themselves under the protection of landowners, effectively renouncing their independence on the assumption that not only would their new status as tenants not carry tax liabilities, but their new lords would be capable of avoiding such responsibilities themselves and consequently would not pass them on. In other words, an unfree labor force now began to emerge that rendered slavery redundant. The former slave owners changed the relations of production by lifting up the slaves they owned to the status of serfs while forcing down the free peasants tenanted on their land to the same level, as a response to the growing shortage of captured slaves and the expense of raising them. The tribal chiefs were meanwhile evolving into settled communities with stable and inherited social divisions between the warrior caste and the peasantry, a process hastened by the establishment of permanent settlements on the former territories of the empire. Both were moving from different directions toward what would become, over several hundred years, a new feudal ruling class. There was also a two-way movement of the exploited, particularly between the ninth and eleventh centuries. On the one hand, the supply of slaves dried up and those that remained were settled as serfs. On the other, the previously free peasants were increasingly brought into a servile condition.[51]

Peasant resistance continued during the transition, but these revolts were different from predecessors under the Roman Empire and successors under the consolidated feudal regime after 1000. Earlier peasant revolts, above all those of the Bagaudae against the Roman Empire in Gaul, were essentially directed against taxation and injustice at a time when the state was weakened and therefore the possibility of change beneficial to the peasantry became possible. Later peasant revolts too were conducted against the state in relation to "military service, laws on status and, above all, taxation."[52] In this period, revolts have a different impetus. Chris

Wickham argues that aristocratic hegemony did function in certain areas where the peasants had to rely on aristocrats for external support, as in eighth-century Luc-chesia (in modern Italy), although this did not, of course exclude "small-scale signs of disobedience," but these are compatible with overall acceptance of ruling values. At the other end of the spectrum, as in eighth-century Paris, the aristocrats domi-nated through "overwhelming physical force" and did not require peasant acceptance of their rule, which they in any case did not receive. Between these lies a third type of area, such as sixth-century Galatia, where neither situation prevailed; that is, where aristocrats could rely on neither ideology nor violence to secure compliance. As Wickham notes, the latter situation is where revolts are most likely to take place, but: "The absence of hegemony is only one reason why peasants revolt, of course; they have to have something concrete to oppose as well."[53] In this case peasant re-volts are signs of resistance to attempts by the emergent ruling class to impose serf-dom. England is exceptional in its lack of peasant revolt, which seems to have two causes. First, because initially landowners had less control over the peasantry than in any other part of Europe, while at the same time they exercised superiority over exceptionally large territories. Second, when the lords did move to subject or ex-propriate peasant communities they did so slowly and in piecemeal fashion, attack-ing the weakest and while leaving the strongest and wealthiest untouched until the basis of possible collective resistance was eroded.[54] Elsewhere, the gradual encroach-ments of the emergent feudal state led to what Wickham calls "frequent small scale resistance," which erupted into one of the great risings of the period: the Stellinga revolt in Saxony during 841–42, a revolt that took the opportunity of a civil war among the local Saxon ruling class to launch a program for the return to the pre-aristocratic social order.[55] I earlier quoted the distinction made by Katz between class struggle within class systems and class struggle between class systems; the types of class struggle enumerated by Wickham for the period of the transition to feudalism are essentially examples of the former. Insofar as they could have resulted in revolutionary changes they were of the sort that would have restored society to what it had been (or what revolutionaries imagined it had been) before the impo-sition of feudal social relations. If they are such, then they were revolutions in the way that Aristotle and Polybius would have understood them: as attempts to restore a former condition, not attempts to establish a new form of society.

The exploited class under capitalism, the working class, will have to achieve the socialist revolution, or it will not be achieved at all. The working class is the first ex-ploited (as opposed to oppressed) class in history that is able to make a revolution on its own behalf. Unlike the peasantry, the working class is structured collectively and is therefore the basis of a new form of social organization in a way that the former can never be. Unlike the bourgeoisie, the working class itself has the numeric size and structural capacity to rebuild society without using another class as an instrument to destroy the existing system. The working class is not an alternative exploiting class to the bourgeoisie and it will not be transformed into one by victory. Even those writers who believe that socialism is impossible and that revolution will only lead to a new form of managerial or bureaucratic society do not claim that the proletariat itself will constitute the ruling class, but rather that it will consist of a technocratic elite or "new class." Consequently, the "everyday" class struggles between exploiters and exploited, and the "transformative" struggles for social revolution are linked by the fact that the same classes are involved: the former always contains the possibility of the latter. To this conception of working-class agency we need to add two qualifications.

First, not all workers will participate in the revolution, at least on the revolutionary side. Gramsci showed that most members of the subordinate classes have highly contradictory forms of consciousness, the most characteristic being a reformist inability to conceive of anything beyond capitalism while opposing specific effects of the system.[56] The alternatives are not, however, restricted to active rejection at one extreme and passive acceptance at the other: there can also be *active* support, the internalization of capitalist values associated with the system to the point where they can lead to action. Marxists and other anticapitalist radicals rightly point out that, rather than men benefiting from the oppression of women, whites from the oppression of blacks, straights from the oppression of gays, and so on, it is capitalism or the bourgeoisie that does so. This is a necessary corrective to the approach typical of many left-wing social movements in which every form of oppression is seen as separate from the others and none have any necessary connection to the capitalist system. Nevertheless, it fails to take seriously the distinction made by Lukács between "what men *in fact* thought, felt and wanted at any point in the class structure" and "the thoughts and feelings which men would have in a particular situation if they were *able* to assess both it and the interests arising from it in their impact on immediate action and on the whole structure of society."[57] We cannot assume that members of the working class are not only capable of the thoughts and feelings "appropriate to their objective situation," but do in fact *have* these thoughts and feelings, and are only prevented from taking the action that these feelings imply because of reformist mis-leadership, lack of confidence due to temporary defeats, or a deeper acceptance that, however desirable an outcome socialism might be, the world can nevertheless not be changed in any fundamental way. But what if workers do not have this level of consciousness? Many of them have either been unaware of "the standpoint of the working class" or have simply refused to adopt it. Instead, a significant minority have taken positions supportive of, for example, racial oppression, which may not have benefited them compared with the benefits they would have received by struggling for racial, let alone full social equality. Without some degree of class consciousness, however, they need not ever consider this alternative: in the immediate context of their situation a stance that is detrimental to working-class interests as a whole may make sense to particular individual members of the working class. Lukács once wrote of revisionism, which in this context can be taken to mean reformism more generally, that: "It always sacrifices the genuine interests of the class as a whole . . . so as to represent the immediate interests of specific groups."[58] In a revolutionary situation, some working-class people will take this a stage further, by sacrificing even the interests of specific groups in favor of their immediate individual interests, usually equated with a supra-class national interest.[59]

Second, the central role of the working class does not mean that it will be the only force involved in the socialist revolution. Lenin wrote in 1916 against those who had criticized the Easter Rising in Ireland: "So one army lines up in one place and says, 'We are for socialism,' and another, somewhere else and says, 'We are for imperialism,' and that will be a social revolution! . . . Whoever expects a 'pure' social revolution will never live to see it. Such a person pays lip service to revolution without understanding what revolution is."[60] The potential allies of the working class have changed in the course of the last hundred years—if the Russian Revolution had successfully spread after 1917, then the peasantry would have played a far greater role, even in Europe, than they will now, just as sections of the "informal" sector in the developing world and the "new" middle or technical-managerial class in the developed will play a far greater role now than they would have in 1917. Similarly there are oppressed groups—of which in the West today the most significant are Muslim communities—whose situation makes them open to argument about the root cause of their oppression. Lenin's notion that socialists must be "tribunes of the oppressed" is as relevant as it ever was—at any rate, any socialism worthy of the name will not succeed without that spirit.[61]

Because the transition to socialism starts with the seizure of power, it must be a conscious process. No socialist economy will blindly emerge from the struggle to develop the productive forces, or to find new ways of exploiting the direct producers who set those forces to work. The struggle for power by the working class requires organization to awaken, consolidate, and maintain class consciousness, but organization is also required as the basis for an alternative form of state power. In short, what the proletariat has to match is not the organizational structures within which the bourgeoisie conducted their struggle for power (in the minority of examples where they did in fact did so), but the centralizing role the state and ideological forms established by the bourgeoisie after its ascendancy. The role of organization in consolidating and maintaining class consciousness is of crucial importance here, from the most basic forms of trade unionism through to revolutionary organization. "The [working] class, taken by itself, is only material for exploitation," wrote Trotsky in 1932: "The proletariat assumes an independent role only at that moment when from a class *in itself* it becomes a political class *for itself*. This cannot take place other than through the medium of a party. The party is that historical organ by means of which the class becomes conscious."[62] The distinction Trotsky draws here between a class in itself (a social group occupying an economic role) and a class for itself (a social group that has become conscious of its own position and what is required to change it) is usually but incorrectly thought to originate with Marx who actually distinguishes between a class "against capitalism" and a class "for itself."[63] The original formulation is preferable in that it suggests not an idealized shift from complete political unconsciousness to consciousness—as few workers accept every aspect of the system as reject every aspect of it, at least before a revolutionary situation emerges—but a process of clarification through struggle.

Socialism would represent the greatest transformation in the human condition since the emergence of class society itself. Indeed, so enormous is the task, so vast is the gulf between the realities of capitalism and the possibilities of socialism, that many on the left have envisaged their goal as simply being a modified version of capitalism, not an entirely new form of human society. The two models of socialism that dominated the twentieth century, Social Democracy and Stalinism, exemplify the problem. Precisely because they have, respectively, defended a modified version of private capitalism where it existed and introduced state capitalism where it did not, any new socialist project for the twenty-first century has to begin by rejecting them both: the dream of human freedom is not realized in either Attlee's Britain or Castro's Cuba, whatever their other admirable qualities. As Draper once pointed out in a rightly celebrated essay, both Social Democracy and Stalinism are examples of "socialism from above": "What unites the many different forms of Socialism-from-Above is the conception that socialism (or a reasonable facsimile thereto) must be *handed down* to the grateful masses in some form or another, by a ruling elite which is not subject to their control in fact." The result is not socialism at all and Draper contrasts it with "socialism from below": "The heart of Socialism-from-Below is its view that socialism can only be realized through the self-emancipation of activised masses 'from below' in a struggle to take charge of their own destiny, as actors (not merely subjects) on the stage of history."[64] Democracy is not merely a desirable feature but a necessity for socialism. Indeed, it will be defined by the way in which democracy becomes the basis for those aspects of human existence from which either the market or the bureaucratic state currently exclude it. It is only through the transformative process of taking power that workers can throw off the legacy of years of enforced servility or misdirected anger that capitalism inculcates: "Both for the production on a mass scale of . . . communist consciousness, and for the success of the cause itself, the alteration of men on a mass scale is necessary, an alteration which can only take place in a practical movement, a *revolution*; the revolution is necessary, therefore, not only because the *ruling* class cannot be overthrown in any other way, but because the class *overthrowing* it can only in a revolution succeed in ridding itself of all the muck of ages and become fitted to found society anew."[65]

With these antipodal examples of social revolution in mind we can now return to the bourgeois case. As we saw in chapter 12, Lenin used two concepts in connection with bourgeois revolution, that of an *era* during which the process unfolds and that of a moment of *consummation* with which it concludes.[66] The following two chapters are structured around these two concepts; more specifically, they ask what makes the former possible and how we know that the latter has taken place.

2
PRECONDITIONS FOR AN ERA
OF BOURGEOIS REVOLUTION

"For Marxists," writes Robert Lochhead, "bourgeois revolutions cover a period of nine centuries."[1] On the basis of this assessment the first episodes of bourgeois revolution took place in the second half of the twelfth century with the communal risings that established the independence of the German and Italian city-states from the Holy Roman Empire. The difficulty with this periodization is that no permanently successful bourgeois revolution took place until four hundred and fifty years later with the consolidation of the Dutch Republic, which suggests that the preconditions for successful bourgeois revolution did not exist until much later than the rise of the towns. Before identifying these preconditions, it is worth clarifying what I mean by the term.

In his famous discussion of the origins of the English Revolution, Lawrence Stone divided the causes into three successive groups, increasingly concentrated in time, which he classified as "long-term preconditions" (1529–1629), "medium-term precipitants" (1629–39), and "short-term triggers" (1640–42).[2] Stone's long-term preconditions were the factors he saw as leading to instability and disequilibrium in the Tudor and Stuart polity. While some of these were rather unspecific ("economic growth," "social change"), others did highlight more concrete aspects of the English situation—the decline of external threats, a crisis of ruling-class confidence, the rise of a parliamentary opposition, and the spread of new ideas and values.[3] My conception of "preconditions" differs from his in three respects. First, they are not a series of loosely connected explanatory factors; instead they take the form of a determinate historical sequence, with each one setting the conditions for emergence of the next. Second, their successive emergence occurred across a longer time-scale, broadly between the arrival of the Black Death in Europe in the 1340s and the beginning of the Reformation in the 1510s. Third, they involved tendencies within the European feudal system as a whole and consequently occurred at a deeper and more general level than those identified by Stone in relation to England—in effect, they constitute an additional, chronologically prior grouping of causes, the impact of which had to be registered before the factors specific to England could begin to take effect from 1529.

These preconditions signaled that what Marx called "an era of social revolution" had begun. Since Marx was clearly thinking of the bourgeois revolutions in the 1859 "Preface" from which this phrase is taken, we can use this classic (and unfairly maligned) text as the starting point for our discussion: "At a certain stage of development, the material productive forces of society come into conflict with the existing relations of production or—this merely expresses the same thing in legal terms—with the property relations within the framework of which they have operated hitherto. From forms of development of the productive forces these relations turn into their fetters. Then begins an era of social revolution."[4] Conflict between the forces and relations of production indicates the emergence of the first precondition: a crisis of feudalism, which became apparent from the late thirteenth century. In this passage Marx, as it were, leaps over several stages of the process by saying that crisis in and of itself necessarily introduces an era of social revolution; in fact, several other preconditions are necessary. A crisis may simply lead to collapse and retrogression, as had happened to earlier societies, such as that of the Maya.[5] Also required is the emergence, from the crisis of feudalism, of a second precondition: capitalism as a potential alternative system with the capacity to resume the development of the productive forces: .

> No social order is ever destroyed before all the productive forces for which it is sufficient have been developed, and new superior relations of production never replace older ones before the material conditions for their existence have matured within the framework of the old society. Mankind thus inevitably sets itself only such tasks as it is able to solve, since closer examination will always show that the problem itself arises only when the material conditions for its solution are already present or at least in the course of formation.[6]

But at what level—national, international, or global—do these new relations of production have to be present? Ellen Meiksins Wood once asked: "Was a revolution necessary to bring about capitalism, or simply to facilitate the development of an already existing capitalism? Was it a cause or an effect of capitalism?"[7] The answer is that bourgeois revolutions could be *either* cause *or* effect. Lukács wrote that during "the transition from feudalism to capitalism": "The rival systems of production will . . . co-exist as already perfected systems (as was seen in the beginnings of capitalism within the feudal order)."[8] In fact, there are no examples where a perfect equilibrium between feudalism and capitalism existed prior to the bourgeois revolution taking place. Bourgeois revolutions are the only types of social revolution that have occurred *during* the transition from the dominance of one mode of production to another; consequently, they were neither the culmination of a socioeconomic process like the feudal "revolution" nor a moment of politico-social transformation like the socialist revolution. The extent to which individual bourgeois revolutions tended toward either the former or the latter varied depended on the stage in the transition to capitalism during which they took place. In some cases, bourgeois revolution was primarily a means of facilitating the further development of capitalism in conditions where key aspects of the transition had taken place before the revolutions began: these cases resemble the transition to feudalism. In other, later cases, bourgeois revolution was primarily a precondition for the emergence of capitalism in conditions where key aspects of the transition had still to take place after the revolutions ended: these cases resemble the socialist revolution.[9] One reason the later bourgeois revolutions took place in less developed conditions was that once the initial breakthroughs had taken place in the United Provinces and England, European absolutism mobilized to prevent any similar revolutions taking place. Consequently, in no other country after England did a capitalist economy grow up relatively unhindered until the point where the classes associated with it could lead an assault on feudal absolutism. But in neither set of cases was capitalism internally either completely dominant (even in England) or completely nonexistent (even in Japan). In the latter cases, however, revolutions took place in a context where capitalist laws of motion were much stronger across the world economy as a whole; indeed, it was this that made them possible. In other words, to speak of a "capitalist alternative" does not mean that one necessarily existed within each individual state territory, but rather that one existed at the level of the world system as a whole. The result was an apparently paradoxical trajectory: the earliest bourgeois revolutions took place where there were high levels of local capitalist development but low levels of global capitalist development; the later bourgeois revolutions took place where the balance was, if not reversed, then strongly weighted in the opposite direction.

Apart from a brief reference to "ideological forms in which men become conscious of this conflict and fight it out," agency is famously absent from Marx's highly compressed and—for reasons discussed in chapter 10—deeply structural formulations.[10] Taking the 1859 "Preface" as his starting point, Gramsci later explored the question of who would be involved in attempting or preventing a solution to what he called "organic" crises:

> A crisis occurs, sometimes lasting for decades. This exceptional duration means that incurable structural contradictions have revealed themselves (reached maturity), and that, despite this, the political forces which are struggling to conserve and defend the existing structure itself are making every effort to cure them, within certain limits, and to overcome them. These incessant and persistent efforts (since no social formation will ever admit that it has been superseded) form the terrain of the "conjunctural," and it is upon this terrain that the forces of opposition organize. These forces seek to demonstrate that the necessary and sufficient conditions already exist to make possible, and hence imperative, the accomplishment of certain historical tasks (imperative, because any falling short before an historical duty increases the necessary disorder, and prepares more serious catastrophes).[11]

As with Marx's original remarks, these general considerations yield quite specific preconditions in the context of the bourgeois revolutions. Capitalism was not brought into existence by victory or defeat in the class struggle, nor—as political Marxists believe—by an indeterminate outcome of the class struggle in England. The outcome of the class struggle did, however, determine whether or not capitalism would be consolidated on a particular territory once it *had* emerged. Christopher Bertram has noted that "class struggle may impede productive development in many different ways," the most important of which from our perspective is the top-down variety where "a dominant class whose domination is absolute may be tempted to derive its wealth simply from greater exploitation of subordinate classes rather than through any development of technique (indeed its exploitation of unfree labor may preclude the development of more sophisticated techniques)."[12]

The third precondition was therefore that the states that acted as the focus for the pre-capitalist ruling classes had—for whatever reason—to be unable to prevent capitalism developing as an alternative means of social organization. Where the state was strong enough to prevent what Marx and Engels called "the revolutionary reconstitution of society," then it could result in what they called "the common ruin of the contending classes."[13] More frequently, however, it did not reach this stage, because the state was able to prevent what Chris Wickham calls "minimum conditions" for the transition to capitalism ever being reached. Wickham is thinking of China in this context, as an example of "high-level equilibrium which can happily continue for centuries, its contradictions, if any in practice dealt with without difficulty, feudal reproduction being not less creative than capitalist reproduction in our own day."[14] When ruin ultimately occurred it tended, as in the case of China, to be the result of the invasions and impositions invited by its social stagnation and weakness, rather than directly through internal conflict and collapse. "As exposure to the atmosphere reduces all mummies to instant dissolution," wrote Marx, "so war passes supreme judgment upon social organizations that have outlived their vitality."[15]

But, like the existence of an organic social crisis, a relatively weak state is a negative precondition. Capitalism is not a disembodied social force and must be liberated or imposed through political action, a fact that implies a fourth precondition: the existence of revolutionary agencies, associated with capitalism but not necessarily consisting of capitalists, with the capacity to remove structural impediments to its ascendancy. The earliest successful examples of bourgeois revolution, in the United Provinces and England, involved leadership by mercantile, agrarian, and—in the case of the latter country—even industrial capitalists, although these tended to be based in the countryside and the colonies rather than the metropolitan centers. There was a difference between the French Revolution and these earlier examples of bourgeois revolution from below. As a consequence of the relative success of the absolutist regime in retarding the development of capitalism, France was internally less developed in 1789 than England had been in 1640. But even those capitalists who had emerged in France were more inclined to reform than their predecessors, not least because of the risk that revolution posed to their property, which tended to be more industrial than agrarian or mercantile. From 1789 on, therefore, the nature of leadership in the bourgeois revolutions became increasingly removed from capitalists in the class structure: Robespierre was a lawyer, Danton a journalist, Roux a priest; only a very few of the leading French revolutionaries, of whom Roederer was the most important, could seriously be described as capitalists. With the exception of the period between 1859 and 1871 during which fractions of the existing feudal classes came to the fore, these noncapitalist sections of the bourgeoisie dominated the leaderships of the bourgeois revolutions until the cycle was complete on a global scale; indeed, as the twentieth century wore on, the social roles that they occupied tended to shift even further from the economic core toward those of military and party bureaucrats.

The fifth and final precondition concerns the motivations of these agencies and here again we need to return to Marx's original discussion: "Just as one does not judge an individual by what he thinks about himself, so one cannot judge such a period of transformation by its consciousness, but, on the contrary, this conscious-ness must be explained from the contradictions of material life, from the conflict existing between the social forces of production and the relations of production."[16] If this insight had been taken more seriously, we might have been spared much subsequent confusion about the role of consciousness and ideology in the bourgeois revolutions. In fact, the agents of bourgeois revolution displayed a range of different levels of consciousness, depending on the classes involved and the periods during which each took place, but all required an ideology that motivated them to move from being a theoretical to an actual revolutionary leadership. In no bourgeois rev-olution did the revolutionaries ever seek to rally popular forces by proclaiming their intention to establish a new form of exploitative society—a goal that peasants, small commodity producers, and workers might have been understandably reluctant to support—but did so instead by variously raising demands for religious freedom, representative democracy, national independence, and, ultimately, socialist recon-struction, although by the last named the dissociation between being and con-sciousness, between reality and representation, had become almost total. Of all the successive, if overlapping, ideologies under which the bourgeois revolutions were waged, only that of the Enlightenment can be genuinely described as originating within the bourgeoisie, rather than being adopted and adapted for bourgeois pur-poses. And of all the victorious bourgeois revolutions, only the French can be said to have been inspired by Enlightenment thought, which is one reason why this greatest of all examples is also the most exceptional.

Initially at least—that is to say in the cases of the United Provinces and Eng-land—all of these preconditions had to be present before a bourgeois revolution had the possibility of success. The specifics of how the various preconditions were met differed from country to country. Each had their own specific versions of what Stone termed, in the English context, "long-term preconditions," "medium-term precipitants" and "short-term triggers," but these variations belong to the individual histories of the successive revolutions. What can be said in an overview of this sort is that in every case the opening of a period of social revolution is usually unmistakable, involving a moment of what Teodor Shanin calls "alternativity," when all their preconditions are met and the fuse of political crisis is lit:

> Long periods pass during which material circumstances (as well as our images of them) and social institutions (reflected in individual cognitions) facilitate the high consistency of social reproduction and foreclose fundamental changes. During these well-patterned, repetitive, socialization-bound and sociologically explicable stages the historical processes behave themselves in a nicely predictable manner, the "alternativity" of history is low. Then, once in a while, comes a period of major crisis, a revolution, an "axial" stage. The locks of rigidly pattered behavior, self-censored imaginations, and self-evident stereotypes of common sense are broken, and the sky seems the limit, or all hell seems let loose. The "alternativity" of history, the significance of consciousness, and particularly the scope for originality and choice, increase dramatically. The "turning" taken then by a society establishes the pattern of development for decades or centuries.[17]

When historical development accelerates to the point where the outbreak of revolution is inescapable three alternatives are then posed: victory for the revolution on a transformative social basis; defeat and the reassertion of the existing order, or—less straightforwardly—confinement within the limits of political revolution. Of course, no revolution can be guaranteed success, even if it is objectively feasible, because of the element of subjectivity—the revolutionary forces may lack effective leadership while the defenders of the existing order may possess precisely this quality. And, as we shall see in the next chapter, even success could prove temporary in the face of counterrevolution from without. But even victory could take two forms—there are, in other words, also "alternatives" in this respect. Here I think we have to take seriously the implications of the first of the three "symptoms" declared indispensible by Lenin for a "revolutionary situation": "When it is impossible for the ruling class to maintain their rule without any change; when there is a crisis, in one form or another, among the 'upper classes,' a crisis in the policy of the ruling class, leading to a fissure through which the discontent and indignation of the oppressed classes burst forth. For a revolution to take place, it is usually insufficient for 'the lower classes not to want' to live in the old way; it is also necessary that 'the upper classes should be unable' to live in the old way."[18] The point, as Lenin was quite aware, is that in the case of the bourgeois revolution, the hitherto feudal ruling class could under certain conditions successfully attempt to rule in a "new" way, involving capitalist social relations, but only after a certain point in history had been reached, the point at which capitalism had become an unstoppable economic force. Thereafter, ultimate victory may have been assured, but the question then became not whether the world would be capitalist but what form would be taken by the bourgeois revolutions and the capitalist nation-states they would create. But these considerations point us toward the end of an era; we must first understand how it began.

THE ACTUALITY OF THE FEUDAL CRISIS

Until the Japanese Meiji Restoration of 1868 all successful bourgeois revolutions were made against European feudal states or their overseas extensions in the Americas; we therefore need to begin with the mode of production upon which they were based. Non-Marxist historians have tended to identify feudalism with a relatively short-lived episode in its development, namely the establishment of land tenure based on military service ("vassalage") during the tenth century in parts of what are now Belgium and France. Under this system, the vassals, themselves members of the ruling class, were obliged to provide military service to the monarch and attend his court in return for land granted directly from the crown. Sub-vassals had the same relationship to their superiors, and so on down the chain of seigniorial command. In Marxist terms, however, feudalism is more than a political relationship between different sections of the ruling class. It is rather a distinct mode of production compatible with several different forms of political rule. Feudalism in this sense is fundamentally defined by the existence of an exploitative social relationship between a class of landowners and another, vastly more numerous, class of peasants, who were by no means always serfs tied to a specific piece of land or a particular master. This relationship had two distinguishing features.

The first was that the main source of income for the landowners was appropriated, in the form of rent, from the surplus produced by the peasants, rather than from the work of slaves or wage laborers.[19] Members of the feudal ruling class did, of course, own slaves or employ wage laborers at different periods in the development of the system but merely to supplement an income already guaranteed by the exploitation of their tenants. Moreover, as Jairus Banaji reminds us, within an economy subject to feudal laws of motion: "The slaves and hired laborers who intervened in this kind of economy were as much part of specifically *feudal relations of production* as the serf population itself."[20]

The second distinguishing feature was the process by which the surplus was extracted. Since the peasants had effective possession of the means of production (land, tools, animals), and would not have handed over part of their produce without external pressure, the relationship between lord and peasant was inevitably coercive, involving either the threat or actual application of force. As a result, the political and judicial institutions through which this pressure was exerted are inseparable from economic relations and must be included in any definition of the system. Key among these institutions were the territorial jurisdictions through which local lords could bring tenants to their own court of law.[21] The general commutation of servile dues and the attendant shifts from labor rent through rent in kind to money rent refined the system without bringing about the domination of capitalist relations of production—the existence of money being a necessary but insufficient condition for this to take place.

The first period of feudal development, following the consolidation of the system early in the eleventh century, saw increases in productivity, measurable by increased crop yields, through the application of technological innovation and direct seignio-rial supervision of the labor process.[22] The evidence of these centuries demonstrates that feudalism was capable of developing the productive forces, to a degree, without the relations of production posing an obstacle—the capitalist component of the European economy was in any case of minor importance at the time, except in parts of northern Italy and Flanders. The significance of this period of development can be seen by the end of the twelfth century: "This was the first time that one could begin to speak of a 'European economy,' at least since the Roman Empire, and certainly the first time that such a trans-regional economy was not dependent on a trans-regional state."[23] The existence of such an economy means that it is pos-sible to speak of a *general* crisis of feudalism, spreading unevenly but inescapably across Europe from the late thirteenth to the early fourteenth century, bringing an end to this period of expansion. Guy Bois has highlighted the extent to which the crisis represented a qualitative shift:

> The watershed at the beginning of the fourteenth century is not simply one episode among the many dramatic conflicts that punctuate the history of feudalism. It must be seen at a deeper level, as the beginning of the crisis of a mode of production. What does this mean? First, that the system had exhausted its possibilities of expansion, having completely occupied all cultivatable land. . . . The economic impasse became a social one. The end of expansion precipitated the fall in seigniorial revenue. How could the lord compel his subjects to make additional contributions when he no longer possessed sufficient powers over them? The impasse was at once political, in-stitutional, and moral. It is this general character of the crisis (which affected all as-pects of social life) that we denote by the expression "crisis of feudalism."[24]

The feudal crisis is usually taken to consist of the following elements, some of which are mentioned by Bois. First, a population that had grown significantly through the centuries of expansion began to reach the territorial limits of lands that could be colonized for clearance or reclamation. In areas of existing settlement, crop yields first stagnated and then began to fall through exhaustion of the land, in part as a result of it being used mainly for arable rather than pastoral purposes, leading to a lack of manure for fertilization. A similar stalling in forces of produc-tion can be detected in the mining industry, which extracted the silver used for monetary exchange: once the near surface seams of the metal had been exhausted, existing levels of technique were unable to penetrate sufficiently far underground to reach new reserves, which inevitably led to the increasing debasement of the currency on the one hand and the hoarding of older, purer coins on the other. The combined effect on the lords of declining rural productivity and currency inflation was to reduce their income at a time when their socially determined levels of ex-penditure were rising.[25]

These causes of crisis varied in intensity across feudal Europe, but there was one further block to development, which had a more universal impact. This lay not in the forces of production but rather in the way in which the relations of production and the state were inseparable under feudalism. As Stephen Epstein has pointed out, "the principle threat to feudalism did not come from trade; up to a point, feudalism thrived on trade," not least because lords "did not exclude markets, they regulated and taxed them for income." As Epstein notes:

> The lords' and towns' main purposes in stimulating trade was to maximize income streams from their fiscal and jurisdictional rights, and those rights were a fundamental aspect of their social and political powers. In other words, "free trade" would have reduced both feudal and urban revenue, and challenged the jurisdictional superiority of lord over peasant and town over country. Consequently, strong feudal jurisdiction was incompatible with long-run economic growth. Not surprisingly, agricultural innovation appears to have been inversely correlated with the intensity of seigniorial rights, and rural industry was inversely correlated with the jurisdictional powers of towns. The fundamental constraint in the feudal economy was not technological inertia, but the market monopolies and other coordination failures arising from political and jurisdictional parcellization.[26]

There was no capitalist solution available to resolve the feudal crisis: indeed, it was only the effect of the latter that generated the possibility of capitalism as an alternative form of society in the first place. It is important to understand the implications of this sequence of developments, in particular it means that any claim that capitalism—as opposed to merchants' and usurers' capital—existed before the fourteenth century involves a form of misrecognition. Feudalism involved economic relationships other than those between lords and peasants. Like all precapitalist modes of production it necessarily involved markets, trade, and consequently the existence of a class of merchants who were integral to its functioning. Throughout early modern Europe mercantile capitalism played an ambiguous role in the development of the system. They drew their profits, not from realizing the value added to commodities in the process of production, but from the discrepancy in price between their initial outlay and the ultimate selling price at the end of long-distance trade routes. Fernand Braudel is right to say: "With few exceptions, the capitalist, that is in this period, the 'important merchant' with many undifferentiated activities, did not commit himself wholeheartedly to production." His central interests made him "a man of the market": "Above all in distribution, marketing—the sector in which real profits were made."[27] Marx noted that even by taking control of production, the merchant "cannot bring about the overthrow of the old mode of production itself, but rather preserves and retains it as its own precondition." More specifically, where "the merchant makes the small masters into his middlemen, or even buys directly from the independent producer he leaves him nominally independent and leaves his mode of production unchanged": for capitalism to develop required either the industrialist to directly become a merchant or the merchant to directly become an industrialist.[28] For all these reasons, their activities were, as Alex Callinicos writes, a "necessary but not sufficient" condition for the dominance of capitalist relations of production: "As long as capitalism did not conquer production it was forced (and indeed largely content) to co-exist with feudalism."[29]

This assessment of the merchant class fraction also has implications for how we understand the territorial bases from which they undertook many of their activities: the towns. Adam Smith was the first thinker to regard these as the spatial embodiment of what he called "commercial society," as opposed to the parcelized feudal authority dispersed throughout the countryside.[30] Subsequently, his position has been endorsed by several important non-Marxist thinkers including Weber and Braudel. It is perhaps best summarized by Michael Postan: "Medieval towns . . . were non-feudal islands in the feudal seas; places in which merchants could not only live in each other's vicinity and defend themselves collectively but also places which enjoyed or were capable of developing systems of local government and principles of law and status exempting them from the sway of the feudal regime."[31] Several Marxists have also accepted this position, often in the form expressed by Postan.[32] Eric Mielants's statement of the case is representative: "Because of the nobility's weakness, division and inability to adequately (re)generate primitive accumulation based on extraeconomic coercion, the elites in charge of the European city-state system were capable of constructing strategies that furthered the ceaseless accumulation of capital (with subsequent reinvestment in their companies)."[33] But like the merchants who dominated them, the towns had an ambiguous position within the feudal system that cannot be treated as one of uncomplicated opposition.

The struggle for urban autonomy during the eleventh and twelfth centuries was not in any sense "anti-feudal"; it was rather an attempt by the local patriciates to establish their own distinct position within the feudal ruling class. Similarly, the urban "revolutions" that pitched the merchant guilds against the magnates were not struggles between "capitalist" and feudal classes but struggles for office within the latter; at most these were political revolutions, as defined in the previous chapter. Unsurprisingly then, in their capacity as corporate bodies the towns often acted as institutional seigneurs for the surrounding countryside, with the burgesses playing the role of collective exploiters of the peasantry, no different in this respect from individual nobles or the Church. As a result, in Italy in particular, peasants would often ally with the lords against the authority of the towns, above all that of imposing and collecting taxes. It was not the role of towns as corporate entities that helped to undermine feudalism, but the fact that they constituted independent spaces of relative freedom—"islands," in Postan's terminology—where lordly jurisdictions did not hold sway. As such, they allowed a forum for the collective exchange of new opinions concerning everything from agricultural production or religious observance, which would have been impossible in more isolated or scattered rural communities; they provided places of physical safety for peasants fleeing the land and their masters (although runaway peasants were by no means always welcomed by the urban guilds, whose function was precisely to restrict entry into the occupations they organized, not open them up to unskilled rural refugees). Did they also play a more directly political role? Here too the record is uneven. The great series of peasant revolts that stretched from maritime Flanders in the 1320s to Catalonia in the 1480s effectively ended serfdom in the West, although not, of course, feudalism itself. Although never themselves instigators of these revolts, towns sometimes contributed to their success, either through empathetic risings of the urban plebeians against their own oppressors (as in Canterbury and London during the English Peasant Revolt of 1381) or the more calculated support of the towns themselves as feudal corporate bodies with their own reasons for opposing the lords (as Paris did during the French *Grande Jaquerie* of 1359). During the most successful of all peasant revolts, in Catalonia between 1462 and 1472, however, the urban patriciate of Barcelona actually allied with the feudal nobility *against* the *Remenscas* peasants.[34] The last example in particular demonstrates that Trotsky was simply wrong to claim, as a general position, that: "In Europe, beginning with the close of the Middle Ages, each victorious peasant uprising did not place a peasant government in power but a left urban party. To put it more precisely, a peasant uprising turned out victorious exactly to the degree to which it succeeded in strengthening the position of the revolutionary section of the urban population."[35] Indeed, the most decisive alliance between peasants and towns (involving both individual burghers and the commune as a collective actor) demonstrates how it was possible for areas to escape from feudal domination without necessarily doing so on a capitalist basis.

The Swiss cantons, largely for reasons of geographical inaccessibility, retained on a greater scale than elsewhere most of the individual peasant freedoms that had been lost elsewhere in Western Europe by the end of the thirteenth century. Alpine society was both effectively (although not always formally) free of feudal lordship and organized communally for certain activities like the sale of dairy products, the protection of mountain passes, and mercenary activity. The importance of the Swiss valleys as a trade route between southern Germany and northern Italy also encouraged the growth of independent towns based on the model of the Italian communes. The difference between the Swiss and, for example, the Italian city-states was that the former retained the alliance with the peasantry who remained armed and in certain circumstances were granted citizenship, while the urban guilds did not seek to undermine rural production. The reliance of the towns on the surrounding countryside also had ideological effects in that the burghers could not celebrate their superior position to that of the peasantry or the urban poor, as their counterparts in the Italian and German lands did, without risking their security.[36] One consequence was that "no large number of dispossessed peasants was available as a source of cheap labor and of any large urban proletariat."[37] When the Austrian Habsburgs attempted to subject the Swiss lands to their seigniory (or rather to extend their seigniory across the entire territory), they were met by an alliance of free burgesses and peasants that established the Swiss Confederation between 1291 and 1393, a process that coincided with the most devastating period of the first crisis of feudalism. The fact that the feudal overlords were external ("foreign" would be anachronistic here) meant that their removal stripped out the ruling class, leaving other relationships in place. Progress toward capitalism was slow. The first cantons to join the confederation in 1291 had thrown off a foreign feudalism before capitalism had a chance to develop, leaving a population of small commodity producers in possession of their land. Although this example is the nearest one we have to a "revolutionary road to simple commodity production," the situation did not remain static but saw the forest cantons and cities either fall under the domination of the various feudal courts of the German crown in the North or develop toward capitalism in South, but without any effective superstructure. By the time Calvin set up his dictatorship in Geneva during the sixteenth century this land of free peasants and urban oligarchs was the very opposite of a centralized nation-state. Divided by language, a fragmented canton structure, and, after the Reformation, opposed religious affiliations, it made much of its wealth by hiring out the population as mercenaries to the very regimes that were stifling capitalist development elsewhere in Europe. If this, "the first independent republic in Europe" was in any sense "a bourgeois republic," it was only in the sense that, as Engels put it, "the Swiss . . . turned their fame as warriors to cash."[38] Feudal crisis on its own could lead to revolution, but not to bourgeois revolution.

THE POSSIBILITY OF A CAPITALIST ALTERNATIVE

The crisis did not of course last uninterruptedly from the late thirteenth to the late eighteenth century, "There is no doubt that feudalism in Europe became reactionary in the thirteenth to eighteenth centuries," writes Tony Cliff, "but this did not prevent the productive forces developing at the same rate as before or indeed of developing at an even faster rate."[39] But in so far as the productive forces did resume their growth after the first crisis it was only to the extent that capitalism had begun to establish itself. How did this new way of organizing production first emerge? The elements that would eventually combine to create the capitalist mode of production—not only market competition but also wage labor and commodity production—preexisted it by many centuries. Political Marxists are therefore right to insist that the existence of these elements does not in itself indicate the existence of capitalism as such. One can further agree with them that the socioeconomic activities that ultimately ended up producing capitalism were not, initially at any rate, necessarily undertaken with capitalism as a conscious goal. Neither of these observations should be taken to mean, however, that capitalism was an unlikely outcome.

There are very few ways in which exploitation or the social relations of production more generally can be organized. "Slavery, serfdom and wage labor are historically and socially different solutions to a universal problem which remains fundamentally the same," writes Braudel.[40] Given this highly restricted range of options, the chances of something like capitalism arising were actually rather high, given certain conditions. Alan Carling has argued that it originally emerged as a result of what he calls "feudal fission": "It was probable that something like English agricultural capitalism would arise out of something like European feudalism." Why? Carling identifies two characteristics of feudalism as crucial to this outcome: political decentralization and the demographic cycle. The first meant that no state was in a position to impose a uniform system of production, with the result that new systems could develop in the spaces where sovereignty did not hold sway. The second meant that population collapse was regularly of such severity that it left spaces of this type (following the desertion of hitherto occupied land, for example), which could be filled by property and productive relations of an ultimately capitalist nature: "If there are 10 or 20 independent fission experiments in each demographic cycle, the probability of at least one 'English' outcome is very high, even if the probability is very low of an English outcome in any single experiment. . . . And England only has to happen once for capitalism to become established. That is why it is not as fanciful as one might suppose to suggest that the transition from feudalism to capitalism was almost inevitable—almost indeed a natural necessity of history."[41]

It is not the demographic cycle in general that is significant here, but rather the specific downturn associated with the general crisis of the fourteenth century, which was in turn massively intensified by the incidence of the Black Death. If capitalism did not preexist the feudal crisis, why did this catastrophe lead people to turn to new ways of economic organization? In order to answer this question we must first revisit some fundamental tenets of historical materialism.

Marxism treats the social world as a whole, or what Lukács calls a "mediated totality." To be part of a totality is to be part of "a total social situation caught up in the process of social change"; to say that a totality is mediated is to overcome "the mere immediacy of the empirical world," in which moments are "torn . . . from the complex of their true determinants and placed in artificial isolation."[42] Two claims are being made here: one is that societies constitute totalities (and Lukács rightly believed that capitalist societies are the most "totalizing" of all); the other is that our method for understanding specific aspects of a society must involve treating them as constituents of a greater whole.[43] For Bertell Ollman, Marxism conceives of reality "as a totality composed of internally related parts" so that each of these parts "in its fullness can represent the totality" and for each aspect "the conditions of its existence are taken to be part of what it is": "Capital, for example, is not simply the physical means of production, but includes potentially the whole pattern of social relations that enables these to function as they do."[44] David Harvey has spelled out the implications of this approach for the type of disciplinary boundaries that became characteristic of academic inquiry after the Enlightenment:

> Put simply, the Marxian method accepts fragmentation and separation for purposes of analysis only on the condition that the integrity of the relation between the whole and the part is maintained intact. The Marxian theory thus starts with the proposition that everything relates to everything else in society and that a particular object of

inquiry must necessarily internalize a relation to the totality of which it is a part. The focus of the inquiry is, then, on the relations of the epistemological object to the enquiry—as Marx does when he commences his analysis of capitalism by an examination of the commodity—is to discover the relations within it that reveal the real nature of the capitalist mode of production. . . . Marx did not disaggregate the world into "economic," "sociological," "political," "psychological," and other factors. He sought to construct an approach to the totality of relations within capitalist society.[45]

And yet, stating "everything relates to everything else in society" without further elaboration is simply to affirm a truism from which few but the most extreme Nietzschians would dissent. Different aspects of the totality form what Derek Sayer calls "a hierarchy of conditions of possibility."[46] In his mature work (that is, post-1847) Marx argued that there were three different forms of human practice, which together explain how societies emerge, develop, and transform themselves. One, the most fundamental, involves those activities that bring together natural and technological capacities and qualities into the cooperative activities that directly produce and reproduce human existence. These activities entail the social relationships of exploitation and conflict within which they take place. These in turn entail those institutions—of which the states system is fundamental—and ideologies by which these relationships are justified, defended, and challenged.[47] For Marx then, "the anatomy of . . . civil society . . . has to be found in political economy" and the anatomy of the state has to be found in turn in civil society.[48]

These three practices have usually been identified by the terms "forces of production" and "relations of production"—together constituting the "base" (or "infrastructure")—and the superstructure. As Benjamin puts it, the superstructure is not a "reflection" of the base, but its "expression": "The economic conditions under which society exists are expressed in the superstructure—precisely as, with the sleeper, an overfull stomach finds not its reflection but its expression in the content of dreams, which, from a causal point of view, it may be said to 'condition.'"[49] I do not intend to use the term "base and superstructure" here, but not because I object to the use of metaphor. As Andrew Collier points out, most abstract terms, like "wave" in physics or—more relevant to this discussion—"market" in economics, start out as metaphors, but tend to lose their metaphoric quality whenever they are closely defined within the particular branch of science.[50] My objection is rather that it is not a very helpful metaphor and, on the contrary, it positively encourages undialectical forms of thought: a building is constructed from the base up, but there is no point at which a society does not have both a base and a superstructure, nor do buildings change their superstructure once constructed. Indeed, outside of the 1859 "Preface" Marx and Engels themselves used the metaphor on less than a dozen occasions and several of these were in explanatory letters by Engels warning against the mechanistic uses to which it was already being put within the Second International.

The underlying concept that the metaphor inadequately seeks to express—of a hierarchy of practices in which a causal chain ascends from the productive forces through the productive relations to the various aspects of the superstructure—is however essential to historical materialism, providing this is understood in properly epochal terms: it is not a mechanism for explaining every historical event that has taken place or every social institution that has arisen. In one of the late letters to which I have already referred, Engels tried to clarify some of the key propositions of historical materialism against trivial applications, noting, for example, the impossibility, "without making oneself ridiculous, to explain in terms of economics the existence of every small state in Germany, past and present."[51] But both Marx and Engels were in no doubt that the productive forces had to develop to a certain extent before capitalism itself could come into existence. For Marx, the core human quality, the one that distinguishes us from the rest of the animal world, is the need and ability to produce and reproduce our means of existence. This is why production, not property, is the *sine qua non* of Marx and Engels's own Marxism, and why their theory of social development privileges the development of the productive forces over productive relations. As Marx wrote in *Capital* Volume 1: "For capitalist relations to establish themselves at all presupposes that a certain level of historical production has been attained. Even within the framework of an earlier mode of production certain needs and certain means of communication and production must have developed which go beyond the old relations of production and coerce them into the capitalist mould."[52] Given the high levels of abstraction at which these debates tend to be conducted, including my own discussion thus far, it might be useful to examine the process through a concrete micro-example from the epoch of the Scottish bourgeois revolution. As late as the Anglo-Scottish Union of 1707, coal mining, lead mining, and salt panning north of the border were activities dominated by the lords, who supplemented their income from feudal rent by exporting the mineral wealth of their lands. The minerals were extracted by men who were legally serfs (although the Scottish Enlightenment reformers tended to refer to them as "slaves," by analogy with plantation labor in the Americas). By the last quarter of the eighteenth century the class position of the men operating this machinery had, however, undergone a decisive change: they were no longer legally bound as serfs to the coal they dug, but were wage laborers whose terms and conditions were at least partly determined by their collective organization. The process discussed here therefore went in sequence from changes to the forces of production (introduction of the new mining technology to increase output), leading to long-term changes in the relations of production (gradual transition to wage-labor to ensure workforce availability), overlapping with the conclusion of the Scottish bourgeois revolution (defeat and abolition of localized military-feudal "dual power" in the last Jacobite Rising of 1745–46), and leading directly to still longer-term changes in the legal-ideological region of the superstructure (juridical recognition and formalization of the shifts in relations of production with Acts of Parliament of 1775 and, more decisively, of 1799).[53]

Despite the existence of this type of historical example, sections of the left have for several decades now tended to downplay or deny altogether this aspect of his thought. In part this has been inspired by an understandable revulsion at the mechanistic and determinist formulae typical of Social Democracy and Stalinism. A passage from the most famous of all Stalinist textbooks, displaying the general secretary's distinctive approach to literary production, provides a classic example: "First the productive forces of production of society change and develop and then, depending on these changes and *in conformity with them*, men's relations of production, their economic relations, change."[54] The critique of what is usually, if wrongly, called "productive force determinism" has two aspects.

One is that it has no explanatory power and fails to square with the known facts. Unsurprisingly, given its emphasis on social property relations, political Marxism has played a leading role in providing intellectual support for this tendency. According to Wood, "the proposition that history is propelled forward by the inevitable contradictions between forces and relations of production" is, in her view, "scarcely less vacuous than the general law of technological development in its simpler form."[55] "Productive force determinism is of little use in explaining the crisis of pre-capitalist modes of production and is redundant in Marx's model of the crisis of capitalism," writes Stephen Rigby: "Neither is the theory of any use in explaining transitions from one mode of production to another, a central issue in Marxist historiography."[56] Only slightly less dismissive is Cornelius Castoriadis, who at least accepts that the development of the productive forces may explain one important historical process:

> It more or less faithfully describes what took place at the time of the transition from feudal society: from the hybrid societies of Western Europe from 1650 to 1850 (where a well-developed and economically dominant bourgeoisie ran up against absolute monarchy and the remains of feudalism in agrarian property and in legal and political structures) to capitalist society. But it corresponds neither to the breakdown of ancient society and the subsequent appearance of the feudal world, nor to the birth of the bourgeoisie, which emerged precisely outside of and on the fringes of feudal relations.[57]

The other aspect of the critique of "productive force determinism," often articulated by the same people, concerns the way in which it supposedly diminishes human agency. James Young complains that: "There has long been a tendency amongst some 'Marxist' historians to portray any expansion of the productive forces as being the key to human emancipation from either nature or feudal oppression."[58] Joseph Ferraro claims that Marx and Engels did not give primacy to the productive forces but to "human activity" and apparently finds it necessary to tell us: "It is humans who are the principal protagonists in history, not the productive forces; and not humans in the abstract, but humans divided into antagonistic classes."[59]

These are not new arguments but ones that have existed in different forms since Marxism began to acquire a mass following, as the following comment from the 1880s suggests: "When the average Russian intellectual hears that in Marx 'everything is reduced to the economic foundation' (others simply say 'to the economic') he loses his head, as though someone had suddenly fired a starting pistol."[60] The local allergic reaction reported here by Plekhanov in the 1880s has more recently acquired global epidemic proportions, but it is no more appropriate now than it was then. The forces and relations of production are not a synonym for "the economic" and study of their interrelation does not correspond to the bourgeois academic discipline of "economics," even though Marx and Engels occasionally used these terms or referred to the "economic element" as a conventional means of expression. A central theme of Marxism is the critique of political economy, and this at times overlaps with consideration of the forces and relations of production (as in Marx's discussions of the "formal" and "real" subordination of labor, or of "primitive accumulation"); but these discussions belong to different regions in the totality of Marxist thought. Insofar as we allow these distinctions at all, the forces and relations of production are aspects of "the social" rather than "the economic," since they are essentially about the organization of cooperation and exploitation within and between classes. In one sense then, Ferraro is quite correct: the productive forces do not "develop" themselves: they are not sentient, nor are they even independent variables, "calling forth" this or "selecting" that response from the relations of production. To say that forces of production have developed is simply to say that human beings have been motivated to change them and have then successfully done so in such a way that the social productivity of labor has risen as a result.[61] Human agency is quite as decisive here as it is in the class struggle.

Eric Olin Wright has argued that, as a general proposition, there is a "weak" tendency for the productive forces to be developed, from the transition to class society onward. Unlike tools or equipment, productive techniques will tend to be retained once they are acquired: no one has a positive interest in causing labor productivity as such to fall, although it may still do so through the effects of war, as in central Europe during the first half of the seventeenth century. On the contrary, ruling classes have a general interest in sustaining or increasing labor productivity, if only to ensure the availability of the surplus that they must appropriate to maintain itself. But more generally, developing the productive forces will create new needs—for types of manufactured clothing, say—whose continued satisfaction depends on the level of development being maintained, so that there are people from more than one class with positive interests in doing so.[62] When people develop the productive forces it creates a situation in which they, or other people, can adopt new, more compatible productive relations, of which there are not an infinite number. As John Torrance argues in his "Darwinian" reading of Marx, "mutations in production relations are not random, but experimental":

> They arise as deliberate attempts to adapt to perceived conditions. To that extent the mechanism resembles the breeding of new strains under domestication. But it also differs from artificial selection, where only desired traits are allowed reproductive success in a controlled environment. For development of the productive forces limits variation in productive relations in much the same way as the natural environment limits biological variation: those variants most capable of reproducing themselves persist while others die out.

Torrance suggests a parallel with "feral species, bred experimentally, but surviving in the wild," which seems appropriate for class societies.[63] But although developing the productive forces makes certain types of society possible, it does not make them inevitable. Here again the role of human agency is decisive. Ruling classes are never passive. By successfully preventing people from developing the productive forces to the point where they can lead to changes in productive relations, they have either ensured centuries of relative stagnation or the repetition of developmental phases that never progress beyond a certain point. In other relatively rare cases, this type of blocking maneuver led to outright regression, as it did across Western Europe in the fifth century, in the fourteenth, and again—although on a more regionalized basis—in the seventeenth; but even in these cases, the "anti-development" of the productive forces also led to transformations in productive relations: change does not always go in one direction. As Alasdair MacIntyre once noted, "it is no use treating the doctrine that the basis determines the superstructure as a general formula in the way Stalinism has done": "For the difference between one form of society and another is not just a difference in basis, and a corresponding difference in superstructure, but a difference also in the way basis is related to superstructure."[64] The process by which human beings first make progressive changes to the productive forces, then the productive relations and ultimately the superstructures can explain the two greatest social transformations that have occurred in human history: the transition from pre-class society ("primitive communism") to various forms of class society (slave, feudal, tributary).[65] The other was the transition to capitalism.

As we saw in chapter 18, political Marxists do not believe that anyone under pre-capitalist modes of production has any incentive to develop the productive forces. Or as Robert Brenner puts it, the process whereby "individual economic actors adopt more effective techniques in bringing in new relations of production simply because the techniques are more productively effective decisively depends on the existence of capitalist property relations." Why? Because only under capitalism "will the individual economic actors necessarily have the motivation . . . to adopt new techniques."[66] Wood appears to believe that saying human beings have the desire and capacity to improve their material conditions is the same as saying that they have always been subjugated by the needs of competitive accumulation. One consequence of this denial that there might have been any positive incentives to embrace capitalist production is a tendency to portray peasant life before capitalism as essentially based on a natural economy of self-governing communities, which have no incentive to develop the productive forces, and into which the lords or the Church only intrude superficially and occasionally in order to acquire their surplus. I do not recognize this picture. In a great passage from one of the early classics of Scottish vernacular literature, *The Complaynt of Scotland*, written by Robert Wedderburn but published anonymously in 1549, the character of "the laborer" [peasant] rages against the misery of his life: "I labor night and day with my hands to feed lazy and useless men, and they repay me with hunger and the sword.

I sustain their life with the toil and sweat of my body, and they persecute my body with hardship, until I am become a beggar. They live through me and I die through them."[67] Four centuries later the power of that final sentence is undiminished. Developing the productive forces seems to me to be at least as rational a response to the feudal exploitation it so vividly describes as the alternatives of "fight or flight" that are usually posed. People have wanted to do the former since the transition to agriculture; they have only had to do the latter since the transition to capitalism. The wish to better the circumstances in which we live has been one the main impulses behind the attempts to develop the productive forces and it is intimately bound up with class society, not least because in situations where the direct producers have to hand over part of what they have produced to someone else, there is a very real motive—one might almost say, an imperative—to increase their output, a motive that need have initially nothing to do with market compulsion. As Peter Musgrave writes:

> The search for profit maximization is as valid an economic objective for early modern Europeans as it is in the modern world. It would certainly be wrong to argue that at no time and at no place in early modern Europe did people or families set out to improve the performance of their own private economies by seeking and following the sort of opportunities which were to lead on to the industrial developments of the nineteenth and twentieth centuries. This economic aim could be followed sensibly in an early modern context only in certain limited and specific circumstances.

Musgrave, like Brenner, assumes that risk is the main factor preventing peasants from opting for profit maximization. What could overcome these concerns? Musgrave argues that it could only have been such insecurity that the risk was worth taking because it could scarcely be worse than current conditions.[68] Increasing production, if it leads to greater disposable income, might give peasants the wherewithal to buy their way out of performing labor services, to hire wage labor to carry out work that would otherwise destroy the health and shorten the life of family members, or perhaps even to acquire heritable property which would remove them from feudal jurisdictions altogether. "Rather than retreating from the market," writes Jane Whittle, "peasants used the market to escape from serfdom."[69] And in conditions of crisis, such as those that shook European feudalism in the fourteenth century, the pressure on the ruling class to raise the level of exploitation, and consequently on the peasantry to look for ways of escape, was of course heightened still further.

The result was a prolonged process of class differentiation among the peasantry. In England, it led to the emergence of a class of richer peasants who were at least as important to English agrarian development as the lords. As several writers—by no means all hostile to the Brenner thesis—have pointed out, without the existence of such a relatively prosperous class it is difficult to see where the lords would have found a sufficient number of tenants, or how these tenants could have afforded the investment that the landlords demanded.[70] Terence Byres writes: "The possibility . . . exists for the peasant to produce surpluses, whether deliberately or adventitiously, and to market those surpluses. This is so given that the lords, their powers of extra-economic coercion notwithstanding, are unable to extract everything above subsistence, even though they may well wish to." Rich peasants "had less restricted resources than middle and poor peasants; had larger plots and greater investment funds, and would, therefore, have been able to produce surpluses and better able to take attendant risks." Not to recognize the existence of this prior process of differentiation, like Brenner, is to assume: "Without explanation the existence of a class with the capacity and strength to take on commercial leases, to cope with and respond to market dependence, to compete in production and so, ultimately, become a class of capitalist farmers. Where did this class come from?"[71]

The period in which this class began to form fell between the onset of crisis and the arrival of the Black Death. Whittle writes of Norfolk: "The active land market, the litigious and market-orientated nature of Norfolk peasants, the large numbers of hired workers and rural craftsmen, not to mention the development of socialized rural industry in the form of worsted weaving, all dated from the late thirteenth and early fourteenth centuries, if not earlier."[72] Nevertheless, population decline and consequent labor shortages from the 1340s strengthened these tendencies. Rodney Hilton writes of Forncett, an estate to the southwest of Norwich, prior to 1381:

> A peasant society governed by customs in which serfdom and labor services played an important part was shattered by uncontrollable peasant mobility and the commercialization of all transactions in land. In 1378 on the very eve of the rebellion about a quarter of the free-holdings and three-quarters of villein holdings on this estate had been abandoned. The remaining tenants, many of them in theory unfree, were dealing briskly and commercially in the available land, taking parcels of, on an average, three to four acres on lease for short terms.

Nor is this the only example: "In Essex, the market in peasant land was developing a social differentiation among inhabitants of villages, dividing the landless and the cottagers from the few well-to-do."[73]

We are in short looking at a general phenomenon, at least across the southern half of England: "Whether we look at peasant life in the south-east, in the Thames Valley, in East Anglia or in the Midlands, we find standing out from the ordinary run of tenants with the fifteen or twenty-acre holdings, a small group of families sometimes free, more often serf, holding a hundred acres or more." These holdings would usually be composites, pieced together from a range of sources, and rarely consolidated. There were inevitably major tensions between the legal status of these larger peasants and their economic position, the former preventing them carrying out the activities which the latter would otherwise have made possible, notably the lack of freedom to buy and sell land, even if they had acquired surpluses. In contrast to the smaller peasants: "Most irritating to them must have been the hindrances to accumulation, rather than the fear of starvation."[74] This class of farmers existed because peasants had already put themselves under the discipline of the market in a situation where they were under no compulsion to do so. "[Brenner] assumes that lords were able to find tenants to take land on lease at a time when we also know that lords were granting land on increasingly favorable terms—without [entry] fines, with rent reductions—because of the overall shortage of tenants."[75] And why was there a shortage of tenants? "Clearly," writes Jaime Torras, "any explanation of the singularity of the English case must take into account those other sectors of the economy, absent from Brenner's model, which may have absorbed available labor and, by vying for it against the agricultural entrepreneurs, may have made wage-saving improvements attractive to them."[76]

These other sectors involved both non-agrarian rural and urban activity. R. B. Outhwaite writes: "The English countryside accommodated nearly one and one half million extra inhabitants before 1650, and by no means were all of them landless agricultural or industrial laborers." Far from being absorbed into large farming units from the mid-fourteenth century, there was a growth in the number of small farms, particularly in fenland, forest, woodland, and pastoral areas:

> The rapid growth of small farms became a problem in some places, a problem that was "solved" by these small farmers and cottagers turning their attentions increasingly to industrial pursuits, such as spinning or weaving of wool or hemp, the knitting of stockings, the making of lace or fishing nets, the manufacture of nails, basket-making or straw-plaiting. Whether such activities developed depended primarily on the availability of local raw materials, the proximity both of markets and of rival manufacturers, and the interest or lack of interest of merchant organizers. Where such activities developed, however, they accentuated many of the tendencies already noted: they became an additional inducement for local populations to stay and an extra attraction perhaps to immigrants; they may have encouraged early marriage—for both sexes; they made small-holdings viable; they may, in some cases, have enabled some landlords to secure higher rents, by permitting the proliferation of small units, than they could by encouraging the process of amalgamation.[77]

The same combinations occur in the towns. Indeed, the basis of the combination often was the connection with the countryside. Donald Woodward writes of the relationship between building craftsmen and agriculture that it "was close in many areas and that, like laborers, building craftsmen often supplemented their craft-earnings by farming both for subsistence and the market." Neither group was composed of pure wage-laborers. "Their modern equivalents are not wage-earning factory workers, but, rather, jobbing joiners, plumbers and electricians." In fact, their modern equivalents are more accurately identified as the semi-proletarians of the Global South who return to farms to work part-time during the year, or who maintain smallholdings to supplement their income or food intake. Nevertheless, Woodward is right to conclude: "English society during the sixteenth and seventeenth centuries had not yet become a predominantly wage-earning society . . . it was above all still a society in which the small unit of production and the small unit of ownership and control prevailed in most trades."[78]

The tripartite class structure of agrarian capitalism in England—capitalist landlord, capitalist tenant farmer, landless laborer—was achieved by a two-way process involving, on the one hand, divisions among the exploited and, on the other, changes from above in the functions of the exploiters. The former began first and may have been the inspiration for the latter. "Would it be too far-fetched to suggest that it was the example of substantial copyholders and the like, with their strictly commercial attitude to their land and produce, that gave lords the idea of adopting commercial rather than feudal relationships, when the former became more promising?"[79] Take, as a specific example of change from the bottom up, the process of enclosure, which Brenner tends to see as imposed on peasant communities by the lords. What is enclosure? The most useful definition, by Wordie, defines it as a situation of "land held in severalty, fell completely under the power of one owner to do with as he pleased, whether or not he chose to enclose his land in the literal sense with hedges and ditches." The essential point is that the land no longer carried common rights.[80] "He" was of course occasionally "she," but more importantly was often a collective, since the dispossession of common land was by no means only carried out by individuals. When did the bulk of enclosures take place? As Wordie carefully explains, making "every effort to err on the side of enclosure where doubt exists," by 1500 England at most 45 percent enclosed and only 47 percent enclosed by 1600, but 75 percent enclosed by 1760, meaning "there was almost twice as much enclosure in seventeenth-century England as in any other century, including the eighteenth."[81]

Who carried out the enclosures? Robert Duplessis has noted that this was in fact often initiated by peasants themselves with the consequence of increasing divisions within the community: "Members of the existing yeoman elite—freeholders on lands their ancestors had acquired after the Black Death or tenants with long-term renewable leases at fixed rents—were often in a position to take on or create enclosed farms." For example: "On the manor of Cheshunt (Hertfordshire), where 20 per cent of the tenants already held slightly more than half the land in 1484, but boosted their share to 70 per cent in 1562, the trend towards concentration was due essentially to transfers among tenants."[82] These changes were in response to market "opportunities": "For example, in order to take advantage of the potentially higher profit margins of pastoral farming, village communities should ideally have rearranged their fields and introduced some form of convertible husbandry. But in order to facilitate this process, they often had to discard the communal features of the open field-system and enclose fields, in other words, alter the property and institutional framework of the entire township."[83]

But even after the lords began to adopt commercial relationships, they were not capable of doing so completely on their own terms, precisely because of the existence of a class of capitalist farmers. As Mark Overton points out:

> There is mounting evidence to show that there was not a coordinated relationship between landlord power, tenure ownership, farm size and capitalist farming. Landlords were frequently unable to exercise the power that Brenner attitudes to them: customary tenancies and leases could give legal protection to tenants, whose rights

were upheld by the courts. In general, economic differentiation was a process which took place among the tenantry. Moreover landlords, especially in the sixteenth century, showed little interest in developing their estates for capitalist tenant farming, and as a rule they were not very adventurous in promoting innovation in agriculture. The pioneers of new methods in the seventeenth and eighteenth centuries (at least in Norfolk) were not the great landowners but smaller farmers, both tenants and owner-occupiers ... the most dramatic advances in output and land productivity came in those areas (such as Norfolk) where leadership was relatively weak.[84]

On the basis of her study of Norfolk during the fifteenth and sixteenth centuries, Whittle writes: "There is no evidence that lords tried to transfer customary or copyhold land to leasehold in the sixteenth century. While considerable amounts of formerly customary or demesne lands were held by leasehold in Norfolk manors during the fifteenth century, this appears to have been because tenants preferred leasehold to customary tenure. It was untainted by the vestiges of serfdom, and its rents were sometimes lower."[85] The number of peasants who were able to achieve security of tenure ("freehold") was generally far greater than Brenner allows. These were often proprietor-tenants who exercised competitive pressure for increased rents on their subtenants and acquired far greater levels of income from doing so than the manorial lord himself. In Rossendale, for example, copyhold tenants were paying three to four times less to the manorial lord than the subtenants on the same holding were paying them.[86]

But what was true for England was also true, if to a lesser extent, of France. According to political Marxist orthodoxy: "Agrarian capitalism did not develop in France, since neither peasants, who formed subsistence communities based on unmediated access to their means of production, nor the upper classes (nobles and bourgeois), which reproduced themselves through land-rents and the spoils of political offices were subject to capitalist imperatives."[87] We should by now be wary about magical incantations involving the term "capitalist imperatives." As Phillip Hoffman comments of seventeenth-century France: "The poor often favored the dissolution of the commons, and in the one instance in which the poor did fight for common grazing rights—in Varades—it was to protect their stake in what was clearly capitalist agriculture."[88] The episode to which Hoffman refers is full of interest. For virtually a hundred years after 1639 the peasants of Varades fought with the local marquis to retain use the commons against his attempts to enclose it. As Hoffman comments, at first glance this looks like another example of enterprising capitalist aristocrat in conflict with traditional peasant agriculture—which would in itself cast doubt on the supposed unwillingness of the French landed classes to improve, but the situation was more complex than this. There was indeed a capitalist interest here, but it lies not with the landowner—in this case we can confirm the stereotype—but with the peasants themselves. For as Hoffman explains, they were attempting to continue to use the common to graze sheep, but as "a commercial enterprise raised for sale because they could be transported over long distances." The problem is where we conceive of "the commons" as invariably being associated with the spaces of peasant collectivity under feudal or tributary modes of production. In this case, at least: "The common pasture was not the preserve of subsistence farming. Rather, it was the meeting place for nascent rural capitalism, the locus for a curious alliance between modest peasants and the agents of commercial agriculture."[89]

Braudel points out, again in relation to the seventeenth century, that large estates up in Brie, near Paris, were being bought by urban owners who generally did not work the land themselves but let it out to tenant farmers who would often hire from several different proprietors at once: "All the signs indicate a 'capitalist' organization, such as the English revolution had instituted: the landowner, the rich tenant and the agricultural laborers." There were differences with England, notably in the absence of technological innovation, but nevertheless, "this tenant-farmer was a new feature of the landscape, the owner of a slowly accumulating capital which was already turning him into an entrepreneur." One indication is the way in which peasant anger was turned against these tenant farmers during the so-called Flour Wars of 1775, an indication of the resentment the latter provoked by raising himself above his class and the way in which they dominated the village life, not least by carrying out the wishes of the proprietors.[90]

Henry Heller has accepted that even the vast expansion of banking and commercial capital, together with the less significant but still not negligible investment in productive technology, can define seventeenth-century France as capitalist. He argues, however, drawing on the work of Le Roy Ladurie and Bois, that in Languedoc and Normandy a differentiation—indeed, a polarization—was already taking place by the first half of the sixteenth century, resulting in people leaving the land to work in the Isle-de-France, Le Havre, and Paris for whatever wages they could get—a factor that meant there was less of a need to develop or invest in labor-saving devices than there was in England.[91] There were changes following the crisis of the seventeenth century: "Thenceforth, intensification did not merely amount to extending the acreage of the land under cultivation, but it also began to affect the structures of agricultural production as a whole." In particular, the expropriation of the French peasantry began to intensify from the 1740s:

> Whereas the peasants were more or less successful in defending the "occupancy" of the land against outside attempts to take it away from them, the landlords also tried to enlarge their estates mainly at the expense of the common land. Thus, common rights were carved up, forests were closed and grazing rights superseded. Production on the estates became more rationalized, also in the sense that the landlords tended to rely on the *gros fermiers*. The latter in turn usually leased the land to the peasants, thus interposing themselves between the landlords and the mass of the peasants.

Clearly this is not exactly the same as the process in England, since an element of both feudal rent and payment in kind was retained within the peasant relationship to the landowners or larger tenants.[92] The dispossession of the French peasantry was a fact, as the area around Toulouse demonstrates. On the one hand, there was "a global decline in the amount of land left in Peasant hands": "In the Toulousian and the Lauragais although [the peasants] constituted between 60 and 70 per cent of the population, they held only a fifth or less of the land by the early eighteenth century." On the other, there was "a dramatic decline in the size of the tenures that survived": More than a third of the peasantry of the Toulousian had less than six-tenths of a hectare (1.48 acres) and, 84 percent less than three hectares (7.41 acres). The French peasants were considerably less secure than Brenner claims: "yet, as the French experience shows, the simple process of proletarianization, albeit a general precondition of capitalist development, was not a sufficient one." Apart from anything else, it is insufficient by itself to create the size of home market necessary for the self-expansion of capital.[93] Nevertheless, we can perhaps conclude this part of our survey in the words of Richard Hoyle: "Whereas Brenner suggested a single road to the capitalist farms of the eighteenth century, it may perhaps be seen that there were several ways in which these forms emerged."[94] Marx himself was clear that not only capitalist agriculture but the capitalist mode of production as a whole had multiple points of origin: "The feudal system, for its part, foundered on urban industry, trade, modern agriculture (even as results of individual inventions like gunpowder and the printing press)."[95] Two examples will illustrate how feudalism helped to generate from within itself the social forces that could potentially destroy it and the social forms that could potentially replace it.

In a critique of Carling's "feudal fission thesis," Vivek Chibber notes that he "is surprisingly vague on what the mechanism is that can serve to transmit new, more congenial production-relations across the terrain of stagnating productive forces, but it appears that the two most likely candidates are, first, their simple imposition through military conflict; and second, through some kind of demonstration-effect." Chibber argues that there are difficulties with both mechanisms. In the case of military victory: "Such transformations of the productive structure presume a capacity on the part of the victors that far exceeds the power required to simply win in war." In the case of demonstration-effect, the rulers of less developed systems may desire to emulate their more developed rivals, but "since the rival economic systems rest on different productive relations, a transition to those production-relations will involve the dismantling of the very social relations on the basis of which these rulers maintain their power."[96] In fact, as we shall see, some ruling classes did consciously choose to adopt different and more productive social relations in circumstances where not to do so would lead to their destruction or subordination. The question of military imposition is more complex. Although I agree with Chibber that the ability to conquer a territory does not necessarily imply the ability to transform the productive relations that are dominant there, the process of making war itself seems to have been more generally important: even in relation to states that sought to restrict further capitalist development, military competition also inadvertently helped to stimulate it.

During the First World War Bukharin wrote in general terms of war that "as a function of state power and a 'non-economic' factor" it was "one of the key factors of the economic process."[97] More recently, Erica Schoenberger has written more specifically of how absolutist states may either create or extend markets as a response to "the problems generated by processes of territorial conquest and control": "Without planning to promote the commercialization of society, the state's efforts to convert fixed and lumpy resources into flows across territory may spur the formation or further development and generalization of markets." These processes were built into the very act of state formation: "This proposition is incompatible with a view that warfare is purely destructive. It is compatible with the argument that one possible outcome of wars—territorial integration—provides a favorable context for market development, but goes further to suggest that the process of fighting wars in itself may spur commercialization."[98]

To anticipate one objection: the point here is not that markets themselves equate with capitalism, but the type of changes that shifts toward extensive production lead to in terms of social relations of production. Prior to the emergence of the absolutist states toward the end of the fifteenth century, for example, the manufacture of armor was subcontracted out by the dominant nobles to artisan workshops that specialized in making individual components, such as helmets or breastplates. Throughout Europe guild regulations forbade any increase in the size or number of workplace units to meet demand: "Until 1507 no more than the master himself, two qualified journeymen and a single apprentice were supposed to work in a single workshop. It is not surprising that such tiny workshops each concentrated on supplying single items of armor . . . to the merchants who put them together."[99] By the end of the fifteenth century, outside of two cities in the German Lands (Cologne and Nuremburg) and another two in Northern Italy (Milan and its satellite, Brescia): "There were no other major production centers for armor elsewhere in Europe, not in France, nor in the British Isles, nor in Scandinavia, nor in Eastern Europe, nor in Southern Italy, nor in any of the kingdoms of the Iberian Peninsula." Christopher Duffy notes: "Artillerymen entered the Age of Reason in medieval guise."[100] They did not leave it in the same way. As military competition intensified, all were forced to varying degrees to produce their own armor and weaponry more generally rather than rely on actual or potential enemies. Ordinance had previously been produced on a diverse, localized basis. The demand for interchangeable parts, whose design was based on practical experimentation and that incorporated technical improvements derived from other parts of the economy (horse harnesses, sights, elevating mechanisms) implied the need for systematic manufacture.

The process of production could not remain untouched by these new demands. "It is not possible to put a blast-furnace—even a seventeenth-century one—in a cottage" writes Donald Coleman, "or to disperse the assembly process inherent in the building of a great house or a great ship."[101] Marx refers to the emergence of forms of production—paper or saw mills, metal works, glass factories—which from the beginning require industrial manufacture on a scale for which the number of workers, extent of investment or size of market was impossible under the guild system could not be conducted.[102] In relation to military competition, change was partly the result of the increased quantities required. During the 1440s the French royal artillery consumed 20,000 pounds of gunpowder a year; by the 1540s this had risen to 500,000. Prussian powder production rose from 448,000 pounds in 1746 and rose to 560,000 pound in 1756. But it was also a qualitative difference. As Sheilagh Ogilvie notes, "military and strategic considerations led central and north Italian states to grant industrial privileges to remote, frontier, or mountainous parts of their territories, enabling the rise of rural proto-industries in the teeth of urban guild privilege."[103] During the reign of Louis XIV (1638–1715) the French army adopted the use of mobile field artillery that would be as effective in the field as in sieges: "Under the enlightened direction of Jean Baptiste de Gribeauval, the calibers, carriages and equipment of the French artillery were standardized, and their parts were made interchangeable (thanks to the ability of industrial plants to mass-produce identical, precise and highly durable metalwork)."[104] Here there are genuine continuities between the pre- and post-revolutionary economy in France. In what can retrospectively be seen as early measures of state capitalism, the Committee of Public Safety effectively nationalized the existing armories and organized the building of new ones in Paris and elsewhere. The majority of forges (about a thousand) were confiscated from their noble and ecclesiastical owners and transformed into state property, leased out to the *maîtres de forges* who had previously run them, Under the Directory and Napoleon they were ultimately sold off to the same individuals who, over the entire revolutionary period, began through a process of internal competition to centralize ownership and control: "The stage was set for a future transformation of this industry—key to the development of nineteenth-century industrial capitalism—under the auspices of these *maîtres de forges* who now operated these means of production as their private property." Steel production nearly doubled between 1789 and 1801. And the new owners prospered too: by 1811 more than a dozen of the *maîtres de forge* had assets of between one and three million francs.[105]

Not every state was capable of producing its own equipment. Portugal remained dependent on imported guns from other, rival states; but at the opposite extreme, Sweden underwent three phases of development in gun manufacture in the middle years of the sixteenth century, from wrought-iron to cast bronze to cast iron. Carlo Cipolla notes of this striking micro-example of uneven development: "Sweden was concentrating into a few decades the evolutionary process that the Continent had taken centuries to accomplish."[106] Three centuries later tsarist Russia saw the most spectacular examples of military development, but the central dynamic was similar. After 1861 an industrialization program was principally undertaken to strengthen the ability of the tsarist autocracy to participate in military competition with rival (and more advanced) states in Western Europe. Clive Treblicock notes, "from 1861 until 1917 Russian industrialization was pursued always in part for military purposes and always within a framework rigidly defined to minimize domestic upheavals."[107] The latter aspect was not destined to be successful other than in the short term, as Peter Gatrell points out: "To promote industrial expansion was to introduce a Trojan horse into the camp of imperial Russia in the shape of new social forces, possessed of their own agenda and aspirations."[108] This Trojan horse contained both a bourgeoisie and—unlike in earlier centuries—an organized working class that threatened the state from within.

It was in relation to shipping, however, that the greatest steps toward capitalist social relations were made: "Power, the ability of the states and the dynasty to impose its will on other states, depended on guns, including guns on board ship, if effectively deployed. In order to pay for the guns, states needed the kind of money which, in the sixteenth century, could only be obtained from trade."[109] The threefold task of protecting the mercantile marine, raiding blockade, and interception saw a massive shipbuilding campaign, particularly after 1588. This affected all the competing states, capitalist and absolutist alike, for war imposes its own symmetry on the participants, if they are capable of taking part. By the 1680s, the French state possessed 221 ships; during the Wars of the British and Irish Succession between 1689 and 1697 they captured 4,000 enemy ships.[110] Where did these ships come from? To an even greater extent than blast furnaces, ships cannot be built by a handful of artisans and their journeymen in a backyard: it requires a dry dock for construction, a steady supply of materials and a large number of laborers—wage laborers. It was not only construction that involved wage labor, however, but the organization of maritime workforce. The following comments by Marcus Rediker are made of Britain after the Glorious Revolution, but the same logic applied in the absolutist states:

> As capital came to be concentrated in merchant shipping, masses of workers, numbering 25,000 to 40,000 at any one time between 1700 and 1750, were in turn concentrated in this vibrant branch of industry. The huge numbers of workers mobilized for shipboard labor were placed in relatively new relationships to capital—as free and fully waged laborers—and to each other: seamen were by their experiences in the maritime labor market and labor process, among the first collective laborers. . . . The completely contractual and waged nature of maritime work represented a capital-labor relation quite distinct from landlord-tenant, master-servant, or master-apprentice relationships. The seaman was both a free wage-laborer located in a critical sector of the economy and a collective laborer located among an unprecedented number of men such as himself.[111]

There was of course one important difference between Britain and its imperialist rivals, but this did not lie in the realm of the labor process in the shipyards or on the vessels themselves. During the early eighteenth century, the suggestion was made by French state managers that one way to raise sufficient taxes to pay for improvements to the French Navy that would enable it to compete with that of Britain was to extend the tax base to those, above all the nobles, who were currently exempt but responsible for collecting it from the peasantry. "Politically," Bruce Lenman dryly observes, "this was not practical."[112] This conception of practicality indicating the self-imposed developmental limits of states where the bourgeois revolution had not yet been achieved.

Where conquest was important in nurturing capitalist development was not in Europe itself but through the establishment of colonies, above all in the Americas. There was of course a connection between the enhanced ability to make war and the expansion of empires beyond Europe, as Smith noted in 1776: "In modern war the great expense of fire-arms gives an evident advantage to the nation which can best afford that expense; and consequently, to an opulent and civilized, over a poor and barbarous nation. In ancient times the opulent and civilized found it difficult to defend themselves against the poor and barbarous nations. In modern times the poor and barbarous find it difficult to defend themselves against the opulent and civilized."[113] Paradoxically, the major contribution of Western European colonization to the transition may have been in the creation of forms transitional to wage labor, rather than from what is normally thought of as the primitive accumulation in its external aspect. James Blaut claimed: "The massive flows of wealth into Europe from colonial accumulation in America and later in Asia was the one basic force that explains the fact that Europe became rapidly transformed into a capitalist society, and the complimentary fact that Asian and African protocapitalist centers began to decline first in relative then in absolute importance." The validity of any theory that ascribes the outcome of world history to "Europe's location near America and because of the immense wealth obtained by Europeans in America and later in Asia and Africa" must be in doubt.[114] As Robin Blackburn points out: "The simple amassing of wealth is a secondary aspect of 'primitive accumulation,' since capitalist industrialization required an appropriate framework of institutions and production relations capable of converting wealth into capital."[115] The same is true for the clearance of "surplus" populations from the land. As Braudel notes in relation to the Mediterranean region, the persecution of vagabonds and vagrants, usually seen as part of the primitive accumulation in England, was in fact common across Europe, but did not produce the same economic results.[116] In other words, enforced transfers of wealth in and of themselves will not necessarily lead or even contribute to capitalist development: in some cases it simply acted as a life-support mechanism for the most economically backward absolutist states. Pierre Vilar described Spanish imperialism as "the highest stage of feudalism": "Occupying land, enslaving the inhabitants, looting treasure—there were no preparations for 'investment' in the capitalist sense of the word."[117] These actions were intended to rescue the existing class structure, as Banaji explains:

> At its inception the colonization of Latin America was a *feudal* colonization, a response to the crisis of feudal profitability which all the landowning classes of Europe were facing down to the latter half of the sixteenth century. In the Baltic and Easter Europe this crisis was partly overcome by territorial expansion into contiguous areas, and then displaced by the production of grain for export; but in the maritime periphery of Europe, in Spain and Portugal where this feudal crisis recurred with peri-

odic sharpness, it expressed itself in a movement of *overseas* colonization. The Spain which launched this movement of expansion was a Spain dominated by feudalism, but a feudalism in crisis.[118]

Similarly, Portugal began from a situation of limited material resources and skilled manpower, which placed great difficulties in the way of creating a large enough military and salaried bureaucracy to efficiently run the empire. Consequently, the crown had to make participation attractive to the nobility—the only class capable of carrying out these roles. But in doing so, the crown also had to allow them to plunder resources to make it worthwhile for themselves and to ensure the participation of their own followers. The effect was to both decentralize and thus diminish royal authority and ensure that resources were endlessly recycled into maintaining military control over the imperium. Unable to control noble expectations and lacking central mechanisms to bring them under control, the crown was reduced to granting offices on short tenures and leasing trading rights on short leases, but these moves only encouraged the noble recipients to exploit the opportunities for short-term gain. "By the end of the sixteenth century the pattern of social and economic behavior had destroyed any burgeoning Portuguese capitalism and left the empire with all the strengths of a decentralized and locally deep-rooted feudalism, but without the financial resources and central authority to further strengthen its armed forces for a long drawn-out struggle to survive in a new and mercantile competition with the Dutch and English."[119]

It might even be said that the plundering of the colonies did more to preserve feudal social relations and absolutist states than it necessarily did to enhance capitalist social relations and states. Colonies established for geopolitical reason such as several of the British possessions in Asia may have been essential for imperial security but were net drains on the exchequer. Mike Davis has rightly argued against "the claim that the Industrial Revolution necessarily depended upon the colonial conquest or economic subjugation of Asia; on the contrary, the slave trade and the plantations of the New World were much more strategic streams of liquid capital and natural resources in boosting the industrial take-off in Britain, France and the United States." Only the industrialization of the United Provinces seems to have been based on the extraction of tribute from the colonies. For Britain in particular, it was only in the latter half of the nineteenth century that India became an important market for Lancastrian cotton or Sheffield steel: "The coerced levies of wealth from India and China were not essential to the rise of British hegemony, but they were absolutely crucial in postponing its decline."[120]

It was trade with the colonial settlers rather than the expropriation of the colonized peoples that provided the greatest impetus to capitalist development in the colonizing states. In the original debate on the transition, both Maurice Dobb and Paul Sweezy noted the importance of long-distance trade was that, to put it in Hegelian terms, quantity eventually changes into quality. Once the demand for commodities expanded beyond a certain point, it had implications for, not simply the division of labor nor the labor process more generally, but how production itself was organized.[121] Marx wrote that trade with the colonies and the consequent expansion of commercial capital "were a major moment in promoting the transition from the feudal to the capitalist mode of production": "The sudden expansion of the world market, the multiplication of commodities in circulation, the competition among the European nations for the seizure of Asiatic products and American treasures, colonial system, all made a fundamental contribution towards shattering the feudal barriers to production."[122] In particular, from the mid-seventeenth century the plantation colonies became major new markets for merchandise that was produced in the European metropolitan centers: "The demands of the new colonial markets could not be satisfied by the relatively small number of urban workers handed down from the Middle Ages, and the manufactures proper opened out new fields of production to the rural population which had been driven from the land by the dissolution of the feudal system."[123] The so-called triangular trade involved merchant exchange of commodities for slaves in the African markets, the slaves were then taken to the Americas to work on plantations to produce the agricultural commodities that were exported back to Europe where they were worked up for re-export. Finally, commodities were traded directly with the plantations, which relied on the imperial homelands for goods they could not produce themselves. It is certainly true that in some cases, like those of the cotton manufacturers at Nantes in relation to West Africa, it tied producers into stable markets that in time became their sole markets, nevertheless it allowed new industries to emerge or new ways of organizing industry were considered in order to meet these new demands.[124]

The most important impacts may, however, have occurred in the colonies themselves, where the most important experiments were under way. In the cases of Portugal or Spain there may have been greater movement toward capitalist relations of production in their imperial possessions than in the metropolitan centers themselves. Before the Spanish conquest of Peru, for example, the native inhabitants worked what they called a *mit'a*, or turn, which was in effect a form of community labor. The Spanish kept the name for this practice, but during the sixteenth century transformed it into a form of forced labor, turning the peasants into temporary workers, "*mitayos*," for set periods during which they had to leave the community—often with their families in train—for the silver mines of Potosi, ranches, agricultural estates, or even as craftsmen in workshops. Were the mitayos slaves? In fact, they were examples of a transitional form of wage labor and this was not their only relationship to the market:

> From the moment his service began a mitayo contended with pressures to enter commercial transactions which reduced his net pay. If daily rations and the foodstuffs brought from home communities proved insufficient to support the mitayo and his relatives who accompanied him, the peasant would need to purchase the remainder from his temporary master or in the market at large.... Even without a food deficit,

mitayos had good reason to turn to the market. Rations did not generally include coca, an indispensable source of sustenance during Andean labor.[125]

The Brazilian sugar plantations of the Portuguese Empire displayed comparable transitional forms. By the end of the seventeenth century these had become something like a model for the rest of the plantation colonies of the Americas, regardless of the nature of the colonial state. The merchants who owned the plantations were involved in the process of production, from cultivation to processing to ultimate transportation to market, to an extent that they very rarely were in the metropolitan centers. And the same process would often happen in reverse, with planters becoming merchants in their turn. Plantations, although often smaller than the average area owned by landowners in Europe, occupied labor forces up to ten times as large. These were more akin to later factories than to the actual manufacturing as it existed in most of Europe at the time in the form of the largely unsupervised putting-out process. Moreover, some of the processes involved skilled labor, but even those that did not saw massive coordinated physical effort on the part of male slaves, which had the same effect upon the laborers as factory work did on a latter generation of wage laborers: it united them as a class—something of which the slave owners were only too aware.[126] Brazil was not unique. Slaves on the sugar plantations of the French Caribbean were in some ways like peasants, both in the fact that they worked the land for subsistence and in the elemental violence with which they rose against their oppressors given the opportunity; but not in others. As C. L. R. James noted, "working and living together in gangs of hundreds on the huge sugar factories which covered the North Plain [of San Domingo], they were closer to a modern proletariat than any group of workers in existence at the time."[127] These similarities between Brazilian and San Dominican slave plantations extended to those of their British rivals in the Caribbean. Of these classically "combined" forms Blackburn writes: "It would . . . be wrong to propose a sharp contrast between English 'bourgeois' colonization and French 'feudal' colonization, since the social forces involved in both—merchants and colonists—were comparable."[128] Although the possession of colonies led to variable outcomes in the imperial centers, in the colonies themselves transitional forms of social relations of production were emerging that tended to converge. These emergent social relations and the trading links connecting them to Europe would form part of a network through which capitalist laws of motion could become operative on a global scale, once the existing states system was overthrown.

Following the resumption of economic growth in the mid-fifteenth century then, increases in productivity ceased to be generated by feudalism itself, but by the now expanding sectors based on capitalist production. As Bois puts it:

> There was not a sort of continuous transition from one mode of production to another, simply through the growth of the "new" within the "old." On the contrary, there were successive waves of accumulation (in the twelfth, thirteenth, sixteenth, and eighteenth centuries) separated by phases of ebb. For obvious reasons, each of these waves broke

further on than the last, since the structures of the feudal system, weakened by the irreversible erosive action (both socially and psychologically) of earlier thrusts of accumulation, offered less resistance.

Capitalist impulses were initially "auxiliary," "but the role of the new impulses, of a capitalist type, grew ever stronger," leading ultimately to a situation in which "the auxiliary becomes the main motor force."[129] When the second general crisis began, nearly three hundred years after the first, it was no longer a purely feudal crisis, but one occurring within a transitional economy in which capitalism was a still subordinate, widely uneven, but growing component. Peter Coveney has summarized the components of this second wave as: "population growth and food crisis in an unreformed agrarian economy; economic stagnation or recession affecting the great majority of the European population; under-employment, pauperism and vagrancy; over-crowded cities becoming the forcing houses of epidemic disease; the states with their wars and oppressive fiscalism, increasing social distress and de-stabilizing the traditional political structures of late medieval Europe."[130]

These afflictions were, however, also experienced outside Europe and its overseas extensions. Jack Goldstone has argued that during the middle decades of the seventeenth century similar underlying causes lay behind the crises of Stuart England, Ottoman Turkey, and Ming China. These arose from the growth of population leading to pressure on resources, price inflation, initial shortfalls in tax revenue as a result of levels being fixed, subsequent dramatic increases in taxation to compensate, rigorous state intervention to enforce monarchical control, resistance, and division among the ruling and popular classes, leading finally to the emergence of ideologies that justified resistance to the ruler. The main differences, according to Goldstone were ideological, rather than economic, social, or political. Puritanism in England was "apocalyptic" and pointed toward an interventionist role for a reconstructed English state in world affairs. Sufism in Turkey and T'ai-chou neo-Confucianism in China were "cyclical" and demanded a return to the uncorrupt ways of some earlier period: "After 1650, the Ottoman and Chinese empires became more rigidly orthodox and conservative than they had been earlier; they turned more inward and eschewed novelty, while rewarding conformity to past habits. State reconstruction on these lines was successful in restoring a measure of prosperity and prolonging the life of these states, but they entered the late-seventeenth and eighteenth centuries without the dynamism of England."[131] If, however, England had been no different in terms of development from Turkey and China, then it is unlikely that the overthrow of the state would have been anything other than temporary, no matter how interventionist the Puritan ideology of the revolutionaries. Here we can agree with Brenner and Christopher Isett that "England's path of economic evolution diverged decisively from that of the Yangtze delta over the course of the early modern period (1500–1750), as it also did from that of most of the rest of Europe at the same time." There was, in other words an "*already existing* divergence" in economy, which had led to the divergence in ideology, and which meant that the crisis in England could potentially lead to a different outcome than those that occurred further east.[132] Where and when capitalism shifted from the periphery to the center of economic life was in very large part dependent on the nature of the pre-capitalist state, to which we now turn.

THE STRUCTURAL CAPACITIES OF PRECAPITALIST STATES

The question of pre-capitalist state power is central in answering the question of why it was not in the hitherto most advanced areas, like the Ottoman and Chinese Empires, that the potentiality of capitalism was first realized but in relatively backward territories of Europe. As Mielants has argued, even if "all the relevant features necessary to ensure a gradual transition from feudalism to capitalism were available" this may still be insufficient unless the situation also involves "the lack of other features," among which he includes "the construction of a well-organized 'world empire' or the recurring destructive raids of pastoral nomads on the emerging centers of capital accumulation."[133] It is in this context that Carling's argument concerning the ability or otherwise of states to maintain noncapitalist modes of production is of decisive importance, if we understand the state to be the complex of institutions and social relations through which existing ruling classes conduct the class struggle. What kind of states were these that acted as obstacles to the establishment of viable nation-states dominated by capitalist laws of motion? As Epstein points out, "the most significant effect of the demographic shock [after 1348] was sharply to accelerate the process of political centralization inherent to the feudal-tributary mode of production"; this was in turn accompanied by greater territorial integration and both processes were "strongly contested by the more powerful feudal lords and towns."[134] Let us leave aside the question of whether we can speak of a "feudal-tributary" mode of production for the moment and focus first on the states that emerged in territories that were unambiguously feudal.

The replacement of the feudal estates-monarchy by absolutism followed the first crisis of feudalism.[135] Under conditions of generalized economic contraction the landowning classes had only two means of maintaining—let alone increasing—their level of income. One was by extending the area controlled by the state to which they owed allegiance and so increasing the number of peasants under their seigniorial control. The other was by intensifying the level of exploitation for both long-standing and these newly conquered peasant communities. The first brought conflict between those states that encroached on each other's territories, a process exemplified by the Hundred Years' War between England and France (1337–1453). The second brought conflict within states, between the lords and the peasants themselves. The latter violently opposed these increased exactions in a great series of risings that began in maritime Flanders in the 1320s and ended, in Western Europe at least, in Catalonia in the 1470s. Both the effective pursuit of external military aggression and the suppression of internal revolt required the agency of a centralized coercive state power greater than the territorially dispersed structures typical of military feudalism. For our purposes two main characteristics of this emergent state form are of central importance.

One was the relative autonomy of the absolutist states from their class base—the feudal lords. The latter did not, in the main, directly control the state apparatus, either through inherited membership of their estate or appointment to regal office. On the contrary, since they regularly went to war with each other and, less regularly, combined to make war on the monarch, it was essential that the state apparatus be operated by a bureaucracy directly responsible to the Crown. Only thus could the collective interests of the feudal ruling class be secured. Inseparable from this strengthening of central power was a twofold weakening of both the collective and individual powers exercised by the lords. Collectively, they were the dominant estate within any parliament, and could still use this position to thwart the wishes of the Crown. The relative success of individual absolutisms therefore depended on (and could almost be measured by) the extent to which they managed to suppress their particular national assembly—the longevity of French absolutism compared to the English variant being very marked in this respect. Individually, the lords held jurisdictional authority within their own superiorities, which provided, on the one hand, a (theoretically) untrammeled supremacy over the peasants and, on the other, a territorial base for resistance to the monarch, particularly when combined with a system of military land tenure. Aspirant absolutists therefore sought to dominate the peasantry directly, without relying on local intermediaries. Where this displacement of power was successfully achieved—as it was in Sweden, France, Spain, Prussia, Austria, and Russia—the responsibility for extracting the surplus from the peasantry had largely been assumed by the central state and the mechanism of surplus extraction changed from rent to tax. The local autonomy of the lords was thereby greatly reduced.

The other main characteristic of absolutist states was the hegemony that they exercised over the class that would eventually supersede the lords—the bourgeoisie. For the bourgeoisie, the absolutist state was important both as a means of controlling civil disorder within the towns and of protecting the towns themselves from the demands of individual lords. For the absolutist state, the bourgeoisie were important as a source of revenue, of personnel to fill the offices of state and, most importantly, as a social force that the monarchy could muster in the face of collective opposition by the lords. Yet this dependent relationship left the bourgeoisie as an influence upon the state, not a codeterminate (with the lords) of its class nature. Absolutism placed the bourgeoisie in a protected but subordinate place within the social order, which had the paradoxical effect of allowing socioeconomic advance while imposing political retardation.

Were absolutist states still feudal? Jane Whittle has argued: "Royal taxes became the early modern equivalent of the feudal exactions of the early modern period."[136] Bois similarly claims, on the basis of the French experience: "The two basic classes of society remained face to face. Only the methods by which one exploited the other had changed. The power of the prince henceforth protected that of the lord, extracting from peasant production whatever was needed to maintain the ruling class. Coexistence between the two forms of levy had become necessary, but it was difficult."[137] Brenner, however, has argued that absolutist France was not feudal. The "difficulty" to which Bois refers is indicative of two different forms of exploitation corresponding to the "two forms of levy." For Brenner, the state in prerevolutionary France "developed . . . as a class-like phenomenon . . . an independent extractor of the surplus."[138] It is difficult, however, to see how this position can be held for France alone, given that it was merely the most developed example of a general tendency. Characteristically, Wood has taken Brenner's position to its logical conclusion, arguing that absolutism was not only "class-like," but a distinct mode of production in its own right: "In some Western European cases, feudalism gave way not to capitalism but to absolutism, with its own non-capitalist modes of appropriation and politically constituted property."[139] More specifically: "The absolutist state was a centralized instrument of extra-economic surplus extraction, and office in the state was a form of property which gave its possessors access to peasant-produced surpluses."[140] Absolutism then, is a pre-capitalist mode of production, not a state form characteristic of the transition from feudalism to capitalism. Benno Teschke has made a similar generalization: "[Absolutism] was a *sui generis* social formation, displaying a specific mode of government and determinate pre-modern and pre-capitalist domestic and international 'laws of motion.'"[141] There is, of course, a mode of production in Marxist theory that the state acts as the prime extractor of the surplus: the tributary mode. Was absolutism effectively its Western variant?

The concept of a tributary mode, if not the actual term, originates with Marx himself: "In the case of the slave relationship, the serf relationship, and the relationship of tribute (where the primitive community is under consideration), it is the slaveowner, the feudal lord or the state receiving tribute that is the owner of the product and therefore its seller."[142] Samir Amin, the figure most responsible for popularizing the concept of the tributary mode, characterizes it as "the separation of society into two main classes: the peasantry, organized in communities, and the ruling class, which monopolizes the functions of the given societies, political organization and exacts a tribute (not in commodity form) from the rural community."[143] Wickham subsequently elaborated on this basic definition, writing that the tributary mode involves a "'state class' based on a public institution, with political rights to extract surplus from a peasantry that it does not tenurially control." Although he subsequently changed his position, Wickham originally argued that the crucial distinction between the tributary and feudal modes lay in the means by which the surplus is collected from the peasantry. In the former, it is through payment of taxation to the state; in the latter, through payment of rent to private landowners.[144] For Wickham, there are two further differences between the tributary mode and the feudal. The first is that a tributary state taxes landowners in addition to peasants. The second is that the tributary mode allows far greater autonomy for the peasantry in the process of production than the feudal mode. As a result: "They represent two different economic systems, even if they can come together in some exceptional circumstances. Their differences, their antagonisms, lie in their divergent interventions in the peasant economy, just as their convergences lie in the fact that both are rooted in it. The same productive forces, however, can, be seen as giving rise to two separate modes of production."[145] Eric Wolf gives an example of this convergence from precolonial India, where the operation of the tributary mode involved domination of the direct producers by the local agents of the state—either military bureaucrats with lifetime grants of land (*jagirdars*) or hereditary chiefs (*zamindars*)—responsible for collecting the tribute, part of which went toward their own revenue, part to the central state. "The critical difference from the later English practice was that these rights were not, properly speaking, rights of property in land, but rather claims on people's labor and the products of that labor." In some cases the central state bypassed the zamindars completely to extract the surplus directly. In others the zamindars had a feudal relationship with the peasants.[146]

One key question is therefore whether extraction of surplus as rent by a landowning class on the one hand and extraction of surplus as tax by a state on the other constitute different modes of production. Marx himself had suggested that there was no essential difference between the feudal and tributary modes. He noted that where peasants form what he called a "natural community," then "the surplus labor for the nominal landowner can only be extorted from them by extra-economic compulsion, whatever the form this might assume": "If there are no private landlords but it is the state, as in Asia, which confronts them directly as simultaneously landowner and sovereign, rent and tax coincide, or rather there does not exist any tax distinct from this form of ground-rent."[147] In response to Wickham, Halil Berktay and John Haldon similarly pointed out that, in terms of the central exploitative relationship with the peasantry, there was no difference between these; the difference lay in the extent and nature of state power.[148] The most serious theoretical attempt to argue this case was subsequently made by Haldon in relation to the tributary states of the East. He argues that there is no fundamental difference between tax and rent such as would allow us to regard them as constituent of different modes of production: "The fundamental difference between these two forms of the same mode of surplus extraction lies in fact in a political relation of surplus appropriation and distribution." On this basis the relationship of peasants to feudal landlords on the one hand and to tributary states on the other is essentially the same, even down to the level of day-to-day interference:

> The forms of intervention vary quantitatively, to a degree; but states and their agents could also be just as involved in the process of production and extraction of surplus as landlords (indeed, in Mughul India, for example, tax-farmers also involved themselves in these relationships). Where both exist it does not imply that there are two

different ruling classes (for the state represents the landlords), merely that the state bureaucracy and the landlords represent different factions of the same ruling class and their conflicts are not based on a different relationship to the direct producers, but over the distribution of the surplus extracted from them.[149]

In other words, the tributary and feudal modes are variations on the same mode of production, but it is the tributary variant that has been the most widespread, both in the sense that it embraced the majority of the world's population after the fall of the Roman Empire and that these areas remained the most economically developed until the eighteenth century. However, it is perfectly possible to accept that there is no fundamental difference between tax and rent without also accepting that there is no fundamental difference between the tributary and feudal modes.

The problem with the latter position is that it restricts the concept of a mode of production solely to relations of exploitation; but as Perry Anderson has pointed out: "*All* modes of production in class societies prior to capitalism extract surplus labor from the immediate producers by means of extra-economic coercion." His solution is to argue "pre-capitalist modes of production cannot be defined *except* via their political, legal and ideological superstructures, since these are what determine the type of extra-economic coercion that specifies them."[150] But this argument too presents problems. As Paul Hirst explains, it "*means that there can be as many modes of production as there are distinct legal-political constitutions and forms of extra-economic sanction which follow on from them.*"[151] There is, however, no need to distinguish between pre-capitalist modes solely on the basis of their superstructural forms. Even if the process of exploitation is essentially the same, modes of production also involve relations between the exploiters themselves, crucially how their relations are mediated by the state. Curiously, Wickham has noted this while retaining his later belief that two modes are identical:

> The basic economic division inside class societies thus becomes simply that between societies based on taking surpluses from peasants (or, for that matter, household-based artisans) and those based on withholding surplus from wage laborers. . . . It does not mean that the Chinese or Roman empires, the Frankish kingdoms, and the feudal world of the eleventh century were exactly the same, for an essential *structural* difference remains between the first two, and tax-raising state systems (with aristocracies subject to them), and the second two, polities dominated by aristocratic rent-taking and Marc Bloch's politics of land.[152]

It is because of these different relationships between their respective ruling classes and their states that Banaji has argued that the tributary mode has to be seen as distinct from feudalism:

> The tributary mode of production may be defined as a mode of production where the state controls *both the means of production and the ruling class,* and has "unlimited disposal over the total surplus labor of the population." . . . The relations of production of the tributary mode . . . involved *both* the control of peasant-labor by the state (the state-apparatus as the chief instrument of exploitation) *and* the drive to forge

a unified imperial service based on the subordination of the ruling class to the will of the ruler. . . . The bond between the ruler and the ruling elite within the wider circles of the ruling class was the basis on which *new* states were constructed, and the state itself bureaucratized to create an efficient tool of administration. The autocratic centralism of the tributary mode and its backbone in the recruitment of a pliant nobility were not just "political superstructures" to some self-contained state, they were essential moments of the structuring and organization of the economy (*of the relations of production*).[153]

The feudal mode of production was a peripheral, mainly Western European mode of production. According to Janet Abu-Lughod: "By definition . . . restructuring is said to occur when *players who were formerly peripheral* begin to occupy more powerful positions in the system and when *geographical zones formerly marginal to intense interactions* become foci and even control centers of such interchanges."[154] The restructuring of the medieval regional systems in favor of the hitherto marginal and peripheral region of Western Europe began from the second half of the fourteenth century, co-extensive with the emergence of capitalism. Abu-Lughod explains this by reference to the "disarray" of the Orient as a result of the "progressive fragmentation" of hitherto unified trading routes and the greater impact of the Black Death in the East, as it was carried along the far more developed urban sea routes.[155] There were however more general problems in the tributary world, some of which have been identified by Haldon:

> Tributary relations of production can in fact only be transformed or replaced by capitalist relations of production when there takes place a proletarianization of the peasantry, that is, when a large proportion of the producing population is separated from their means of production, hence creating a free and available supply of labor which can then be exploited within capitalist production relations. . . . The "capital" available to merchants and traders is always only potentially capital, insofar as, without a proletariat whose labor-power can be transformed into relative surplus value, it functions merely as a medium of simple exchange.

The proletariat began to form in Europe, but not in the Eastern tributary empires:

> Partly this was because expansionist European traders arrived in time to dominate Asian trade and to invert the pre-existing relations of commercial exploitation between the Indian sub-continent and its periphery. In addition, the different ways in which the institutional forms of tributary relations were structured in India—in particular, the self-contained and semi-autonomous nature of rural production relations, the integration of merchant and trading groups into a balanced set of social relationships through lineage identities and demands—are central elements in this picture.[156]

The most serious obstacle to capitalist development—and here we return to the first of Carling's enabling conditions—lay however in the very nature of these states. The significance of the distinction between feudal and tributary modes lies in their relative ability to prevent the development of capitalism beyond a certain point and consequently the possibility of overthrow by a potential new ruling class based on that mode of production. Mielants rightly warns: "One must be careful to avoid the construction of a new and more sophisticated version of typical Oriental Despotism vs. European free-market orientated and democratic urban communities. It seems unlikely that the European nobility as a whole was less 'despotic' than the non-European nobility."[157] The European nobility was not intrinsically less oppressive than its Asian equivalents, but simply operated within a different structural context. Notwithstanding his belief in the identity of the feudal and tributary modes, Wickham has rightly emphasized how the state under the latter enjoys two advantages over that in the former. First, "tax-based states were ... richer and more powerful than rent-based, land-based, states." Second, and more important even than wealth, was stability, which Wickham illustrates with the Byzantine example:

> Even at the weakest point of the eastern empire, roughly 650–750, Byzantine political structures were more coherent than those of even the best-organized land-based states, such as Lombard Italy in the same period; tax-based structures had more staying power, and the risk of decentralization, a feature of all land-based states, was less great. If taxation disappeared as the basis of any given state, then, no matter how much cultural, ideological, or legislative continuity there was ... it would not prevent fundamental changes in political resources, infrastructure and practice.[158]

Callinicos too has emphasized the effectiveness of the Asian tributary states in preventing the growth of an independent class of lords and their transformation into capitalist landlords or manufacturers while, at the other end of the class spectrum, preserving the peasantry as a source of tax income. It is therefore precisely the weakness of feudal compared to tributary societies that provides capitalism with the most fertile ground to develop, notably through the greater direct involvement of the lords in the productive process and the existence of fragmented power structures which encourage the flow of commodities.[159]

The spaces that allowed the emergence of capital should not be understood as synonymous with the towns but instead identified with what Patricia Crone refers to as the "extreme dispersal of power" characteristic of feudal Europe.[160] In fact, as I have already argued, towns were no more intrinsically capitalist than the countryside was intrinsically feudal. In the case of both town and country the issue was how far capitalist production had been established and to what extent those controlling that production had achieved political power on their own behalf. Examples of this could be found in England, Flanders, and the Netherlands where, as Ogilvie notes, "craft guild and merchant companies could easily be evaded by moving industry outside the towns," because in all these cases either "the state was too weak to provide support or enforcement for the institutional privileges of towns over the countryside," or "the large number of cities created too much inter-urban competition for effective capture by a single city of state enforcement for its privileges against all the other cities."[161] Medieval cloth production in England was policed by both guilds and local governments that were also dominated by the guilds, which inspired the flight of production to the countryside: "Free of borough and guild taxes, and with easy access to cheap wool and a good water supply, rural cloth workers in Yorkshire increased production.

As early as 1300, York and Beverley were facing competition from at least eight other cities. Thereafter, and at an accelerating pace, the manufacturing and finishing, especially of the cheaper kerseys, was undertaken away from, and at the expense of, the older urban centers."[162] Ironically, in some parts of England in particular, rural industry was established in the "common" areas, which fell outside feudal control altogether: "The heath and woodland system were often outside the parochial system, or their large parishes were left with only a distant chapelry, so there was freedom from parson as well as squire. . . . In such areas feudal ties of subordination hardly existed, and there was little obstacle to the intrusion of rural industry in search of cheap part-time labor."[163]

There were of course regional variations even within Western Europe; those areas that remained decentralized had the advantage here, at least in the period before the bourgeois revolution. Bois has argued that feudalism both originated in and reached its highest level of development in France. England, on the other hand: "Sufficiently near to the most advanced feudal societies to have high levels of technical resource at her disposal, she was also sufficiently underdeveloped to have escaped the consequences of the fossilization of social relations which feudal reorganization induced." What Bois is in fact describing is the operation of uneven development, "the relative backwardness of England's social evolution as compared to France was to prove its trump card in the transition from feudalism to capitalism."[164] But if "the advantages of backwardness" were indeed decisive, then there is no need to invoke such ahistorical causations as the "luck" invoked by John Hobson to explain how in Western Europe the last came to be first.[165] The tributary world was hampered precisely because the greater level of development had produced a state capable of preventing systemic challenges—as opposed to, say, periodic peasant revolts—from emerging.

The Chinese Empire encompassed a great civilization with important scientific and technical accomplishments, surpassing those of Europe. As Chris Wickham has pointed out, there is no reason to suppose that Europe, even Western Europe, was in a privileged position to begin development toward industrial capitalism during the early feudal period. Similar and, in some areas, superior, levels of development can be found in Song China at exactly the same time: "Chinese ploughs were in many respects more sophisticated than European ones until the eighteenth century." Rice yields were far higher than cereal yields (50–100:1 compared to 4:1):

> Furthermore, no one could claim that the sophisticated and complex irrigation techniques of the Yangtze Delta were not intensive, or that they did not need highly organized local collective cooperation, at least on the level of the northern European common field and probably rather more so. By the twelfth century, several substantial areas of China specialized in cash crops such as tea or fruits that could be exchanged for staples in a structured market system. The social division of labor was developing, and merchant capital was based on a complex credit system. Under the Sung, population density was higher than Europe's with no signs of Malthusian dangers (new strains of rice could crop twice or three times a year). Artisanal work was flourishing, and in

the crucial areas of textiles and ceramics was technologically highly sophisticated, well above European levels.[166]

"Overall," claims Kenneth Pomeranz, "China was closer to market-driven agriculture than was most of Europe, including most of Western Europe."[167] It was closer, but it never arrived and the key reason was political. As Mark Elvin points out, from the advent of the Song dynasty in AD 960, China also began to "diverge significantly" from Europe, not only in respect of its inventiveness and productivity, but in the development of the state: "Chinese society, like that of Europe at this time, developed in the direction of manorialism . . . but since the state retained control over defense functions, as it did not in Europe, there was no feudal superstructure . . . in the sense of a dominant specialist military class disposing of fiefs granted in return for military service and ruling these as more or less unquestioned lords."[168] It is important to understand that these developments did not lead to absolute retardation of the economy. John Hall writes: "For market relations to gain autonomy, extensive networks are needed. In China, such extensive networks were provided by the polity. However, imperial rule was, perhaps could only be, based upon the negative tactics of horizontal linkages that it could not control, and it was because of this that bureaucratic interference eventually proved deleterious for the economy."[169] But "market relations" did exist in China; as we have already seen, markets and merchants are quite compatible with non- or, more precisely, precapitalist modes of production and may even have been essential to them, as was certainly the case in China.[170] What did not exist were capitalist social relations. The Chinese bureaucratic tributary state acted to suppress emergent class forces and the dangerous ideas associated with them. As late as the eighteenth century critical writings were censored or destroyed. The high point of this "literary inquisition," as it was known, ran between 1779 and 1789—the events of the latter year showing the distance that had opened up between China and Europe.[171] Reading the work of one leading intellectual in seventeenth-century China, Wang Fu-Chih (1619–92), it is difficult not to see him as a predecessor to Smith in Scotland or Barnave in France; but unlike them, his thoughts led to no immediate results.[172] "China has been long one of the richest, that is one of the most fertile, most cultivated, most industrious and most populous countries in the world," wrote Smith himself in 1776: "It seems, however, to have been long stationary." Yet as he also noted, "Though it may perhaps [have] stood still, [it] does not seem to go backwards."[173] These comments embody the contradictions in the late eighteenth-century Enlightenment view of China: in many ways admiring, but in others seeing it as an example of the stationary state that Political Economy most feared. Adam Ferguson noted that China was an exception to the pattern of stadial development he and his cothinkers detected in Europe: "The succession of monarchs has been changed; but no revolutions have affected the state."[174] It was not that revolutions failed to take place: China had seen dynasty after dynasty fall to successive peasant revolts, to an extent quite unknown in Europe. The point, however, is that although the dynasties may have fallen, tributary relations of production, and the state associated with them, continued unaffected in any fundamental way. After initially welcoming the Taiping rebellion in China on its outbreak in 1851, Marx was subsequently to see this as another manifestation of the recurrent Chinese dilemma of "constant immobility in their social substructure, with unceasing change in the persons and clans that gain control of the political superstructure."[175]

The Ottoman imperial state did not display the same underlying continuities of the Chinese, and may only have achieved its final form, like the Austrian and Russian, in response to the second crisis of feudalism during the seventeenth century.[176] Nevertheless, the empire imposed severe restrictions on private property in land and therefore little space for new approaches to production and exploitation to arise. There is nothing in the either the Koran or the Sunnah that is intrinsically hostile to capitalism.[177] Nor is there anything inherently stagnant about Islamic societies; but they stand as further examples of how ruling classes are consciously able to use state power, "the superstructure," to prevent new and threatening classes from forming, with all that implies about the thwarting of intellectual developments. Abbasidic relations were never classically feudal, since the state refused to grant land in perpetuity, but only in the form of the *iqta*, by which it was held for a limited period of time, thus preventing both the establishment of local sovereignty and the possibility of hereditary possession but also discouraging improvement: "The grantees, who lived in the cities and knew that before long the estates would be taken from them or that they themselves would ask for a change, did not look after their maintenance."[178] There was a period toward the end of the twelfth century when the urban bourgeoisie did manage to take advantage of the temporary fragmentation of the empire to assume a political role and even establish city-republics comparable to those in Central and Southern Europe, but also like their European counterparts they fell to a combination of local princes and the imperial state. With the reassertion of tributary power came the suppression of the intellectual and technological advances that had been characteristic of the Arab-Islamic world during the European "Dark Ages": "The great technological progress had been made when freedom of enterprise and the *tiraz* system—factories which were great industrial enterprises—was flourishing. These great enterprises could afford experiments which resulted in technological innovations. In the age of the Seldjukids and the Ayyubids the princes curtailed freedom of enterprise, established monopolies, and impose heavy taxes on the workshops."[179]

As representatives of the main exploiter, state officials displayed a quite conscious hostility to potential alternative sources of power, hence the bias it displayed toward small-scale commerce and the hostility it displayed toward large mercantile capital. Consequently, merchants tended to be from external "nations," Jews, Greeks, or Armenians—not from the native Arab or Turkish populations. As Mielants writes, "the socioeconomic splendor of the medieval Islamic society cannot be denied" and mer-

chant capitalists contributed toward it: "But the presence of capitalists does not necessarily imply the successful creation of an endurable capitalist system in the long
run."[180] "Asking why the Scientific Revolution did not occur in Islam," writes Pervez
Hoodbhoy, exaggerating only slightly, "is practically equivalent as asking why Islam
did not produce a powerful bourgeois class."[181] Take the example of the Tunisian
writer Ibn el Khaldun (1332–1402), author of the *Kitab Al-Ilbar* or *Book of Examples*
(usually referred to in English as *The Muqaddimah* or *Introduction to History*). His sociological insights identified the continuing struggle between civilizations based on
the one hand on towns and traders (*hadarah*) and on the other on tribes and holy
men (*badawah*), the two endlessly alternating as the dominant forces within the Muslim world.[182] Smith and his colleagues in the Historical School of the Scottish Enlightenment could develop a theory that saw societies develop and progress upward
from one "mode of subsistence" to another because they had seen this movement in
England, and wished to see it reproduced in Scotland. Ibn el Khaldun saw only cyclical repetition in the history of Islamic society and could not envisage any way to break
the cycle. His work could not transcend the society it sought to theorize.

Of all the great tributary states the Mughal Empire was perhaps the one in
which progress toward capitalist relations of production were most advanced. By
the seventeenth century, several changes to Indian economic life, including the increased monetary basis of commercial activity, had established the necessary conditions for capitalist development to at least the same extent as those areas of
Western Europe still under absolutist rule. Irfan Habib makes this assessment:

> We find that in both agricultural and non-agricultural production, production for
> the market formed a very large sector. In agriculture, there existed *khwud kast* culti-
> vation, based on hired labor, representing an advance, in form, towards capitalist farm-
> ing. In handicrafts, merchant capital had developed considerably and had brought
> artisans under control through forms of the putting-out system. But manufacturing
> as an established form was yet largely outside of the sphere of commodity production.
> In other words, capital was by and large merchant capital, and though the economy
> was fairly highly monetized, domestic industry still predominated.[183]

A merchant class with large amounts of money capital had emerged, particularly
along the western coastal regions, tied closely to the Mughal rulers and the markets
provided by their empire. But Christopher Bayly has argued that capitalist relations,
if anything, became more dispersed with a range of different actors including "the
petty kings, the revenue and military entrepreneurs, the great bankers and warrior
peasant lords of the villages" at their centers.[184] The decline of the Mughals between
1680 and 1750 did not in itself lead to the dissolution of indigenous Indian capitalism, but it did mean that there was no longer a central authority to balance or
mediate between these different competing interests, which were now overlaid with
princely political rivalries:

> Rulers and revenue farmers needed credit to tide them over the periods between
> harvests as they were required to equip and pay armies month by month throughout

the year. This encouraged them to squeeze the merchants and village magnates. Merchants for their part avoided direct management of agrarian taxation and were reluctant to disburse resources which they might need in commodity trades. It was in the interest of the village magnates to construct their own networks of credit in the countryside. Above all, the successor states to the Mughals were often in conflict with each other, fighting for cash revenues and for the still limited pool of agricultural and artisan labor.[185]

It is quite conceivable that, undisturbed, at least part of the former Mughal Empire could have developed into a fully developed capitalist economy, initially in the spaces which were opening up across this increasingly fragmented society, in the same way as had happened in parts of Western Europe. But its inhabitants were not permitted the time in which the process might have taken place, and into the void entered the Western Europeans themselves, in the form of the British East India Company. As Satish Chandra concludes: "It is not necessary to enter into the controversy whether Indian society was capable, on its own, of developing from merchant capitalism to industrial capitalism. What is significant is that the growth of merchant capitalism itself was arrested in the eighteenth century, and industrial capitalism hardly showed any signs of developing till the third quarter of the nineteenth or the early twentieth century."[186]

The consequences of failing to make the breakthrough to capitalism then left these societies vulnerable to the predations of those that had. As John Darwin has written, from around 1830, the peoples of what he calls the "Outer World" beyond Europe and North America "found themselves in a race against time: a race to 'self-strengthen' before European power and wealth could overwhelm their defenses."[187] One indication of their decline consequent on a failure to win this race can be seen in the decreasing ability of these states to cope with natural disaster. Davis has shown that in 1743 and 1744 the Qing regime in China was able to provide relief to the northern area of Hebei after an El Niño event had caused the monsoon to fail, with consequent drought and crop failure, at the same time as millions in feudal Europe were dying. "Whereas in 1876 the Chinese state—enfeebled and demoralized after the failures of the Tongzhi [T'ung-chih] Restoration's domestic reforms—was reduced to desultory cash relief augmented by private donations and humiliating foreign charity, in the eighteenth century it had both the technology and political will to shift grain massively between regions and, thus, relieve hunger on a larger scale than any previous polity in world history." Even the Mogul regime in India, although weaker and lacking the resources of the Qing, was able to provide grain and to hold the price down to the extent that starvation was avoided: "Although the British insisted that they had rescued India from 'timeless hunger,' more than one official was jolted when Indian nationalists quoted from an 1878 study published in the prestigious *Journal of the Statistical Society* that contrasted thirty-one serious famines in 120 years of British rule against only seventeen recorded famines in the entire previous two millennia."[188]

The Chinese "restoration" to which Davis refers—the T'ung-chih or "union for order," might seem comparable with the Japanese Meiji or "enlightened rule," but as the outcome he describes suggests, the former in reality was quite different. "What this great effort could not achieve (and was not meant to achieve) was the transformation of China into a modern state on the Western model," writes Darwin: "It might even be argued that the real priority of the 'restoration' was precisely that: to restore the authority of the Confucian state and its ethos of frugality and social discipline, not to break the Confucian mold."[189] The only example of a tributary state that was overthrown before any significant capitalist development had taken place therefore remained Japan, largely because it contained a social group capable of recognizing that what was happening to China could foreshadow their own fate, if no challenge to the existing order was successfully mounted, enabling the transition to capitalism to be achieved. But no matter which societies had developed capitalism first, they would have been compelled to respond in the same way to the imperatives of the system. There is no basis for thinking that a Chinese or Turkish capitalism would have been immune to these imperatives any more than Japanese capitalism was: cultural "difference" is of little significance before the demands of competitive accumulation.

All the great tributary empires were venerable when absolutism was a novelty. "Unlike Asiatic monarchy," writes Victor Kiernan, "absolutism was an unstable transitional form, even if over a wide area it was prolonged for centuries."[190] There is then a connection between the tributary and absolutist states. Russia, in particular, might best be considered not as an example of what Anderson called "the Eastern variant" of absolutism, but rather of "the Western variant" of the tributary state.[191] Indeed, the emergence of absolutism can be seen as an attempt to introduce into Europe the mode of production and corresponding state form typical of Asia, the Middle East, North Africa, and even parts of Latin America (Mexico and Peru), in order to impose a similar "fetter on production." Amin suggests that absolutism would have been the Western variant of the tributary mode, but that it arrived too late to arrest the development of capitalism in the same way that the Chinese state repeatedly succeeded in doing after 1300.[192] Capitalism already existed in Western and Central Europe—albeit unevenly and with varying degrees of implantation—at the point when the absolutist states were in the process of formation. It was this lag that created the conditions of possibility for the initial breakthroughs in those territories where capitalism was strongest and absolutism weakest. Nevertheless, even if the absolutist states were incapable of completely containing capitalism, they could still prevent it from achieving dominance unless they were overthrown. Who achieved this task?

THE BOURGEOISIE AS A REVOLUTIONARY LEADERSHIP

In his book, *Categories and Methods of Historical Science* (1984), the Russian historian Mikhail Barg distinguished three "projects" in the bourgeois revolutions, past, present, and future. These have been summarized by Christopher Hill:

In the German Reformation and Peasant War "the project of the past" mobilized a medieval-type social movement—peasantry and burghers: it was the culmination of past history. The "project of the present" was that of the capitalist class forces grown up within feudal society. Two modes of production were in conflict, and so the revolution turned into a national political struggle for *national* ends. This was a new type of *class war*, distinct from peasant revolts which had great destructive force but no constructive national policy. The peasantry *could* not change the social structure. Hence the bourgeoisie could claim to be genuinely "national" in a way the peasantry could not. The "project of the present" represented the maximum possible at the time: hence bourgeois hegemony. It was transcended only by the "project of the future"— the leveling aspirations of the plebs, which would have led to the most complete clearing of the country from the Middle Ages. The "project of the future" emerged at the highest point of the revolution (Diggers, Babeuf), but it was not feasible at that stage in history.[193]

Although Barg's model involves the schematicism typical of Stalinist Russian historiography, his assessment of the capacities of the various classes is essentially correct. As we saw in the previous chapter, not every class is capable of making a social revolution. We can see these limitations most clearly in relation to the peasantry. Even after the dissolution of serfdom in Western Europe, which had been accomplished by the late fifteenth century, the peasantry remained the central exploited class in feudal society, the class upon whose labor that society was based. Yet although the peasants certainly continued to struggle against the landowners who exploited them, they were not ultimately victorious in the sense of replacing the landowners as a new ruling class within a new society based on a new mode of production. The peasants may have attempted to moderate or remove the effect of the feudal system, but they had no alternative to it, simply a desire to escape the source of their exploitation. In this sense peasant revolts resemble those of slaves, although the former were of course vastly more numerous. There were three main obstacles to the peasantry becoming an independent revolutionary force during the transition to capitalism.

The first was that where collective activity by peasants did take place it was not always directed toward their masters but sometimes against other exploited or oppressed groups. When Pope Urban II preached a crusade to drive the Seljuk Turks from Asia Minor in 1095 the call was not only answered by feudal knights intent on plunder, land, and, of course, enacting God's will. The preaching of itinerant *prophetae* like Peter the Hermit also aroused thousands of the insecure peasant masses living in overcrowded, disease-ridden conditions to set off for Jerusalem and retake it from the infidels. At the heart of this movement—the so-called People's Crusade—was certainly deflected class anger: the cry of the quasi-mythical leader King Tafur—"Where are the poor folk who want property? Let them come with me!"—encapsulates the rational core of their religious enthusiasm. The way this was expressed, however, was not only in the massacre of Muslims in Jerusalem—for in this they were matched death-for-death by the knightly crusaders themselves—but in the massacres of Jews. In May and June 1096 the Episcopal towns of the Rhine, from Speyer to Worms to Mainz to Cologne and beyond were attacked by three armies of popular crusaders. The Jewish communities, which had been settled there for many centuries, were massacred, often against the wishes of the local ruling class, who found them useful. One group led by the itinerant preacher Gottschalk, entered Hungary where they began to pillage the local peasantry until they were massacred in turn by royal troops at Stuhlweissenburg.[194] And this was followed by four further explosions of anti-Semitic persecution "from below" between 1200 and 1450, as far north as Flanders and as far south as Spain.[195] When Marx and Engels wrote of the "idiocy of rural life," they were not suggesting that this was all there was to peasant existence, but neither was it simply a gratuitous insult.[196]

The second obstacle was that, even when collective activity was directed at the ruling class rather than convenient scapegoats, the lack of a societal alternative proved a fatal weakness. The local nature of the peasant vision, their inability to conceptualize the system as a whole, has led them, historically, to exonerate the ruler from the crimes of his officials. The peasants of 1381 in England believed the false promises of Richard II, but even if they had not, what could they have done with London? Even the examples of peasant success prove the point. None of the great European peasant revolts actually overthrew a state; but as Jean Chesneaux writes of China:

> The most important contribution of peasant movements in the historical play of forces in imperial China was in the overthrow of dynasties. The Ch'in regime (221–207 BC) was destroyed by peasant revolts; their leader Liu Pang proclaimed himself emperor and founded the Han dynasty (206–23 BC). In their turn, the later Han (AD 25–220), the T'ang and the Sung (AD 960–1279) were overthrown or irreparably weakened by great waves of peasant discontent. The Ming dynasty (1368–1644), which achieved power through popular revolts against the Mongols, was itself brought to an end by peasant rebellions under Chang Hsien-chung and Li Tzu-ch'eng, which were subsequently suppressed by the Manchus.[197]

As we saw in the previous section, none of these huge convulsions resulted in any fundamental change. As Trotsky observed:

> In ancient China revolutions brought the peasantry to power, or rather, the military leaders of peasant insurrections. That led each time to a redivision of the land and the establishment of a new "peasant" dynasty, after which history would begin again from the beginning with new concentration of land, a new aristocracy, a new system of usury, and a new uprising. So long as the revolution maintained its purely peasant character, society is incapable of emerging from these hopeless and vicious circles. Such was the basis of ancient Asiatic history, including ancient Russian history.[198]

We can see a similar pattern near the end of the era of bourgeois revolution. During the Mexican Revolution the armed Zapatista peasantry had succeeded in taking control of Mexico City by December 1914: six months later they had abandoned it, without establishing a new governmental apparatus. Eric Wolf writes of the "tragic ineptitude" revealed by both Villa and Zapata in their failure to "create a political machine that could govern the country." In one sense this is unfair: not personal inadequacy but class incapacity lay behind the incomprehension of the Mexican revolutionaries.[199] Adolfo Gilly explains why the conquest of the Mexican capital involved not the seizure of state power but the creation of a power vacuum: "The exercise of power demands a program. The application of a program requires a policy. A policy means a party. The peasants did not have, could not have, any of these things."[200]

The third obstacle was that 'the peasantry' were not homogenous, but internally differentiated with often opposed interests; indeed, one of the major effects of peasant success in ending serfdom, in both Western Europe after the crisis of the fourteenth century and Russia after 1861, was to allow a layer to emerge whose interests were separate from both the tenants below them and the great landowners above them. We have already discussed this process in England and France: did the Russian *mir* develop in a different way? There is in fact some doubt as to whether it ever existed in the form that is usually thought. The idea of the peasant commune seems to have originated with the German Catholic nobleman, August von Haxthausen, a major figure in the Romantic Movement in the German Lands.[201] Haxthausen claimed that the commune was the basis of peasant economy and society in a book published in 1846 after his travels in Russia, and his views were subsequently adopted by early populists like Herzen and Chernychevsky. Partly as a result of his influence over Russian reformers the Emancipation Act of 1861, which formally ended serfdom, introduced collective ownership of the land, but this was an innovation or, at best, a generalization from a geographically limited form of social organization. Recent investigation into one average estate, Voshchazkniko, in Yaroslav province, has produced the following conclusions:

> Communal land was not the basis of a self-sufficient household economy, its repartition was far from being harmonious, and the larger shares allocated to richer peasants seem to have been a form of progressive taxation. There was no correlation between family size and size of communal holding. There was no communal property in anything but land. The commune was not "patriarchal" either in the sense that its eldest members ran it, or in the sense that an unusually high proportion of households were headed by men. Communal offices were shirked or avoided; those elected often hired others in their place. Poverty was far from impossible and in some cases extreme, though welfare provision was resisted by the commune and had to be enforced by the landlord. Private property in land and dwellings was widespread. Far from avoiding market transactions, serfs were active participants in land, labor and credit markets. Equality was neither aimed at nor achieved; social stratification was at least as pronounced as in pre-industrial or early industrial western and central Europe, and was reinforced trans-generationally through inheritance.[202]

In the Russian case as in the English, a minority had effectively left their peasant origins behind to become part of the rural capitalist class. It was this minority, rather than the peasantry as a whole, which would provide part of the leadership of the bourgeois revolutions, which observation brings us back to the question of the bourgeoisie itself.

As we saw in chapter 15, skepticism over the revolutionary capacity of the bourgeoisie has of course become the stock-in-trade of revisionism, particularly in relation to the French Revolution. Sarah Maza argues that in "a society in crisis," where "new sources of social order and cohesion had to be sought . . . the bourgeoisie in either its narrow or wider senses would have been a most unlikely place to start."[203] Other historians have been more generally dismissive. According to Murray Bookchin:

> In the Marxist and liberal view of these [bourgeois] revolutions, it was bankers, merchants, manufacturers, and other entrepreneurs—the predatory men who were amassing enormous wealth in the eighteenth century—who formed the class vanguard of the great revolutions, presumably in spite of themselves. . . . But if it is true that capitalism is globally supreme today, no class in history has been more craven, cowardly, and fearful of social change (especially change involving the "dark people," as they called the underprivileged) than the entrepreneurs who peopled the commercial centers of Europe and America during the eighteenth century. As a class the bourgeoisie has *never* been politically revolutionary, let alone insurgent.[204]

There have indeed been liberals who have held this view; but as we saw in Part Two, from Marx onwards thinkers in the classical Marxist tradition took a much more nuanced view of the bourgeoisie than Bookchin suggests, without dismissing altogether its role as a revolutionary class.[205] Nevertheless, it is true that several different social groups or fractions other than the bourgeoisie have been responsible for leading the transformation in pre-capitalist or colonial states in ways conducive to capitalist development. In this context it may be worth temporarily refocusing the title of this book to ask another, related question: how revolutionary were the bourgeoisie in the bourgeois revolutions?

We first need to establish what it meant to be a member of the bourgeoisie during the feudal era. Paul Corcoran writes:

> In France the term "bourgeois" originally had a reasonably precise meaning, dating back to the period of feudal consolidation and referring to the inhabitants of the enclosed or fortified area surrounding the castle of the local lord for whom they also performed particular duties and for which they were afforded a certain legal status. It is from this point of origin that the notion of bourgeois as a town-dweller derives.[206]

Most European languages have analogous terms to *burgeis* in the original Old French: *burgerij* in Dutch, *burgher* in German, *borgesia* in Italian, *burzuazja* in Polish, and *burguesía* in Spanish. Some Marxists appear to believe that these etymological origins remove any need for further discussion. "A bourgeoisie, if the term is to mean anything at all, is a class based on towns; that is what the word means," wrote Anderson in 1966: "It is ludicrous to call a landowning class a 'bourgeoisie'—one might as well call artisans a peasantry.[207] Wood agrees: "The burgher or bourgeois is, by definition, a town dweller."[208] But, as Corcoran further notes, over time the original topographical terms began to be used in an additional, normative sense: "As feudal society developed and the capitalist element within, the term also took on a pejorative meaning in the mouths of the aristocrats, for whom the bourgeois were avaricious, hypocritical, servile, uncultivated and interested in money above all."[209]

For revisionists, it is this lack of social definition that characterizes the bourgeoisie. Maza writes that "bourgeois" is "an extremely slippery term"; to be bourgeois was to be consigned to a "holding category," both the term and the social experience it suggested were "unstable": "To be bourgeois was to be in transit, uncomfortable about your social identity, with workers muttering against you and noblemen sneering at your manners."[210] The bourgeoisie apparently had no internal coherence as a class "for itself," but was defined instead almost entirely by forces external to it. David Bell claims that the revisionists have demonstrated the impossibility of identifying either "a 'bourgeois' social group possessing a distinct relationship to the means of production," or "a group united by a common assertion of 'bourgeois' identity" in 1789.[211] Maza, for example, writes: "Unlike both aristocracies, whose existence usually rests on a combination of legal distinctions and kinship patterns, and rural and urban working classes, which are united by common forms and objects of labor, the middle class exists only in relation to other groups." In fact, *all* social classes exist, "only in relation to other groups," or more precisely, in relation to other social classes. Nevertheless, the supposed exceptionalism of the bourgeois case allows Maza to reduce its existence to a question of "discourse": "whether and how it is named and invested with social, political, moral, or historical importance."[212]

For political Marxists the bourgeoisie is in any case irrelevant: our attention should be focused instead on capitalism and capitalists. This is a subject that has particularly exercised Wood:

> We have got so used to the identification of bourgeois with capitalist that the presuppositions secreted in this conflation have become invisible to us . . . in its French form, the word used to mean nothing more than someone of non-noble status who, while he worked for a living, did not generally dirty his hands and used his mind more than his body for work. That old usage tells us nothing about capitalism, and is likely to refer to a professional, an office-holder, or an intellectual no less than to a merchant.[213]

Neal Wood summarizes the supposed distinction in this way: "One can be bourgeois, in the narrow traditional sense, without being a capitalist, and the converse is also true."[214] On this basis, Benno Teschke can claim that, "while the English revolution was not bourgeois, it was capitalist; and while the French Revolution was bourgeois, it was not capitalist."[215] Do these authors then see the bourgeoisie as a distinct class in its own right, separate from but overlapping with the capitalist class? If so, given that Marxists do not treat class as culturally defined, what socioeconomic role does the bourgeoisie play, if not that of personified capital? In effect, they seem to regard the bourgeoisie either as a Weberian status group or as a residual (or as Maza has it, a "holding") category for those who do not fit into one or other of the main economic classes. For supporters of capitalism the elevation of capitalists above the bourgeoisie poses no difficulties, theoretical or otherwise. "The dramatic difference between the two classes is obscured by Marxist periodization," writes Liah Greenfield:

> But the fact is that these two classes had nothing in common (or, at least, as little as any two different classes in society): One [the bourgeoisie] was docile, interested in security, ashamed of its social position; the other [the capitalist class] adventurous, achievement-orientated, and self assertive. Their collective tempers, their interests, outlooks, and styles—everything that could characterize them as communities, that is, classes in a meaningful sense—were different. Moreover, in distinction to the bourgeoisie, which was many centuries old, the capitalist class was only emerging in France in the late eighteenth century. It evolved out of the bourgeoisie, it is true, but also out of sectors of the nobility, and, in any case, like other new social groups, such as the intellectuals, it did not cultivate collective memory that would emphasize its genetic lineage: there was a break in continuity.[216]

In fact, the kind of theoretical convolutions implied by the distinction between "bourgeois" and "capitalist" are quite unnecessary. As Elizabeth Fox Genovese and Eugene Genovese point out: "The use of a single term for ... different social entities causes problems, but when most Marxists speak of the [French] Revolution as bourgeois they are referring specifically to the national consolidation of bourgeois social relations of production in the sense that all the great nineteenth-century social theorists understood them, not to the specific careers of a small merchant from Arles, or a *rentier* from Nimes."[217] By the time Marx and Engels—surely two of the "great nineteenth-century social theorists"—used the term "bourgeoisie" in the 1840s, it stood, in relation to town-dwellers, for something both shallower than previously (because it excluded the new class of urban industrial laborers) and wider (because it included rural capitalists). There is therefore no inherent contradiction in Edward Thompson referring to the rule of an "agrarian bourgeoisie" in England after 1688.[218] In part then, "bourgeoisie" meant capitalists, both urban and rural, in the literal sense of those who owned or controlled capital; but it also meant something wider.

In what is by far the most sensible discussion of this issue, Hal Draper describes the bourgeoisie as a whole as involving "a social penumbra around the hard core of capitalists proper, shading out into the diverse social elements that function as servitors or hangers-on of capital without themselves owning capital."[219] It is important to understand that the components of this "penumbra" are *not* members of the petty bourgeoisie, who stand outside the capital-labor relationship and "earn their living by dint of their own labor and their own property."[220] On the contrary: according to Anderson, membership of the non-capitalist bourgeoisie "is typically composed ... of the gamut of professional, administrative and technical groups that enjoy life-conditions similar to capitalists proper—everything customarily included in the broader term 'bourgeoisie' as opposed to 'capital.'"[221] One way of thinking about the bourgeoisie is therefore to divide the notion of a socioeconomic class into its constituent parts: the bourgeoisie in general comprise the class in its "social" aspect; the section of the bourgeoisie who specifically own or control capital comprise the class in its "economic" aspect; the connection between capitalist and non-capitalist sections of the bourgeoisie is that both derive their income, directly or indirectly, from the extraction of surplus value from the proletariat.[222]

As we have seen, the bourgeoisie was originally as necessary, as intrinsic to feudalism as the peasantry—not in the sense that it was similarly exploited, but in the sense that the system required bankers and merchants as well as lawyers and bureaucrats to function. Once capitalism, as distinct from merchants' or usurers' capital, came into existence, it changed the nature of the bourgeoisie: the center of gravity of the class shifted. And if nothing else, the various fractions of the capitalist bourgeoisie can be credited, with recombining the preexisting elements of the feudal economy in an entirely new way. In this sense, as Louis Althusser wrote, the capitalist bourgeoisie "is indeed nothing other than the element predestined to unify all the other elements of the mode of production, the one that will transform it into another combination, that of the capitalist mode of production."[223] One might say that the decisive moment in the transformation of the bourgeoisie into a potential ruling class was when the non-capitalist sections began to either derive, or at least see the possibility of deriving, their income from the exploitation of workers rather than of peasants. It was not inevitable however that these possibilities would result in revolutionary consciousness.

Braudel long ago identified "the defection of the bourgeoisie" in Spain and Italy, areas in which crises took place in conditions where capitalism had either never developed or had regressed: "The bourgeoisie in the sixteenth century, committed to trade and the service of the crown, was always on the verge of disappearing." Their lack of self-consciousness was in part due to the very insecurities of commerce, in part because their relatively small numeric size made it difficult to see themselves as a distinct class, and in part because they wished to avoid the hostility of the nobles who constituted a major part of their market. Their impulse was always to compromise, to attempt to join the minor ranks of the aristocracy and invest in landowning, to accumulate capital, but because of the guaranteed return that land promised. "The bourgeoisie was not always pushed out, brutally liquidated," writes Braudel: "It turned class traitor."[224] Henry Kamen points out, however, that this was not the result of a moral failing on its part, because "if sectors of the bourgeoisie failed, it was because external conditions, rather than a conscious defection, determined their situation." In these conditions "the bourgeoisie felt that they belonged ultimately not to their present condition but to the rank which they aspired," which was that of the existing ruling class—although Kamen notes that the adoption of aristocratic ideals "did not necessarily lead to the withdrawal of capital from wealth formation."[225]

> There is indeed nothing to indicate that the sixteenth-century Castilian was congenitally unsuited to a business life.... All the signs ... seem to indicate that in the early sixteenth century there were very fair prospects for the development of a dynamic

"capitalist" element in Castile, which—like its equivalents in England and Holland—might gradually have imposed some of its ideas and values on the rest of society. The fact that these prospects were not realized would suggest that at some point adverse circumstances proved too strong, and that the enterprise of the north Castilian *bourgeoisie* failed to withstand a serious change for the worse in the country's economic and social climate.[226]

The decline of the Castilian bourgeoisie was not simply a consequence of the government incompetence and mismanagement that Elliott identifies as occurring in the sixteenth century, which need not itself have proved fatal; it was instead a purposive process undertaken with the intention of subduing bourgeois power. This was accomplished in part through the depletion of liquid capital in order to pay for Spanish participation in the Thirty Years' War, the accompanying forced reduction of interest rates and the consequent restoration of feudal land ownership as the primary source of income; in part through the conscious intervention of the monarchy to strengthen traditional aristocratic hierarchies by blocking social mobility.[227] "The contempt for commerce and manual labor, the lure of easy money from investment in censos and juros [taxes and mortgages], the universal hunger for titles of nobility and social prestige—all these, when combined with the innumerable practical obstacles in the way of profitable economic enterprise, had persuaded the bourgeoisie to abandon its unequal struggle, and throw in its lot with the unproductive upper class of society."[228]

John Berger has painted an evocative portrait of the type of bourgeoisie that remained in the condition of subalternity, drawn specifically from the Spanish case. Here the bourgeoisie was a creation of the imperial state and played the role of an economically unproductive bureaucracy, which could be sustained only as long as wealth flowed from the Americas and Flanders. Once this ceased:

> Chronic impoverishment set in; there was no attempt to develop the economy because this so-called middle class did not understand the link between capital and production: instead they sank back into provincial improvidence, proliferating only their "connexions." ... The Spanish middle class ... had—even if they wore the same clothes and read some of the same books—little in common with their French or English or German contemporaries. Such middle-class virtues as there were in Spain were not created of necessity: if they existed they were cultivated theoretically. There had been no successful bourgeois revolution. In an absolutist state the middle class had no independent power and so the virtues of initiative, industriousness, non-conformism, thrift, scientific curiosity, had no reason to exist. On the contrary the history of the Spanish middle class had encouraged the very opposite traits. ... The state bureaucracy had discouraged initiative and put a premium on safe laziness. It came to be thought that to work hard was to lose one's dignity. The energy of the Spanish middle class was turned to ritual, which bestows on events a significance gathered from the past and precludes innovation or the thought of it.[229]

But not all territorially based bourgeoisies could be accommodated and consequently adapt themselves to the pursuit of heroic inertia. Some made the shift from incorporation to at least partial independence. Hans Baron notes that the early Florentine bankers and financiers did not represent a threat to the feudal order: "Forming, as they did a foreign body in the noble feudal world and yet living at its expense, they were not the potential bearers of a new outlook on economic life." A distinction, however, needs to be drawn between them and the merchants who entered into production, thus—potentially at least—embodying a new form of social organization: "The new industrial merchant class of the woolen gild, whose interests were bound up with the majority of the population, was socially much more consistent than [the financiers] and had an outlook on life more independent of the traditions of the feudal world." Baron summarizes the difference as being that, "merchants and bankers in the thirteenth century had lived on the edge of the feudal world; in the fifteenth-century Florence they lived on the edge of an industrial society."[230] Jürgen Habermas writes in similar terms of the Hamburg bourgeoisie before the disasters of the Thirty Years' War:

> The "capitalists," the merchants, bankers, entrepreneurs, and manufacturers (at least where, unlike Hamburg, the towns could maintain their independence from the traditional rulers) belonged to that group of the "bourgeois" who, like the new category of scholars, were not really "burghers" in the traditional sense. . . . Unlike the great urban merchants and officials who, in former days, could be assimilated by the cultivated nobility of the Italian Renaissance courts, they could no longer be integrated *in toto* into the noble culture at the close of the Baroque period.[231]

As Habermas suggests with his reference to "scholars," as the bourgeoisie began to take shape as a potential alternative ruling class to the feudal nobility, new professions and social categories arose that immediately became part of it: journalists, doctors of medicine, public intellectuals who were not—or not necessarily—clerics or theologians.

In neither Italy nor Germany did the bourgeoisie succeed in making a revolution and consequently was forced backward into a position reminiscent of its earlier dependence. In those states where members of the bourgeoisie at least managed to retain an independent position in feudal society, they underwent a common experience of individual pride in their own achievements and class humiliation at the restrictions still imposed upon them. Members of the bourgeoisie in the broad sense were both conscious of and angered by the discrepancy between their growing wealth and their exclusion from certain social positions, let alone their distance from the exercise of political power. The contempt of the absolutist rulers was palpable. Here is James VI (of Scotland) and I (of England) writing in his late sixteenth-century guide to kingcraft, *Basilicon Doron*, nominally a letter to his eldest son, Henry. James refers to "our third and last estate, which is our Burgesses" as being "composed of two sorts of men; Merchants and Craftsmen": "The Merchants think the whole common-wealth ordained for making them up; and accounting it their lawful gain and trade, to enrich themselves upon the loss of all the rest of the people, they transport from us things necessary; bringing back sometimes necessary things, and at other times nothing at all. . . . And the Craftsmen think, we should be content with their work, how bad and dear soever it be: and if in any thing they be controlled, up goeth the blue blanket."[232] When James's successor Charles I attempted to prevent movement between social classes during the period of his personal rule after 1629, "the inspiration came from the old-fashioned noble and gentry families, who were resisting bitterly the aspirations of well-to-do middle sort of people—yeoman farmers as well as clothiers—to be regarded as gentlemen": "The achievement of the formal title of 'gentleman' could not ensure a man of acceptance as a gentleman by the leading county families, who ostracized or cold shouldered the *nouveaux riches*."[233]

One factor was necessary to channel resentment into the active pursuit of social change. As Eric Olin Wright has argued, feudalism was in its own way as hegemonic a system as capitalism, at least in relation to the subaltern capitalist class: "So long as they were able to 'feudalize' their capitalist exploitation (that is, buy into the feudal class in various ways) they generally supported feudalism. It was only in the period of the long crisis of late feudalism, in part perhaps stimulated by the expansion of capitalism itself, that the bourgeoisie became stridently antifeudal."[234] In other words, once the crisis of feudalism made the possibility of being satisfactorily incorporated into the existing system a diminishing possibility, at least some sections of the bourgeoisie began to see the social relations in which they were involved as an alternative to, rather than a subordinate component of feudalism. David Harvey has argued that the oppositional bourgeoisie operated across "seven different activity spheres":

> Capitalism did not supplant feudalism by way of some neat revolutionary transformation resting on forces mobilized within only one of these spheres. It had to grow within the interstices of the old society and replace it bit by bit, sometimes through main force, violence, predation and seizure of assets, but at other times with guile and cunning. And it often lost battles against the old order even as it eventually won the war. As it achieved a modicum of power, however, a nascent capitalist class had to build its own alternative social relations, administrative systems, mental conceptions, production systems, relations to nature and patterns of daily life as these had long been constituted under the preceding feudal order.[235]

These spheres might be seen as aspects of the transition as a social rather than purely economic process. The key issue then is the role the bourgeoisie did play in what Harvey calls "main force, violence, predation and seizure of assets"; in short, revolution. As Thompson once noted: "Mill-owners, accountants, company-promoters, provincial bankers, are not historically notorious for their desperate propensity to rush, bandoliers on their shoulders, to the barricades. More generally they arrive on the scene when the climatic battles of the bourgeois revolution have already been fought. . . . What need did these bourgeois have of courage when their money served them better?"[236] But in some cases money would not serve and it was in these cases that the distinction between the capitalist and noncapitalist sections of the bourgeoisie acquired decisive significance, since sections of the latter were less adverse to bandoliers and barricades, and tended to form the revolutionary leaderships. Which sections?

There is a famous schema, widely but erroneously ascribed to Lenin, in which ideological leadership could only be provided to the working class "from outside."[237] In his discussion of the formation of the seventeenth-century French Jansenism, Lucien Goldmann suggested, without direct reference to Lenin, that the formation of an "external" leadership might explain the influence of this movement for reform of the Catholic Church:

> The ideology is first of all elaborated outside the social group by a few professional politicians, and essentially, by ideologists . . . It is the circles which are outside the main group which combine to provide both the ideologues and the extremist leaders . . . However, shortly after the birth of the movement, it is the *élite* or vanguard of the group itself which takes control, providing the leaders of the main body of opinion, and offering the real resistance to the king's authority. What might, in modern times, be called the sympathizers or fellow travelers come from the *officiers* and in particular from the *Cours souveraines* and the *parlements*. It is thanks to them that the ideas of the *élite* produce the great effect which they do upon the rest of the country.[238]

Generalizing from Goldmann's work, Michael Mann argued that the process he described was applicable to the way in which leaderships were formed for the bourgeoisie. On the one hand: "Left to itself the bourgeoisie was only capable of economism—in the eighteenth century of segmental manipulative deference." But on the other: "An ideological vanguard might articulate best the experience and needs of other power actors (economic, military, and political), but its ideology was then appropriated by them."[239] The difficulty with Mann's argument is that of "externality": leaderships came from outside the capitalist wing of the bourgeoisie, but were part of it in the wider "non-economic" sense. The notion of an "ideological vanguard" has a family resemblance to Gramsci's notion of "organic intellectuals," but the latter conveys greater sensitivity to the integral nature of this group to the bourgeoisie: "Every social group, coming into existence on the original terrain of an essential function in the world of economic production, creates together with itself organically, one or more strata of intellectuals which give it homogeneity and an awareness of its own function not only in the economic but also in the social and political fields. The capitalist entrepreneur creates alongside himself the industrial technician, the specialist in political economy, the organizers of a new culture, of a new legal system, etc."[240]

The most decisive bourgeois leaderships therefore tended to emerge from those sections of the class without direct material interests in the process of production. What made it possible for this section of the bourgeoisie to provide leadership to the class as a whole? One way of answering this question is to take a negative example; where a group of highly developed capitalist societies failed to complete the bourgeois revolution: the Italian city-states.

The republics of Northern and Central Italy displayed the same ambivalence toward the feudal system as elsewhere in Europe.[241] Nevertheless, the Italian experiment may have proved to be a historical dead end, not because of the extent to which it remained part of feudalism, but because of the extent to which it did not. For, in one important respect, they displayed a characteristic of the mature capitalist system even in this formative period: competition raised to the level of state rivalry. Giovanni Arrighi noted that, historically, there have been two kinds of competition between capitals. The first is more "a mode of regulating relationships between autonomous centers which are in fact *cooperating* with one another in sustaining a trade expansion from which they all benefit, and which the profitability of each centre is a condition of the profitability of all the centers." The second is not restricted to firms, but is carried on by states, beginning with the behavior of the Italian city-states during the Hundred Years' War when "an overaccumulation of capital leads capitalist organizations to invade one another's spheres of operation; the division of labor that previously defined the terms of their mutual cooperation breaks down; and, increasingly, the losses of one organization are the condition of the profits of another." The situation ceases to be "positive-sum" and becomes "zero-sum."[242] This level of economic competition prevented the city-states from forming a unified nation-state under Frederick II and led to the resultant submission of the communes, over several centuries, to the feudal barons of the surrounding countryside; a defeat compounded by conquest at the hands of the Spanish Habsburgs at the end of the fifteenth century.

It was not simply capitalism that then went into retreat but everything associated with it. John Breuilly takes two essays by Dante to argue that national consciousness could be found as early as the thirteenth century, although not yet nationalism. In one, "On Vernacular Language" Dante claims to have discovered an Italian language, which he in turn identifies with the Italian nation and argues for its use by poets. In the other, "On the Monarchy," Dante argues for the establishment of a universal monarchy to establish harmony across Christendom as a whole, not only in the Italian Peninsula. Breuilly argues that the divergence between these two positions is proof of both "the existence of some kind of national consciousness and concern with national language and cultural identity in late thirteenth and early fourteenth-century Europe" and "the non-existence of nationalist consciousness."[243] The "illustrious vernacular" of which Dante spoke was in fact the Florentine dialect adopted by intellectuals like himself who belonged to the bourgeoisie of the most advanced Italian city-state. As Gramsci rhetorically asked: "Does not this mean that two conceptions of the world were in conflict: a bourgeois-popular one expressing itself in the vernacular and an aristocratic-feudal one expressing itself in Latin and harking back to Roman antiquity?"[244] With the decline of the Communes and the reimposition of feudalism, the attempt to establish a vernacular means of expression was destroyed along with its social basis: "After a brief interlude (the communal liberties) when there is a flourishing of intellectuals who come from the popular (bourgeois) classes, the intellectual function is reabsorbed into the traditional caste, where the individual elements come from the people but where the character of the caste prevails over their origins."[245] In other words, the proto-national consciousness expressed above all by Dante was linked to the very early development of capitalism in Italy, whose defeat meant that the possibility of national unification was taken off the historical agenda. The failure to make Italy meant that no Italians would be made for another five hundred years. In these circumstances the aspiration for a universal monarchy was an *alternative* to a nationalism that had been blocked, and whose literary manifestations would soon themselves be abandoned. National consciousness could not flourish, or even take root, where the conditions for capitalist development were no longer present, and for it to be consolidated across Europe, even if only among the bourgeoisie, there had to be at least one case where it successfully made the transition to nationalism and then became embodied in a nation-state. Insofar as identification with the state did take place, it was with the existing city-states: "This identification then led to the relatively easy outbreak of warfare between different city-states, which perceived their competitors as dangerous rivals (as do modern nation-states)."[246]

Drawing on the Italian example, we might therefore say that existence of capitalism and capitalists was not enough to guarantee that a bourgeois revolution would even be attempted. The non-economic bourgeoisie were therefore central for three reasons. First, precisely because they were not subject to competitive economic divisions within their class, these groups were often more able to express the common interests of the bourgeoisie as a whole than capitalists: they were tactful cousins smoothing over the tensions between the hostile band of warring brothers. Second, and conversely, they were also prepared to temporarily transgress capitalist property rights in order to better permanently enshrine them. Third, because these revolutionaries still belonged to a minority exploiting class, albeit one broader than their feudal predecessor, they needed to involve other social forces to expel the Spanish and overthrow the English absolutist states. As I noted earlier, the bourgeoisie should not be confused with the petty bourgeoisie, but the former did have a close *relationship* with the latter, which, until 1848 at least, invariably provided the foot soldiers for the struggle with feudal absolutism. Anderson writes that the bourgeoisie "will normally lack a clear-cut frontier with layers of the petty bourgeoisie below it, for the difference between the two in the ranks of the small employer is often quantitative rather than qualitative."[247] These links are strongest before the transition from agrarian and mercantile capitalism to industrial capitalism, as Gareth Stedman Jones explains: "In general, the more industrial capitalism developed, the stronger was the economic power of the *grande bourgeoisie* in relation to the masses of small producers and dealers from which it had sprung, and the greater the distance between their respective aims. Conversely, the less developed the bourgeoisie, the smaller the gulf between "bourgeois" and "petit bourgeois," and the greater the preponderance and cohesion of the popular movement."[248]

The capacity of these organic intellectuals to represent a collective bourgeois interest, to abandon when necessary the immediate economic manifestations of that interest, and to unite classes outside the bourgeoisie were only possible because they tended to act from motives that were not strictly economic in nature. These motives varied over time but tended to be more concerned with religious or constitutional liberties than with removing absolutist impediments to the exploitation of wage labor. What ideologies then helped shape the revolutionary consciousness of the bourgeoisie?

THE FIRST IDEOLOGY OF TRANSFORMATION

Mikulas Teich has described a series of three "historically demarcated sequences" encompassing "the long-drawn-out transition from feudalism to capitalism": the Renaissance, the Reformation, and the Enlightenment.[249] Yet the relative importance of these sequences is quite different. In the initial cases of the United Provinces and England, opposition to absolutism was at least partly expressed in terms of religious belief; in the later case of France, far more consistently in grounds of Enlightenment rationality; the link between England and France in particular was provided by nationalism, which was compatible with both positions. As this suggests, in the context of our discussion the Renaissance is the least significant. In part this was because a movement primarily concerned with aesthetics and philosophy the Renaissance was the most removed from questions of state power, at least until the late figure of Machiavelli who, as I argued in chapter 1, was not a bourgeois revolutionary. Perhaps more to the point, however, there is a respect in which, as we shall see, the Renaissance period was expressive precisely of the absence of the bourgeois revolution in the Italian city-states. This absence gives the great productions of humanist culture a retrospectively elegiac quality, as if the achievements of Michelangelo were compensation for the unwillingness or inability of his Medici patrons to unify the peninsula. Ultimately, the visual arts too would decline into the decadence of Mannerism, the aesthetic equivalent of the static formalism characteristic of the feudal courts that began to dominate Italy from the late fifteenth century. It is, as they say, no accident that the emergence of Mannerism can be dated to the same decade of the 1520s that saw the final assertion of Spanish royal power in Italy, even over Rome itself.[250] Gramsci wrote of there being "two currents" in the Renaissance, "one progressive and the other regressive, and that in the final analysis the latter triumphed after the general phenomenon had reached its full splendor in the sixteenth century (though not as a national and political fact, though, but as a prevalently but not exclusively cultural fact)." As he also notes, "the people were preparing the reaction against this splendid parasitism in the form of the Protestant Reformation" and it was this process that constituted the first ideology of bourgeois revolution.[251]

The revolt begun by Luther in 1517 was by no means predestined for success. There was, after all, nothing new in schisms within the Catholic Church taking a political form. After the Great Schism of 1378 Christendom divided between two (and at one point three) different contenders for the papal throne. Yet neither this nor any of the lesser schisms had threatened to lead to the creation of a new faith to rival the established church. Nor was heresy previously unknown. Heresies, often millenarian in content and drawing their main support from peasants and urban plebeians, had given ideological focus to several of the most explosive social movements of the Middle Ages. Yet no actual or potential ruling class in Europe, with the partial exception of the Bohemian, embraced these doctrines. The fifteenth-century Hussite Revolt, which led to the independence of the kingdom of Bohemia, is in fact of great relevance to our theme, since it presents a picture of what could happen when a great revolutionary movement arose, united by a radical religious ideology, but which lacked the socioeconomic basis that would enable it to develop into a bourgeois revolution.

The Hussite movement between 1419 and 1434 was, in effect, a proto-Reformation, a form transitional between the various forms of medieval heresy and Protestantism.[252] Like the establishment of the Swiss Confederation, the Hussite Revolt was successful because it involved an alliance between peasants, individual burgesses, and the towns as corporate bodies. Indeed, the Bohemian case had an even wider class base in that it also involved additional forces in the form of the minor nobility and the lesser gentry. Like the Swiss Confederation, the Kingdom of Bohemia sought to overthrow the local authority of the Austrian Habsburgs, but the key antagonist of the Hussites was the church—as landowner, as secular power, and as the source of religious authority. The success of the revolt established the first territorially based, schismatic church in Western Europe, based on recognition of the Bible as the final authority in all matters of religion, yet this did not directly lead to similarly novel developments in economics and politics. If anything, the nobles and gentry consolidated their positions through expropriation of church lands and property, and acquisition of Crown domains on what amounted to permanent leasehold, while the Crown itself was reduced to a relatively weak form of elected estates-monarchy.[253] Ironically, insofar as the Hussite Revolt contributed toward capitalist development in the longer term it was through the one feature that it shared with the earlier peasant revolts: the effective ending of serfdom.

Even the Reformation proper did not in and of itself lead to capitalist development. Attempts to explore the relationship between Protestantism (the Calvinist variant in particular) and capitalism often involve a pair of false alternatives. One is a supposedly Marxist position that sees the capitalist economy producing Protestantism as a form of ideological legitimation. The other is a supposedly Weberian position that sees Protestantism as an independent factor that inadvertently provided the psychological motivation for believers to undertake capital accumulation. Neither position accurately represents the views held respectively by Marx or Weber: both men have been ill-served in respect of this subject, often as much by their supporters as by their opponents. It is therefore necessary briefly to review what they actually had to say on the role played by the ideologies of the Reformation.

Many writers start from a set of wrong assumptions about Marxist theory and how it explains the nature of Calvinism. In a defense of Weber, exemplary in the accuracy with which it represents his thought, Gordon Marshall writes: "[Marxism] states that since ideas, such as those conveyed by Calvinist doctrines, are merely 'reflections' of underlying economic conditions, then Calvinism (indeed the Reformation in general) was a historically necessary development following upon prior economic changes. In other words, the new capitalist class utilized Calvinist beliefs in order to excuse their prior class interests, these being to accumulate capital in the manner prescribed by the 'spirit of capitalism' as conceived by Weber."[254] On reading this passage, one wishes that Marshall would show the same scrupulousness of exposition when discussing Marx that he does when discussing Weber. What he outlines here is not classical Marxism, but the crude reductionism characteristic of the Second International at its worst and Stalinism at its most typical. Furthermore, although one might suppose that Marshall is summarizing Marx on the subject of Calvinism, he is not, for Marx nowhere wrote a systematic account of any aspect of the Reformation. His contributions on the subject were in fact restricted to a number of suggestive but unsystematic observations, the two most relevant of which both appear in *Capital*, Volume 1.

One observation is specifically concerned with the—largely unintended—economic consequences of the Henrican dissolution of the monasteries and seizure of church property in England after 1537. Church land acquired during this process by "speculating farmers and townsmen" was subject, in some cases, to consolidation and the introduction of commercial agriculture, and often accompanied by the eviction of existing church tenants who then went on to form part of the rural proletariat.[255] In other words, Marx sees one economic aspect of the Reformation—the expropriation of church wealth—as contributing in England to primitive accumulation and the formation of capitalist relations of production in the countryside. Marx says nothing here about ideology, but notes the economic effects of the establishment of the Anglican Church, which in all of Protestant Europe was the one doctrinally closest to Catholicism. Theoretically, the insight could be generalized to take account of similar events in any other countries that did have Calvinist reformations. In practice, it simply does not square with the evidence. In the case of Scotland, church wealth was simply squandered by the rapacious feudal nobility and consequently contributed nothing toward capitalist development. In the case of the United Provinces, capitalist development certainly took place, but the wealth of the Catholic Church seized during the Eighty Years' War with Spain was more often used to pay for the Dutch military effort rather than to invest in production.[256]

The other observation is a generalization and deserves to be quoted in full: "For a society of commodity producers, whose general social relations of production consists in the fact that they treat their products as commodities, hence as values, and in this material form bring their individual, private labors into relation with each other as homogeneous human labor, Christianity with its religious cult of man in the abstract, particularly in its bourgeois development, i.e., in Protestantism, Deism, etc., is the most fitting form of religion."[257] Here Marx emphasizes the ideological appropriateness not of Calvinism specifically, nor even of Protestantism more generally, but of Christianity *per se* as the confessional counterpoint to generalized commodity production.[258]

Neither of these observations therefore deals specifically with Calvinism. The only direct suggestion that Marx makes concerning a homology between accumulation of capital and the Protestant worldview is in the *Grundrisse*: "The cult of money has its asceticism, its self-denial, its self-sacrifice—economy and frugality, contempt for mundane, temporal and fleeting pleasures; the chase after the *eternal* treasure. Hence the connection between English Puritanism, or also Dutch Protestantism, and money-making."[259]

It was in fact Weber who introduced the supposed affinity of Protestantism with capital accumulation, in the essays written in 1904 and 1905, which comprise *The Protestant Ethic and the Spirit of Capitalism*.[260] But Weber makes clear that he is indeed referring to "the *spirit* of capitalism," which he defines as an "ascetic compulsion to save" or more generally as "rational conduct on the basis of a calling," and specifically denies as "foolish and doctrinaire" the idea that only the Reformation could have produced this type of *mentalité*, "or even that capitalism as an economic system is a creation of the Reformation."[261] Weber was of course aware that capitalist production pre-dated the October 31, 1517, when Luther pinned his ninety-five theses to the door of the castle church in Wittenberg; indeed, as we saw in chapter 15, he believed it had existed to some degree in virtually every previous form of human society. The notion of a calling could even be found in the work of Petrarch and the Humanist school of the Renaissance, as Baron notes: "The claims that man should indeed wish for more than to fill his traditional station, that he should be a miser of his time and contemplate his life in the light of continuous progress and unlimited activity—these claims seemed to the men of the Renaissance a cultural as well as an economic need."[262] Weber's point was rather that the adoption of the form of rationality associated with Calvinism and the other Puritan sects, in certain concrete circumstances, assist in the consolidation of capitalism as a systematic method of organizing economic life. This is a much weaker and more defensible claim than Weber is often thought to have made and, as such, it is compatible with a Marxist account of the origins of capitalism.[263] Where capitalist production was weak, as it was in most areas of Europe in the sixteenth century, the capitalist spirit alone was not enough to transform the conditions of action.[264]

What then is the source of the view that Marxism sees Calvinism as the ideological reflection of capitalism? It would appear to be a handful of relatively late comments by Engels.[265] But these see the importance of the Reformation to capitalism primarily in political rather than economic terms, as in the later Weberian tradition. Engels himself described the Reformation as a whole as "the No. 1 bourgeois revolution" that had "triumphed in Switzerland, Holland, Scotland, England," and adding that it had also been successful "to a certain extent" in Sweden and Denmark.[266] His claims for the extent of the bourgeois revolution here are simply unsustainable, as the massive differences between Switzerland and Scotland on the one hand and the United Provinces and England on the other suggest. His more considered verdict treated England as "the second act of the bourgeois revolution" after the United Provinces: "Here Calvinism justified itself as the true religious disguise of the interests of the bourgeoisie of that time, and on this account did not attain full recognition when the revolution ended in 1689 in a compromise between one part of the nobility and the bourgeoisie."[267] The problem with this formulation is the unnecessarily conspiratorial image of a "religious disguise" masking other, economic interests. The Reformation in fact provided the first ideology for "non-economic" bourgeois revolutionary leadership, although in several respects it was less intrinsically bourgeois than the Renaissance had been.

The crisis of feudalism had generated an enormous uncertainty concerning the human condition that the Catholic Church, committed as it was to the existing and supposedly unchanging order of Estates, could not address. Protestantism was the first movement of international significance that sought to provide assurance of salvation in a world where assurance was gone, and it did so by asking believers to look into their hearts for proof that they were among the saved. By proclaiming that everyone had as much (or, more plausibly, as little) chance of salvation, regardless of the Estate to which they belonged, Protestantism represented a relatively democratic element in European feudal society. The general nature of the spiritual crisis meant that Protestantism appealed to individuals among many different social groups—German knights and Scandinavian peasants as much as Dutch merchants. It was only bourgeois elements like the last named, however, who experienced new social tensions specifically produced by the clash between their own practice as capitalists and the teachings of the Catholic Church. As Mann writes, these tensions took three forms:

> First, there was a tension between the centralized authority of the Catholic Church and the decentralized decision-making required in a market system by those who owned the means of production and exchange. Second, there was a tension between a fixed order of statuses legitimated by the church and the requirements of commodity production, in which nothing apart from property ownership is given a fixed and authoritative status. . . . Third, a tension existed between the social duty of the rich Christian to be "luxurious" (i.e., to maintain a large household, provide extensive employment, and give to the poor) and the capitalist's need to claim private ownership rights over the surplus so as to provide a high level of reinvestment.[268]

The Reformation, however, saw both a successful and permanent split in the church, and the adoption of the new religion by significant sections of both the existing and potentially alternative European ruling class. In essence, the Reformation consisted of three related developments; the spread of Protestantism as a personal faith among individual believers, the formation of new "national" churches, which provided the doctrinal basis and congregational structure for the practice of that faith, and the adoption of these churches as the religious arm of the local state—although all three developments were subject to reversal. Ultimately, however, the success or failure of Protestantism in a particular area did not depend on the extent of individual conversion, or the motivation behind it. As Ewan Cameron writes: "To become established the Reformation had to 'affiliate' itself to some social unit."[269] More precisely, it had to affiliate itself to a series of states. But which states? In feudal terms, the wealthiest and most developed areas of Europe lay to the west and the south, in France, Italy, and Spain. These powers were the main contenders in the struggle for control over the papacy and, through that institution, exploitation of those areas of Europe that fell within the Holy Roman Empire. There was no reason for these ruling classes to embrace the new religion, since they had the potential to dominate the Catholic world from inside and therefore had no need to escape from its control.[270] The center of the Reformation lay, not in the most developed economic regions of Europe but in the most backward.

Those actual or potential ruling classes that embraced one or other variety of Protestantism fell into three broadly identifiable types. The first was typical of the north German principalities and Scandinavia, where Lutheranism, the initial ideological and organizational form of Protestantism, first established a base. The Lutheran creed was quite compatible with feudalism (as the German peasantry discovered to their cost in 1525), but it fulfilled a function for those states that wanted to escape the respective financial and political demands of the pope and the emperor. It provided an ideological banner for those princes with no hope of competing for control of the papacy to make themselves independent from its control instead. The second consisted of only one case: England. Here the state under Henry VIII retained many of the organizational and ceremonial forms of Catholicism, while detaching from Rome as a source of doctrinal authority and political allegiance. Initially, the greater geographical inaccessibility of England meant that even the limited gestures toward popular acceptance adopted by Lutherans on the continent were unnecessary to the regime. In time, England would eventually give rise to the most socially radical Protestant sects in Europe, but until the reign of Mary Tudor forged a lasting association between Protestantism, English protonational consciousness and the defense of state sovereignty, it was the most conservative reformation of all.

There was, however, a third type, linked by adherence to what Trevor-Roper calls "the Calvinist International."[271] The more conservative types of reformation, the Anglican and Lutheran, were those where the state itself imposed Protestantism (regardless of the initial degree of popular support) for reasons of domestic and, more importantly, foreign policy. "The more hostile the state," writes Owen Chadwick, "the more likely that the Protestants would be Calvinist, for Calvinism established an authority of the ministry free from the spiritual subjection of the state authorities."[272] As we saw in chapter 1, where the state was hostile, Calvinists either attempted to free the church of state control or, failing that, to overthrow the state. For this reason, as late as 1616 the Catholic propagandist Kaspar Schoppe could claim that Calvinists were the "worst enemies" of the Holy Roman Empire and desired to turn Germany into either a "tyrannical oligarchy" or a "revolutionary democracy."[273] Yet, as Quentin Skinner has argued, there is no Calvinist theory of revolution as such; indeed the Calvinist doctrine of resistance is very similar to that of the Lutherans (Luther did not oppose all resistance to princes, only popular resistance) and both drew from the existing Conciliar tradition. Skinner draws attention, in the context of Scottish political theory, to the influence of the Catholic John Major on the Protestant George Buchanan, but this was an example of a more general continuity: Calvinist theorists attempted to win over Catholics by appealing to a tradition which the latter recognized as legitimate.[274] The real distinctive feature of Calvinism was in its attitude toward the state—not equality in different realms, but superiority of the church over the state.

The relationship between Calvinism and the bourgeois revolution is therefore a complex one. All bourgeois revolutionary movements down to and including the English Revolution involved Calvinism, but very few Calvinist movements down to and including the English Revolution led to bourgeois revolutions. Calvinism was a doctrine that gave support to those who wished to overthrow a state, but there were many different social forces seeking to overthrow states in mid-sixteenth-century Europe, very few of them remotely bourgeois in composition. It was the need to challenge state power that explains why sections of the Scottish or Transylvanian nobilities embraced Calvinism rather than the Lutheranism favored by, for example, the German knights and princelings to which they were otherwise quite similar in social terms. The class content of Calvinism therefore varied from country to country. In France, for example, as Henry Heller has pointed out, Calvinism "was essentially a movement of artisans and bourgeoisie," but one in which the latter "were eager to subordinate themselves to the nobility," a minority of whom had turned to Calvinism for quite other reasons. Heller explains that the reasons for noble hegemony over French Calvinism were, on the one hand, that the bourgeoisie "had been unable to develop at this time an economic basis strong enough to enable it to make a stand independently of the nobility" and, on the other, that no consistent allies could be found among popular social classes: "apart from a minority of the more literate and skilled artisans," most small producers were as hostile to the bourgeoisie as they were to the nobility and clergy.[275]

Those societies most faithful to the teachings of Calvin himself were generally the least compatible with capitalist development. As Gramsci noted: "The Lutheran Reformation and Calvinism created a vast national-popular movement through which their influence spread: only in later periods did they create a higher culture ... the phase of popular development enabled the protestant countries to resist the crusade of the Catholic armies tenaciously and victoriously."[276] There is no doubt that Calvinism represented a retreat from the sophistication of late Renaissance Humanism, as exemplified by Erasmus, but by weakening the power of the Catholic Church, and providing the ideology for of the first successful bourgeois revolutions, it paved the way for later intellectual advances, without necessarily contributing directly to them. The point is well made by Trevor-Roper: "If Calvinism was intellectually retrograde and repressive, a positive, vindictive enemy of enlightenment, politically it nevertheless performed an essential service. . . . Politically, therefore, Calvinism may well have been necessary to the intellectual progress of Europe in the seventeenth century . . . but the fact that Calvinist resistance was necessary to the continuation and development of an intellectual tradition does not entail any direct or logical connection between them."[277] Once victorious, the Dutch bourgeoisie did not allow Calvinism to constitute an obstacle to the operation of capitalist economy. Baruch Spinoza, in many ways the most radical figure of his time, attacked the "dogma" of organized religion in 1670 for "degrading rational man to a beast, completely inhibiting man's free judgment and his capacity to distinguish true from false. . . . Men who utterly despise reason, who reject and turn away from the intellect as naturally corrupt . . . are believed to possess the divine light!"[278] In this respect at least Spinoza was expressing the beliefs held tacitly by the most advanced sections of the Dutch bourgeoisie, albeit in more vigorous terms than most were prepared to use. Calvinism could be a siege engine for destroying the fortifications of feudal absolutism; it was not scaffolding for constructing a capitalist economy. As Luciano Pellicani writes:

> The entrepreneurial bourgeoisie . . . had no intention of seeing Calvinist bigotry substitute [for] Catholic bigotry. . . . Thus it was the spirit of Erasmus, not of Calvin, which in the end set the tone of economic and cultural life in Dutch society, which became the most capitalist nation of Europe. And it succeeded in this precisely in that it institutionalised the typically bourgeois separation between business and religion: a separation which, to the custodians of Calvinist orthodoxy, seemed blasphemous, but against which they could do nothing.

Pellicani notes that, unlike the English, the Scots failed to adopt this separation, but embraced instead the views of "the bigoted and anti-capitalist Holland," which had been vanquished in its country of origin: "Thus, whereas England started down the road that was to lead her to become the main capitalist power in the world, Scotland remained immersed in the stagnant waters of Calvinist orthodoxy and underdevelopment."[279] But Pellicani reverses the actual causal order. Even if Protestantism offered ideological support to those who felt economically confined by Catholicism, it could not by itself ensure that capitalism would become the dominant mode of production in any given area. As Gordon Marshall has argued, the reason why Scottish capitalism failed to develop in the seventeenth century did not lie in "the worldview or motivation of the capitalists themselves"—for in his view they were indeed motivated to accumulate capital—but were "frustrated by the backwardness of the economic structure of the country . . . by the conditions of action that circumscribed their activities."[280] Marshall exaggerates the number of "capitalists" operating in Scotland in the seventeenth century, but the point is well made: Protestantism, even in its Calvinist form(s) was not an independent factor in the transition to capitalism. Its efficacy in this respect depended not only on whether members of the bourgeoisie adopted it as their religion, but also on the circumstances under which they did so.

The potential for this discrepancy between ideological intention and practical result lies in the very fusion of the economic, political, and ideological, which was characteristic of feudalism, and which reached its apogee under the absolutist state. One aspect of Bertram's notion of "evolution by international competition" is relevant here in relation to the overcoming of precapitalist state forms or, in his terms, the adoption of a capitalist "legal and political superstructure": "The proximate cause may be religious or political. . . . But those countries or cultures that fail to select structures conducive to the development of the productive forces will either be eliminated (or assimilated) by their rivals, or will undergo a crisis that will force them to select anew their basic structures. In either case, the unsuccessful, if they survive, will tend to adopt structures resembling those of their successful rivals."[281] There are two aspects to this claim: one about how "structures" are adopted in the first place and other about how they are then spread. I will return to the latter in the next chapter, but it is the former that concerns us here. Let us assume that Bertram's "social structure" includes the state: the establishment of a social structure "that permits a high rate of development may be the consequence of the class struggle, of military adventure, of religious doctrine, or anything else."[282] Regardless of what motives various groups had for opposing absolutism then, if they were successful in destroying it, the integrated structures associated with that state form would also be removed, making it possible for capitalism in all its initial myriad forms to experience unimpeded expansion. Under these conditions, government could always be delegated, provided the state was rededicated to the accumulation of capital. In England between 1649 and 1660, for example, the New Model Army could act as a substitute for a capitalist class, which, although economically dominant within society, was not yet capable of assuming political leadership within the state. The "new" colonial merchants who ruled in alliance with the major-generals during the 1650s were "significantly below, or outside, the traditional governing classes," and unrepresentative of the capitalist class in general: "The alliance of . . . moderate republican forces that governed nationally and in London under the Commonwealth exerted an influence that could not possibly be justified by its real social weight within English society."[283]

But the discrepancy between intention and outcome is also what produces the sense of "the revolution betrayed." I mean by this not simply that the interests of the petty bourgeoisie, small commodity producers, and laborers were ignored or attacked, although this was obviously the case in the English Revolution; but also that the ideological aims under which the bourgeoisie *themselves* went into battle had come to nothing. The ascendancy of King Jesus over King Charles is a different matter from the ascendancy of the English East India Company over the Dutch East India Company. The problem was perhaps first recognized after the Restoration by Milton in *Paradise Lost* (1667), in what is quite possibly the first major literary work to express these postrevolutionary feelings of betrayal. As Tom Paulin writes, Milton's Archangel Michael "voices the embattled puritan sense of how the written record can be falsified by the forces of reaction."[284] But he also voices the sense in which the inheritors have assumed the outward forms of revolutionary ideology while availing themselves of material benefits that were never the original goals of the movement:

> *Their Ministry performed, and race well run,*
> *Their doctrine and their story written left,*
> *They die; but in their room, as they forewarn,*
> *Wolves shall succeed for teachers, grievous Wolves,*
> *Who all the sacred mysteries of Heaven*
> *To their own vile advantages shall turn*
> *Of lucre and ambition, and the truth*
> *With superstitions and traditions taint,*
> *Left only in those written Records pure,*
> *Though not but by the Spirit understood.*
> *Then shall they seek to avail themselves of names,*
> *Places and titles, and with these to join*
> *Secular power, though feigning still to act*
> *By spiritual, to themselves appropriating*
> *The Spirit of God, promised alike and given*
> *To all Believers; and from that pretense,*
> *Spiritual Laws by carnal power shall force*
> *On every conscience; Laws which none shall find*
> *Left them enrolled, or what the Spirit within*
> *Shall on the heart engrave . . .*

Inevitably, those who maintain the original motivations of the revolution can no longer be tolerated by those who have emerged victorious:

> *Whence heavy persecution shall arise*
> *On all who in the worship persevere*
> *Of Spirit and Truth; the rest, far greater part,*
> *Well deem in outward Rites and specious forms*
> *Religion satisfied; Truth shall retire*
> *Bestuck with slanderous darts, and works of Faith*
> *Rarely be found: so shall the World go on,*
> *To good malignant, to bad men benign,*
> *Under her own weight groaning till the day*
> *Appear of respiration to the just,*
> *And vengeance to the wicked . . .* [285]

And so did the world go on indeed, down to the last days of the bourgeois revolution. But if they did not bring about what their organic intellectuals sought, what did they achieve?

3

PATTERNS OF CONSUMMATION

According to Eric Hobsbawm, the seizure and maintenance of state power is not enough to bring a revolution to an end: "Revolutions cannot be said to "conclude" until they have either been overthrown or are sufficiently safe from overthrow."[1] This observation is accurate with regard to political revolutions, but profoundly misleading in relation to social revolutions, which are liable to be overturned by a mixture of external pressure and internal subversion as long as they remain isolated in a world where different and hostile systems prevail. Only when the cumulative impact of several revolutions has established a new social system can safety be assured; as Perry Anderson rightly notes, in relation to the bourgeois revolutions: "The idea of capitalism in one country, taken literally, is only a bit more plausible than that of socialism [in one country]."[2] What Alexander Chistozvonov calls the point of "irreversibility" must therefore be understood in relation, not only to the overthrow of individual precapitalist states and the removal of the obstacles they posed to internal capitalist development, but also the cumulative effect of these events: an international environment in which individual revolutions could no longer be suppressed, undermined, or simply contained by external feudal-absolutist or tributary counterrevolution.[3]

NECESSARY OUTCOMES

Understanding that the earliest bourgeois revolutions were never fully secure until this point of systemic irreversibility had been reached, we can nevertheless identify the two main characteristics of a post-bourgeois revolutionary society: an economy subject to capitalist laws of motion and a state committed to competitive accumulation. Take capitalist laws of motion first: do they necessarily involve the complete removal of all feudal (or other pre-capitalist) relations of production? A famous passage by Marx from the *Grundrisse* suggests that this is not necessarily the case: "In all forms of society there is one specific kind of production which predominates over the rest, whose relations thus assign rank and influence to the others. It is a general illumination which bathes all the other colors and modifies their particularity. It is a particular ether which determines the specific gravity of every being which has materialized within it."[4]

The succession of metaphors that Marx employs here are intended to convey a more complex relationship than simple quantitative "dominance." "I doubt," writes Ashok Rudra, "that it may be possible to establish scientifically which mode is dominant over what other mode in a particular context." Nevertheless he has a try, suggesting that "one can count the number of persons entering into a particular productive relation (say, tenancy) and find out whether that is more or less than the number of persons entering into another production relation (say, wage labor) and settle which is more important."[5] "Tenancy" is not a productive relation in and of itself, but no matter, the entire premise is wrong. As Geoffrey de Ste. Croix has pointed out, the key issue in determining the class nature of any society is not necessarily how most labor is performed but rather how the labor that produced the surplus accruing to the ruling class is performed.[6] Just as a precapitalist society can contain—in the sense of both "including" and "limiting"—capitalist relations of production, so too can a capitalist society contain pre-capitalist social relations. In the latter case these might even involve a majority of the direct producers, as long as the ruling class, which by definition includes those in ultimate control of the state, occupied their position through the competitive accumulation of capital based on wage labor.

But although different precapitalist modes of production (such as slavery and petty commodity production) have coexisted in the type of dual economy discussed by Ste. Croix, capitalist and precapitalist modes cannot, at least after the bourgeois revolutions. Once consolidated, the former contextualizes and structures ("bathes," "modifies," "determines") the latter, so that their constitutive relations of production acquire a new content. For example, Marx emphasized that, during the transition to capitalism, small independent producers involved in agriculture or handicrafts or both could carry on production in their traditional manner, but on behalf of the usurer or merchant, even though the latter pair may play no direct role in organizing the labor process. He referred to this process as the "formal subsumption of labor," in contrast to the "real subsumption of labor," which occurred when the capitalist began to organize production and the labor process, culminating in large-scale factory manufacture.[7] As Preobrazhensky noted, until that point it might appear that independent small commodity production continued: "Finally, as a last transitional stage to genuinely capitalist surplus value we may cite the work of handicraft men in their homes, for a buyer [putter-out], when they work up the customer's raw material, with tools belonging to him, and are in essentials already actual wage-workers, even though they retain the external attributes of independent producers."[8] The central point, as Lenin explained, was that during the period when formal subsumption is maintained, "capital always takes the technical process of production as it finds it and only subsequently subjects it to technical transformation."[9] Taking over the existing labor process also involves taking over the form of property to which it corresponds: "Capital finds the most diverse types of medieval and patriarchal landed property—feudal, 'peasant allotments' [the holdings of bonded peasants]; class, communal, state, and the other forms of land ownership."[10]

Jairus Banaji has drawn a series of general conclusions from these and similar observations by figures from the classical Marxist tradition. He argues that Marx used the term "mode of production" (*produktionsweise*) in two ways: one to refer to the technical process of production, or the labor process more generally; the other to encompass an entire epoch in the history of the social organization of production, in which particular laws of motion predominate. The existence of wage labor, for example, does not necessarily signify the emergence of the capitalist mode of production; wage labor also took place under feudalism, but primarily as a means of meeting the consumption requirements of the lords rather than contributing to the self-expansion of capital. It is rather that the existence of the capitalist mode of production determines that wage labor becomes the central means through which surplus extraction takes place. Equally, however, various types of unfree labor associated with precapitalist modes of production, including slavery itself, can also take place within the context of the capitalist mode of production and, in the terms Marx uses in the *Grundrisse*, both posit and produce capital.[11]

The relevance of this argument to our theme is that it is perfectly possible for feudal, absolutist, or tributary states to be overthrown, thus removing the last obstacle to establishing what Alex Callinicos calls "an independent centre of capital accumulation," while some social relations remain, initially at least, those associated with precapitalist modes in the purely technical sense.[12] The decisive fact is that these technical relations are subordinated to capitalist laws of motion. Political Marxists repeatedly highlight the radical difference between capitalism and preceding modes of production. This emphasis is useful up to a point, but beyond it we lose all sense of what capitalism has in common with other exploitative class systems. Indeed, if capitalism did not possess this commonality, then it is difficult to see how it could have successfully incorporated aspects of these earlier modes, as it has in most of the world outside of a handful of countries at the core of the system where, quite exceptionally, capitalism exists in more or less pure form. Feudal lords were able, in some circumstances, to transform themselves into capitalists, just as ancient slave owners before them were able, in other circumstances, to transform themselves into feudal lords. The continuing fact of exploitation is what makes these adaptations possible. In this respect, as in many others, it will surely be socialism rather than capitalism that is distinct from all previous modes of production.

What then of the capitalist nation-state? Heide Gerstenberger writes: "The concept of 'bourgeois state' . . . implies an idea of 'bourgeois revolution.' This means nothing more—though nothing less—than the assertion that the emergence of bourgeois state power does not simply involve a change in organizational structures or modes of behavior in the exercise of 'state' power, but the creation from scratch of a public instance."[13] Gerstenberger claims that there is a complete break between the "personal" power of the absolutist state and the "public" power of the capitalist state, which suggests that the latter should not bear any traces of the former. In fact, this is no more necessary than it is for a capitalist economy to eliminate all traces of feudal social relations.

There are certain activities that capitalist states must perform, of which three are particularly important. The first is the imposition of a dual social order: horizontally over competing capitals so that market relations do not collapse into "the war of all against all"; and vertically over the conflict between capital and labor so that it continues to be resolved in the interest of the former. The second is the establishment of "general conditions of production," which individual competing capitals would be unwilling or unable to provide, including some basic level of technical infrastructure and welfare provision.[14] These are mainly "internal" to the territory of the state; the third is the way in which each capitalist state has to represent the collective interests of the "internal" capitalist class "externally," in relation to other capitalist states and classes. Capitalism is a system of competitive accumulation based on wage labor and these two defining aspects point to the reasons for the persistence of the states system: the first because of the need for capitals to be territorially aggregated for competitive purposes; the second because of the need for that territory to have an ideological basis—nationalism—which can be used to bind the working class to the state and hence to capital.

There are of course complex issues involved in identifying collective ruling class interests, especially given that one central characteristic of capitalism is competition between capitals; but the state managers who have to resolve this do not need to be themselves capitalists any more than the revolutionaries who created the state in the first place; indeed, in some respects it is essential that they are not. If policies were framed for the benefit of sectional capitalist interests this would constitute a problem for the local capitalist class as a whole. In other words, whatever their own origins or inclinations, state managers and politicians have to identify their interests, not with *specific* national capitals or even specific *sectors* of national capital, but with national capital as a whole. In the case of those bourgeois revolutions, such as the Japanese, which were carried out to develop capitalism from a minimal preexisting base, this was in any case unavoidable, since a capitalist class barely existed. Bertell Ollman comments: "The *samurai* who made the Meiji Revolution refused to become new feudal rulers (as happened after earlier successful revolts), opting instead to make themselves into a capitalist ruling class. But before they could do that they had to create capitalism and a capitalist class of which they could be part." Ollman includes in "capitalist class," not only capitalists but also "the higher state bureaucrats and the leading politicians in the ruling party," with the former group initially playing the most important role.[15] What happened to the pre-Meiji ruling class? As Ann Waswo records, the former *daimyo* or feudal lords "no longer exercised political control over the land they owned, and although they were represented in the

House of Peers, that body was at no time the center of political power": "Unlike England, then, where the landed aristocracy maintained its political influence and by means of the Corn Laws protected the agricultural income on which its power was based until a relatively advanced stage of industrial development, Japan in the decade after the Meiji Restoration was ruled by bureaucrats, the former Samurai who had led the Restoration movement and who had been divorced de facto from the land for centuries."[16] The differences are in fact less significant than they at first appear. The British landed aristocracy after 1688 in effect played the same role as the Japanese samurai bureaucrats after 1868, as Hobsbawm points out: "A plainly bourgeois society—nineteenth-century Britain—could, without serious problems, be governed by hereditary peers."[17] What is it about a capitalist state that makes the absence of direct capitalist rule possible, perhaps even essential?

Under all precapitalist modes of production exploitation took place visibly through the extraction of a literal surplus from the direct producers by the threat or reality of violence: economics and politics were "fused" in the power of the feudal lord or the tributary state. Under the capitalist mode of production exploitation takes place invisibly in the process of production itself through the creation of surplus value over and above that required in reproducing the labor force. Ellen Meiksins Wood identifies a "resulting division of labor in which the two moments of capitalist exploitation—appropriation and coercion—are allocated separately to a 'private' appropriating class and a specialized 'public' coercive institution, the state: on the one hand, the 'relatively autonomous' state has a monopoly of coercive force; on the other hand, that force sustains a private 'economic' power which invests capitalist property with an authority to organize production itself." Furthermore, unlike previous exploiting classes, capitalists exercise economic power without "the obligation to perform social, public functions." "Capitalism is a system marked by the complete separation of private appropriation from public duties; and this means the development of a new sphere of power devoted completely to private rather than social purposes."[18] This is the reason for what Hal Draper calls "the political inaptitude of the capitalist class" compared to other ruling classes in history: feudal lords combine an economic and political role; capitalists perform only the former— although the necessity for capitalists to devote their time to the process of accumulation and their own multiple internal divisions also militate against their functioning directly as a governing class.[19] This is quite compatible with the exercise of bourgeois hegemony over society as a whole, although even in this respect, some sections of the bourgeoisie tend to play a more significant role than others. Adam Smith shrewdly remarked of merchants and manufacturers:

> Their superiority over the country gentlemen is not so much in their knowledge of the public interest, as in their having a better knowledge of their own interest than he has of his. It is by this superior knowledge of their own interests that they have frequently imposed on his generosity, and persuaded him to give up both his own interest and that of the public, from a very simple but honest conviction that their interest,

and not his, was the interest of the public. The interest of the dealers, however, in any particular branch of trade or manufactures, is always in some respects different from, and even opposite to, that of the public.[20]

But the failure of the bourgeoisie to transcend their self-absorbed pursuit of profit drove some conservative supporters of capitalism to despair. Carl Schmitt complained that, unlike working-class ideologues, members of the bourgeoisie no longer understood the friend-enemy distinction, which was central to "the political"; the spirit of Hegel, he thought, had moved from Berlin to Moscow.[21] More prosaically, Bernard Porter notes that capitalists "tend to be hostile to 'government' generally, which they see mainly as a restraint on enterprise and, on a personal level, don't find 'ruling' half so worthwhile or satisfactory as making money."[22]

The Moment of Systemic Irreversibility

We can now return to the process of bourgeois revolution at a global level. Immanuel Wallerstein has claimed: "By 1650 the basic structures of historical capitalism as a viable social system had been established and consolidated."[23] In fact, in many cases, these structures had been dismantled at a local level. Bohemia, for example, was less developed than the Italian city-states that had been re-feudalized during the previous century, but unlike them it was a coherent territorial state with a population ideologically bound together by the Hussite protoreformation of the fifteenth century. Defeat and reversal came suddenly at the hands of the armed counterreformation during the early stages of the Thirty Years' War. After the Battle of White Mountain in 1620 the Austrian Habsburgs abolished the defeated estates, expropriated the lands of the disloyal nobility, reestablished the Catholic religion for the population as a whole and reimposed serfdom on the peasantry.[24] More importantly, however, even the two states that were fully founded on capitalist relations of production by 1650 were not entirely secure. It is true, as Victor Kiernan writes: "In England and Holland social relations, immobilized over most of Europe, were relatively free to evolve in accordance with what may be termed Europe's historic logic."[25] Yet this was far from signaling the consolidation of the capitalist system. In fact, it was by no means certain that capitalism would survive in those territories where it had been realized until the new mode of production and the emergent states system associated with it had achieved stability at the international level. Even by the 1690s, when both the United Provinces and England had achieved irreversibility in relation to their own individual territories and united under the Orange monarchy, they were still within a world dominated by hostile absolutist and tributary states in which France, the most powerful of the former, sought to undo them from without and within. What then determined whether these new capitalist nation-states would survive in a still hostile environment long enough to transform it? The decisive issue was the type of capitalist state that had emerged from the bourgeois revolution. The Italian city republics had been unequal to the task; did their Dutch and English successors prove more capable?

The Dutch Revolt was the first permanently successful bourgeois revolution. Marcel van der Linden has rightly opposed attempts to reduce it "to a series of rebellions which had little to do with each other," noting that "it has been proved time and time again . . . that the same group and class specific motives are consistently present: freedom of religion, anti-absolutism, and revolt against economic misery."[26] Nevertheless, the United Provinces by no means escaped the trajectory of its Swiss and Italian predecessors, as its wealth also depended partly on servicing the existing feudal regimes—not, like Switzerland, through the supply of military manpower, but like the Italian city-states, through its vast trading and financial networks.[27] Yet there was also a difference with Italy, as Gramsci pointed out: "In the Netherlands and only in the Netherlands was there an organic passage from the commune or city-state to a regime that was no longer feudal."[28] After the Swiss Confederation, the United Provinces was the second example of "city-state consociationalism," an alliance of independent political communities who cooperate jointly on a contractual basis while preserving their separate rights and privileges: "The republic of the Seven United Provinces emerged relatively early as an independent political unit, from what was in fact little more than an accidental, military alliance of seven separate territories which successfully rebelled against their common Hapsburg Overlord."[29] Yet, as Liah Greenfield writes: "The political organization of the Dutch Republic was the very opposite of a centralized state."[30] An unwieldy compromise between a federal and confederate polity was one of the structural reasons it was unable to sustain its pre-eminent economic position.[31] The governments of the main provinces, especially Holland, were too closely aligned with particular capitalist interests for the central apparatus of the States General to make decisions that could advance their collective interest. The other reason was that the Dutch Republic suffered from both the crises of feudalism—at second hand via the absolutist regimes that it serviced—and the risks associated with capitalism. As Pepijn Brandon has pointed out, the stagnation of the Dutch economy in the latter half of the seventeenth century did not mean re-feudalization, as it had in the case of the Italian city-states; it meant decline in capitalist terms:

> Although the strength of merchant-capital went hand-in-hand with substantial changes to production, the core of the capitalist class always remained focused primarily on trade. This started to become a serious hindrance to further capitalist development once the Dutch were outcompeted or forced out of international markets by political means from the 1650s onwards. Financialization, based on the strong integration in international capital-flows, proved the easier option for the Dutch ruling class over a restructuring of production, leading to the long eighteenth-century depression. Meanwhile, the consistent localism and small-scale of production meant that drawing up the walls of urban protectionism remained the preferred answer to increased competition for much of the urban middle classes. The federal state-apparatus, probably more directly populated and controlled by the leading families than

any state before or afterwards, could never act as a counterweight to these trends. Instead, it helped to enforce economic policies that were characterized by the absence of protectionism on a national scale and strong protectionism on a local scale.[32]

It is in respect of competition at the level of the state that the parallels between the United Provinces and the Italian city-states are perhaps strongest. The three Anglo-Dutch Wars of the seventeenth century, in 1652–54, 1665–67 and 1672–74, saw the two regions most advanced in capitalist terms in the world—on the one hand Holland and Zeeland in the United Provinces, on the other London, the southeast counties and East Anglia in England—pitched against each other, but although they "provided the sinews of war in material, money, and personnel, they were not responsible for the outbreak of any of the wars." There were economic reasons for the wars, but mediated through the geopolitical interests of the only two capitalist states in the world: "From the Dutch perspective the English aim in all three wars was no less than the conquest of the seas, and the reduction of the Dutch to a state of total and helpless submission."[33] The United Provinces were to remain a bulwark against French expansionism, but that role was also played by such notably non-bourgeois regimes as Austria. It was not to be at the center of a new world system. Brandon is right to reject Hobsbawm's description of the United Provinces as "a feudal business economy," but the latter's verdict is surely correct: "If the only 'capitalist' economies available in the seventeenth century had been like the Dutch, we may doubt whether the subsequent development of industrial capitalism would have been as great or as rapid."[34]

The English state did not simply play Venice to the Dutch state's Genoa: it suffered from none of the disabilities associated with its Italian predecessors or its Dutch rival. Indeed, as a result of the reversals and accommodations they had experienced England was by 1688 the only surviving source of a systemic alternative to feudal absolutism. "The absolute power of the sovereign has continued ever since its establishment in France, Spain, etc.," Smith told his students in the 1760s: "In England alone a different government has been established from the natural course of things."[35] Peter Coveney writes of the European political landscape at the opening of the eighteenth century:

> For all the turbulence of the mid-seventeenth century, when the stabilization came, when the European ancien regime consolidated in the later seventeenth century, the old social structure remained remarkably intact. . . . The Europe of 1700 was still in a very real sense more "medieval" than "modern." The large majority of the population still lived within a seigniorial framework or within medieval municipalities still largely untransformed. It was a society still stratified, formally, in terms of "feudal" hierarchy, of medieval "orders." . . . In most states some form of *modus vivendi* between centralizing authority and "reactionary" interests, usually landed and aristocratic but sometimes mercantile, established itself as the social and political basis of the European ancien regime.[36]

From Marx himself onward, the majority of Marxist historians have claimed that the events of 1688–89 in England ended the revolutionary process begun in

1640 by confirming a new capitalist ruling class in power and establishing a state geared to the accumulation of capital.[37] In these accounts it is accepted that the state had still to undergo several subsequent transformations, largely to accommodate the process of industrialization and the classes that it produced, but on the essential point—that there was no longer any question of a retreat to feudal economic relations or absolutist political rule in England—the decisive nature of the Glorious Revolution has never seriously been in doubt. In his outstanding history of the revolution of 1688–89, Steve Pinkus asks whether it can be considered as a bourgeois revolution and answers his own question thus: "Not in the sense that a self-conscious class, the bourgeoisie, overthrew another class to place itself in power." His conclusion, however, is quite compatible with the consequentialist position taken here:

> The Whig revolutionary triumph brought with it a new bourgeois culture. The revolution in political economy brought with it a revolution in cultural values. Political economic transformation—new tax structures, new institutions, and a new imperial agenda—encouraged the new cultural dominance of the urban middle classes. . . . The Revolution of 1688–89 represented the victory of those who supported manufacturing, urban culture, and the possibilities of unlimited economic growth based on the creative potential of human labor. The effect of the revolution meant that traders felt no need to aspire to the culture and estates of the landed elite. In fact, the aristocracy and the gentry began to act more bourgeois in the wake of the Revolution of 1688–89.[38]

Yet there is a difficulty associated with this virtually unanimous verdict. In fact, as Roy Porter writes, "1688 could in nowise be a final solution."[39] The finality usually ascribed to that year is only possible if events in England are treated in complete isolation. As Fred Halliday has noted:

> There is an extensive literature on the origins of the English revolution and indeed the character of this, the second—after the Dutch—"bourgeois" revolution. The overwhelming majority of this literature focuses on changes in the social and economic structure of Britain prior to the 1640s and on variant interpretations of the social character of the parliamentary cause. One can, indeed, say that virtually the whole of this literature is written as if England was not just an island, but was a closed entity, separate from the political, economic and intellectual world of the rest of Europe.[40]

More specifically, it is not possible to separate developments in England from either the wider struggle with France for European and colonial hegemony, or the impact of that struggle on the other nations of the British Isles, as the English ruling class themselves were only too well aware at the time. Counterrevolution can have both external and internal sources.

The external danger to England after 1688 mainly lay in France. Benno Teschke sees the unintended consequences of the British pursuit of "security and order" during the eighteenth century as "forcing continental states to respond to and finally adjust to the superior socio-political British model, especially under the impact of the Industrial Revolution."[41] This was eventually the case, but the first response of this greatest of the absolutist powers was not to accept the existence of England/Britain and emulate it, but to attempt to overthrow the new state form. Frank McLynn writes: "Britain and France were for the entire Jacobite period [1688–1746] engaged in a titanic economic and commercial struggle, waged worldwide." At the heart of this struggle lay the fundamental difference between the two states, "the divine right of kings versus the divine right of property."[42] The essential difference between Britain and France is however perhaps best illustrated by focusing on a subject that in different ways was dear to the hearts of both ruling classes: money.

Far from occurring "prematurely," the English Revolution took place in time to prevent the absolutist state consolidating and acquiring the massive state debts and parasitic bureaucracies that characterized its European rivals. John Brewer writes: "In this respect, the *timing* of the emergence of the English fiscal-military state is crucial." And here the English then British states did draw on the most useful aspects of the Dutch experience: "When its mobilization occurred, it happened under the auspices of a regime which not only exploited the techniques of Dutch finance but also, though parliamentary scrutiny placed a rein on the more egregious instances of venality."[43] As Colin Mooers has stressed, the nature of taxation and office holding in England were unique in Europe at the time. The principle form of taxation was the Land Tax, which was self-imposed on the landowners by the Parliament that they controlled, then assessed and collected by the lower levels of that class and their tenants. This preference for a land tax over customs and excise was conditioned by the connections there had always been under the Stuarts between custom and excise, the financial independence of the Crown, and its attempts to impose absolutist rule. There was, however, another aspect of the Land Tax that marked it as bourgeois in nature. English landowners were taxed on capitalist ground rents paid to them by tenants whose incomes derived from the employment of wage labor.[44] In this respect Britain had an advantage over France.

The internal threat to Britain lay in Scotland. After the new constitutional monarchy was established in 1688 the English ruling class regarded Scotland as a disruptive element to be contained rather than a potential ally to be transformed. But as long as Scotland remained untransformed, there was always the possibility that the feudal lords who had found it convenient to remove James VII and II might, through a further change in circumstances, wish to bring him back, and with him his French backer—the global rival of the English state. Neither the English Revolution nor the new world system that it promised (or threatened) to bring into being would be secure while this possibility remained. The oft-stated desire of the exiled Stuarts to reclaim all their previous kingdoms, combined with the French need to remove their opponents from the international stage, meant that the English ruling class was faced, not only with impoverishment, but also with a threat to its continued survival on a capitalist basis. Had the Jacobites, and through them, absolutist France, been

victorious, Britain, the most dynamic economy in the new system and the only significant state geared to capitalist accumulation, would have been severely weakened
and its greatest opponent given a further lease on life. The Jacobites would have been
incapable of reimposing feudalism over the whole of Britain—the relative economic
weight of Scotland was still too slight, and the development of capitalist agriculture
elsewhere too great for that to be possible—but they could have established a regime
more subservient to French absolutism than even that of Charles II during the previous century. In practical terms this would have removed the main obstacle to
French hegemony in Europe, allowed France to inherit British colonial possessions
and, at the very least, reversed the land settlement—particularly in Ireland—that resulted from the Revolution. Britain would have necessarily been reduced to a satellite
of France, for the very lack of a firm social base in England would have forced the
new regime to rely on the force of French arms for its existence.

These internal and external threats were overcome during the 1740 and 1750s.
First, with the defeat of the Jacobites at the Battle of Culloden in 1746, then with
a spectacular series of victories directly over the French state in the Seven Years'
War, most decisively in India and Canada during 1759. As McLynn writes:

> The entire history of the world would have been different but for the events of 1759.
> If the French had prevailed in North America, there would have been no United
> States (at least in the form we know it), for it is inconceivable that France would ever
> have ceded any of its North American possessions and, without the Louisiana Pur-
> chase of 1803, even if we assume the thirteen British colonies had revolted success-
> fully against their French overlords—a questionable assumption—they would have
> been hemmed in on the Atlantic seaboard, unable to expand westwards to the Pacific.
> If France had won in India, the global hegemony of the English language could never
> have happened. . . . The consequences of 1759 really were momentous; it really was a
> hinge on which all of world history turned.[45]

Similarly, Wallerstein writes that "the Treaty of Paris of 1763 marked Britain's
definitive achievement of superiority in the 100 years struggle with France."[46] Lenman has criticized the ascription of decisive significance to the Treaty, writing
specifically of Wallerstein:

> The attempt to reconcile this particular peace with conviction that somehow, some-
> where, there has to be a "Bourgeois Revolution"—however complex and veiled in
> form—and that this is part of a predetermined pattern of global social evolution, no
> longer even serves to over-simplify world history conveniently (as the convoluted na-
> ture of Wallerstein's material shows), and is much better dumped in historiography's
> rubbish bin. Apart from anything else, the Peace of Paris was not the irreversible con-
> clusion of a century of predictable evolution. It was a new balance of power between
> the Crowns of France and Great Britain, much of it based on remarkable successes
> for British arms in the previous five or six years. The balance was extremely fragile,
> indeed arguably self-destructive, and it was to be shattered within twenty years.[47]

There was nothing remotely premeditated about the result of the Anglo-French
conflict between 1688 and 1763, nor was Wallerstein claiming that it involved a

bourgeois revolution of any sort. Yet for once we can agree with him that it was more than another temporary shift in the balance of power, not because it saw Dutch hegemony replaced by British—as Wallerstein and those who have followed him like Arrighi believe—but because it marked a global turning point or moment of irreversibility for the emergent capitalist system as a whole.[48]

The ultimate global dominance of capitalism may now have been assured, but colossal struggles were still to follow, involving not so much the survival of the new system as the relationship it would have with surviving precapitalist modes of production and the nature of the capitalist states that would comprise the nation-stat system. In classifying the bourgeois revolutions we have hitherto distinguished between them on the basis of whether their main impetus came from below or above; but to this must be overlaid another, nonsynchronous feature: whether they took place before or after this moment of systemic irreversibility. The vast majority fell afterward and took the form of revolutions from above. "It was," writes Anderson, "the world *economic* strength of the capitalist mode of production—its spontaneous power of social transformation—which rendered possible the limited political thrust of these revolutions."[49] There was one exception, the last and greatest of all the bourgeois revolutions from below and the only one to occur after the moment of systemic irreversibility had passed: the French Revolution.

Toward International Structural Adaptation (1): The Uniqueness of the French Revolution

The editors of one recent collection of essays may be justified in resetting the beginning of the Age of Revolution back from 1789, or even 1776, to the conclusion of the Seven Years' War in 1763; but their new endpoint—the commencement of the Anglo-Chinese Opium War in 1839—while commendably avoiding Eurocentrism, also demonstrates the difficulties attendant on a refusal to differentiate between revolutions on the basis of their class nature or relationship to the state.[50] In fact, of all the revolutionary upheavals that shook the world in this period of nearly eighty years, only the French Revolution and those associated with it, above all in San Domingo, constituted even temporarily successful *bourgeois* revolutions.

How did the preconditions for bourgeois revolution combine in the French case? Here the feudal crisis and the capitalist solution were both simultaneously manifest, but the latter as an external model to be adopted rather than a set of internal developments ready to be imposed. For, if the French bourgeoisie had any conception of the society to which they aspired, then it was one very like Britain.[51] This is not to succumb to the myth that there was no capitalist development in France before 1789 (or 1830, or 1848, or 1871, or 1959 . . .); but as a consequence of the relative success of the absolutist regimes in retarding the development of capitalism, France was internally less developed in 1789 than England had been in 1640, although the global environment was more developed. The crisis of the

French state therefore took a different form, not least in that it involved geopolitical competition to a far greater extent than in the latter and it was the latter that revealed the structural incapacity of the state to prevent revolution from beginning.

The American War of Independence took place against a backdrop of a naval arms race in which the absolutist monarchies of France and Spain collaborated, particularly from the late 1760s, to overwhelm the British. Although they attained superiority (sixty-six French and Spanish ships facing forty-four British ones across the Channel) it was never on the kind of overwhelming scale that could have guaranteed victory.[52] It was an example, however, of the kind of military spending that strained the French state to the limits of its capacity: "It was through state military competition that the backwardness of French productive relations was initially, and disastrously, demonstrated. The coercive force of England's more advanced system of social relations was experienced by France in a succession of military defeats and the ultimate bankruptcy of the absolutist state."[53] The fiscal crisis of the state, particularly as a result of the increased share of taxation falling on the commoners, was a major precipitant of the revolution. Not only were the nobles largely exempt from these taxes, but they also increased their own income levels by squeezing greater rents from their tenants. Henry Heller has insisted, however, that the financial crisis was simply a manifestation of a more all-embracing economic crisis, which had two other aspects. In industry and commerce there was a shortage of investment capital, "because too much of the economic surplus was drained off in the form of agricultural rents": "In the final analysis the paralysis of the leading sectors of an emergent capitalism reflected the ongoing stranglehold of the seigniorial class over the economy." In agriculture itself: "The growth in population rendered the holdings of many of the peasants progressively smaller and increasingly fragile." Both aspects were connected by the limitations of French development: "The domestic market was clearly inhibited by growing rural poverty. But the market was also blocked by the persistence of tolls and tariffs, local systems of weights and measures, a lack of adequate means of transport, and the burden of indirect taxes. Such a situation encouraged the persistence of too large a degree of domestic or local subsistence inhibiting urbanization and the commercialization of agriculture." In short, the Revolution had three underlying economic causes. Two of these, the crisis of industrial underinvestment in the capitalist manufacturing sector and "a classic Malthusian" crisis of subsistence in feudal agriculture, triggered by a combination of population increase and harvest failure, were primary. They set the context for the third, "the financial insolvency of the state," which in turn "led to an ultimate political crisis."[54] The alignment of the joint crises of capitalism, feudalism, and the absolutist state suggest the transitional, combined nature of the French economy, but also that the transition had reached the point where it would be increasingly difficult for the process to continue without radical political change: "The crisis of absolutism, rooted in the collision of two quite contradictory sets of productive relations, left the bourgeoisie with only one way forward: the abolition of seigneurialism, the creation of legal equality and guaranteed property rights, and the unification of France into a single economic market—all of which were central to capitalist development."[55]

What then of the two remaining preconditions: bourgeois leadership and its ideology? Elizabeth Fox Genovese and Eugene Genovese described the French revolutionaries as "those who, for whatever reasons, could no longer tolerate the national backwardness, social degradation, and political corruption and injustice attendant upon the contradiction between the emerging social relations of production and the entire 'superstructure' of legal relations and moral sensibilities, indeed of the very idea of humanity, could launch a successful assault on the state because possessed of an emerging ideology rooted in new productive forces and class relations."[56] By 1789 this intolerance on the part of the French bourgeoisie had increased in intensity, not least because its members were aware of the quite different and more favorable status afforded their equivalents in the United Provinces and Britain. Heller points out that, in terms of social weight, there were many more members of the bourgeoisie in the broad sense by the end of the eighteenth century than at the beginning: "It is estimated that the size of the bourgeoisie grew from 700,000 to 800,000 at the beginning of the eighteenth century to perhaps 2.3 million in 1789, vastly outnumbering the 120,000 or so nobles." Partly because of this, from 1720 onward the nobility began to force through measures that excluded the bourgeoisie from joining them, including the ending of ennoblement through office in 1728. The bourgeoisie were opposed to the tax exemptions of the nobility, particularly as taxation increased, although membership of the nobility based on merit was still their goal. As this suggests, the development of their class consciousness was subject to contradictory pressures. Further, their capacity for collective self-organization was limited, for fairly obvious reasons: "Before the onset of the Revolution, the sphere of autonomous political activity was quite circumscribed by the authorities of the ancien regime as a matter of policy." Nevertheless, a bourgeois way of life involving distinct forms of dress, manners, and speech began to develop, associated with which were semi-clandestine organizations like the Freemasons in which new ideas could be discussed and economic activities undertaken: "The meeting of the lodges became sites not only for philosophical discussions but for the creating and financing of new business partnerships." It was clear to many young bourgeois the careers were not open to their talents: "As a result, late eighteenth-century France produced a large stratum of alienated intelligentsia who played an important role in the Revolution."[57] As William Sewell points out:

> Revisionist historiography has tended to assume that if the bourgeoisie and the aristocracy were not distinct classes in a Marxist sense and if wealthy commoners could still rise into the nobility, then there was no reason for relations between the nobility and the bourgeoisie to be fraught with conflict. The French Revolution, therefore, could only be a political, not a social, revolution. I think this line of reasoning is based on a false premise. While it is certainly true that Old Regime society was much more

fluid than the classical Marxist historians of the Revolution claimed, it remained profoundly hierarchical. Where elaborate hierarchy was combined with fluid social relations, social status was never secure. Even those bourgeois who had wealth, education, and good social position had to be constantly vigilant to preserve their honor against threats from above and below. Social intercourse, consequently, was bathed in a continual cascade of disdain. Each group was subjected to multiple, if often petty, humiliations from above and returned the favor to those immediately below. In Old Regime society, disdain—and its inevitable complement, resentment— were produced abundantly by the ordinary experiences of bourgeois life. And although these resentments were by no means generated solely by slights at the hands of the nobles, the nobility and its privileges remained the pinnacle and the paradigm of hierarchy.[58]

If Calvinism was a non-bourgeois ideology that could, in certain conditions, be adopted by the bourgeoisie for revolutionary purposes, the Enlightenment was more closely connected to capitalist development. Critics of the Enlightenment have no doubt that there is a connection, although they are less certain what it is. For Michel Foucault the Enlightenment-as-regime-of-truth "was not merely ideological or superstructural; it was a condition of the formation and development of capitalism."[59] If Foucault credits the Enlightenment with giving rise to capitalism, Partha Chatterjee sees the Enlightenment as dependent upon it: "For ever since the Age of Enlightenment, Reason, in its universalizing mission has been parasitic upon a much less lofty, much more mundane, palpably material and singularly invidious force, namely the universalist urge of capital."[60] Faced with reductive arguments of this sort, it is tempting to deny that any connection exists. This is the strategy pursued by Wood, who writes of such criticisms: "We are being invited to jettison all that is best in the Enlightenment project—especially its commitment to a universal human emancipation—and to blame these values for destructive effects we should be ascribing to capitalism."[61] In fact, like the bourgeois revolutions themselves, the Enlightenment was both a product of capitalist development and a contributor to its further expansion. The transition displayed marked geographical and temporal unevenness between initiation and completion across, or even within the nations. In an early example of uneven development, Enlightenment thought tended to manifest itself simultaneously, or after only a brief delay, on the different components of the international scene. As a result, their class content and social meaning differed depending on whether the nation in question was nearer to the beginning or the end of the process of transition. In this respect, the Enlightenment shared two characteristics with the Reformation. "First, individual Enlightenments almost always involved a combination of different classes: The promoters of the Enlightenment were socially a heterogeneous group, and from that point of view, the Enlightenment was a mixed 'aristocratic-bourgeois' movement. Insofar as it is possible to ascribe to it a common program it was reformist. Insofar as it was undermining the reigning feudal order it was revolutionary."[62] The cross-class nature of Enlightenment thought manifested itself in these different programmatic orientations, although the dividing lines were often indistinct and the bourgeoisie itself was divided. The latter position recognized the logic of seeking to transform the absolutist state, as Jonathan Israel indicates: "Since the royal absolutism against which radical thinkers reacted could not easily be reformed or corrected piecemeal, this, in turn, and for the first time in European history, engendered an implicit and incipient, but nevertheless real and enduring preoccupation with revolution."[63] Israel has distinguished between a "radical" enlightenment on the one hand and a "conservative or "moderate" enlightenment on the other: "For the difference between reason alone and reason combined with faith or tradition was a ubiquitous and absolute difference."[64] The distinction captures an important truth, but here too the dividing line is also less distinct than Israel perhaps allows. The categories of "reformist" and "revolutionary" may roughly correspond to those of "moderate" and "radical," but much depended on context. According to Israel's classification, the Scottish Enlightenment was largely a moderate, reformist affair, and in purely intellectual terms so it was; but insofar as it was concerned with Political Economy, it also provided a program for the most rapid and decisive agrarian transformation in European, perhaps world, history down to the second half of the eighteenth century. Moderate theoretical positions could in certain circumstances lead to radical social effects.

The second similarity with the Reformation is that there was no necessary correspondence between prior capitalist development and the extent of Enlightenment radicalism. The Scottish case itself indicates the extent to which the Enlightenment was subject to the law of uneven development. Enlightenment thought was originally expressed in the context of the most developed capitalist economies, the Dutch and the English, but once it had emerged as a set of ideas they became available to anyone who aspired to live under the same conditions—in some cases backwardness acting as a spur to their adoption, producing forms of thought more focused on social change than that of the forerunners. Franco Venturi contrasts England with Scotland to the advantage of the latter: "It is tempting to observe that the Enlightenment was born and organized in those places where the contrast between a backward world and a modern one was chronologically more abrupt, and geographically closer."[65] But whether or not Enlightenment thought, conceived in these conditions, would actually become a material as well as intellectual force was by no means assured. As John Robertson has pointed out, Enlightenment thought in both Scotland and Naples was based on "Epicurean intellectual foundations," furthermore, "those foundations were of much longer and securer standing in Naples than they were in Scotland," but: "There was no high road from Enlightenment to revolution in Naples, any more than from Enlightenment to industrial revolution and empire in Scotland."[66] Again, in both cases the geopolitical context was decisive.

Where did the French bourgeoisie stand along the reformist-revolutionary axis? Pamela Pilbeam has written of "the real revolutionary impulse of the bourgeoisie in 1789 and subsequent years" that it "sought institutional, never violent change"; in other words it was primarily reformist in orientation.[67] This assessment tends to be supported by historians who see the real revolutionary social class as being the petty bourgeoisie; in these accounts the bourgeoisie is entirely consistent and consistently moderate:

> It is misleadingly simple to think of this process in terms of a bourgeoisie moving to the right and "betraying" its "mission" in face of the rise of a proletariat, for its opposition to the old order had always been moderate. In the first French Revolution, it was not a nascent class of capitalists, but the pressure and relative strength of small men that produced Jacobitism, revolutionary defense, the terror, democratic politics and revolutionary religion. These were not the essential components of a "classic" bourgeois revolution, but the results of a specific constellation of social forces at a particular historical juncture.[68]

There are two problems with this analysis. First, it fails to allow for the possibility of class differences between the leadership and the rank and file; in other words, views of the bourgeoisie might well have been temporarily congruent with those of the petty bourgeoisie—or at least the former might have persuaded the latter that this was the case. Sarah Maza accuses Marxists of believing that members of the bourgeoisie were "promoting their own class interests under the cover of something broader and nobler sounding," but, she asks: "Why should the bourgeoisie, if it existed, refuse to name itself, why should it feel compelled to conceal its own existence and purpose?"[69] But insofar as members of the revolutionary bourgeoisie were conscious of the underlying economic aims of their class as a whole, they could scarcely declare these openly to their allies among the other classes, who were the very ones likely to find themselves simply with a change of masters at the end of the process. This is not to suggest that the bourgeoisie necessarily engaged in deliberate deceit: their cadres required some "ethico-political" justification for their actions and had at least to try to convince themselves that what they were doing was in a greater "national" interest, even if it was primarily in their own. In this respect the role of the noncapitalist "professional" bourgeoisie was particularly important: "In its civic form, professionalism legitimated the attack on privilege, even when the latter was defended by corporative values. It stimulated a conception of the state as something which was not so much embodied in the dynast as present in the "nation," an ideological construct which developed *pari passu* with the growth and elaboration of the market."[70]

The identification of the bourgeoisie with the emerging modern concept of "the nation" was a decisive ideological maneuver. Greenfield argues that "the results" of the French Revolution "were favorable to capitalism because capitalism was consistent with nationalism, and the Revolution, which owed to nationalism its character, direction, and the very fact of its occurrence (though not timing), established nationalism as the foundation of the social order."[71] In his study of the thousand or so pamphlets published in France between January 1788 and June 1789, Boyd

Shafer identified the way in which the grievances of the opposition were treated as violations of the French national interest:

> The commercial treaty of 1786 with England was denounced on the ground that it harmed French industry, and Frenchmen were urged to use only French products. The nobles were asked to abandon privileges which harmed French agriculture and commerce, in order "to save the country," as England with machines was outstripping France. Economic freedom was demanded by an "awakening bourgeois" because "true liberty, as well as the interests of the nation," did not permit the continuation of restrictions on commerce, such as internal tariffs, and *jurades* and *maitreses*. The "passion of regulating everything to oppress everything," this writer complained, had not only produced "absurd annoyances to business," but had sapped the "sources of national wealth" as well.[72]

The second problem with foregrounding the role of the petty bourgeoisie is that claims for bourgeois moderation wrongly treat that bourgeoisie as a homogenous bloc. It is true that those capitalists who had emerged in France were more inclined to reform than their Dutch or English predecessors, not least because of the risk that revolution posed to their property, which tended to be more industrial than agrarian or mercantile. In this respect, Ralph Miliband's claim that "extreme bourgeois class consciousness appears to impose severe limits upon successful political practice" can be sustained, but is only true if we understand "bourgeois class consciousness" to mean something like: "extreme awareness of the potentially destructive short-term effects of revolution from below on capital accumulation and the personal safety of individual capitalists."[73] Full class consciousness might even have been an obstacle to adopting the necessary revolutionary conclusions, as it ultimately was for Barnave, but not for Robespierre, even though he had a similar class position. If my claims for the decisive role of the noncapitalist bourgeoisie are correct then, precisely because they were not directly involved in the process of production and hence of exploitation, they could potentially adopt more extreme revolutionary positions than the majority of actual capitalist members of their class, positions more typical of the small producers to whom Stedman Jones refers, which allowed members of both classes to unite under the banner of Jacobitism. Colin Lucas has written of how the "professional men" of the Third Estate became the leaders of the revolution as a result of two "confusions." First, because they presented their own grievances in general terms, as those of the entire estate, they were able to ideologically focus peasant and artisan hostility onto the noble landowners, rather than onto the ruling classes in general, deflecting attention from the fact that they belonged to one of those classes. In any circumstances other than revolution they would not have been able to make these connections. Second, the professionals first identified the nobility as a distinct privileged group, and then further identified the interests of the nobles with those of the absolute monarchy—a task made easier precisely by the way in which sections of the nobility rejected the Revolution. The constitution of 1791 defined the ruling class by possession of landed property, which in turn made the possessors eligible for election to public office: "The Revolution did therefore provide a social framework within which the acquisition of nobility was to be increasingly irrelevant and which allowed elite status to develop into the attribute of men of wealth however acquired and however expressed. In this sense, we may say that the Revolution made the bourgeoisie even if it was not made by the bourgeoisie."[74]

The noncapitalist bourgeoisie began to temporarily detach themselves from the economic goals of their class only when the revolution itself came under existential threat and could not be defended by means acceptable to businessmen. "Citizens," Robespierre asked members of the Convention in 1792, "did you want a revolution without a revolution?"[75] Many of them wanted precisely this; their difficulty was that it was not on offer. It was at this point, in 1792, that the rhetoric of Classical Republicanism was adopted by the Jacobin leaders to fill the ideological void. The recourse to antiquity, which Marx famously identified in *The Eighteenth Brumaire of Louis Bonaparte* as an example of the general tendency of bourgeois revolutions to clothe themselves in the garb of earlier historical periods, was in fact a much more specific response to the threat of counterrevolution, as Sewell explains:

> During the relative calm of 1789 to 1791, the revolutionaries needed no self-deception to mask their establishment of the legal conditions for capitalist enterprise. They promulgated revolutionary transformations of the nation's administrative, constitutional, and juridical structures under the banner of enlightened reason, efficiency, and natural law, without significant recourse to Roman and Greek masks. But when the affairs of the Revolution grew desperate, when the very survival of the Revolution was threatened by external war and internal revolts and the legislature was faced with the awful task of trying and executing the king for treason, the language of political economy— indeed the language of Enlightenment rationalism more generally—no longer sufficed. Political economy, whose leading advocate in the French Revolution was Sieyes, lacked a heroic vision.[76]

Sewell's point about the limitations of Enlightenment rationalism as a mobilizing ideology is true but underestimates the extent to which some leading Jacobins came to actively reject it:

> Robespierre delivered a keynote speech to the assembly condemning what he called the arid materialism of the *encyclopédistes* (Diderot and d'Holbach in particular), *philosophes*, who waged war not just upon the great Rousseau but on sentiment, common opinion, and the simple virtue and beliefs of common people.... Here, ironically, Robespierre's Jacobinism closely converged with royalist Counter-Enlightenment ideology, both propagating the myth of the Enlightenment as a coldly clinical, unfeeling machine of rational ideas, brutalizing natural sentiment and destroying instead of furthering what is best in human life.[77]

Nevertheless, the extremity of Robespierre's position was precisely why it was only tolerated by the majority of his class as a response to a moment of danger. The majority of the Jacobins saw political dictatorship, economic centralization, the Law of the Maximum, and similar measures as temporary in nature, made necessary by civil war and invasion. Only at the outer edges of Jacobinism did members see them as being anticapitalist in themselves, and this was the anticapitalism of the small producers, not workers.

When was the moment of irreversibility for France? Here the national experience was different from those of earlier bourgeois revolutions. In the case of Britain the Restoration of 1660 involved a reaction within the revolutionary process, rather than outright counterrevolution, although the latter remained a threat until both the second English revolution of 1688–89, the climax of the Scottish Revolution in 1745–46, and victory over France abroad during the 1750s and 1760s. In the case of France the restoration of 1815 effectively signaled the end of the bourgeois revolution. Several revolutions followed, of course, but they were either political, involving the redistribution of power within the bourgeoisie (1830), or failed socialist revolutions (1871) or a combination of both (1848). To argue that the French state underwent further changes as a result of these events and indeed into the twentieth century is not to declare the Great Revolution incomplete, it is merely—as I argued in chapter 15—to notice something important about the nature of all capitalist states, namely that they never attain a condition of perfection, but are regularly subject to restructuring in response to forces unleashed by capitalist accumulation. The point is that after 1815 the French state was compatible with capital accumulation whereas before 1789 it was not.

Higher levels of economic growth have often taken several decades to achieve in the aftermath of bourgeois revolutions and, in the French case, productivity actually fell in ways that might be more characteristic of the aftermath of socialist revolutions. Nevertheless, the revolution put in place a juridical superstructure, itself a crucial component of the state, which enabled such growth to take place, not least by encouraging initiatives that would have previously not been worth undertaking, rather than acting as a barrier to them: "Under the Old Regime, it would have paid to drain marshes or to irrigate the soil, but the path was blocked by overlapping property rights and a judicial system that encouraged debilitating court suits." The Revolution changed these conditions: "Once the local and administrative reforms were securely in place, water projects proliferated." Not every region of France was capable of benefiting from innovations of this kind, but where they did "the economic consequences proved dramatic."[78] There were of course more dramatic examples of how the legal framework was changed to facilitate capitalist production, most notably in the legislative program of the Convention during the first half of 1791: under the Law of Allaire of March 2, feudal guilds were abolished and restrictions on businesses removed; the decree on agrarian property rights of June 5, the most important of a series of enactments concerning agriculture, established freedom of ownership, including the right to enclose common land; and finally, the Le Chapelier Law of June 14–17, banned combinations and industrial action.[79] In other words, as David Parker asks, can the French Revolution not simultaneously have "removed the legal and institutional impediments to the operation of the free market" *and* temporarily "deepened and prolonged the economic crisis of most sectors of the economy"?[80]

As we saw in chapter 15, revisionists have claimed that the existence of a mass of peasant smallholders left in secure possession of their holdings after the French Revolution acted as an economic break, thus casting doubt on the connection between the Revolution and the subsequent development of capitalism. Similar claims have subsequently been made by political Marxists like George Comninel. There are, however, perfectly good reasons why this might have occurred that have nothing to do the nature of social relations in postrevolutionary France. As we saw in the previous chapter, preparation for war had the effect of stimulating capitalist development in feudal-absolutist Europe; but war itself could lead to catastrophic retrogression. The effect of the Thirty Years' War on the north German lands is perhaps the best example of this, despite the tendency among modern historians to downplay the consequences for economy and society. Even when allowance has been made for the fact that economic development in the German lands had already stalled in the years directly before 1618, the overall impact of the war was to throw it into reverse. Conservative estimates suggest that the German population may have fallen from between 15 to 20 percent or from twenty million people to sixteen or seventeen million. In the areas directly affected by the fighting, such as Mecklenburg or Pomerania, the population may have fallen by as much as 50 percent. The majority of these deaths were not directly due to the war, but the result of famine or epidemic disease on a population weakened by food shortages and other privations. Of equal importance was the massive burden of municipal debt that afflicted cities required to pay both for the upkeep of their own forces and "contributions" toward enemy troops in order to spare themselves from occupation (debts that were often owed to wealthy noblemen), the abandonment of land by formerly independent peasants, and the formation of large-scale estate farming based on serfdom.[81]

France did not suffer the same levels of devastation as the German lands, but as Phillip Hoffman points out, the cumulative effect of the revolutionary years was to retard economic development. Hoffman also argues, however, that expecting otherwise is indicative of a rather unrealistic conception of what revolution and revolutionary war involve:

> That the Revolution harmed farming should come as no surprise, given what we know about the effects of warfare on agricultural productivity. Warfare and troop movements nearly always jolted farming. They did so during the Revolution, just as they had during the Wars of Religion. Requisitions were hardly beneficial either. When we add how the Revolution cut off sources of agricultural capital and dissipated trade—the great source of productivity growth under the Old Regime—the deleterious effects on the economy are almost predictable.[82]

And in this respect the French experience was scarcely unique. Productivity did not instantaneously increase after the American Civil War either; indeed, the decade of the 1860s saw the lowest growth in the entire century between the 1830s and

1930s, but these figures include the South, and therefore completely ignore the devastation of its economy and this too has more general implications. The North was eventually prepared to wage total war in order to destroy the social order based on slavery, even though the South would be an integral part of the reconstituted United States. It took the South nearly a hundred years to recover and for at least part of that period precapitalist or noncapitalist social relations of production—in the "technical" sense discussed above—continued to exist, at least in the countryside.[83] In other words, the survival and ultimate expansion of the capitalist system across the subcontinent was more important to Northern politicians than immediately achieving either uniformly intensive growth or "real subsumption" in the vanquished South.[84]

To return to the French Revolution, it is by no means clear that the small peasant agriculture sustained by the French Revolution *did* retard capitalist economic development other than in the very short term. Following the work of the Russian historian Anatoli Ado, Heller argues that Jacobin encouragement for "petty commodity production as a prelude to primitive accumulation, social polarization, and the emergence of a vibrant agrarian and industrial capitalism" was an attempt to reproduce the American version of capitalism rather than that of the Britain: "The short-lived Jacobin state may be seen as a bold if unsuccessful attempt to install such a capitalism from below." The division of the land did indeed initially retard capitalist development: "But under free market conditions it would have speeded primitive accumulation over the medium term by unleashing the path of small-scale commodity production in both town and country." This position was actually theorized under the Directory from 1795 by the proponents of what James Livesey calls "commercial republicanism," who saw it as a conscious alternative to the British path of "enclosure, tenant farming, and agricultural innovation": "Comparing Great Britain to France, the commercial republicans argued that Britain could not fulfill the promise of economic liberty, because unlike the republican French, the British under their monarchy did not enjoy full political liberty." But these were a minority. The post-Thermidorian reaction refused the demands of the peasants for land and upheld the ownership and dominance of "nobles, bourgeoisie, and rich peasants." We therefore may have to revise the traditional view of the agrarian settlement and consider whether it was not "the persistence of large property and the burden of rent, not small peasant property, which inhibited a more rapid development of French capitalism." In turn, this might suggest "the popular revolution based on the petty producers ought to be seen as an essential element of the capitalist dynamic characteristic of this upheaval." Heller agrees with Livesey that "revisionist attempts to measure the economic consequences of the Revolution in terms of short-term costs and benefits are historiographically misconceived." This does not mean that there were no benefits. In particular, Heller questions the conventional view that British manufacturing was superior to the French in the immediate aftermath of the Revolution. First, Britain was actually less mechanized during this period than is traditionally thought; only in the latter half of the nineteenth-century did machinofacture come to dominate production. Second, mass production was not the only method of industrialization: "With its higher quality production, France inserted itself differently into the international division of labor . . . [growing] at a rate comparable to that of its neighbors but based its secondary sector on small craft and manufacturing enterprises."[85] These arguments have by no means achieved general acceptance, but they demonstrate that it is possible to interpret the continued existence of small-scale peasant agriculture in France without simply repeating the narrative of precapitalist backwardness.

The French Revolution was one of the great turning points in human history, as every intelligent contemporary, friend or foe, recognized at the time. Yet, paradoxically, the cataclysmic force it unleashed also ensured that nothing like it would ever happen again. Even at the time the French Revolution had no successful imitators with the exception of the revolution in San Domingo; yet this extraordinary process, the significance of which is only now being fully realized, was at least partly directed *against* the French Republic, to the extent that it refused to apply in the colonies the principles that it declared in the metropolis. Nor was it capable of leaping over the material constraints within which it took place. "Given the immediate historical context of a slave labor based world-system, from the moment Napoleon abandoned the revolutionary ideals of 1789 and decided to reinstate French slavery, it is doubtful if an entire nation composed solely of small farmers could have remained free from slavery beyond 1802. . . . No true freedom, one that would allow for the sustained development of both liberty and social equality, was ever possible for Haitians in such an unfree totality as was Western modernity in 1804."[86]

In Europe, those who sought to emulate the French Revolution were either defeated, as in Ireland or, more commonly, a minority within their own societies who relied on the external support of the French in order to achieve power and who consequently could not retain it. Indeed, the next revolution to bear any real comparison to the French in terms of its internal dynamic and pattern of development was the Russian Revolution of 1917, which had a quite different class basis. "The French Revolution was and remained *sui generis*," writes Tim Blanning: "It was the war which brought it to the outside world, and it did so with shattering impact."[87] The revolutionary and Napoleonic Wars to which Blanning refers directly contributed to capitalist development by attacking feudalism outside the borders of France. The intervention of the New Model Army in Scotland between 1651 and 1660 had been the first example of "externalizing" the bourgeois revolution; far more significant, however, were these attempts by the French "people's armies" to crush the local nobility, abolish feudal tenures and jurisdictions, and generally rationalize the economy and society throughout Europe, even after the internal reaction began with Thermidor. Their failure to do so permanently was an important factor in determining why capitalist stabilization had to take place on the conservative basis of a restored monarchy, as it had in England beforehand.

The extent to which the French were able to establish sister republics in conquered Europe depended on whether indigenous forces existed that were willing to be involved in the process of reform; but precisely because of their isolation, their minority status, they were not necessarily those with popular followings, as the Spanish rebellion against France and its local supporters after 1808 was to prove. Although the Napoleonic armies that invaded Spain in 1809 were clearly the bearers of a more advanced social system than the Bourbon monarchy they sought to overthrow, the fact that change was being imposed at bayonet point provoked a popular resistance that ultimately aided the reactionary alliance against France. Where there were social forces committed to republican politics, it tended to be in those areas, principally Holland, where bourgeois revolutions had already taken place and consequently where these forces were opposed to the imperial role of the French armies.[88] In Britain, the most advanced of all, the majority of the ruling class were violently opposed to France and prepared to ally with absolutist reaction to defeat her, partly because the British bourgeoisie feared a successful rival—as they had the Dutch in the 1650s—and partly because the very violence of the Revolution had acted as an inspiration to nascent working-class forces in England and Scotland and to bourgeois revolutionaries in Ireland. In some territories, like Hanover and Westphalia in 1807, the French abolished serfdom only for it to be restored after Napoleon withdrew in 1813. In other parts of the German lands, notably in the Rhineland, it proved impossible to restore seigniorial rights, but these examples were too few to be the immediate basis for a Europe of independent states on the French model.

Nevertheless, as I noted in chapter 7, Europe after 1815 was not "a world restored." François Crouzet argues that the preconditions for industrialization "existed thanks to the French Revolution and its exportation to neighboring centers, especially by Napoleon": "A whole deadwood of time-honored institutions (such as guilds or the manorial system), which had been hampering economic progress had been wiped out; and a bourgeois laissez-faire social and economic system, much more akin to the British system than to that of the Ancien Regime had been established—and was not much tampered with by the post-Waterloo 'Restorations.'"[89] It is important to note that the discrepancy between intention and result, which I highlighted in the previous chapter in relation to the English Revolution, also applies to the Napoleonic period of the French Revolution. Chateaubriand, a survivor, comes close to capturing the full complexity of Bonaparte's role in his memoirs "from beyond the grave":

> That Bonaparte, continuing the successes of the Republic, sowed everywhere the principle of independence, that his victories helped loosen the links between peoples and kings, tore those peoples free from the power of old customs and old ideas: that in this sense he pursued social liberation, all that I can in no way contest: but that of his own will, he consciously worked for the political and civil liberation of nations; that he established the most narrow despotism with the idea of giving Europe, and France in particular, the broadest constitution; that he was only a tribune disguised as a tyrant, that is a supposition it is impossible for me to adopt: the revolution, which was Napoleon's source, soon appeared to him as an enemy; he fought it ceaselessly.[90]

Between 1815 and 1848, no revolution comparable to that of 1789–94 took place, although liberal conspiracies and military coups were relatively commonplace. The difficulty was simple enough: the French, indeed the European bourgeoisie as whole, had a reasonably clear program of demands before 1789; but as Marx asked, "had any eighteenth-century Frenchman the faintest idea *a priori* beforehand of the way in which the demands of the French bourgeoisie would be accomplished?"[91] He had not. Revolutionaries invented the practices and structures that we associate with the French Revolution in response to events; but in situations where quite different conditions prevailed would-be revolutionaries could repeat the familiar slogans to virtually no effect. The idea of the French Revolution dominated the first half of the nineteenth century, but it had no successful imitators.

TOWARD INTERNATIONAL STRUCTURAL ADAPTATION (2): FROM REVOLUTION TO REFORM

Earlier in this chapter I noted how, by the conclusion of the Seven Years' War, the British capitalist-constitutional state form had triumphed over its French feudal-absolutist competitor. The very same British capitalist-constitutional state form had by the end of the Napoleonic Wars also triumphed over its French Jacobin rival and this was to prove equally decisive, for the results of the next phase of revolutionary state formation resembled the conservatism of England after 1688 rather more than the radicalism of France after 1789. It was highly compressed, beginning with the launch of the first Italian War of Independence in 1859 and ending with the Franco-Prussian War of 1870–71, with an aftermath in the form of the Paris Commune pointing toward the possible socialist future. From this period almost nothing resembles the great popular insurgencies of 1567, 1642, or 1792; instead we find that negotiated constitutional settlements (Canada), military-bureaucratic coup d'état (Japan), and above all, conventional warfare (Italy, Germany, United States) were the methods by which these transformations were accomplished. The only revolutionary movement comparable to the earlier movements from below was the Polish Insurrection of 1863, not coincidentally the one significant failure of the entire period. More successful bourgeois revolutions were carried out in these years than in any other, but as these formal shifts suggest, the significance of the individual preconditions discussed in the previous chapter had also changed—indeed, in many respects they were no longer distinguishable as separate factors. The outcomes, however, remained constant.

The expansion of capitalism beyond Europe and consequently the increased pressure for states to adapt to the new system was the indirect result of British victory over France in the Napoleonic Wars: the collapse of the European empires in the Americas, the substitution of informal British influence and influx of British manufactures; the end of existing trade monopolies with Asia; the global domination of British sea power—all these developments contributed to the establishment of the world capitalist economy dominated by Britain and policed by the Royal Navy.[92] By the middle of the century the momentum began to sweep all before it: "The drive to exchange more, to seek out new markets, to find 'new' products and commodities, and to draw the commerce of the world into one vast network centered on the great port cities of the West . . . was the main dynamic behind the gradual formation between the 1860s and the 1880s of a 'world economy'—a single system of global trade."[93] As far as the balance between feudal crisis and capitalist alternative was concerned, the attempts to establish unified nation-states in the 1860s were made on the basis of economies that were internally less developed in capitalist terms than even France had been in 1789, but which now existed within the overall context of a rapidly developing world capitalist economy. As a consequence Prussia and Piedmont suffered from the economic slump that had helped stimulate the revolutions of 1848, but were not able to participate fully in the boom of the 1850s that followed. Within the absolutist states feudalism was no longer so much in crisis as subject to the slow, inexorable collapse and reconstruction of its constitutive social relations on a capitalist basis, often without any conscious decisions having been taken to achieve this end. These were the outcome of long-term trends dating back to the French Revolution, which had forced some of the absolutist state bureaucracies and even some individual members of feudal ruling classes to begin the process of reform that would ultimately culminate in the revolutions from above between 1859 and 1871.

Scotland provides an interesting precursor, since the actions of the Scottish lords in the latter half of the eighteenth century inadvertently provided the prototype for the top-down transitions that would follow in mainland Europe during the nineteenth. The former process was the first transition to agrarian capitalism to be carried out almost entirely by an existing class of feudal landowners who realized that the only way to reverse their decline was to adopt the very methods of the capitalist agriculture that they had hitherto resisted. In this way they could at least remain members of a dominant class, albeit within a new set of social relations, using new methods of exploitation. There are obviously major differences between what might be called the Scottish path and, for example, its better-known Prussian successor. The Scottish landlords took part in a ferment of theoretical exploration during the Enlightenment that was unprecedented in the history of Europe or its overseas extensions; their Prussian successors merely inherited the operational conclusions without experiencing the liberatory intellectual process by which they were produced. The Scottish landlords were able to begin reform safe in the knowledge that they would not be met with widespread peasant resistance; their successors began reform in part to prevent peasant revolt from assuming the terrifying proportions that it had already done during the French Revolution.[94]

These differences aside, however, two striking similarities remain. One is that military defeat precipitated the reform process. In the case of Scotland, it was the Jacobite defeat at Culloden in 1746. In the case of Prussia, it was defeat by the Napoleonic armies at Jena and Auerstadt in 1806, the outcomes of which seemed to demonstrate the superiority of free peasants over serfs as a source of manpower, while the indemnities imposed by the victorious French demanded an increase in revenues that was unlikely to be produced as long as serfdom endured. The other similarity is that, because of a comparable primitiveness of economic relations, both landlord classes appropriated the peasant surplus in the form of labor rent. One unintended consequence of the reassertion of absolutist power in Central and Eastern Europe after the failure of the bourgeois revolutions of 1848 was to accelerate this process, as Jerome Blum points out:

> It is difficult to imagine, much less to document, the thesis that bourgeois capitalists in Russia or Romania or Hungary, or, in fact any of the servile lands, had sufficient influence to persuade governments to end the servile order, or that governments freed the peasants out of their concern for the needs of bourgeois capitalism. . . . The final reforms that freed the peasants from their servility, and afforded them civil equality with the other strata in society, were the last great triumph of royal absolutism over nobility—and, in truth, its last great achievement.

The revolutionary regimes of 1848–49 passed legislation that was never implemented, but "when the absolutists gained control, as they quickly did, they carried out the revolution's agrarian reforms because these reforms suited their own interests." What were these? One was "reducing the power of the nobility" and the other "enabled the throne to hold the loyalty and support of the peasantry": "These men, advocates of the bureaucratic sovereign state, opposed the traditional order because it interfered with and impeded the welfare and power of the state."[95] But in an environment in which capitalist market conditions increasingly prevailed, the slackening of feudal agrarian social relations could only result in adaptation to it. Hobsbawm has described how in Bohemia and Hungary in the latter half of the nineteenth century: "The large noble estates, sometimes helped by injections of finance from the compensation payments for the loss of labor services, transformed themselves into capitalist undertakings."[96] This was a general trend after 1848, in Latin America and East Asia as much as Central Europe and it meant that landowners now came to have new expectations and requirements of the state. "The landowners were trying to maximize profits by turning themselves into big local agro-business or efficient tax-collectors," writes Christopher Bayly, who mentions "Prussian junkers, Mexican *hacendados*, and Javanese *regenten*" as examples. "Entrepreneurial landed interests like this needed the government to put in roads, railways, and canals for them. Equally, the administrators needed the support of big landowners, provided they could be persuaded to reform sufficiently to head off peasant revolt and the hostility of urban dwellers."[97]

But very few of the existing states had the structural capacity to make these provisions on the scale required. Pressure therefore began to be exerted by emergent capitalist landowners for, at the very least, reform; what made at least some fractions among the existing feudal ruling class opt for revolution was the need to respond to more immediate danger: defeat in war:

The impetus towards these reforms had been the success of Great Britain and the failure of most of the continental countries in the middle of the century. In 1856, Russia had been humiliated in the Crimean War's outcome. Austria had been defeated in 1859 by the French and the Piedmontese, who established the kingdom of Italy in 1861. Prussia had been humiliated in 1850 by the Austrians. In the 1850s, most countries experienced financial confusion, and needed serious reforms and considerable loans to make good. But financiers would not give money unless there were reforms. One of these was that the running of the state should be entrusted, not to a Court and its hangers-on, but to experts, with the backing of law.[98]

The untransformed state therefore acted as a block to supporting capitalist expansion, restoring military capability, and achieving the financial stability necessary for either. "To be a Great Power—and in Central Europe or Japan merely to survive—it was useful to have a central government wielding infrastructural coordination of its territories than confederal regimes could muster. Self-styled Modernisers everywhere regarded this as essential. Neither German nor Japanese confederations nor transnational dynasties could provide this. Their survival in war or anticipated war was in jeopardy, and so they fell."[99] They fell, or at least some did; but who pushed them? Not the bourgeoisie, for reasons that once again can be traced back to the French Revolution. When pan-European revolutionary upheaval took place in 1848, the non-capitalist bourgeoisie would not reprise the audacity of the Jacobins. Why?

One reason, already extensively discussed in part 1 of this book, was their fear of the consequences of popular insurgency, now heightened by the greater social presence of the working class among the ranks of "the people," a presence that was also indicative of the larger levels of capitalist fixed investment that stood to be destroyed. The necessity for alliances brought with it the danger that, even if these peasant and plebeian allies were unable to achieve their own goals, they might still push matters further than any section of the bourgeoisie was willing to go. The English capitalist class had learned the lesson as early as 1688, when it called on an invasion by the regime of their Dutch predecessors to complete their revolution for them and thus exclude or minimize the threat of popular interventions of the sort had characterized the years from 1640–48. For the European bourgeoisies that developed later, it was the Great French Revolution that provided the same lesson. This assessment should not be historically foreshortened: the problem in 1848 was not that members of the bourgeoisie were unwilling to take part in the revolutions, but rather that they were unwilling to conduct the revolutions in the only ways that would overthrow the absolutist regimes. The radicalism of the French Revolution was inherited, not by the bourgeoisie, but by the emergent working-class movement. "If the bourgeoisie no longer thought in terms of 1789–1794," writes Hobsbawm, "the democratic and social-revolutionary radicals still did."[100]

Another factor contributed to these levels of self-defeating restraint, one that also concerned the role of the popular masses. In this case it was not, however, fear of their radicalism, but instead fear of their potential for reaction or, more precisely, the way in which elements of the ancien régime were able to mobilize popular feeling against religious or agrarian reforms.[101] "The bourgeoisie is naturally bound to fear the stupidity of the masses as long as they remain conservative," wrote Marx, "and the discernment of the masses as soon as they become revolutionary."[102] It is important in this context to remember that the Parisian sansculottes were not the only and certainly not the most typical participants "from below" in the upheavals between 1789 and 1815. During the Napoleonic Wars the French occupying armies attempted to impose bourgeois revolution "from above and outside" on the absolutist regimes of Western and Southern Europe, in alliance with local Liberals. Yet in at least two important cases, those of Spain and Naples, the republics established by Napoleon were resisted, not merely by representatives of the feudal ruling class, using conscripts and mercenaries but by popular uprisings dedicated to restoring church and king, often operating completely outside the command or control of the elites. It is meaningless to describe these revolts as nationalist in inspiration, since the kingdoms of Spain and Naples that the insurgents sought to defend were, in their different ways, the antithesis of modern nation-states. Indeed, in both cases modern nation-states were precisely what the hated Liberals were attempting to construct. Yet the mass of the population, who might have benefited from the overthrow of feudalism, were isolated from the Liberals by the latter's bourgeois status and relative wealth. The Liberals then heightened their social distance from the masses by their reliance on a foreign power and by offering no positive reforms to the peasantry. Presented by a mere change in the mechanism of exploitation, but one that would nevertheless destroy the only aspects of society that offered stability and consolation, and simultaneously offered the opportunity to exercise a power normally denied them, the masses rejected the new order arms in hand.[103]

There were deep contradictions within a popular resistance dedicated to restoring one of the most reactionary regimes in Europe, contradictions captured by Goya in *The Disasters of War* in a way that expressed both his awareness of the tragedy and his ambivalence toward the forces involved. Yet if the meaning of the movement was ambiguous, that of the outcome was not in doubt: the restoration of church and king.[104] A similar story could be told of events in Naples, where the French-established republic failed to abolish feudal relations on the land and instead raised taxes on the peasants and urban poor. The retaking of Naples by Calabrian forces and the British involved a slaughter that continued for two weeks in which Republicans were massacred by the urban poor and the lumpenproletariat.[105] The Spanish peasants and Neapolitan urban masses, faced with the choice of two evils, actively embraced the one that was familiar to them and at least preserved their existing life world. Nevertheless, these struggles, the Spanish in particular, involved self-sacrifice and collective organization linked to overt forms of class hostility, albeit one focused almost entirely on the external foreign enemy and its internal supporters, who were seen as both betraying the kingdom and seeking to impose new forms of exploitation. The liberal revolutionaries could offer the masses nothing, and the resulting

absence of popular opposition to the old regimes was one reason the bourgeois revolutions in both Spain and what would eventually become Italy were delayed for so
long after these initial top-down attempts. Nevertheless, in spite of their awareness
of these historical episodes the French bourgeoisie supported the coup by Napoleon
III, which brought the revolutionary period begun in 1848 to an end, even though
Bonaparte was supported in this and the subsequent referendum precisely by the
reactionary elements of the peasantry which it most feared. More than anything
else, this accommodation demonstrated which social force the bourgeoisie now regarded with the greatest dread, with all the attendant consequences for its own role
as a revolutionary class.

At least sections of the bourgeoisie had participated in the revolutions of 1848.
Hobsbawm notes of the motivations of students and intellectuals in that year: "It was
largely based on the (as it turned out temporary) inability of the new bourgeois society
before 1848 to provide enough posts of adequate status for the educated whom it
produced in unprecedented numbers, and whose rewards were so much more modest
than their ambitions."[106] In the decades that followed the noncapitalist sections of
the bourgeoisie, which had previously given revolutionary leadership, might have been
less paralyzed by fear of working-class radicalism and more prepared to face down
peasant reaction, were increasingly integrated into a society in which their former
frustrations and humiliations were rapidly becoming things of the past.

Leadership would therefore have to come from sections of the existing ruling
classes of Europe and Japan, such as the Prussian landlords led by Bismarck, which
had previously resisted revolution but now embraced a top-down version in order to
make their states capable of competing militarily with their rivals—or in the case of
Japan, to avoid the fate of colonization and dismemberment which had befallen
China. They had models to follow, and here again uneven development, "the advantages of backwardness," was central, as Crouzet notes of the European powers:

> They had to *transform* existing industries, to "modernize" them by large scale intro-
> duction of the new techniques which had been invented and perfected in England,
> and did not need to build up completely new industries from scratch. . . . The Conti-
> nentals, once peace and normal relations with Britain had been established in 1815,
> were theoretically able to take advantage of the experience accumulated by the British
> during the preceding decades, to tap the reservoir of technical expertise and borrow
> straight away the best British practice.[107]

If industrial Britain provided a model for the organization of production,
Napoleonic France and its European Empire provided a model for the formation
of the nation-state: "The same techniques of administrative uniformity, linguistic
imposition, and pressure for social integration that had marked Bonaparte's attempt
to remold Europe were transferred by the statesmen of the new states of Europe
within their national boundaries in order to eliminate what were regarded as the
disaggregative forces of local identities."[108] The contrast between the German (1871)
and Austro-Hungarian (1867) empires is illustrative in this respect. In the former:

"The regime was strengthened. The bourgeoisie mobilized behind it, disparaging federalism as reactionary. The opposite was occurring in Austria, where modernizing ideologies were snatched from centralizing liberals by regional 'nationalists.'"[109]

The postrevolutionary states in Italy, Germany, and Japan continued to be ruled by kings or emperors but, in terms of capitalist development, this is of less significance than it at first appears. An analogy can be drawn here with the distinction between the formal and real subsumption of labor that we have already discussed in relation to the socioeconomic transition from feudalism to capitalism. As we have seen, capital initially took over the existing technical mode of production and only later created the labor process anew in factories specially designed for this purpose; in a similar way, state managers took over the outer forms of the existing absolutist states, but internally transformed them into apparatuses capable of building an autonomous center of capital accumulation. Between 1870 and 1918, virtually all the great powers consciously emphasized the archaic, imperial role of their monarchies. Bayly has noted that these "were useful to the political forces trying to mediate an increasingly complex society." The role played by Kaiser William II is typical in this respect: "By astute manipulation of the press and acquiescence in the views of elected politicians, he could serve the interests of the new middle classes of Germany's industrial cities. As commander of the forces and descendant of Frederick the Great, he was the symbolic leader of the junkers of East Germany and of their brothers and sons in the imperial army. As emperor of Germany, he could pacify the interests of the states and regions, both Catholic and Protestant, that had seemed locked in battle at the time of Bismarck." Bayly makes the obvious comparison with the Japanese emperor, but also another that is perhaps less obvious: "The real parallel with late-imperial Germany was not imperial Russia . . . it was Britain," where "the royal ritual of coronations, parades, and state openings of Parliament became more elaborate and more beautifully choreographed as the century wore on."[110]

To the inattentive this may look like the assertion of "feudal" elements within the state, indicating an incomplete transition. Tom Nairn, for example, claims that in the earlier case of the British state after 1688, "an in-depth historical analysis shows that, while not directly comparable to the notorious relics of the 20th century, like the Hapsburg, Tsarist, or Prussian-German states, *it retains something in common with them.*" What is the basis of this commonality? "Although not of course an absolutist state, the Anglo-British system remains a product of the general transition from absolutism to modern constitutionalism; it led the way out of the former, but never genuinely arrived at the latter."[111] These arguments confuse form and content. In fact, the enhanced eminence of the British monarchy after 1870 was consciously engineered by the representatives of the capitalist ruling class for the same reasons and in much the same way as their equivalents did in imperial Germany and imperial Japan. There was only one respect in which Britain was exceptional: unlike the American president on the one hand or the German kaiser on the other, its monarch wielded no real power.[112] In all these cases the preexisting symbolism of the Crown was imbued with a sense of national unity against two main challenges: internal class divisions and external imperial rivalry. The point was well made by Bukharin, writing of the ideology of the imperialist powers in the First World War:

> These sentiments are not "remnants of feudalism," as some observers suppose, these are not debris of the old that have survived in our times. This is an entirely new socio-political formation caused by the birth of finance capital. If the old feudal "policy of blood and iron" was able to serve here, externally as a model, this was possible only because the moving springs of modern economic life drive capital along the road of aggressive politics and the militarization of all social life.[113]

In other words, Britain could indeed be compared with Germany and Japan: all three were capitalist states that could be strongly contrasted with feudal absolutist Austria-Hungary or Russia, even down to the role of the emperor and empresses: "Russia represented the opposite pole to Japan within the spectrum of authoritarian monarchy—no corporate regime strategy, much depending on the monarch him-self."[114] The most striking contrast is however between Japan and China, the two states that, until the mid-1800s had been most inaccessible to Western power. Su-perficially, the Japanese revolutionaries had taken a reactionary position of restoring a previous form of rule ("Revere the Emperor!"); but as Ben-Ami Shillory notes, "the Meiji leaders, wishing to make Japan the leading force of East Asia, adopted Chinese Imperial trappings which had not previously existed in Japan."[115] But unlike the Chinese imperial attempts to "expel the barbarians," the Japanese also derived their new method of socioeconomic organization from these self-same barbarians. Success or failure in the case of any bourgeois revolution can therefore be deter-mined by assessing whether or not it has achieved the essential changes in the nature of the state required by capital, regardless of formal continuities.

A further cluster of transformations occurred more or less contemporaneously with the revolutions from above in Germany, Italy, and Japan; those in the white colonial-settler states. Marx noted that, although mercantile capital existed in both, two distinct types of production prevailed in these territories. The first is where the colonists are essentially subsistence farmers who do not carry out capitalist pro-duction, the majority of whose products are not traded as commodities.[116] The key to the retention of small-commodity production in these circumstances is the su-perabundance of one of the most fundamental forces of production: land. In these circumstances it is impossible for the expropriation of the producers to take place: "In the colonies the separation of the worker from the conditions of labor and from the soil, in which they are rooted, does not yet exist, or only sporadically, or on too limited a scale."[117] But this is not the case everywhere. The second type, where plan-tation slave labor (and often varying degrees of unfree peasant labor) is used to produce commodities like sugar and cotton for the world market, is formally nearer to that of capitalism, even though wage labor is not involved.[118] With one great exception to which I will return, none of the societies in either variant required a bourgeois revolution in the form we have hitherto discussed.

Colonial settlements in which small-commodity production was initially dominant tended to be British. Samir Amin has discovered this pattern, "in New England between 1600 and 1750, in the South Africa of the Boers between 1600 and 1880, and in Australia and New Zealand from the beginning of white settlement to the rise of modern capitalism." What is interesting about these societies was that, historically, they were the *only* ones to be based on this mode of production, which was otherwise coexistent and subordinate to another modes: "These societies of small farmers and free craftsmen, where the simple commodity mode of production was not tacked on to tribute-paying or slave-owning modes constituted the principal mode of social organization, would be inexplicable if one did not know that they were a by-product of the break-up of feudal relations in England (and, secondarily, in the Netherlands and France)." Amin adds: "Such formations have a strong tendency to develop into full-fledged *capitalist* formations."[119] But did they require revolutions to do so? The settlers were not required to overthrow feudalism, which was marginal in North America and nonexistent in Australasia and Southern Africa, but against the indigenous populations, which were subjected to genocidal onslaught in the former two areas and to systematic racial subordination in the latter. Can these also be regarded as bourgeois revolutions? Rosa Luxemburg once noted:

> A natural economy thus confronts the requirements of capitalism at every turn with rigid barriers. Capitalism must therefore always and everywhere fight a battle of annihilation against every historical form of natural economy that it encounters, whether this is slave economy, feudalism, primitive communism, or patriarchal peasant economy. The principal methods in this struggle are political force (revolution, war), oppressive taxation by the state, and cheap goods; they are partly applied simultaneously, and partly they succeed and complement one another. In Europe, force assumed revolutionary forms in the fight against feudalism (this is the ultimate explanation of the bourgeois revolutions in the seventeenth, eighteenth and nineteenth centuries); in the non-European countries, where it fights more primitive social organizations, it assumes the forms of colonial policy. These methods, together with the systems of taxation applied in such cases, and commercial relations also, particularly with primitive communities, form an alliance in which political power and economic factors go hand in hand.[120]

This suggestive passage compares the bourgeois revolutions against feudal-absolutist states with "colonial policy" against indigenous societies in which the state was still in the process of formation. The latter, despite the savagery involved in displacing and exterminating the Native American and aboriginal peoples, and partly because it was not directed against a state, took the form of a more prolonged process than the former, even when they involved more than one episode. There is no law, however, which states that bourgeois revolutions can only be conducted against states associated with the feudal and tributary modes of production out of which capitalism emerged; in a context where a capitalist world economy was consolidating they could also be conducted against tribal societies still in the "Asiatic" stage transitional to full class society. The decisive periods in the destruction of these indigenous social structures and the seizure of the land that had previously been occupied—"owned" would be anachronistic here—overlapped with those of the revolutions of above, unsurprisingly, since the pressures of the world market was decisive in both cases. In New Zealand, for example, the wars between the colonial settlers and the Maori population reached their climax in the 1860s, after which the construction of the bourgeois order began: "Between 1870 and 1914 central government policy was designed to create a modern state, with a balanced population structure, the infrastructure for a primary producing and trading economy, a streamlined political system, and the administrative and social institutions necessary for a maturing society."[121] A unified nation-state still had to be created, but in the absence of a precapitalist state to be overthrown, this was essentially a technical and administrative task rather than a political and social one.

Colonial settlements based on slavery and other forms of unfree agricultural labor tended to be formerly Spanish and Portuguese. The Latin American revolutions that spread through these territories after the fall of the Bourbons in 1808 are sometimes referred to as the wars of independence, and the allusion to the US revolution of the previous century is apt, since the former were also ultimately political revolutions and left the social structures essentially intact following the expulsion of the Iberian powers. Although the rhetoric of the Latin American revolutions was derived from that of the French Republic their real reference point was 1776 rather than 1789, still less 1792. "The new nationalism was almost devoid of social content," writes John Lynch:

> The creoles [white colonialists] were haunted by the specter of caste war. And to some degree the chronology of their conversion to independence depended on two factors—the strength of popular agitation, and the capacity of the colonial government to control it. In Mexico and Peru, where viceregal authority had the nerve and the means to govern effectively, the creoles did not hasten to desert the shelter of imperial government. But where the colonial regime was thought to be weak and social explosion imminent—in northern South America—then the obsession of the creoles with law and order and their anxiety to preserve the social structure persuaded them to make a bid for power from the very beginning. . . . There was therefore, a causal connection between the radicalism of the masses and the conservatism of independence. Spanish America retained its colonial heritage not because the masses were indifferent to the creole revolution but because they were a threat to it.[122]

Although each country had its individual peculiarities, Lynch's general analysis is applicable in the specific cases of all the successor states of the Spanish and Portuguese Empires; thus Luis Tapia writes of Bolivia after 1825: "The constitutions of the nineteenth century acknowledged a political change—the replacement of Spanish colonial rule by a new state that responded to the dominant economic and social power groups within it—but brought no social change as such. That independence took place without changing the social structure is reflected in the constitutions of the time, conceived as these were more as a political transformation than a social one."[123]

Revolutions, albeit of a mainly top-down variety, had still been necessary where a coherent territorial state needed to be formed from preexisting, precapitalist fragments (as in Italy and Germany) or where a centralized precapitalist state was incapable of defending its territory against imperialist incursions as in Japan). The history of the former colonies of Latin America (and indeed that of their former colonial powers) suggests, however, that by the middle decades of the nineteenth century and the formation of the capitalist world economy, bourgeois revolutions were no longer essential for either the initiation or consolidation of capitalist development on any given territory, provided it was formally independent of external control. Under these conditions a prolonged process of adaptive reform, perhaps punctuated by a succession of political revolutions, could achieve the same result that had previously required a social revolution. Joseph Choonara writes, again in relation to Bolivia:

> As the system develops on a world scale and capitalist political domination becomes the norm, subsequent "bourgeois revolutions" can take on an even more disjointed and episodic form in late developing capitalisms. Often it is difficult to specify a moment or even a decisive period in which quantity transformed into quality. At what point, for example, did Bolivia cease to be "feudal" and become "capitalist"? Along with a long societal process of economic development, a whole series of upheavals were required, combining blows struck from below and maneuvers at the top, through successive political revolutions with a social dimension. This must include the great indigenous struggles of 1780–82 and the liberation from colonial rule in the early 19th century, the various coups and countercoups at the start of the 20th century to the great popular nationalist revolution of 1952 and beyond.[124]

Although I do not believe that identifying capitalist states and laws of motion is quite so difficult as Choonara suggests, this type of approach is nevertheless likely to prove more fruitful than attempts to play the game of "Hunt the Bourgeois Revolution." Alan Knight, for example, writes in relation to the Mexican Revolution of 1910–20 that, insofar as it produced "new circumstances" that "involved market production, labor mobility, and capital accumulation, it is entirely valid to regard the Mexican Revolution as, in some sense, a bourgeois revolution," above all, "because it gave a decisive impulse to the development of Mexican capitalism and of the Mexican bourgeoisie, an impulse which the preceding regime had been unable to give."[125] However, even in cases where a single decisive moment of bourgeois revolution is impossible to identify, it is important not to move so far from turning point analysis that we are left with a process without beginning or end. According to Enrique Semo, Mexico experienced three waves of bourgeois revolution: the wars of independence after 1810; the mid-century reform wars against the Catholic Church, the native inhabitants and the French; and the revolution of 1910–20. For

Semo the Mexican bourgeoisie remained progressive until 1940 but were only able to play this role in "the absence of the proletariat."[126] In fact, the decisive period in the transformation of most Latin American states was concentrated into decades rather than the centuries invoked by Choonara in relation to Bolivia or Semo in relation to Mexico.[127]

In relation to Mexico, Adolfo Gilly argues that the transition to capitalism began in 1867 after the decisive victory of the Liberals over the Conservatives and their French allies in the "Reform War." The difference with France was that "the barely nascent Mexican bourgeoisie had to rely upon mass support and Jacobin methods in order to sweep away the institutions and structures inherited from colonial times that now impeded its development," but it—or its representatives—did so from a position of state power that they used to crush resistance. Political change through the state set the conditions for economic change: on the one hand the nationalization of feudal church property (and the separation of church and state); on the other, the division of indigenous Indian land into individual and unsustainable plots, both types of property bought or simply seized by great landowners to establish latifundia:

> Just, as in the struggle to liquidate the feudal structures of Church property, it had been compelled to lean on the masses and employ the plebeian forms and methods of Jacobinism, so, in its struggle against the peasant masses, the bourgeoisie had to rely upon the barbaric methods of appropriation and plunder everywhere characteristic of primitive capitalist accumulation. In other words, it had to combine its own backward capitalist relations of production with other, still more primitive forms: pre-capitalist relations of peon-type dependence upon the hacienda.... Unlike the original period of capitalist accumulation, however, this process of accelerated accumulation at the expense of pre-capitalist economic forms took place during the worldwide expansion of capitalism. In some ways then, it resembled the plunder of the North American Indians, and in other ways the colonial wars conducted by imperialist countries. But the colonial war was waged by the Mexican landowner-bourgeois government in its own country and against its own people.[128]

The experience of Argentina, at the opposite end of the subcontinent is similar. Here too is the struggle against foreign aggression, in this case from the navies of the British and the French; here too the primitive accumulation, in this case by the clearing of the Pampas Indians for the privatized cattle herds of the great ranches. Both processes were associated with the rancher and general José Manuel Rosas. The turning point in transforming the state began in 1852:

> The laborious process of national organization begins with the defeat of Rosa's army by Urquiza's federal troops, continues with the passing of the first effective national constitution, and ends in 1881 when Buenos Aires becomes the nation's capital. During this period of time, a unified state structure is set up, the Buenos Aires customs houses are nationalized, the internal customs are eliminated, a single national currency is issued, a national legal code is established and a single army is organized. Simultaneously ... a major boost is given to primary education, immigration, and the construction of new railways with public capital.[129]

There was however one great revolution during the 1860s that was in other respects quite distinct from those contemporary with it: the American Civil War. Barrington Moore described it as "the last revolutionary offensive on the part of what one may legitimately call urban or bourgeois capitalist democracy."[130] In fact, it is even more distinctive than this suggests. The Civil War resembled the German and Italian experiences in that it took the form of a conventional war for unification (or, more precisely, reunification); but unlike them and indeed every other bourgeois revolution of whatever period it involved the leadership of an industrial capitalist class. In this respect, as Charles Post points out, "the social origins of the US Civil War indicates that it, almost alone among the 'bourgeois revolutions' identified by the historical materialist tradition, actually fits the classical schema." Leaving aside what may or may not be involved in the "classical schema," the essential point is correct; in this case: "Capitalist manufacturers and commercial family-farmers, organized in the Republican Party, take the lead in organizing the political and military struggle to remove the impediment posed by slavery and its expansion."[131] Why did the United States not simply follow the general pattern of development in white colonial-settler regimes? It was, after all, already more developed in capitalist terms than any of them by midcentury. The answer lies in the fact that the social basis for opposition to capitalism was also more highly developed than elsewhere. George Novack once outlined the forces that US capitalism had to overcome:

> The three most important powers based on precapitalist forms of labor were the Indian tribes, the semifeudal proprietors, and the slaveholding planters. All contributed to the building of the bourgeois order in its formative stages: the Indians through the fur trade; the landed proprietors by importing capital, labor, tools, and provisions into the new settlements; the planters through the crops they grew and the wilderness areas their forced laborers cleared and cultivated. But, after performing useful services, they were themselves cleared away as they became obstacles to the further expansion of bourgeois property, production, and power. . . . The Indians were wiped out; the British overlords and their feudal dependants were expelled; the insurrectionary slaveholders were "gone with the wind" of the Civil War.[132]

The destruction of Native American tribal society, already well advanced before 1861, was essentially completed in the quarter century after 1865, as the colonization of the West drove them from their remaining lands. Feudalism was never of any great significance, even before 1776; the real obstacle to capitalist development was the existence of slavery in the South. Why did the Southern planters not simply adopt the same adaptive attitude as the Prussian Junkers toward the introduction of wage labor? Why, in other words, did members of the latter class not similarly transform themselves into capitalist landlords? Not only did they recognize no comparable necessity to do so, the pressures upon them were pushing in the opposite direction.

Both forms of white-settler colonial production identified by Marx existed in the southern United States before 1865, but they were neither separate nor equal in their relationship. Slavery was widespread in the South, but in most cases, relatively small scale. On the eve of war, over 97 percent of slaveholders owned fewer than fifty slaves and only 0.1 percent had estates with more than two hundred.[133] But the majority of Southerners were not slave owners and there were major class differences between the former and the latter. As Barbara Fields explains: "The domination of plantation slavery over Southern society preserved the social space within which the white yeomanry—that is, the small farmers and artisans who accounted for about three-fourths of the white families in the slave South just before the Civil War—could enjoy economic independence and a large measure of local self-determination, insulated from its characteristic form of capitalist market society."[134] The problem for the ruling class was not so much with the yeomen, however, as with the whites below them in the social structure, those who did not own slaves and who had little or no chance of ever owning them. As Theodore Allen has pointed out, it was in order to prevent the emergence of solidarity between this group and black slaves that the condition of racialized slavery had to be absolute.[135]

Both Prussian Junkers and the Southern planters understood that commercial success was essential if they were to continue as landed classes, but the Prussian serfs were not a group distinct from the rest of their society and the Junkers were consequently more vulnerable to the threat of a democratic movement uniting all the oppositional forces against them, perhaps in the form—long hoped-for by Marx—of a repetition of the Peasant War of 1525 alongside an urban insurrection by the modern working class.[136] In one sense, the Southern planters were in a stronger position than their German contemporaries, precisely because the slaves had been absolutely separated from all other subordinate social groups and were not in a position to make common cause with them. But the paradox of this position was that, unlike serfdom, slavery was not a system that could be reformed out of existence because the entire social structure was based on the position that blacks were racially inferior, incapable of any other role than as slaves, and could be expected to revert to savagery and exact revenge if freed from the supposedly paternalistic but firm restraints imposed by their masters.[137] There was manufacturing, but it too was constrained by slavery. Firms tended to be smaller and less productive than in the Midwest, and were often operated on a part-time basis as a supplement to income mainly derived from agriculture. There is no reason to suppose that Southern manufacturers were intrinsically less capable of being successful capitalists than their Northern cousins, but the restricted market characteristic of the Southern economy acted as a barrier to them, both in terms of the limited consumption demands of the large proportion of the workforce who were slaves and the fact that the larger farms and plantations produced their own small-scale goods for use.[138] It is not that the Southern slave economy was incapable of either dynamic spurts of growth or of adaptation to changing conditions, in fact it displayed both characteristics at different times between 1783 and 1861. It is rather that a system of absolutely racialized slavery tended toward self- imposed limits on expansion. Was there any way for the South to circumvent them?

The fact that social relations of production were based on an absolute connection between skin-color racism and exploitation might have been overcome if the South had been an imperial or colonial outpost of a metropolitan power; but it *was* the metropolitan power. These two factors made reform impossible and consequently made the South different not only from other societies with slaves but other slave societies. In these, like other societies with unfree labor, slaves were closer to peasant status in that they generally had their own land with which to cultivate crops, thus providing for their own subsistence and perhaps even giving them the opportunity to sell any surplus in local markets. In the South, even this was much restricted, as the masters suspected any arrangements that would diminish slave dependence upon them.[139] More importantly, while there was undoubtedly racism toward the enslaved blacks who worked on the sugar plantations in, for example, the British colony of Jamaica, whether or not they remained enslaved or became wage laborers and peasants was not crucial to the survival of the British state and society. In the end, slavery was abolished in Jamaica in 1838 as a result of calculations over profitability and the reproduction of the labor force, together with concerns over a repetition of the slave rebellion of 1831.[140] In both of the other slave societies of the Americas, Cuba and Brazil, the state began to lessen the necessity for slave labor by introducing other types of unfree labor, which formed a bridge between slavery and free labor, in Cuba these involved Chinese and even Spanish coolies.[141] In Brazil free blacks and mulattoes could serve in the militia and, crucially, could own slaves themselves.[142] None of this was possible in the South.

Individual plantations could only grow by moving or adding new land; but the same was true of the society that they supported. Slavery in one society was never going to remain viable unless it could be guaranteed further territory. In the North, capital expanded, labor productivity grew and, potentially at least, both could continue indefinitely. In the South, increased productivity was achieved from moving operations to or extending existing plantations into more fertile soil, a process to which there were limits.[143] Those limits could of course be overcome if the boundaries of Southern slave society were widened, up into the Northwest or south and east into the Caribbean and the Americas beyond the United States. "If the Northern capitalist system was an expansive one, so too was the Southern slave system," writes Morris Berman: "The fight was at least in part a conflict of two expansionist systems, and it was not possible for both of them to win."[144] Robert Fogel has pointed out that the Confederacy could have dominated Central and South America, and even formed alliances further afield with other slave-trading nations, although this might have brought it into conflict with Britain that was still applying diplomatic pressure on Brazil and in Africa.[145] But given Britain's reliance on Southern cotton, and her tacit support for the Confederacy during the Civil War, it is very likely that British state managers would have overlooked these transgressions in the spirit of compromise on which they tended to rely when their material interests were in conflict with their moral values. There was, however, a much more serious obstacle to territorial expansion, emblematic of a tension between the individual and collective interests of the slave owners.

Individual slave owners may have wanted to increase cotton production in order to boost their income; but collectively they had an interest in restricting it on the grounds that generalized increased supply would have the effect of lowering prices. Similarly they did not want the slave population to grow too quickly as this would have a comparable downward impact on the relatively high price of slaves. As Gavin Wright notes, "these attitudes had roots in their property interest and reflected the kind of economy which that property interest had created": "By slowing the growth of the regional population, both free and slave, that property interest also retarded territorial expansion and political weight. Since this political weight was a factor in secession, and since sheer manpower was a factor in the South's military defeat, in these ways we may say that the economics of slavery contributed to its own demise."[146] It was therefore important for the Southern slave owners to move into areas where other crops than cotton could be produced on the basis of slavery; the crucial failure of that class was to delay establishing a state until its Northern opponent was in a position to defeat it.

What then was the nature of the Old South? What mode of production exercised its laws of motion there? The societies over which the slave owners ruled cannot be directly assimilated to those of the ancient world; the insertion of the South into the emergent capitalist world economy meant the context for the social relations of master and slave was unimaginably different from that of the tribal and tributary formations in which the Greek and Roman city-states developed. But nor can the South simply be regarded as a peculiarly backward variant of the capitalist societies that were consolidating in Western Europe, Australasia, and the rest of North America; the surplus accruing to the landowners did derive from the exploitation of slaves. Perhaps the solution is to regard the South as a society transitional to capitalism, but one in which the transition had never been able to progress beyond a certain point. The South therefore retained a form of production with the accompanying social relations, namely chattel slavery, which elsewhere had been merely one, albeit crucial, element in the primitive accumulation of capital. In other transitional societies the importance of slavery and other forms of unfree labor diminished over time, but in the South it remained and indeed became more central to the economic and social structure rather than less.

Nevertheless, this case of arrested development might simply have led to the South remaining, like the Scottish Highlands or the Italian Mezzogiorno, as the more backward component of a "dual economy," within a nation-state in which the laws of motion were set by the capitalist mode of production. It did not. In order to survive, the Southern ruling class established, on the basis of this retarded early stage in the transition to capitalism, a new and expansionist state, the Confederate States of America and it did so with the support of the overwhelming majority of the inhabitants who were not themselves slaves. In most societies where the economy was transitional from precapitalist modes of production to the capitalist mode, states remained under the control of the precapitalist ruling class, although they adapted to the new conditions, most typically in the emergence of absolutism: society became increasingly opposed to the state. As we have seen, these tensions were resolved either by a direct external challenge to the state from the new social classes created by capitalism or, in order to avoid this outcome while enabling the ability to compete in geopolitical terms, by internal pressure from sections of the existing ruling class who themselves undertook the process of transforming the state—or some combination of these two paths, with one predominating. None of these options was possible in the South. There was no alternative ruling class capable of overthrowing the plantocracy, but, because of the unbreakable divisions associated with racialized slavery, neither could the slaveowners engage in self-transformation without unleashing the very social conflicts that, in Europe, the process had been undertaken to avoid.

Strictly speaking, the South was therefore *sui generis* and its ideologues were more justified than they knew in referring to the "peculiarity" of Southern institutions. The South was exceptional; very few other societies—effectively only Cuba and Brazil—were so absolutely dependent on one particular transitional form of labor exploitation and no other society became both developmentally "frozen" at such a fundamental level while embodying that stage of development in the state form. The South was exceptional; but it is not therefore inexplicable in Marxist terms—providing we reject the assumption that all immediately precapitalist states have to map tidily and conveniently onto our categories of tributary, feudal estates, or feudal absolutist monarchy.

Within the North as a whole the dominant reason for opposition to slavery was the perception that its citizens were potentially or actually oppressed by what they called the "slave power," an attitude that involved hostility to the slave owners without necessarily displaying any sympathy for the slaves. Accordingly, attitudes within the working class were complex, dividing those who supported the war on abolitionist grounds, those who supported it on anti-secessionist grounds (which could be quite compatible with racism toward the slaves), those who opposed it on grounds of opposition to the draft or the economic hardships it caused ("a poor man's fight"), and those who opposed it on straightforwardly racist grounds. What the bourgeoisie did not face was a revolutionary working class attempting to drive the revolution forward *in the North* in a more radical direction, in the manner of the "permanent revolution" envisaged by Marx in 1850. Indeed, the biggest upheavals were directed against the war and the free black population in the shape of the New York anti-draft riots of 1863. It is in this context that the territorial dimension assumes great importance. The fact that revolutionary violence could be directed outward to a now effectively external enemy, through the mechanism of disciplined state power, meant that a far greater degree of radicalism could be attempted than if the struggle had been a purely internal one conducted, as it were, by civilians. In other words, the Northern bourgeoisie were ultimately prepared to embrace the logic of total war rather than face defeat, even if this meant the emancipation of the slaves and harnessing the freedmen against their former masters as part of the Union's military apparatus.

According to Charles and Mary Beard: "The main economic results of the Second American Revolution would have been attained had there been no armed conflict for the census returns with rhythmic beats were recording the tale of the fates."[147] James McPherson concludes in perhaps the greatest single-volume history of the Civil War with essentially the same argument: "Of course the northern states, along with Britain and a few countries in northwest Europe, were cutting a new channel in world history that would doubtless have become the mainstream even if the American Civil War had never happened. Russia has abolished serfdom in 1861 to complete the dissolution of ancient institutions of bound labor in Europe."[148] What McPherson ignores here is that it took the Russian Revolution of 1917 to complete the liberation of the serfs. The assumption, which I used to accept, is that, even if the Confederacy had won that battle and gone on to win the Civil War, the ultimate victory of industrial capitalism across the entire territory of what is now the United States of America would sooner or later have followed, either through a renewed attempt by the North or adaptation by the Confederate plantocracy to the new order, in the manner of the Prussian Junkers or Japanese Samurai.[149] But this view ignores the fact that a Confederate victory or—what amounts to the same thing—a Northern refusal to oppose the expansionist drive of the South in the first place, would have altered the conditions under which capitalism would then have developed, on a continental and ultimately global scale. John Ashworth notes that "the ending of slavery in the American South was part of a broader movement transcending national boundaries by which unfree labor systems were dismantled across the long nineteenth century" and lists the extensive number of countries and territories, many of them in the Americas, in which slavery was abolished before 1861. He then argues that "the same processes or factors that doomed unfree labor systems elsewhere on the globe resulted in the collapse, on the battlefield, of the South's slaveholding Republic and the ultimate triumph of the Union armies": "The fundamental, inescapable fact is that throughout much of the developed and even semideveloped world unfree labor systems were being dismantled partly because they were thought to obstruct or impede economic growth and development."[150] The Confederacy, after all, was not intent on preserving a compromise with the North but imposing a new and—in the literal sense of the word—reactionary settlement on the United States as a whole. The American Civil War was therefore the most decisive and significant of all the nineteenth-century bourgeois revolutions.

The exceptional nature of events in the United States can be illustrated by comparing the process of bourgeois revolution to the north in Canada. Successive British governments had considered combining the remaining colonies in British

North America into a single nation-state, but had never acted, partly because there was little demand within Canada itself, except as a lever to gain concessions from the British. The main pressure to do so was the developmental block posed by the remnants of feudalism in the former French colonies. Three quarters of the population of Lower Canada (now Quebec) lived on the countryside under a tenurial arrangement called the "seigniorial system," which the British had preserved after the conquest in 1763. The ruling class in the province resisted attempts to integrate Lower Canada with the other major territory, Upper Canada (now part of Ontario) because of the threat this posed to the system: "The French Canadians masquerading in the fashionable hues of liberal democracy, were heart and soul in defense of the *ancien regime*. When . . . the British government made possible, though not obligatory, the commutation of feudal tenures in the province, the assembly protested in the name of the priceless heritage of feudalism which had been secured for all eternity by the Quebec Act."[151] The rebellion of 1837 has been described by two French Canadian historians as "an attempted bourgeois revolution . . . without the presence of a true bourgeoisie in its midst."[152] The Act of Union between the two provinces that followed in 1840 was intended to numerically overwhelm the French-speaking population with British colonists, but misfired in that allowed greater cooperation between radicals of both French and British origin. However, the seigniors maintained their hostility: "The French Canadians were determined to resist immigration, for immigration would inevitably affect the law, the agricultural system and the static culture of the lower St. Lawrence. . . . The *patriotes* preferred to save subsistence agriculture on feudal lines at the expense of large-scale trade in the new staples."[153] In the end the British abolished the seigniorial system in 1854 in order to allow English-speaking immigration into Lower Canada, since no British colonist would willingly submit to tenurial arrangement that has disappeared in England by 1688 and in Scotland after 1746; as was often the case by this stage in history, the impulse was tactical rather than embodying a principled opposition to feudalism. And, although there is a parallel here with the United States, in which Quebec plays the role of the South, these should not be taken too far, since the former territory was an obstacle rather than the existential threat posed by the latter.

As in the cases of Piedmont in Italy, Prussia in Germany, and the North in the United States, one area within the territories themselves took the initiative in the unification process. "Fundamentally, Confederation was the creation of a vigorous and confident Upper Canada, which saw it as the best way of escaping from the political log-jam of the existing province and as an acceptable framework for the prosecution of other projects."[154] This underestimates the colonial interest. By the 1850s at least some important political figures in Britain began to see unification as essential in order to act as a counterweight and ally against the power of the United States, not least by enabling the construction of the intercolonial railway, which would act as a carrier of both commodities and troops. The threat of US annexation became more intense as it became clear that the Union would win the Civil War. The Quebec Conference of September 1864 at which confederation was first systematically discussed coincided with the beginning of the end for the Confederacy. Donald Creighton writes of the majority of the delegates: "They did not realize that the war was coming to an end and that their long immunity from possible external danger was over."[155] As one historian of the event notes, by this stage, "the British government . . . was in favor of strengthening the central government even more than the delegates were ready to do."[156] The American abrogation of the reciprocity treaty of 1854 was intended to force Canadian politicians to apply for incorporation into the United States; instead it pushed them in the other direction: "The acceptance of the 'federal' principle against their own political traditions and wishes was the great concession that the English-speaking delegates at Quebec were prepared to make to French Canada; but they agreed to make it only on the clear understanding that the resulting British American union was to be a strongly centralized federation, a federation radically different from that which had helped to precipitate the American Civil War.[157]

In the achievement of Confederation in Canada, the key players were civil servants rather than military commanders and the stage was the conference chamber rather than the battlefield. It highlighted the diminishing need for revolutionary transformation in Europe and its overseas extensions: a process of cumulative structural adaptation had become the rule, even before the decade of the 1860s was out. With the exception of Britain's Irish colony, which liberated most of its territory between 1916 and 1921, the location of the bourgeois revolutions after 1871 shifted inexorably east and south of Europe, beginning with the old feudal absolutist and tributary empires, the Russian (1905), Persian (1905), Ottoman (1908), and Chinese (1911). But the failure or incompleteness of these revolutions indicated how difficult it now was to establish new capitalist formations in an established nation-states system already structured around the imperialist powers: the possibility of escape from precapitalist stagnation that had briefly been available between 1848 and 1871 closed after the latter date, with only Japan having taken the opportunity it presented.

THE END OF AN ERA

In one sense, that of historical possibility, the moment when the era of the bourgeois revolution ended can be timed and dated with some precision to around 9:00 p.m. on November 8 (October 25, old calendar) 1917, when Lenin began his report to the Second All-Russian Congress of Soviets with the words: "We shall now proceed to construct the socialist order."[158] The majority of the world still lay under the domination of colonial or precapitalist states, or some combination of the two; consequently, these societies were still required to liberate themselves, but the Russian Revolution now offered an alternative way of achieving their liberation. In other words, bourgeois revolutions were still possible, but they were no longer necessary, because the process of permanent revolution, at least in the form identified by Trotsky, opened up the possibility of an alternative path out of imperial domination, leading not toward occupying a subordinate position of formal independence within the capitalist nation-states system, but toward a socialist world in which both capitalism and nation-states would be historical relics.

But in another sense, that actually inscribed onto the historical record, the bourgeois revolutions now entered the period of their greatest proliferation, adding many more to the roster in the two and a half decades between the proclamation of the People's Republic of China in 1949 and the fall of Haille Salassie in 1974 than had been achieved in the three and a half centuries between the Dutch Revolt of 1567 and the Russian Revolutions of 1917. The former events are, however, rarely categorized as bourgeois revolutions. One reason is that, within little more than a decade of the Bolshevik leader rising to address delegates at the former Smolny Institute for Noble Girls, an extraordinary form of collective false consciousness had arisen, first in Russia itself, then spreading to the colonial and semicolonial world. Starting in China, twentieth-century bourgeois revolutionaries began to adopt the language and symbols—in Milton's terms, the "outward rites and specious forms"—of the socialist tradition. Their inspiration was not however the society promised by the Bolshevik revolution of 1917, but the one delivered by the Stalinist counterrevolution of 1928. False consciousness had been a characteristic of almost all previous bourgeois revolutions, but the level of cognitive dissonance here was of quite a different order, because it did not involve an ideology that was merely tangential to capitalism but one that was supposed to represent the society that would succeed capitalism. Puritanism in revolutionary England sought to establish the rule of the Saints and ended up facilitating the rule of a very unsaintly landed, mercantile, and banking elite; outside of Russia, Stalinism sought to establish state capitalist societies and succeeded in doing so, but mistook—in most cases it appears quite sincerely—what they had achieved for socialism.

These modern bourgeois revolutionaries were not necessarily organized in national Communist parties formally affiliated to the Soviet Union—in Africa in particular they tended not to be—nor did they necessarily look to full state capitalism on the Russian model as a goal; hybrids involving both state and private capital, often combined with long-standing forms of petty-commodity production, were common as decolonization was achieved. In many ways these revolutionaries were not particularly different in class terms from their predecessors between 1789 and 1848. In the colonial and semicolonial world after 1945, the local capitalists tended to be very weak and, even when not closely linked to the colonists, inherited the long-standing class fear of mass involvement in any revolution. Members of the "revolutionary intelligentsia" and the noncapitalist bourgeoisie more generally tended to treat the capitalist bourgeoisie with contempt, which is one reason the former looked to the state as an alternative. Frantz Fanon's discussion of the inadequacies of native African capitalist bourgeoisie is classic:

The bourgeoisie of an under-developed country is a bourgeoisie in spirit only . . . it will always reveal itself as incapable of giving birth to an authentic bourgeois society with all the economic and industrial consequences this entails. . . . It does not go in for investments and it cannot achieve that accumulation of capital necessary to the birth and blossoming of an authentic bourgeoisie. At that rate it would take centuries to set on foot an embryonic industrial revolution. . . . If the government wants to bring the country out of its stagnation and set it well on the road towards development and progress, it must first nationalize the middle-man's trading sector.[159]

The hostility between the capitalist and noncapitalist bourgeoisie in the colonial world during the twentieth century was far greater than in Europe and the Americas during the nineteenth. What remained similar was the sense of humiliation, and consequently hatred, felt by members of the revolutionary noncapitalist bourgeoisie for their oppressors in the old or colonial regime—so obviously inferior to them in every respect. The point was well expressed in an autobiographical passage by the leading figure in the revolutionary movement of Guinea-Bissau, Amilcar Cabral: "To take my own case as a member of the petty bourgeois group who launched the struggle in Guinea, I was an agronomist working under a European who everybody knew was one of the biggest idiots in Guinea; I could have taught him his job with my eyes shut, but he was the boss: this is something which counts a lot, this is the confrontation that really matters. This is of major importance when considering where the initial idea of struggle came from.[160]

This final phase in the history of the bourgeois revolutions involved two main variants: one involved the overthrow of precapitalist states, preserved beyond their natural life by one or other of the imperialist states for reasons of geopolitical strategy or access to raw materials, usually oil; the other involved the dismantling of actual colonial regimes that had constrained local capitalist development in order to meet the economic requirements of the metropolitan power. In the former, the process of transformation was initiated by an army coup, as in Egypt in 1952, Libya in 1969, or Ethiopia in 1974—although the first example actually occurred before the advent of Stalinism with the opening of the second phase of the Turkish Revolution in 1919. In the latter variant, the option of a coup did not exist and the revolutions therefore tended to combine elements of earlier bourgeois revolutions from below *and* above: "from below" in relation to the existing state, since it required an external military force—usually waging guerrilla warfare in the initial phases—to overcome it; but "from above" in relation to the popular masses, whose self-activity was either suppressed, minimized, or channeled into individual membership in an instrumentally organized party-army apparatus. This was the pattern in China between 1928 and 1949, North Vietnam between 1945 and 1954, and Algeria between 1956 and 1962.

Yet it would be wrong to identify every episode of national liberation that followed the Second World War as a bourgeois revolution. In some cases, such as Czechoslovakia from 1945 to 1948 and Cuba after 1959, external or internal forces replaced one model of capitalism with another. In others cases, such as that of India, liberation movements contributed toward making the position of colonialists untenable, but the successor regimes simply inherited the state apparatus bequeathed by the colonial power; native elites occupied the offices vacated by the departing Westerners, while peasants and workers returned to fields and factories as before. All these cases and many others were examples of political revolutions, in which the class basis of the state remained essentially unchanged. In still other cases, such as Malaya from 1947 to 1957 and Kenya from 1952 to 1963, liberation movements were actually defeated prior to British withdrawal, with independence then being granted on imperialist terms; but the states and societies that emerged were no more or less capitalist than those in which the movements had succeeded. It is perfectly possible for nation-states to be weak players within the world system and their economies to have little impact on the world market, as was the case in most of the former colonies, without this having the slightest bearing on whether or not they are capitalist nation-states with capitalist economies.

The Russian Revolution should have signaled the end of the era of bourgeois revolution and the opening of its proletarian successor. Given that it did not, the era finally came to an end in 1973–75, when the feudal-absolutist regime of Ethiopia was overthrown, the Portuguese colonies of Guinea-Bissau, Angola, and Mozambique were liberated, and the United States was defeated in Indochina with the fall of its client states in Cambodia, Laos, and South Vietnam. The climax of the bourgeois revolutionary era coincided with the retreat from, and in the case of Eastern Europe and the Societ Union, the collapse of the state capitalism model that had been the characteristic outcome of its last phase. It was in China, home of the greatest of these revolutions, that one important entry point to the neoliberal era was first opened, when Deng announced the Four Modernizations to the Third Plenum of the Eleventh Central Committee Congress of the Chinese Communist Party in December 1978.[161] When Deng looked back from 1992 on the transformation he had initiated in China he used the slogan "to get rich is glorious"; the echo of Guizot advising disenfranchised French citizens to "enrich themselves" if they wanted to be able to vote was unlikely to be accidental. And perhaps this is appropriate. Regardless of the vast differences between them in most respects, what the Frenchman and his Chinese successor had in common was that they represented not counterrevolution, but the consolidation of the bourgeois revolution that brought them to power and that is now over.

IS THERE A FUTURE FOR PERMANENT REVOLUTION?

If, as I have suggested, the bourgeois revolution is now a purely historical category—and no one seriously contends that there are still outstanding bourgeois revolutions waiting to be accomplished, other than perhaps at the very margins of the world system—is there any sense in which "permanent revolution" continues to be relevant?

Does retaining the term and the cognate notion of "deflection" have any benefits for Marxists other than providing the consolations of familiarity? It is possible, of course, to explicitly detach permanent revolution from the "tasks" of the bourgeois revolution, real or imagined, and instead focus on other characteristics associated with the term. The difficulty with this strategy is that these characteristics tend not to be specific to permanent revolution.

Take, for example, the following claim by Paul D'Amato: "All countries … need a permanent revolution, because though the material prerequisites for socialism exist on an international scale, they do not within a purely national framework."[162] While this is true, it is irrelevant to an argument for retaining the concept of permanent revolution. The claim that socialism was only possible on the basis of a global revolution had been central to historical materialism since its origins in the mid-1840s, antedating even the original (pre-Trotsky) concept of permanent revolution.[163] The reason Trotsky originally emphasized the requirement for the international extension of the Russian Revolution in his writings during and immediately after 1905 was precisely because he conceived it as developing into a proletarian revolution rather than remaining within the confines of a bourgeois revolution. Had it been the latter, as virtually everyone else in the Second International expected, the necessity for internationalization would not have arisen since, long before the early twentieth century, individual bourgeois revolutions had been able to survive because they were entering a preexisting capitalist environment. The reason permanent revolution is associated with international revolution is because Stalin chose to counterpose it to the doctrine of Socialism in One Country in the debates from 1924 onward; but in this context the debate was initially about the conditions of survival for the revolution in Russia, not about the character of the revolution in China. Stalin was of course ostensibly attacking a deviation peculiar to Trotsky, but he was in fact abandoning a central tenet of Classical Marxism as such. International revolution is simply a necessary condition for the existence of socialism anywhere in anything other than the very short term, but the first major countries in which opportunities to achieve this were aborted or squandered were, after all, Germany (1923) and Britain (1926): to argue that revolutions in these heartlands of developed capitalism would, if successful, have been "permanent" is to denude the concept of any specificity and consequently of any meaning.

A further argument for the continued relevance of permanent revolution emphasizes the necessity for it to be retained as a strategic alternative to Stalinist conceptions in which socialism is preceded by a "bourgeois-democratic" or—where democracy was restricted but state and economy were already clearly capitalist—a "national-democratic" phase. Here is a late but typical example of this type of argumentation by a leading figure in the South African Communist Party: "At this, the stage of the national democratic revolution the main component of which in the South African context is the national liberation of the African people, the main thrust of the revolutionary forces is to forge the broadest possible unity of the masses and of all the strata of the people for the overthrow of the hated racist regime."[164] Two points are worth making in this connection.

First, no Stalinist organization, certainly none that was in a position to take state power, ever genuinely intended the revolution to pass through a "democratic" stage of any sort—this was rhetoric designed to disarm or incorporate bourgeois opponents of colonial and precapitalist regimes or right-wing dictatorships by pretending adherence to representative democracy; the real intention was always to establish exclusive party regimes and state capitalist economies as soon as possible. In some countries, notably in India, Stalinist parties have either been unable or unwilling to challenge for total power and here the necessity for stages during which outstanding "tasks" will be accomplished is simply a justification for parliamentary deals. Achin Vanaik writes: "The Indian left that still speaks of semi-feudalism and semi-colonization or believes in a stage-ist approach—and hence rationalizes electoral-political alliances with non-Congress and non-BJP parties—is unprepared to recognize that India is a sub-imperialist, regional power."[165] Since 1917 at least the counterposing of "permanent revolution" to "stages," has therefore always been slightly unreal, since only adherents of the first position have actually been presenting their genuine position. The only situation in which a democratic stage seems to have been put forward in good faith was in South Africa, where the normal Stalinist methods of manipulation were less effective because of the size, combativity, and democratic traditions of the working class.

Second, and more important, whatever may have been the case before 1989–91, since then the basis for the entire strategy of stages has been removed. With the fall of the Stalinist regimes and the neoliberal turn in China, those who formerly argued this, with whatever degree of honesty, no longer believed that a socialist "stage" was possible: there was now nothing beyond capitalism, although there could be varieties of capitalism and they could be more or less democratic. Today the African National Congress exudes this sense of curtailed possibilities. Writing in 1976, Joe Slovo argued that the black bourgeoisie in South Africa was "pathetically small" and had "arrived too late on the historical scene to play a classic role either as a leading element in the national struggle or as the main beneficiary of mass revolutionary sacrifice": "Indeed, for a black bourgeoisie to gain ascendancy, the whole "normal" process would have to be reversed, in the sense that *its real class formation would have to follow and not precede political power.*" The trajectory outlined by Slovo in which bourgeois economic formation postdates the revolution was in fact historically far more common than he suggests, but in any case he thought it implausible in a South African context: "Since the aspirations of all the main classes among the oppressed majority can, at the moment, only be served by the destruction of the economic and political power of the existing ruling class, the question which remains is whether the all-white bourgeoisie could conceivably be assumed by a black equivalent in the future which could act to stop the revolution in its tracks and subvert the social aims of real national emancipation."[166] What Slovo does not seem to have considered is that blacks could join the existing white bourgeoisie as a new component of the South African ruling class, still less that this would be made possible by the organizations to which he belonged, the ANC and the SACP.[167] In an interview with Paul Kingsnorth from 2003, the former organization's then head of policy and research Michael Sachs explained why it had been so conservative since the overthrow of apartheid:

> "You know," he says, gesturing at nothing in particular, "you can't just go and redistribute things, in this era. Maybe if we had a Soviet Union to defend us we could do that but, frankly, you've got to play the game—you've got to ensure that you don't go on some adventure—you know, you *will* be defeated. They were defeated in Chile, they were defeated in Nicaragua . . . you can't do it now . . ."[168]

Sachs makes clear that it is not only socialism in the sense in which that was once understood that is impossible, but even social democratic reformism: "I have no doubt that if we had embarked on some kind of Keynesian socialist project in 1994, we would have been defeated by now, as the ANC."[169]

In effect, what has been constructed in South Africa is a version of what Jeffery Webber has called, in the context of Bolivia post-2006, "reconstituted neoliberalism."[170] Unsurprisingly then, leading figures in the government of Evo Morales have drawn similar conclusions to those of Mandela, Mbeki, and Zuma. When the Bolivian vice-president, Álvaro García Linera, was asked by Trotskyist interlocutors whether he thought that socialism was viable in Bolivia today, he replied:

> There are two reasons why there is not much chance of a socialist regime being installed in Bolivia. On the one hand, there is a proletariat that is numerically in a minority and politically non-existent, and you cannot build socialism without a proletariat. Secondly, the potential for agrarian and urban communities is very much weakened. There is an implosion of community economies into family structures, which have been the framework within which the social movements have arisen. In Bolivia, 70 percent of workers in the cities work in family-based economic structures, and you do not build socialism on the basis of a family economy.

The goal of the Morales government, he said, was to build an "Andean capitalism," and this was a long-term perspective: "Bolivia will still be capitalist in 50 or 100 years."[171] Choonara cites this interview as an example of the type of position against which permanent revolution is intended to offer an alternative.[172] It is true that the argument for internationalization could be used to rebuff García Linera's claims for the incapacity of Bolivia to achieve socialism in one country, but as I have already argued, that argument is not exclusive to permanent revolution. The main point, however, is that García Linera, like his equivalents in South Africa, is not seriously proposing a stage beyond capitalism but rather how it might, in the fullness of time, be restructured and reformed: the real question is whether socialism is conceivable as an alternative system at all.[173]

There is however a more plausible extension of the concept, which also involves the question of democracy and can claim some support from Trotsky himself: permanent revolution as the transition from democratic to socialist revolution. As I argued in chapter 14, there are texts in which Trotsky used this formulation, but in many of these all that is involved is a contraction from "bourgeois-democratic" to "democratic"; on other occasions, Trotsky more accurately contracted the former term in the opposite direction, that is, to "bourgeois," and this is usually what he means. It would be possible, however, to drop the misleading notion of "democratic revolution" with its Stalinist overtones and substitute that of "political revolution," as defined in chapter 20. As Choonara explains:

> Permanent revolution in this conception involves the combination of democratic and socialist challenges to the existing order of things. The former cover a range of potential demands, including the dissolution of large landed estates across much of the Global South, the introduction of parliamentary democracy in Egypt or Tunisia today, the resolution of the "indigenous question" in Bolivia in the struggles of 2003 or 2005, or the overthrow of colonialism in India in 1946–47. None of these demands are, in themselves, incompatible with capitalist social relations, but achieving these in the context of uneven and combined development can lead to an anticapitalist dynamic raising the possibility of social revolution.[174]

Trotsky himself changed the meaning of the term permanent revolution and it could be argued that doing so again simply involves a creative response to new circumstances. Furthermore, political revolutions for democracy are likely to increase. Jeff Goodwin has argued that "revolutionary movements are rather less likely to arise and social revolutions less likely to occur during the contemporary period than during the Cold War era—especially, but not exclusively, movements and revolutions that would seriously challenge the capitalist world system." Rejecting both the argument that globalization has reduced the power of individual states—thus rendering them less meaningful as the site of revolutionary overthrow—and the removal of the Soviet Union as a support for revolutionary movement as explanations, Goodwin claims instead that the real reason is the spread of representative democracy, which he regards as inimical to social revolution, although not to "political radicalism and militancy," which seek to influence the state, but not to seize it, still less to transform it.[175] The problem with this analysis, which may have been superficially plausible in the early years of the third millennium, is that representative democracy is now in retreat. A key characteristic of the Global South is relative and in some cases absolute poverty and it is this that leads to the absence or precariousness of democracy; under conditions of economic crisis this is unlikely to change. Moreover, the tendency has been for the crisis to lead to technocratic restrictions on democracy within the weaker areas of Europe, in Greece and even Italy. Nevertheless, there are several reasons I think that a further change in meaning of permanent revolution to encompass these developments is likely to lead to confusion.

What tends to happen is that the new meaning is "read back" into an earlier period in which the term meant something quite different (as in the case of terms like "nation" or "revolution" itself), with the effect of distorting the historical record. Trotsky's reworking of permanent revolution is a case in point as it produced numerous attempts by Trotskyists of a devotional persuasion to demonstrate that his conception in 1905 was essentially the same as that of Marx in 1850. A further objection concerned with historical understanding is that no social revolution from below, from the Dutch Revolt onward, has ever begun with a majority of the participants intending to totally transform the society, but rather by making ("political") demands for reform within the existing system. Wim Klooster writes of the "Atlantic" revolutions of the half century after 1776: "Overthrow of the old regime was not even necessarily the *initial* goal of the aggrieved."[176] In that sense it is only possible to identify revolutions as being either political or social once they are over: the English and French Revolutions began as the former and ended as the latter, but to describe them as examples of permanent revolution is effectively to say that all modern social revolutions (bourgeois or proletarian) can be described in these terms, which is once again to divest it of any specificity.

The most important reason for not adopting this new meaning of permanent revolution is that it misrepresents the nature of contemporary revolutions by assuming that socialism is their normal or expected outcome under current conditions, so that when it does not occur this must be a process of "deflection." As we saw in chapter 19, Cliff introduced the concept of "deflection" in the early 1960s to explain how, instead of permanent revolution leading to socialism, the postwar period had been characterized by modern forms of the bourgeois revolution leading to partial or total forms of bureaucratic state capitalism. This represented a real theoretical advance, but it nevertheless involved several difficulties that subsequent attempts to cling to the concept of permanent revolution and its "deflected" variant effectively reproduce. It elided the difference between two types of revolution: social—in this case bourgeois—revolutions that created new capitalist states in place of the existing precapitalist or colonial states and political revolutions that reconstructed the existing capitalist state, even though the rhetoric of "socialism" and national liberation may have been the same in both cases. In a sense the issue became clearer when the non-working-class actors no longer used the rhetoric of socialism. In an important article on political Islam, Chris Harman claimed that although Cliff had originally used the category with reference to "Stalinism, Maoism, and Castroism," it was equally applicable to "the Islamist intelligentsia around Khomeini in Iran," who "undertook a revolutionary reorganisation of ownership and control of capital within Iran while leaving capitalist relations of production intact."[177] Iran was a capitalist state before the revolution, during the revolution the working class was defeated, and consequently one wing of the bourgeoisie emerged triumphant over another on the basis of a different strategy for accumulation. But at least in the case or Iran there was a serious workers' movement that was in a position to challenge for power; this was not always the case.

Looking back from the mid-1980s Peter Binns observed, in relation to the Nicaraguan Revolution of 1978–79, that "the rise to power of a state capitalist ruling class on the back of a popular revolution in which the working class had become subordinated to a layer of petty bourgeois intellectuals" had not occurred. Instead, "in spite of the severity of the crisis, both economic and military, that has beset the Nicaraguan Revolution, this by now classic trajectory along the path of a 'deflected permanent revolution' toward state capitalism has itself been interrupted." Binns referred to this process, which he saw occurring in Angola and Mozambique as well as Nicaragua, as "doubly deflected permanent revolution," in which the beneficiaries were a section of the traditional bourgeoisie rather than a state bureaucracy.[178] This is conceptual overstretch with a vengeance. By 1978 the moment of state capitalism had passed. The Nicaraguan Revolution began as an attempt to replace a state run as a murderous, corrupt personal dictatorship with a constitutional bourgeois-democratic regime committed to a degree of social reform and ended by achieving this goal. The bourgeoisie did not seek a state capitalist outcome and the working class—although it participated heroically in the insurrection that overthrew Somoza—did not attempt to seize power on its own behalf. The second point is central here. Political revolutions, changes of regime by nonconstitutional methods, are a fact of life in the Global South and likely to remain so, but these can take place without involving any independent working-class intervention. For deflection to take place there must first be, not simply the potential for proletarian revolution in the abstract, but an *actual* working-class movement engaged in self-activity to the extent that the conquest of power is possible. This was true in China in the 1920s and Iran in the 1970s, but in many cases between and since there was no such movement and consequently nothing to be deflected.

Permanent revolution and, consequently, deflected permanent revolution may now be historical concepts, but uneven and combined development, the underlying process that made the former possible is not, with important implications for the possibility of socialist revolution beginning in the Global South. Following Trotsky, Tim McDaniel argues that there were four reasons why what he calls "autocratic capitalism" of tsarist Russia tended to produce a revolutionary labor movement. First, it eliminated or reduced the distinction between economic and political issues. Second, it generated opposition for both traditional and modern reasons. Third, it reduced the fragmentation of the working class but also prevented the formation of a stable conservative bureaucracy, thus leading to more radical attitudes. Fourth, it forced a degree of interdependence between the mass of the working class, class-conscious workers and revolutionary intellectuals.[179] McDaniel claims that a comparable situation has arisen since only in Iran, but this seems to unnecessarily restrict the applicability of the model to situations that resemble prerevolutionary Russia closely in formal terms.[180] In fact, the relentless expansion of neoliberal globalization, and the consequent irruption of industrialization and urbanization into areas they had previously bypassed, often under conditions of intense state repression, means that the responses identified by McDaniel are being reproduced in places as distinct as China and Dubai.[181] But these are only the most extreme examples of a general trend that is the most characteristic of the current phase of capitalist development. Two points need to be made in relation to the process.

One is that it is not limited to the Global South but to the relatively undeveloped parts of the First and former Second Worlds. As Beverley Silver writes:

> Strong new working-class movements had been created as a combined result of the spatial fixes pursued by multinational capital and the import substitution industrialization efforts of modernizing states. In some cases, like Brazil's automobile workers; labor militancy was rooted in the newly expanding mass production consumer durable industries. In other cases, like the rise of Solidarność in Poland's shipyards, militancy was centered in gigantic establishments providing capital goods. In still others, like Iran's oil workers, labor militancy was centered on critical natural resource export industries.[182]

Take, for example, the Italian Mezzogiorno, where Italian unification was followed by a pronounced process of deindustrialization, which led to a steady drain of capital to the North, with a long-term reservoir of cheap labor power, cheap agricultural products, and a docile clientele in the South; here the process of uneven and combined development led to similarly high levels of militancy to that seen in countries characterized by more general backwardness, the key episode being the revolt of the Italian in-migrants against their living conditions and low pay during the "industrial miracle" of the late fifties and early sixties. What is interesting about the Italian example, however, is that the process has continued, in different forms until the present day.[183]

The second point to be made is that, in the Global South proper at least, it is still unable completely to transform those societies. The state "containers" within which the process of uneven and combined development unfolds, including China, will never achieve the type of total transformation characteristic of the states that formed the original core of the capitalist world system, at least in any foreseeable timescale. One intelligent conservative commentator, Edward Luttwak, has referred to "the perils of incomplete imitation" whereby developing world ruling classes "have been importing a dangerously unstable version of American turbo-capitalism, because the formula is incomplete." What is missing? On the one hand, the legal regulation to control what he calls "the overpowering strength of big business" and on the other the internal humility by the winners and acceptance of the essential justice of their personal situation by the losers from the system.[184] Uneven and combined development is therefore likely to be an ongoing process, which will only be resolved by either revolution or disintegration. But in the meantime, China and other states like India and Brazil where growth has been less dramatic remain both inherently unstable in their internal social relations and expansive in their external search for markets, raw materials, and investment opportunities. It is in this inherent instability that the possibilities for socialist revolution in the Global South lie. This does not mean that wherever uneven and combined development exists today the working-class movement will automatically adopt what Trotsky called the "boldest conclusions of revolutionary thought." In circumstances where Marxist ideas (and those of secular radicalism more generally) are either unavailable or discredited after the experience of Stalinism, movements will reach for whatever ideas seem to assist them in their struggle, regardless of their antiquity—but they will transform them in the process, contrary to what is asserted by reactionaries in the West.

▫ ▫ ▫

The late Fred Halliday once expressed his own disillusionment after the fall of the Soviet Empire, rejecting the revolutionary possibilities of uneven and combined development:

> The insight of Trotsky was that of locating the history and revolution of any one country in a broader, contradictory context, in seeing how ideas, and forms of conflict, like forms of technology or economic activity, could be transposed to contexts very different from that in which they originated. The mistake of the Marxist approach was to conclude that, in the end, the combination would prevail over the unevenness. The unevenness, evident above all in the widening income gaps between rich and poor on a world scale, has continued to grow, and is replicated dramatically in an era of capitalist globalization. But because of the fragmentary character of states, the spatial and political distributor of that unevenness, the combination, *the world revolutionary cataclysm*, did not occur.[185]

To this we reply: combination is not "the world revolutionary cataclysm," it is one of the objective enabling conditions for it to take place. And if the cataclysm has not yet occurred, this is largely because of the absence of the missing subjective condition, which Trotsky recognized in 1917, and which Cliff highlighted back in the 1960s: the revolutionary organization capable of giving focus to the social explosions that the process of uneven and combined development brings in its wake. In that respect, whatever else may have changed since both men wrote, the necessity for the party remains, if the incredible energies unleashed by uneven and combined development are not to be wasted yet again, with terrible consequences for the world and those who live in it. If we are not successful, matters will not simply continue in the old oppressive way, perhaps getting a bit better, perhaps getting a bit worse. Socialism is necessary simply to remove the threats to existence for millions from starvation, epidemic, and war, and for everyone, including the capitalists themselves, of environmental catastrophe. And this perhaps is the fundamental difference between the bourgeois and socialist revolutions, beyond all questions of structure, agency, and organization, important though they are. In the case of the bourgeoisie, to quote one of its greatest poets: "The world was all before them."[186] The working class does not have this luxury. The point was well made by W. H. Auden in relation to Spain during the 1930s, one of the supposedly "bourgeois democratic" but in fact potentially socialist revolutions of the twentieth century:

The stars are dead. The animals will not look.
We are left alone with our day, and the time is short, and
History to the defeated
May say alas but cannot help or pardon.[187]

The task of socialist revolutionaries is to arrive at a situation where they do not need history to help or pardon.

Old Calton Cemetery, Edinburgh. Photograph by the author

EPILOGUE: REFLECTIONS IN A SCOTTISH CEMETERY

All the great cities that have their origins in medieval Europe and the colonial Americas display the physical traces of the bourgeois revolutions if you know where to look. Edinburgh is no exception and many local examples are revealed by a short walk, of no more than a mile, between two graveyards in the Old Town. The second of these will provide the occasion for some reflections on the meaning of the bourgeois revolution today. Even on the short journey to this location, the final destination of many a Scottish luminary, the contradictions of the bourgeois revolutions are clearly visible.

We begin in Greyfriars Kirk on Candlemaker Row. Here, on February 28, 1638, public endorsement of the National Covenant signaled the onset of the revolutionary challenge to Charles I across Britain, the ignition of a multinational conflagration that was, until relatively recently, all too often subsumed within the episode known as the English Civil War. At the most southern part of the same kirkyard we find the prison where over a thousand artisan and peasant Covenanters were thrown after their uprising against Charles II was defeated at Bothwell Brig on June 22, 1679.[1] Leaving the kirk, we turn right onto George IV Bridge then left onto the High Street and the site of the old Parliament House where, in the dying months of 1706, crowds of several thousand Scots petitioned, demonstrated, and rioted against the political leaders and their clients within who were preparing to ratify the Treaty of Union with England in their own, essentially feudal, class interests.[2]

The High Street also contains modern representations of key figures of the Scottish Enlightenment, whose full flowering followed the defeat of the last Jacobite rising at Culloden on April 16, 1746. Outside the High Court is the statue of David Hume completed by Alexander Stoddard in 1995. We will visit the tomb in which the philosopher's remains are interred at the end of our journey, and so have no need to dwell on this depiction of him in classical garb, holding a scroll and looking suspiciously less portly than contemporary portraits would lead us to believe. The ludicrous effect is partly offset by the same sculptor's companion piece of Adam Smith, situated across the High Street and outside Saint Giles Cathedral.

Smith at least is represented in the costume of his age, standing in front of a scythe and sheaf of corn, symbols that rightly reflect the agricultural focus of *The Wealth of Nations*. Funded by private subscription and unveiled on July 4, 2008, this first statue to Smith in the Scottish capital seems unexceptional—certainly compared to the travesty of Hume across the street—until we notice among the list of subscribers listed on the back the name of Dr. Eamonn Butler of the Adam Smith Institute, a body whose views bear as much resemblance to those of Smith as the views of the Institute of Marxism-Leninism of the Central Committee of the Communist Party of the Soviet Union bore to those of Marx and Lenin. This hints at some of the issues we will have to consider at the end of our tour.

Continuing across North Bridge and further down the High Street we encounter a fine example of what Donald Horne calls "the tourism of the bourgeois revolution," relating in this case to its very earliest Scottish manifestation: the reformation of 1560. Here we find a sixteenth-century building, now operating as a souvenir shop falsely purporting to be "John Knox's House," where the unbending founder of Scottish Calvinism has, in Horne's words, been "reduced to tourist coziness."[3] Turning back up the High Street, right onto North Bridge and hence to Princes Street, we discover another respect in which Edinburgh has been marked by the bourgeois revolution: the organization of space. For Princes Street conveniently divides the city in two. To the south, where the sites described so far are situated, lies the old Edinburgh of tenements and wynds and open sewers that had grown chaotically but organically throughout the feudal period. To the north lies the New Town, the ultimate spatial expression of Enlightenment rationality and conscious design.[4] North Bridge, leading out of Edinburgh's feudal past and pointing toward the capitalist future, was itself one of the first examples of the new architecture, signs of how Edinburgh was as much shaped by the particularities of the Scottish Revolution as Paris was by those of the French.[5] Heading east along the last few yards of Princes Street, we pause only briefly to glance leftward at the bronze statue of the Duke of Wellington, designed by Sir John Steele and erected in 1852 to commemorate the victory of Britain and its allies over Napoleon at Waterloo on June 18, 1815. Inadvertently, of course, it also symbolizes the victory of a model of bourgeois revolution derived from 1688 over one derived from 1789. Passing onto Regent Road we arrive at our destination, the entrance to what has been, since 1718, the Old Calton Cemetery or Burial Ground.

Old Calton Cemetery contains many monuments, the most arresting of which is the great obelisk commemorating the martyrs of the first Scottish reform movement, the Friends of the People. Funded by public subscription, it was completed in 1844, a full fifty years after Fyshe-Palmer, Gerrald, Margarot, Muir, and Skirving were transported to Australia for daring to campaign for manhood suffrage. Yet these heroes of the 1790s were already operating in a post–bourgeois revolutionary context, their struggles linking the possibility of a cross-class political revolution to democratize the British state and—at that time—the more distant prospect of proletarian social revolution to overthrow it. Two other monuments, only feet away from each other, are more relevant to our theme and, in their different ways, suggest both the promise of the bourgeois revolution and how it was broken, how it was always destined to be broken.

⬚ ⬚ ⬚

One of these monuments is Hume's mausoleum, a squat cylindrical tower designed by Robert Adam and built in 1778, two years after the philosopher's death. As we saw in chapter 3, Hume is an important thinker for anyone concerned with the theory of bourgeois revolution, both as a historian of the English case and as a political economist working at the very moment in which capitalism achieved systemic irreversibility. But it is perhaps in his work as a philosopher that most clearly illustrates not only the limits of even the most radical bourgeois thought but also the way in which those radical qualities that it did possess have been abandoned; until what remains today can be used for purposes quite different from those that the thinkers originally intended.

The distinction between "reason" and "the passions" long preexisted Hume. In the British tradition of political philosophy these two terms were usually seen as standing in opposition to each other—Hobbes and his critics, for example, both thought that to succumb to the passions was to surrender the ability to reason, although this led them to different political conclusions.[6] For Hume the relationship was different. If we understand the passions as corresponding to "needs" or "desires," then, Hume wrote: "Reason is, and ought only to be the slave of the passions, and can never pretend to any other office than to serve and obey them."[7] In other words, we can act rationally in response to our passions, but the passions themselves are not susceptible to rational analysis. In some ways Weber was later to reformulate Hume's distinction between reason and "the passions" as that between instrumental rationality and value rationality. For Weber values (ends) were fundamental beliefs that may themselves be irrational (the "warring gods" between whom he believed we all have to choose), but to which adherence can be given by rational means. Weber thought that capitalist accumulation is a rational end, although one that may be chosen for irrational reasons, such as his famous "Protestant ethic."[8] Hume had already identified one consequence of the influence the passions exercised over reason: "Men often act against their interest; for which reason the view of the greater possible good does not always influence them."[9] There is however a more fundamental difficulty with reason that becomes apparent precisely when people *do* act in their own interests, as Max Horkheimer explains: "The difficulties of rationalist philosophy originate from the fact that the universality of reason cannot be anything else than the accord among the interests of all groups alike, whereas in reality society has been split up into groups with competing interests. . . . Reason's claim to be absolute presupposes that a community of interests exists among men."[10]

But there is no community of interests in class societies. Capitalists follow their class interests and in doing so pursue courses of action that, however rational they may be for individual members of their class, can be terrifyingly irrational for everybody else. The tobacco companies that are currently opening up huge new markets in Southeast Asia for their drugs will, in due course, be responsible for a cancer epidemic which will in turn put intolerable pressures on the fragile health services of those countries, the costs of which will be borne by the working class and peasantry. A similar logic applies to the nuclear fuel and oil companies lobbying Congress to resist even the most limited attempts to reduce gas emissions; the waters rise in Bangladesh and Mozambique, condemning thousands to homelessness or death, but not until shores of the United States are covered by the Pacific Ocean will this be factored into their calculations—and, if the recent experience of New Orleans is anything to go by, perhaps not even then. The overleveraged risk-taking of financial institutions prior to 2008 requires no further comment. These are all examples of what George Ritzer calls "the irrationality of rationality," the term that he uses for how McDonald's and its competitors promote the efficient delivery of food while destroying the environment and human health.[11] Once accumulation is engaged upon it is not a choice, rational or otherwise, because there are no alternatives, other than ceasing to be a capitalist: if this option is rejected, then capitalists are subject to a compulsion terrible, severe, and inescapable. "The seventeenth and eighteenth centuries opened the way for reason into technical areas and, in part, into the governmental sphere," wrote Trotsky: "But the bourgeois revolution proved incapable of bringing reason into the realm of economic relations."[12]

There is, however, another way of understanding the different aspects of rationality apart from counterposing ends and means, and it is one that suggests how Hume's own reasoning has been abandoned by his self-proclaimed admirers. This alternative is presented most clearly by Fredrick von Hayek, a thinker influenced by Weber, but whose fanatical insistence on the necessity of the market lacks any of the ambiguities of his predecessor. Hayek described himself as an "anti-rationalist," by which he did not mean that he considered himself irrational. On the contrary, Hayek believed that there were two types of rationalism. Adherents of the first, "constructivist rationalism" "believe that human societies can be mastered by human beings and remodeled according to rational criteria. Human societies can be organized so as to abolish social evils such as poverty and violence." Adherents of the second, "evolutionary rationalism," among whom he numbered himself, show "a distrust of the powers of human reason, a recognition of the extent of human ignorance about the social and natural worlds, and therefore a stress upon the unexpected, unintended consequences of social action." According to Hayek, constructivists included Bacon, Condorcet, Godwin, Hobbes, Jefferson, Paine, Priestley, Price, Rousseau—and Marx; evolutionists had among their number Burke, Constant, Ferguson, Mandeville, Smith—and Hume. Leaving aside the question of whether this classification is accurate in respect of these thinkers (it is not), Hayek did identify a real distinction, for it is clear that Marxism and socialist thought more generally belongs to the constructivist camp. Hayek rejects constructivism on the grounds that it is not really rational at all, since any attempt to assert human control over the market will ultimately result, not simply in failure, but in social regression to a state of premodernity in which an economically unfree population is ruled by a dictatorship—although Hayek is inconsistent on this point since he does not object to dictatorships as such, only those that abolish or constrain the market.[13] In effect, Hayek is saying that only the rationality of market-based economic activity—capitalism, in his definition—is really rational. Beyond this, Hayek's evolutionary rationality is quite compatible with religious mystification: "Mythical beliefs of some sort may be needed to bring [the construction and spread of traditions] about, especially where rules of conduct conflicting with instinct are concerned." The traditions to which Hayek refers are of course those of the market order: "We owe it partly to mystical and religious beliefs, and, I believe, particularly to the main monotheistic ones, that beneficial traditions have been preserved and transmitted long enough to enable those groups following them to grow, and to have the opportunity to spread by natural or cultural selection."[14] In effect, Hayek is saying that it is irrelevant how irrational a belief may be, so long as it leads the holder to accept the market order.

We should be clear that it is not by holding this instrumentalist position on religion that Hayek has broken with the Enlightenment tradition. As Jonathan Israel has documented, one of the divisions between what he calls the moderate and the radical wings of the Enlightenment was precisely over whether their views were compatible with religious belief. But there is a further aspect of this issue that united at least some members of both wings, namely the extent to which it was safe for doubts about the existence of God to be the held among the masses. Spinoza, a radical, wrote that "the masses can no more be freed from their superstition than from their fears . . . they are not guided by reason."[15] There was no point, therefore, in the common people reading his work, since they would not understand it.[16] Voltaire, a moderate (and himself a believer), wrote in a letter of 1768: "We have never intended to enlighten shoemakers and servants—this is up to apostles."[17] As Paul Siegel astutely remarks, Voltaire's attitude to the dissemination of Enlightenment ideas to the masses lies behind one of his best-known slogans: "If God did not exist, it would be necessary to invent him."[18] Religion was "necessary" for the common people, who might otherwise seek to apply reason to areas quite as uncomfortable to denizens of the coffee shops of Paris as habitués of the Palace of Versailles. Spinoza and Voltaire were both brilliant and courageous men, but there is no need to deceive ourselves that they saw the Enlightenment—in this respect at least—as extending much beyond their own class. Although also a moderate according to Israel's classification, Hume was probably nearer to Spinoza with respect to religion than to Voltaire. It would be wrong, however, to describe him as an atheist in the way that we can contemporary figures like Richard Dawkins or Christopher Hitchens: Hume's skepticism prevented him from holding any position so dogmatic. Nevertheless, his essay "Of Miracles" makes it clear that, because of the indispensability of the miraculous to all religions, including Christianity, he regarded them as incompatible with reason.[19] In the terms that Hume uses elsewhere in the *Treatise of Human Nature*, religious belief is a form of passion.

Surprising though it may seem, the point at which Hayek breaks with Hume and with the Enlightenment more generally is over their attitude to capitalism. In fact, Hume and his contemporaries argued for what they called "commercial society," in very conditional terms and on the assumption that it would indirectly provide social benefits. Hume himself argued: "Commerce increases industry, by conveying it readily from one member of the state to another, and allowing none of it to perish or become useless. It increases frugality, by giving occupation to men, and employing them in the arts of gain, which soon engage their affection, and remove all relish for pleasure and expense. It is an infallible consequence of all industrious professions, to beget frugality, and to make the love of gain prevail over the love of pleasure."[20] As Albert Hirschman notes, in "Hume's statement . . . capitalism is here hailed by a leading philosopher of the age because it would activate some benign human proclivities at the expense of some malignant ones—because of the expectation that that, in this way, it would repress and perhaps atrophy the more destructive and disastrous components of human nature."[21] Ever since the end of the Middle Ages, and particularly as a result of the increasing frequency of national and civil wars in the seventeenth and eighteenth centuries, the search had been on for a behavioral equivalent for religious precept, for new rules of conduct and devices that would impose much needed discipline and constraints on both rulers and ruled, and the expansion of commerce and industry was thought to hold much promise in this regard. Drawing also on the work of Montesquieu in France and Sir James Steuart in Scotland, Hirschman shows that "the diffusion of capitalist forms" were not, as Weber had claimed, incidentally the consequences of the desperate Calvinist "*search for individual salvation*," but "the equally desperate search for a way of avoiding society's ruin, permanently threatening at the time because of precarious arrangements for internal and external order." But the effects of capitalism were anything but peaceful and conducive to order, and consequently the reasons these arguments were raised in the first place have been "not only forgotten but actively repressed." For Hirschman, this is necessary for the legitimacy of the capitalist order: "what social order could long survive the dual awareness that it was adopted with the firm expectation that it would solve certain problems and that it clearly and abysmally fails to do so?"[22] What actually happened, as Hirschman notes with entirely justifiable distaste, is that intellectual defenders of the system, as different in other ways as Keynes and Schumpeter, continued to argue as if the failure of capitalism was not apparent, the first by claiming that the acquisition of wealth was still less damaging than the pursuit of power, the second by claiming that imperialism was the result of the domination of European states by precapitalist ruling elites.[23]

Hayek and the neoliberal thinkers who have followed him show the same bad faith. Of all the things that might be said about the effects of capitalism, that it promotes "benign human proclivities" is evidently not one of them; yet faced with the resumption of economic crisis on a greater scale than at any time since the 1930s, neoliberal defenders of the system argue that, far from demonstrating its inherently destructive nature, it is a consequence of the constraints and distortions to which markets are still subject in the form of government regulation, trade union bargaining, and environmental campaigning.[24] It is not their passions that have overcome their reason but their interests. Indeed, faced with impending environmental crisis, to name only one potentially irreversible consequence of capitalism, it may be that support for it is increasingly incompatible with reason in *any* form other than a blinkered cost-benefit calculation of individual short-term personal benefits.

As we saw in chapter 6, Hume's friend Adam Smith also based his support for commercial society on a hypothesis concerning its likely positive effects compared to those associated with feudal absolutism. The hope, which Lukács rightly describes as being universal among bourgeois intellectuals at this time "that this democratic, bourgeois freedom and the supremacy of economics would one day lead to the salvation of all mankind" was not to be fulfilled:

> The glory and the pathos of this faith does more than fill the history of the first bourgeois revolutions—above all the Great French Revolution. It is this, too, which confers upon the great scientific pronouncements of the bourgeois class (e.g., the economics of Adam Smith and Ricardo) their forthrightness and the strength to strive for the truth and to reveal what they have discovered without cloaking it. The history of bourgeois ideology is the history of the destruction of this faith in its mission to save the world by making the whole of society bourgeois.[25]

The revolutionary thinkers of the bourgeoisie were grappling with a new phenomenon and can therefore be forgiven for not fully comprehending their subject. Now that the consequences of "actually existing capitalism" have been experienced for more than two hundred years, and it is clear that, for the majority of humanity, the dehumanizing effects of the division of labor already identified by Smith were not an unfortunate by-product but the very essence of the system, there is less excuse for such misrecognition. Political economy was the central discipline of the Enlightenment, the greatest intellectual achievement of the bourgeois revolutions.[26] The expectations that political economists like Hume and Smith had of capitalism have been disappointed, the predictions they made for it have been falsified; to defend capitalism now, to further claim these thinkers in support of such a defense while ignoring the discrepancy between their models and our reality is to attack Enlightenment values quite as comprehensively as did the feudal obscurantists to whom Hume and Smith were opposed.

▣ ▣ ▣

In front of Hume's mausoleum stands the Emancipation Monument, designed by George E. Bissell and built in 1893 to commemorate the Scottish soldiers who fought for the North during the American Civil War, six of whom are interred under or near it. It is the only memorial dedicated to any national group of combatants outside the United States, and depicts in bronze Abraham Lincoln with a freed slave crouching at his feet, the latter lifting one hand in gratitude at his redemption and with the other holding a book—we assume it to be the Bible—to demonstrate his newly acquired literacy. Several companies and regiments of Scottish immigrants were raised to fight for the Union and some, such as the Highland Scots of the 79th New York, adorned themselves in the full regalia of kilted dress uniforms, in their case consciously modeled on the 79th Cameron Highlanders of the British Army.[27] But resources that the Scots provided for the Union cause extended beyond manpower and the invented fashion accoutrements of Highland warriors to the expressions of radical Enlightenment political thought. Writing after the Civil War about the unity of humanity beyond race or nation, Frederick Douglass expressed the hope that "the American people will one day be truer to this idea than now, and will say with Scotia's inspired son: 'a man's a man for a' that'"—a line from Robert Burns he had previously used in arguing for black men to enlist in the Union army.[28]

It would be disingenuous to pretend that Scots did not also fight on the Confederate side. Moreover, if the North used Burns to support their struggle, the South too could draw on another of Scotland's literary giants, although of a very different political persuasion. Mark Twain was being his usual hyperbolic self when he held Sir Walter Scott personally responsible for the Civil War.[29] There is no doubt, however, that Scott's romanticism contributed to the self-identity of the southerner, as did the entire mythical heritage of Scottish clanship, not least in the formation of the Ku Klux Klan in December 1865.[30] One young Confederate, the son of a South Carolina planter, wrote to his mother during the War: "I am blessing old Sir Walter Scott daily, for teaching me, when young, how to rate knightly honor, and our noble ancestry for giving me such a State to fight for."[31] There is a double irony here. One is that Scott, for all his conservatism, was a characteristic figure of the Scottish Enlightenment whose novels were intended to demonstrate to his contemporaries that no matter how heroic Scottish feudal society had been, the warlike pursuit of honor was rightly doomed to be replaced by commerce and the peaceful pursuit of money: in the South his elegies were misunderstood as celebrations. The other is that, in due course, the Southern planters were to be destroyed in the way that in history most closely corresponded to the demise of the Highland chiefs and feudal lords traced by Scott in the Waverley novels.

But could the Civil War have gone further simply destroying the planters as a rival ruling class to that of the North? "Nothing renders society more restless than a social revolution but half accomplished," wrote Carl Schurz, veteran of the German revolution of 1848, Northern commander, and politician, at the end of the war: "The South will have to suffer the evil of anarchical disorder until means are found to effect a final settlement of the labor question in accordance with the logic of the great revolution."[32] Yet the Northern politicians, including figures like Schurz himself, are usually seen as "leaving the social revolution unfinished" and in some cases the Republican Party is accused of "betraying" the former slaves.[33] This seems to involve a misunderstanding of what bourgeois revolutions in general and this one in particular involve.

Once the Confederacy had been defeated, once the coherence of the South as a society had been shattered and its potential to dominate the United States ended, once actual slavery had been dismantled and the threat of subjugation to the former British colonial power removed, the majority of the Northern ruling class—many of whom were themselves racists—had no particular interest in ensuring equal rights and democratic participation for the black population. In the end, the "anarchy" invoked by Schurz—or the process of black liberation as we would see it— could not be endured when it was no longer absolutely necessary for the security of US capitalism, particularly if the possibility existed of black radicalism in the former South coinciding, or even overlapping with renewed worker militancy in the North. "The North's conversion to emancipation and equal rights was primarily a conversion of expediency rather than conviction," writes James McPherson: "It became expedient for Northern political and business interests to conciliate Southern whites and end to federal enforcement of Negro equality in the South was part of the price of that conciliation."[34] The necessary importance given by socialists to the question of racism has perhaps obscured the way in which this outcome was absolutely typical of the bourgeois revolutions from above to which the American Revolution in most respects belongs. The fate of the rural masses in the Italian Mezzogiorno, for example, remained unchanged after the Risorgimento, as they continued to labor on the same latifundia for the same landowners. Indeed, in many respects the South resembled the Mezzogiorno in that they were both effectively economic dependencies of the Northern regions of their respective nations.[35] Racism added another deeper level of oppression to the black population of the South, but their abandonment by a triumphant bourgeoisie, now safely in command of state power, was entirely typical. Free labor as conceived in the ideology of the prewar Republican Party was very distant from the types of labor into which blacks were now forced, such as sharecropping, let alone a prison system in which inmates were forcibly conscripted into production; but the latter were perfectly compatible with capitalism—as indeed, were several other identity-based restrictions on the freedom of labor. As Lisa Lowe notes: "In the history of the US, capital has maximized its profits not through rendering labor 'abstract' but precisely through the social production of 'difference,' restrictive particularity and illegitimacy marked by race, nation, geographical origins, and gender. The law of value has operated, instead, by creating preserving and reproducing the specifically racialized and gendered character of labor power."[36] And in that sense, the actual outcome of Reconstruction foreshadowed how US capitalism has developed ever since.

Was there the potential for a more democratic outcome to Radical Reconstruction? We are not dealing with a situation in which the objective was literally impossible to realize, like Anabaptist or Digger attempts to achieve communism in sixteenth-century Germany or seventeenth-century England. The issue is rather one of balance between objective and subjective conditions. Those who refer to "betrayal" by Northern politicians have to accept the implications of this position, which is that the achievement of equality was dependent on the actions of the reunified state and its military and juridical apparatus. For the reasons given in chapter 22, the Northern bourgeoisie was always collectively going to be more influenced by the necessity for social stability than the desirable but, from its point of view, optional quest for political equality. This is virtually an objective condition. In these circumstances the decisive issue was whether the former slaves could form an alliance with the majority of non–ruling-class whites, and both groups then allying with the organized working class in the North and forcing through a democratic (that is, political) revolution "from below." Obviously the Southern ruling class did everything they could to prevent such an outcome. The question—and this still seems to me to be an open question—is whether its success in doing so was preordained by the strength of a racism that was impossible to dislodge in the decade following Lee's surrender, or whether a different strategy on the part of the Radicals could have overcome it. This at least introduces the possibility that the subjective element might have been determinate here. The issues that it left unresolved could not have been resolved by the bourgeoisie and cannot now: they will have to be accomplished by a genuine second American Revolution, which can only be socialist in nature.

◻ ◻ ◻

The abandonment of the former slave population was not the only aspect of the Civil War that casts doubt on the extent to which the bourgeois revolutions could be harbingers of liberation. Another was the way in which, even before the Northern victory, the final onslaught against the societies of the indigenous population began. In March 1862 John M. Chevington led Union troops in the most important Civil War battle to be held in the Far West, at Glorietta Pass in New Mexico. Virtually as soon as the possibility of Confederate control of the Southwest was ended, the Union forces were turned against the Apache and Navajo peoples. Chevington himself commanded the Third Colorado Volunteers in the infamous massacre at Sand Creek on November 29, 1864, where a camp of five hundred Cheyenne, who believed that a peace treaty had been secured, were attacked while they slept, one hundred and fifty killed, and their bodies mutilated: "The volunteers returned to Denver to cheering crowds that admired the scalps and severed genitals displayed like trophies of battle."[37]

Analogous horrors can be found even in those classic revolutions from below that have provided most of images of bourgeois heroism. During the French Revolution, a counterrevolutionary peasant rising in the Vendée began in March 1793.

After it had been defeated in December, the terror unleashed on the area continued for six months, involving the destruction of houses and crops, in addition to people, many of whom were drowned in the River Loire, due to the inability of the guillotine to kill the numbers involved with sufficient speed. How many died will never be known, since it is difficult to separate out mortality from, on the one hand, those killed in battle during the rising itself and, on the other, the reduction in birth rates and increase in death rates, but between two thousand and three thousand may have died between December and January alone, and the final total may have reached tens of thousands.[38] During the English Revolution, Cromwell and the New Model Army stormed the Irish town of Drogheda on September 11, 1649, massacring twenty-six hundred members of the garrison and perhaps as many as a thousand civilians and clergy, an action that seemed to have been inspired partly by a desire for revenge and partly in order to frighten other towns into surrendering. A month later, Wexford fell while negotiations were still ongoing, leaving as many as two thousand dead, including civilians as well as soldiers.[39]

All bourgeois revolutions contain episodes of this sort. The English Revolution cannot be separated from the massacre at Drogheda. The French Revolution cannot be disassociated from the slaughter of the Chuans. The American Revolution cannot be cordoned off from the genocide committed against the Native Americans. These events are the other side of the coin to the popular insurgencies that characterized the cycle of bourgeois revolutions from below. There are therefore great difficulties involved in ascribing a progressive role to the system responsible for such events, and these difficulties are not a new discovery by contemporary radicals but ones that have troubled socialists of any sensitivity for many generations. Raymond Williams expressed the essential point:

> For it has been commonplace since Marx to speak, in some contexts, of the progressive character of capitalism, and with it of urbanism and of social modernization. The great indictments of capitalism, and of its long record of misery in factories and towns, have co-existed, within a certain historical scheme, with this repeated use of "progressive" as a willing adjective about the same events. We hear again and again this brisk, impatient, and as it is said realistic response: to the productive efficiency, the newly liberated forces, of the capitalist breakthrough; a simultaneous damnation and idealization of capitalism, in its specific forms of urban and industrial development; an unreflecting celebration of mastery—power, yield, production, man's mastery of nature—as if the exploitation of natural resources could be separated from the accompanying exploitation of men. What they say is damn this, praise this; and the intellectual formula for this emotional confusion is, hopefully, the dialectic. All that needs to be added, as the climax to a muddle, is the late observation, the saving qualification, that at a certain stage—is it now?; it was yesterday—capitalism begins to lose this progressive character and for further productive efficiency, for the more telling mastery of nature, must be replaced, superseded, by socialism.[40]

Williams was both reacting against a Stalinist attitude that saw as unproblematic the suffering caused by economic development, either historically (in the case of capitalism) or contemporaneously (in the case of what was mistakenly believed to be socialism in Russia). Stalinism died as a coherent ideology in 1991 with the state that gave it birth. Since then, defenders of the role played by capitalism in the past have tended to come from the ranks of those who defend the system in the present and who wish to see all remaining barriers to its dominance swept way. This alone may explain why campaigners against neoliberal globalization and imperialist war are dismissive of claims concerning capitalist progressiveness. Classical Marxism might seem to be the obvious source of an alternative to these beliefs, but it has fallen under deep suspicion precisely because of its supposedly uncritical attitude to progress. Immanuel Wallerstein expresses surprise that: "Even so stalwart a denouncer of historical capitalism as Karl Marx laid great emphasis on [capitalism's] historically progressive role."[41] Wallerstein was writing in the early 1980s and his tone suggests that the enthusiasm displayed by Marx for capitalism was a blind spot in an otherwise valuable body of work. Today, the prevailing attitude is far more hostile to Marx's work as whole, to the point that his praise for the achievements of capitalism is held to be, not a regrettable inconsistency, but an all-too-consistent indication of his willingness to sacrifice whole peoples and ways of life to the imperatives of modernity and development.

A unifying theme unites these criticisms. For want of anything better I will refer to it as "ahistorical anticapitalism," meaning a rejection of contemporary capitalism that is then read back into the historical record, so that the system is deemed always to have played a simply negative role in human affairs. Marxists see capitalism as a tragedy but a necessary one in that it establishes the material basis for socialism— understood as a society of free and equal human beings without exploitation or oppression. Ahistorical anticapitalists see only the tragedy. For them, the enclosures, clearances, and penal laws directed against people at the core of the system and to an even greater extent the extermination, enslavement, and colonial oppression of the people at its periphery were crimes of such magnitude that they render any notion of capitalism being "progressive," in however relative a way, an obscenity. There are two versions of ahistorical anticapitalism.

One concludes that the scale of the suffering caused by capitalism was so great that humanity would have been better off without it, regardless of whether it has made socialism possible or not. Indeed, adherents of this version tend to argue, on the basis of the Stalinist experience, that socialism is simply another example of Western industrialization and therefore not worth achieving. From this perspective, Marxism and neoliberalism are simply different sides of the same coin, both representing the counterfeit currency of progress. Jay Griffiths, for example, writes that:

> Progress is a one-word ideology and one which has suited both the Marxist world-view and also that of the Neoliberal far right of multinationals and global free marketeers. . . . Those who stand in the way of progress are called ridiculous, backwards, and reactionary. . . . Progress has an enormous appeal for ideologues, of both left and right and for ideologues-of-technology, all of whom use its highly political character,

while pretending that it is non-political. . . . Progress, described as inevitable, is thus not only treated as non-political but also subtly denoted as "only natural," as if it works like a law of nature, which is perverse indeed, considering how modernity's progress destroys nature. . . . For, as in the first colonizing era, it was the non-white races who suffered from the European definition of Progress-As-Genocide: so in this second era of corporate—or Marxist–colonialism, it is people of the land who suffer from modernity's progress away from nature.[42]

Griffiths is right to oppose the Chinese occupation of Tibet—one of the supposed examples of "Marxist colonialism" to which she alludes—but there is no reason to disguise the fact that Tibet before 1957 was a feudal theocracy and not some happy Hobbit-land where peasant and yak harmoniously communed with nature. Roger Burbach makes essentially the same point as Griffiths in more theoretical terms: "Capitalism in this century vied with the communist parties and the national liberation movements primarily over which system could best introduce or carry forward the project of modernization." He laments "the failure of many Marxists and neo-Marxists to recognize the heavy toll that modernism has taken on the third world, where modernization and development marked the discourse that the capitalist powers and the Soviet Union used to impose on the so-called underdeveloped world."[43]

The other form of ahistorical anticapitalism concludes that the suffering caused by capitalism had actually led to socialism it might ultimately have been, if not acceptable, then at least bearable, but it did not, will not, and has therefore been completely pointless. Murray Bookchin expresses well the logic of this position: "It is quite unclear that an industrial capitalist development of the kind that exists today was ordained by history. That capitalism greatly accelerated technological development, at a rate that had no equal in history hardly requires detailed discussion. . . . But capitalism, like the nation-state, was neither an unavoidable "necessity," nor was it a "precondition" for the establishment of a cooperative or socialist democracy."[44] Wallerstein similarly states the basic position concerning capitalist development with admirable clarity: "Not only do I believe that the vast majority of the populations of the world are objectively and subjectively less well off than in previous historical systems . . . I think it can be argued that they have been politically less well off also. So imbued are we all by the self-justifying ideology of progress which this historical system has fashioned, that we find it difficult even to recognize the vast historical negatives of this system."[45]

As the two versions tend to overlap, I do not distinguish between them in the argument that follows. Ahistorical anticapitalists tend to regard the system, from its genesis in Europe during the sixteenth century to the present day, as what Wallerstein calls a "virus," infecting other—presumably healthy—societies and preventing them developing in alternatives ways.[46] From this perspective the only difference between the genocide conducted by Spanish or Portuguese conquistadors against Native Americans while the system was still in embryo and the genocide conducted by the Nazis against European Jewry in its maturity is the extent of the destructive power at their disposal: "Capitalism in both its infancy and dotage is a terrifying social system," writes Alan Armstrong.[47] And at one level this is incontestable: for the victims the experience of suffering and death was the same. The issue is not simply an existential one, however, but one of historical meaning and of the possibility of historical alternatives. There was an alternative to the rise of Hitler in that the German working class objectively had the power, the structural capacity, not only to politically reverse the rise of fascism but to transcend the capitalist society from which it arose. Was there an alternative in this sense to the Hispanic conquest of the Americas and comparable events? Ahistorical anticapitalists tend to claim that two alternatives did exist, even when the system was only in the process of becoming dominant and that these continued to be available throughout the period of that dominance.

The first was found in the societies that fell victim to Western expansion. These supposedly embodied different and more egalitarian social structures to those of the West, as Bookchin explains: "It is important to remember that class society is not the creation of humanity as a whole. In its most ruthless form, it is the "achievement" of that numerically small proportion of "advanced peoples" who were largely confined to Europe. By far, the great mass of human beings who occupied the planet before the Age of Exploration had developed alternatives of their own to capitalism, even to class society."[48]

The second alternative is said to be inside Western Europe itself. Traditions of communal agriculture, supposedly comparable to those of the Native Americans, had survived within the feudal system but were threatened by the emergence of capitalism. Bookchin writes that "capitalism as we know it today was not predestined to gain the supremacy it presently has; rather ... popular revolutionary movements offered, and fought for, more rational and democratic social alternatives to the present society and to so-called 'bourgeois revolutions,' to use the label that has so often been given to the English, American, and French Revolutions."[49] Different paths of development would have been possible if at some point, often identified as the mid-seventeenth century, forces based on these "commons," forces other than the bourgeoisie, forces which in fact cleared the way for the bourgeoisie—had taken power instead in alliance with the indigenous peoples. According to Peter Linebaugh and Marcus Rediker English seamen returning from the Americas in the early seventeenth century reported how the native peoples lived "without property, work, masters, or kings," and claim that by so doing "brought together the primitive communism of the New World and the plebeian communism of the Old":

> There existed a particular English open-field system of agriculture, including provision for common fields, which seems to have been replicated successfully in Sudbury, Massachusetts, until it, too, was overcome by the onslaught of private accumulation. Yet the commons were more than a specific English agrarian practice or its American variants; the same concept underlay the clachan, the sept, the rundale, the West African village, and the indigenous tradition of long-fallow agriculture of Native Americans—in other words, it encompassed all those parts of the earth that remained

unprivatized, unenclosed, a noncommodity, a support for the manifold human values of mutuality.[50]

John McMurtry draws similar parallels. The economics of what he calls "the real market" have their social equivalent in "the civil commons," which is not composed of natural resources themselves, but the social process by which they are protected and husbanded by the peoples who rely on them as, for example, the Turkana people of the Turkwel River in northwest Kenya treated the acacia trees as a common resource before they were enclosed and turned into commodities:

> In fact, the traditional village commons of England—before they were enclosed by early agribusiness capitalism—were regulated like the Kenyan acacia trees of the Turkwel River. That is, there were strict village rules or customs to ensure both that the natural resources were preserved and that there was continued access of all members of the community to their life-wealth (for example, the rule that a commoner could only turn out as many head of livestock to the shared pasture as were kept in the household corral over the winter).... The civil commons is society's long-evolving system of conscious human protection of the larger life-host humanity lives from. We saw it in early form in the commons of Kenya and English villages before their destruction.[51]

Here, once again, the connection is drawn between the socioeconomic organization of the indigenous peoples of Africa and the Americas, and those of Europe before the victory of capitalism; but as Robin Blackburn points out, the later often suffered from a form of misrecognition in relation to the former, one that apparently still occurs today: "Given the manifold uncertainties and frequent obscurity of the new market order, and the novel encounters on which it was based, it is not surprising that it bred new anxieties and truncated perceptions. Thus early modern Europeans, encountering Native Americans or Africans, believed them to be living outside culture and morality in some 'wild' or 'natural' state. This aroused both phobic fears and fantasies, and utopian longings and projections."[52] Bookchin at least suggests that some non-European societies had developed different forms of class society to that of European capitalism. In which case the argument is whether the alternative forms of exploitation on which they were based had comparable potential to ultimately lead to human liberation. Bookchin does not answer the question, but many do not even pose it. Thomas Patterson, for example, writes: "Assertions that [Western] civilization is desirable, beneficial, or superior to societies that lack similar hierarchical social relations merely perpetuate and promote the views of the powerful, self-proclaimed bearers and arbiters of culture and knowledge."[53] Here we simply have the conventional neoconservative polarization between the West and the Rest, but with plus and minus signs interchanged, so that latter are now presented as noble primitives untouched by class society. Neil Young gives this idea classic expression in his great song "Cortez the Killer," in which he describes the Aztec kingdom of present-day Mexico prior to the Spanish conquest:

Hate was just a legend
And war was never known

The people worked together
And they lifted many stones

They carried them to the flatland
But they died along the way
And they built up with their bare hands
What we still can't do today[54]

Now, it so happens that Patterson has written an important scholarly work on the other main pre-Columbian empire in the Americas, the Inca kingdom of present-day Peru, in which he presents a less attractive picture: "The Inca empire and the Andean states that preceded it were based on coercion and violence and on their capacities to construct and sustain political systems that allowed the group defined as the conquerors to expropriate land and extract surplus Labor from the subjugated communities." The Spanish inherited the empire from the Incas after their arrival in the 1530s and effectively maintained the same mode of production: "Like the Incas, the Spaniards were also outsiders who, by virtue of the *encomiedas* they received, claimed the right to appropriate surplus Labor and tribute from local communities."[55] Let us therefore leave unresolved for the moment the question of external alternatives, while noting that there is at the very least a question mark over their freedom from exploitative and oppressive social relations. "Plebeian communism" or the "civic commons" in seventeenth-century Western Europe were in any case radically different from native social organization in the Americas. Although "no land without its master" was the slogan of the feudal ruling class, communal village lands still existed in spaces between the competing jurisdictions claimed by different masters—the urban communes, churches, lords, and monarchs. In some cases, particularly in the North, these were descended from pre-feudal tribal properties; in others, mainly in the West and the South, they were more recent institutions won from the nobility before the system was consolidated at the end of the first millennium. Whatever their point of origin, however, these forms of property were for the feudal system as a whole both marginal (the bulk of production was not carried out there) and functional (it allowed the peasants to retain more of their product than they would otherwise have been able), not islands of communism opposed to it.[56] This was not the basis of an alternative system.

Was there then an alternative to the actual outcome? Christopher Hill has argued that there was:

> There were, we may oversimplify, two revolutions in mid-seventeenth-century England. The one which succeeded establishing the sacred rights of property (abolition of feudal tenures, no arbitrary taxation), gave political power to the propertied (sovereignty of Parliament and common law, abolition of prerogative courts), and removed all impediments to the triumph of the ideology of the men of property—the protestant ethic. There was however another revolution which never happened, though from time to time it threatened. This might have established communal property, a far wider democracy in political and legal institutions, might have disestablished the state church and rejected the protestant ethic.[57]

Hill's formulations were still phrased with care (the other revolution only "threatened," and that "from time to time"). Contemporary historians, including those working within a Marxist framework, have been less careful. In the most important recent example, *Ehud's Dagger*, James Holstun has produced what is probably the most determinedly theoretical work of Marxist history for the last twenty years, and one that every socialist can learn much from reading. Nevertheless, at several points Holstun goes beyond merely recognizing the importance of popular involvement to implying that they might have been successful in their own right, rather than on behalf of the bourgeoisie.

On the one hand, he argues like Thompson against "three sorts of teleological error," which he refers to as "necessitarian," "meliorist," and "winner's teleology." In other words, errors that see history as inevitable, progressive, and justifiable:

> Some Marxists, and Marx himself, insofar as he subscribed to a rigorous modes-of-production narrative inherited from Adam Smith, fall into all three sorts. Necessity comes with the "stageist" movement from feudalism to capitalism. Meliorism is trickier, since Marxism sees no smooth increase in human happiness, but it is at least implied in the promise that class struggle and the development of the productive forces will eliminate most human suffering. And winner's teleology appears when some misty-eyed but stiff-lipped emissary of Stalin or the Shining Path contemplates the "inevitable" (and therefore hastenable) demise of tribal peoples, monks, aristocrats, peasants, kulaks, and small producers inhabiting the soon to be superseded modes of production.[58]

On the other hand, Holstun argues like Hill that "the English Revolution" was "the first capitalist and anti-capitalist revolution."[59] The triumph of Parliament during the first phase of the civil war was followed by an increasing division between two factions: "A capitalist faction struggling to prevent the resurgence of absolutism, establish capitalist state forms, and stifle a popular faction that struggled in turn to create a genuine social revolution enfranchising a political nation of male small producers."[60] Taken together, the implication is clearly that "the popular faction" could have emerged victorious, and the course of history changed. More recently, Holstun has moved the date of the first anticapitalist rising back in time to Kett's Rebellion in 1549, which he also describes as the "greatest" in English history: "But perhaps because its particular form of anticapitalism resisted assimilation to the long-dominant 'bourgeois-revolution' model of social change, it has drawn surprisingly little attention from the British Marxist historians."[61] The key moment of possibility is however still more generally seen as occurring one hundred years later, as Peter Linebaugh makes clear in a rather ungenerous review of Robin Blackburn's book, *The Making of New World Slavery*:

> The destruction of the Diggers' experiments of agrarian organization without commodity exchange, or servile bondage, at the time of the campaign against the Levelers was a defeat of liberty which reverberated across the common lands of England, not to mention elsewhere. It was the consolidation of the bourgeois state from, say, the execution of Charles I to the compromise of 1689 which unleashed not only the Slave Codes, but the Penal Code in Ireland, Albion's bloody code, and the martial laws of

army and navy. 1649 was a hinge in world history, a point of turning. There were actual alternatives to the development of slavery, to the development of addictive drugs as the "exotic luxury" or "dynamo of colonial development," to the promotion of greed as a principle of distribution, to the instrumental rationality which replaced commonism, to the nationalism and racism, all of which Blackburn takes to define "modernity." But the door was shut upon these alternatives.

With the failure (as Linebaugh would have it) of these alternatives, capitalism, although always contested, was able to consolidate its dominance, first within England, then Western Europe, before extending its reach across the rest of the globe. Both sets of "commons" suffered as a result.[62] When history failed to turn, capitalism, although always contested, was able to consolidate its dominance, first within England, then Western Europe, before extending its reach across the rest of the globe. The question that has to be asked here, however, is whether the proffered alternatives were feasible at the time, or are simply exercises in counterfactual history by modern radicals unwilling to acknowledge that historical actors have not always had the choices we might wish for them? Holstun, for example, has argued that agrarian communism was possible in seventeenth-century England on the basis of the communities established by Gerrald Winstanley and the Diggers: "Any sincere critic of the Whig theory of history should be very nervous about the leap from saying 'the state and the gentry crushed the Diggers' to saying 'the Diggers couldn't have succeeded.'"[63] But why should we be nervous, if the latter statement is true? The Levelers and the Diggers are often spoken of together, but were of course quite different in ideology, class composition, size of membership, and virtually every other respect. The former group had members who represented numerically significant sections of the petty bourgeoisie, an organization with roots in both the army and urban society, especially in London, and held beliefs that were relatively unencumbered by religious ideology. They failed to achieve a more democratic outcome to the English Revolution, but the possibility of them doing so was not completely implausible. This is not true of the Diggers. We know of fewer than a dozen settlements in the southern half of England, none with more than a hundred inhabitants, all faced with apathy or even hostility from the local populations from whom they would have had to rely on for support.[64]

According to these authors the fact that capitalism has continued the process of expropriation down to the present day means that a resumption of the failed seventeenth-century alliance between Western "commons" and primitive communism also remains an ongoing possibility. Accordingly, the significance of 1649 (or 1792, or 1848, or whatever date is taken as emblematic of the bourgeois triumph) is that victory for the "commons" then would have prevented the system from arising in the first place, not that defeat ruled out the possibility of overturning it afterward. Armstrong claims that Marx—a "late Marx," apparently remorseful of his youthful enthusiasm for capitalism—saw the victory of popular radicalism as predicated on an alliance with survivals of primitive communism within Western Europe itself:

"Marx saw that where communal property still existed, it might be possible to move directly to higher stages of social organization, without passing through the capitalist stage. It increasingly depended on an alliance with the new popular forces, which also had an interest in opposing private property relations."

Armstrong gives a series of examples scattered across time and space. England in 1649: if the Levelers had continued their mutiny against being sent to Ireland and, as representatives of the "new democracy" of smallholders and artisans, allied with the "old democracy" of clan society. France in 1792: "If the French revolution had lived up to its original ideas and set up a commune state, the counter-revolutionary Chuan movement might not have made much headway in Brittany." Central Europe in 1848: if German revolutionaries had been able to "transcend their own national and middle-class backgrounds" they might have prevented "Slav peasants moving to the side of counter-revolution." Russia in 1921: if the Bolsheviks had maintained the alliance with the Makhnovists against the Whites and supported the re-creation of the rural *mir* they might not have alienated the peasants and produced the tensions that led Stalin to eliminate them as a class.[65] Leaving aside Armstrong's seeming inability to distinguish between bourgeois and proletarian revolutions, one is tempted to ask how plausible an "alliance" this was, if it so consistently failed to materialize in every situation.

At their most radical, above all in France, the petty-bourgeois component of the bourgeois revolutionary movements were aiming for an egalitarian republic based on commodity exchange between small property owners, a society based on what Marx called "simple commodity production."[66] But how feasible was this? Simple commodity production was based neither on communal property nor on cooperative production, nor yet did it involve the redistribution of the product; it rather "supposes private property, a social division of labor, and production for sale by individual producers (and their families) who own the means of production." More to the point, Marx did not treat simple commodity production as a mode of production with a historically independent existence but as a concept by which he could identify what was specific to capitalism: "It is commodity production without wage labor and capitalist profit."[67] Insofar as simple commodity relations have ever existed, they have usually been subsumed within another dominant mode of production. Wherever capitalism has become dominant this process of subsumption, partial under feudalism, becomes total. As Rosa Luxemburg wrote:

> We must distinguish three phases: the struggle against natural economy, the struggle against commodity economy, and the competitive struggle on the international stage for the remaining conditions of accumulation.... Since the primitive associations of the natives are strongest protection for their social organizations and for their material bases of existence, capital must begin by planning for the systematic destruction and annihilation of all non-capitalist social units which obstruct its development. With that we have passed beyond the stage of primitive accumulation; this process is still going on.... Natural economy, the production for personal needs, and the close connection between industry and agriculture must be ousted and a simple commodity

economy substituted for them. Capitalism needs the medium of commodity economy for its development, as a market for its surplus value. But as soon as simple commodity production has superseded natural economy, capital must turn against it. No sooner has capital called it to life than the two must compete for means of production, labor power, and markets. The first aim of capitalism is to isolate the producer, to sever the community ties which protect him, and the next task is to take the means of production away from the small manufacturer. . . . The general result of the struggle between capitalism and simple commodity production is this: after substituting commodity economy for natural economy, capital takes the place of simple commodity economy. Non-capitalist organizations provide a fertile soil for capitalism; more strictly; capital feeds on the ruins of such organizations, and although this non-capitalist milieu is indispensable for accumulation, the latter proceeds at the cost of this medium nevertheless, by eating it up.[68]

A position that holds that it would have been better if capitalism had been avoided is understandable, given the daily disasters for which the system continues to be responsible. Marxists must nevertheless reject it. Without capitalism, we would have no possibility of developing the forces of production to the extent that will enable the whole of the world's population to enjoy what is currently denied most of them—a fully human life. In fact, without capitalism there would be no "us"—in the sense of a working class—to seriously consider accomplishing such a goal in the first place. To me, at any rate, it seems to be completely implausible to think that if only capitalism had not come into existence we could all be living in a world of free peasants, independent small producers, and tribal commons. It is true that capitalism was not inevitable, of course, but the alternative was a world divided between endlessly warring feudal-absolutist and tributary states without even the possibility of escape that capitalism provides.

What then should our attitude be to the society that emerged from the bourgeois revolutions? Consider these descriptions of the same events, at the beginning of the capitalist world economy, from two different sources. The first is from Marx and Engels in the *Manifesto of the Communist Party* (1848):

> The discovery of America, the rounding of the cape, opened up fresh ground for the rising bourgeoisie. The East indian and Chinese markets, the colonization of America, trade with the colonies, the increase in the means of exchange and in commodities generally, gave to commerce, to navigation, to industry, an impulse never before known and thereby, to the revolutionary element in the tottering feudal society, a rapid development.[69]

The second is from Marx alone in *Capital* (1867):

> The discovery of gold and silver in America, the extirpation, enslavement, and entombment in mines of the indigenous population of that continent, the beginnings of the conquest and plunder of India, and the conversion of Africa into a preserve for the commercial hunting of blackskins, are all things which characterize the dawn of the era of capitalist production. . . . The treasures captured outside Europe by undisguised looting, enslavement, and murder flowed back to the mother country and were turned into capital there.[70]

The tone is very different. Which is the real position? The answer is that they both are; each reflects a different aspect of the same reality. There is no inconsistency. Marx early on criticized Proudhon precisely for trying to distinguish between the "good" and "bad" side of a social system, since it is out of the antagonism between them, the contradictory whole, that progress comes.[71] Fredric Jameson has captured this duality well:

> Marxism powerfully urges us to do the impossible, namely, to think this development positively and negatively all at once; to achieve, in other words, a type of thinking that would be capable of grasping the demonstrably baleful features of capitalism along with its extraordinary and liberating dynamism simultaneously within a single thought, and without attenuating any of the force of either judgment. We are somehow to lift our minds to a point at which it is possible to understand that capitalism is at one and the same time the best thing that has ever happened to the human race and the worst.[72]

For as long as class societies have existed, human beings have dreamed of and fought for a world without inequality. But these attempts were impossible to consummate as long as the historical basis of inequality, relative material scarcity, prevailed. It is interesting, in this context, to survey the highlights from the period of what Linebaugh and Rediker call "the revolutionary Atlantic," with which they end their book:

> English sailors and commoners wanted to stay in Bermuda rather than sail on to Virginia, and some, after they got there, deserted to Algonquinian villages. Diggers built communes upon the "earthly treasury" on George's Hill as the light shone in Buckinghamshire. Resistance to slavery extended from Putney Common to the estuarial waters of the river Gambia. Renegades who fought with Bacon against slavery in Virginia escaped to the swampy commons of Roanoke. Pirate rovers of the deep hindered the advance of West African slaving and offered occasional refuge. The outcasts gathered at John Hughson's tavern in New York for laughter and hospitality. Black preachers searched the Atlantic for a place to build a new Jerusalem. Sheffield cutlers pocketed the "wasters." Colonel Edward Marcus Despard redistributed land in Belize. Elizabeth Campbell staged a little Jubilee in Jamaica. The mutineers escaped the regimen of the *Bounty* for the beautiful ecology and people of Tahiti.[73]

Most of these examples are concerned with escape from the encroaching world of capital or the defense of the old world, not the creation of a world beyond. The fundamental difference that capitalism has made to the human condition is that for the first time in history the goal of overcoming scarcity, and consequently that of overcoming inequality is now not inevitable (despite what Marx and Engels may have said in their more unguarded or exhortatory moments) but possible, which it was not for Spartacus, John Ball, or—more importantly in this context—Gerrard Winstanley or Gracchus Babeuf. How then should we regard these figures and the movements they led?

Edward Thompson famously wrote of his disagreement with the "orthodox" historiography of the early labor movement because of the way in which "the period is ransacked for forerunners-pioneers" and the orthodoxy "reads history in the light of subsequent preoccupations and not in fact as it occurred": "Only the successful (in the sense of those whose aspirations anticipated subsequent evolution) are remembered. The blind alleys, the lost causes, and the losers themselves are forgotten. . . . Our only criterion of judgment should not be whether or not a man's actions are justified in the light of subsequent evolution. After all, we are not at the end of social evolution ourselves."

These are important considerations, but Thompson's own concern for "the poor stockinger, the Luddite cropper, the 'obsolete' hand-loom weaver, the 'utopian' artisan, and even the deluded follower of Joanna Southcott" did not involve the claim that they posed an alternative to actual course of events, merely that we should reject "the enormous condescension of history" that ignored or marginalized their struggles.[74] Thompson was not involved in writing counterfactual history but with bringing to light that which had been hidden from history, a quite different project from asserting the type of position set out here by Bookchin:

> In general, Marx's views tend to render the historical process highly fatalistic, obliging us to assume that in all the great movements for freedom over the past four centuries, there was never an alternative to the ultimate triumph of capitalism—in my view an unacceptable case of historical teleology. We would be obliged to assume that the German peasants who revolted in the 1520s were "reactionaries" because they were trying to retain their archaic village life; that the Roundhead yeomanry who formed Cromwell's new model army historically "doomed" as a social stratum by industrial inventions and forms of production that had yet to be developed; that the radical Minutemen farmers had to disappear like their English yeoman cousins; and that the sans-culottes who established the first French republic were déclassé riffraff or mere "consumers," as more than one historian has called them—and so on, up to fairly recent times.[75]

Here Bookchin elides two different questions: our understanding of the historical process on the one hand and our attitude toward historical actors on the other. It has been the case that thinkers or movements whose goals could not be realized or whose impact was negligible in their own time can be—in Walter Benjamin's terms—"torn" from their historical context and given new and vibrant meaning in ours; the contemporary struggle for socialism may be precisely the terrain in which their significance is finally comprehensible, as is certainly the case for Winstanley and the Diggers. Daniel Bensaïd has captured the attitude that is actually expressed in Marx's work:

> No pre-set course of history, no predestination, justifies resignation to oppression. Non-current, untimely, "mal-contemporaneous," revolutions cannot be assimilated to the pre-established schemas of "supra-history" or "pallid, supra-temporal models." Their occurrence does not observe the dispositions of a universal History. They are engendered at ground level, out of suffering and humiliation. It is always right to rebel. If "correspondence" has the force of normality, should we embrace the cause of the victors in opposition to impatience construed as a provocation? Without hesitation or reservation, Marx was on the side of the beggars in the German peasants' war, the Levelers in the English Revolution, the Equals in the French Revolution, the communards set to be crushed by Versailles.[76]

It seems to me to be both mistaken and unnecessary to pose the question in either/or terms. In *Discovering the Scottish Revolution* I argue that we have to distinguish between two different sets of historical actors in the bourgeois revolutions. One set consists of our socialist *predecessors*—that is, those who looked toward collectivist solutions that were unachievable in their own time, like the Diggers in England or the Conspiracy of Equals in France. The other set consists of our bourgeois *equivalents*—that is, those who actually carried out the only revolutions possible at the time, which were, whatever their formal goals, to establish the dominance of capital.[77] Clearly, our attitude to these groups is very different. But since one aspect of bourgeois revolutions is to establish the most successful system of exploitation ever seen, it is scarcely surprising that the people who carried them through should, like Cromwell or Robespierre or Lincoln, leave a complex and contradictory legacy. Given the type of exploitative system that capitalism is, however, could we expect it to have come into being in any other way than, as Marx put it, "dripping from head to toe, from every pore, with blood and dirt"?[78]

⬚ ⬚ ⬚

At the end of his great trilogy on the Enlightenment, Jonathan Israel asks whether radical thought could respond to "today's fundamentalism, anti-secularism, Neo-Burkeanism, Postmodernism, and blatant unwillingness to clamp down on powerful vested interests," before concluding: "There are few grounds for optimism."[79] Given the history of the twentieth century, to go no further back, that conclusion is perfectly comprehensible and has at least one well-known Marxist precedent. "I'm a pessimist because of intelligence," wrote Gramsci in a prison letter to his brother, "but an optimist because of will."[80] But being conscious of the likelihood of failure does not remove from us the responsibility to continue wagering on the possibility of success. Did the bourgeois revolutions contribute any resources that can be used to enhance this possibility? Or, to put the question in another way: did our bourgeois equivalents do any more for the possibility of human liberation than simply provide the material basis for future socialist development? These questions return us to the starting point for our reflections, beside Hume's mausoleum in Old Calton Cemetery where we can consider for a second time the trajectory of the movement to which he made such a central contribution.

Enlightenment thought did not simply involve a wager on the future benefits of commercial society. As Daniel Gordon writes, it was already subject to massive internal tensions since it "was designed not merely to convince people to regard commercial society as the best regime, but also to dramatize the personal qualities of courage, patriotism, and refinement that one should cultivate in opposition to the very same regime." In this "double-edged mentality . . . we should see the dialectic as a process internal to the Enlightenment—a process in which a certain degree of historical optimism immediately produced doubts about the completeness of the society desired."[81] From these doubts came the radicalized Enlightenment at the heart of Marxism.[82] In the *Manifesto of the Communist Party* Marx and Engels summarized the role of the Enlightenment in the bourgeois revolution: "When Christian ideas succumbed in the eighteenth century to rationalist ideas, feudal society fought its death battle with the then revolutionary bourgeoisie." Capitalism needed to free the power of rational thought, but reason is not the possession of single class, and once it became apparent that human beings had the power to transform their world along capitalist lines, the question inevitably arose of a further transformation. "The weapons with which the bourgeoisie felled feudalism to the ground are now turned against the bourgeoisie itself."[83] The weapons of which Marx and Engels write included the universalism of Enlightenment thought at its best.

The complexities of the doctrine of universality are best expressed in the American Declaration of Independence. Along with the French Declaration of Rights of Man and Citizen, this is one of the most famous political expressions of Enlightenment thought. In the immortal words of the second paragraph: "We hold these truths to be self-evident, that all men are created equal, that they are endowed by their Creator with certain unalienable Rights, that among these are Life, Liberty and the pursuit of Happiness."[84] Anyone wanting to raise an ironic postmodern chuckle at the supposedly fraudulent claims of Enlightenment universalism need only quote the opening passage and then point out everyone it excludes: all women, Native Americans, slaves, so on. From this, some people conclude that the oppression is endemic to the Enlightenment itself. Michael Bérubé points out, "Poststructuralism tends to argue that the emancipatory narratives of the Enlightenment are in fact predicated on—and compromised by—their historical and social origins in eighteenth century racism and sexism" and "the social violence of the last two centuries of American society is not something to be corrected by a return to the Enlightenment rhetoric of rights but is, rather, a fulfillment of the symbolic violence constitutive of the Enlightenment itself."[85]

Is it true that universality is 'tainted' in this way? In fact, as Terry Eagleton remarks, it is "one of the greatest emancipatory ideas in world history . . . not least because middle-class society could now be challenged by those it suppressed, *according to its own logic*, caught out in a performative contradiction between what it said and what it did."[86] This is certainly the attitude taken by one famous former black slave whose work I have already quoted: Frederick Douglass. In a speech given during the crisis decade before the Civil War Douglass began by pointing out the "performative contradiction":

> What, to the American slave, is your 4th of July? I answer; a day that reveals to him, more than all other days of the year, the gross injustice to which he is the constant victim. To him, your celebration is a sham; your boasted liberty, an unholy license; your national greatness, swelling vanity; your sounds of rejoicing are empty and heartless, brass fronted impudence; your shouts of liberty and equality, hollow mockery;

prayers and hymns, your sermons and thanksgivings, with all your parade and solemnity, are, to Him, mere bombast, fraud, deception, impiety, and hypocrisy—a thin veil to cover up crimes which would disgrace a nation of savages. There is not a nation on earth guilty of practices more shocking and bloody than are the people of the United States, at this very hour. . . . You invite to your shores fugitives of oppression abroad, honor them with banquets, greet them with ovations, cheer them, toast them, salute them, and pour out your money to them like water; but fugitives from your own land you advertise, hunt, arrest, shoot, and kill.

But later in the same speech Douglass returned to the Declaration of Independence in a way that suggested that different meanings could be found there: "In that instrument I hold that there is neither warrant, license, nor sanction of the hateful thing; but interpreted as it ought to be interpreted, the Constitution is a glorious liberty document. . . . While drawing encouragement from 'the Declaration of Independence,' the great principles it contains, and the genius of American Institutions, my spirit is also cheered by the obvious tendencies of the age."[87] In another speech from the same period Douglass discussed the Constitution in the same connection: "Its language is 'we the people,' not we the white people, not even we the citizens, not we the privileged class, not we the high, not we the low, but we the people; not we the horses, sheep, and swine, and wheel-barrows, but we the people, we the human inhabitants; and, if Negroes are people, they are included in the benefits for which the Constitution of America was ordained and established."[88] During the bourgeois revolutions there were occasions when those on the revolutionary side were forced to register their own failure to uphold the values associated with their cause and acted accordingly. Susan Buck-Morss gives examples from the Haitian Revolution of how such an awareness could lead to "clarity in action": "The French soldiers sent by Napoleon to the colony who, upon hearing these former slaves singing the 'Marseillaise,' wondered aloud if they were not on the wrong side; the Polish regiment under Leclerc's command who disobeyed orders and refused to drown six hundred captured Saint-Dominguans."[89]

William Morris's novel *A Dream of John Ball* is set during the English Peasants Revolt of 1381, the first great breach in the feudal order in that country. To paraphrase the most famous line, the thing that at least some of the bourgeoisie fought for turned out to be not what they meant, and other people have since had to fight for what they meant under another name.[90] But what we fight for is not to accomplish outstanding "tasks of the bourgeois revolution" in the sense I have rejected throughout this book. We fight rather for those universal principles of freedom and justice that the bourgeois revolutions brought onto the historical agenda but, for all their epochal significance, were unable to achieve. We should therefore remember the bourgeois revolutionaries in the hour of their greatness, which often struck in the most unexpected places. During the 1790s William Ogilvie declared, in that combination of the Promethean and the prosaic that characterizes the "practical" improvers of the Scottish Enlightenment: "There is no natural obstacle to prevent the most barren ground from being brought by culture to the same degree of fertility with the kitchen garden of a villa, or the suburbs of a great town."[91] Behind these reflections on cultivation lies an attitude that rejects all forms of determinism, that affirms the unlimited possibilities for human beings to transform their world—possibilities that their wretched bourgeois descendants have long since abandoned—and are best summarized in these great words by Adam Ferguson, from *An Essay on the History of Civil Society*: "If we are asked therefore, where the state of nature is to be found? We may answer, it is here; and it matters not whether we are understood to speak in the island of Great Britain, at the Cape of Good Hope, or the Straits of Magellan. While this active being is in the train of employing his talents, and of operating on the subjects around him, all situations are equally natural."[92]

NOTES

A NOTE ON THE REPRODUCTIONS

1. Hobsbawm, *The Age of Revolution*, 268. This edition of Hobsbawm's book features a reproduction of the entire painting on the front cover.
2. There were attempts to publicize the painting by inventing a real model for Liberty, in the person of a laundress, Anne-Charlotte D., who finding the body of her brother Antoine riddled with ten bullets, supposedly promised to kill as many Swiss Guards but was herself shot on the barricades as she was about to claim her tenth victim. See Pointon, *Naked Authority*, 64. It is possible that the model was actually based on the cover illustration from the 1725 Dutch edition of Charles Johnson's *General History of the Pyrates*, which depicts the cutlass-wielding female pirates Anne Bonny and Mary Read beneath the Jolly Roger. See Rediker, *Villains of All Nations*, 121–26.
3. Timothy J. Clark, *The Absolute Bourgeois*, 16–20; Paul Wood, "The Avant-Garde from the July Monarchy to the Second Empire," 36–39.
4. Fraser, *Napoleon's Cursed War*, 470–75; Gwyn A. Williams, *Goya and the Impossible Revolution*, 141–63.
5. See the classic discussions in Greenberg, "Avant-Garde and Kitsch," 6–11 and "Towards a Newer Laocoön," 27–30. See also the commentary in Timothy J. Clark, "Clement Greenberg's Theory of Art," 52–55.
6. Crow, "The Tensions of Enlightenment," 78–80, 83, 94–96.

PREFACE TO THE ABRIDGED 2017 EDITION

1. Davidson, *Discovering the Scottish Revolution*, 9–15, 73–76, 170, 182, 272–79, 290–94.
2. Holstun, *Ehud's Dagger*, 9–140; Ste. Croix, *The Class Struggle in the Ancient Greek World*, 3–111.
3. Davidson, "How Revolutionary Were the Bourgeois Revolutions?"; Davidson, "How Revolutionary Were the Bourgeois Revolutions? Continued." A rather more abbreviated version of the lecture appeared as "Bourgeois Revolution: On the Road to Salvation for All Mankind."
4. I have allowed my concluding comments on the Middle East and North African revolutions—whose outcome was still uncertain in 2012—to stand. Since the Syrian catastrophe continues to unfold while this preface is being written, it seems particularly important to remember that the revolution in that country was second only to the

Egyptian one in its levels of militancy and mass involvement. Subsequent attempts by Western leftist cheerleaders for Bashar al Assad and Vladimir Putin to portray it as having been inspired by Islamism from the start are a disgraceful example of the type of historical rewriting discussed in the original preface to the 2012 edition below, At the very least the left should be principled enough to oppose *all* imperialist interventions in Syria, not *only* those originating in the West. The main enemy is certainly at home, but it is not the only enemy, and consequently the slogan "neither Washington nor Moscow" retains all its relevance, even in post–Cold War conditions where Russia no longer even pretends to have surpassed capitalism.

5.   See "Revolutions between Theory and History: A Response to Alex Callinicos and Donny Gluckstein," in *We Cannot Escape History: States and Revolutions* (Chicago: Haymarket Books, 2015).

Preface to the 2012 Edition

1.   Eagleton, *Why Marx Was Right*, 182.
2.   Acemoglu and Robinson, "Why Did the West Extend the Franchise?," 1182–86; Therborn, "The Rule of Capital and the Rise of Democracy," 4, 17.
3.   Appleby, *The Relentless Revolution*, 433–34.
4.   Gordon S. Wood, "No Thanks for the Memories."
5.   Lepore, *The Whites of Their Eyes*, 14.
6.   Benjamin, "On the Concept of History," 391.
7.   Orwell, *Nineteen Eighty-Four*, 199.
8.   Acemoglu and Robinson, *Why Nations Fail*, 362. For their more detailed discussion of the Glorious Revolution and its consequences, see ibid., 191–212.
9.   Ibid., 457–58.
10.   Norman Stone, "Owning Up to a Revolution."
11.   Denyenko, "Middle Class Backs Orange Revolution."
12.   Kurlantzick, "The Bourgeois Revolution."
13.   Hitchens, "The Old Man," 52.
14.   Hitchens, "A Liberating Experience," 469.
15.   Hitchens, *Regime Change*, 30.
16.   Ibid., 48.
17.   Ibid., 56.
18.   Ibid., 101.
19.   Douglass, "West India Emancipation," 428, 436, 437.

1. Between Two Social Revolutions

1.   Hayek, "History and Politics," 23–24.
2.   Zagorin, *Rebels and Rulers*, vol. 1, 16.
3.   Lakatos, "Falsification and the Methodology of Scientific Research Programmes," 117–18.
4.   Alasdair MacIntyre, "Notes from the Moral Wilderness," 54.
5.   Grossman, "The Evolutionist Revolt against Classical Economics: II," 517.
6.   Marx, *Grundrisse*, 100–102.
7.   Marx and Engels, "The Manifesto of the Communist Party," 67.
8.   Alasdair MacIntyre, "Breaking the Chains of Reason," 151. MacIntyre had evidently read the *Grundrisse* by the mid-1960s, before it had been translated into English. See, for example, "Marxist Mask and Romantic Face," 322–23.
9.   Losurdo, *Liberalism*, 321.

10.   Marx, "Preface to the First Edition," in *Capital*, vol. 1, 90.

11.   Marx and Engels, "The Manifesto of the Communist Party," 69, note 15.

12.   Engels, "Preface to the Third German Edition of *The Eighteenth Brumaire*," 302–3.

13.   Hobsbawm, *The Age of Revolution*, 62.

14.   Cliff, "The Class Nature of the People's Democracies," 65–66.

15.   Eley, "The English Model and the German Road," 85.

16.   Poulantzas, *Political Power and Social Classes*, 183.

17.   Perry Anderson, "The Notion of a Bourgeois Revolution," 113.

18.   Perry Anderson, "Foreword," 6.

19.   Abbott, "On the Concept of Turning Point," 250.

20.   Pinkus, *1688*, 32.

21.   Lukács, "Legality and Illegality," 258.

22.   Skocpol, *States and Social Revolutions*, 4–5.

23.   Ibid., 141.

24.   Draper, *Karl Marx's Theory of Revolution*, vol. 2, 19–20.

25.   Ibid., 19.

26.   Choonara, "The Relevance of Permanent Revolution," 179–80.

27.   Eley, "The British Model and the German Road," 82–83. See also Hobsbawm, "Revolution," 10.

28.   Neocleous, *Administering Civil Society*, 94.

29.   Edward P. Thompson, *The Making of the English Working Class*, 889 and 887–915 more generally.

30.   Perry Anderson, "Geoffrey de Ste Croix and the Ancient World," 17. See also Perry Anderson, *Arguments within English Marxism*, 55–56.

31.   Callinicos, *Making History*, 229.

32.   I agree with Pinkus that the two episodes are inseparable: "Because the mid-seventeenth century crisis and the Revolution of 1688–89 were part of the same process, they need to be integrated into a single story." *1688*, 486. But taken seriously, this would mean treating 1637 or 1640 as the beginning of "the first modern revolution," rather than, as he insists, 1688.

33.   Webber, "Rebellion to Reform in Bolivia, Part II," 58; Webber, *From Rebellion to Reform in Bolivia*, 46.

34.   Ossowski, *Class Structure in the Social Consciousness*, 84.

35.   Katz, *From Feudalism to Capitalism*, 181.

36.   Gouldner, *The Future of Intellectuals and the Rise of the New Class*, 93.

37.   Giddens, *The Class Structure of the Advanced Societies*, 91–92.

38.   Althusser, *Machiavelli and Us*, 50.

39.   Godelier, "The Concept of the 'Asiatic Mode of Production and Marxist Models of Social Evolution'," 241.

40.   Duby, *The Three Orders*, 147–66.

41.   Bois, *The Transformation of the Year One Thousand*, 152, 171. Although the term "feudal revolution" is not used, the same concept and chronology can also be found in Dockes, *Medieval Slavery and Liberation*, 105–10 and Poly and Bournazel, *The Feudal Transformation*, 2–3, 118–40, 351–57. Duby was later to reject both the term and the notion. See *France in The Middle Ages*.

42.   Bonnassie, "The Survival and Extinction of the Slave System in the Early Medieval West," 43 and 38–46 more generally.

43.   Wickham, *Framing the Early Middle Ages*, 207; Harman, "Change at the First Millennium," 94–95.

44.   Marx and Engels, *The German Ideology*, 48–49.

45.   Lukács, "Critical Observations on Rosa Luxemburg's 'Critique of the Russian Revolution'," 283.

46.   Ibid., 281.

47.   Bukharin, "The Economics of the Transition Period," 125–28.
48.   See, for example, Albert, *Parecon*; Callinicos, *An Anti-Capitalist Manifesto*, chapter 3; and Pat Devine, *Democracy and Economic Planning*.
49.   Peter Green, "The First Sicilian Slave War," 24.
50.   Dockes, *Medieval Slavery and Liberation*, 17, 219. For an attempt to imagine how a victory by the Spartacus revolt might have led to the emergence of capitalism by c. 500 AD, see MacLeod, *The Restoration Game*, 188–93, an example of the type of speculation which is entirely appropriate for science fiction, but not for historiography,
51.   Finley, *Ancient Slavery and Modern Ideology*, 132–49; Ste. Croix, *The Class Struggle in the Ancient Greek World*, 226–59, chapter 8; Wickham, "The Other Transition," 12–30.
52.   Wickham, *Framing the Middle Ages*, 529–33.
53.   Ibid., 441.
54.   Ibid, 350–51.
55.   Ibid., 578–88.
56.   Gramsci, "The Study of Philosophy," 333–34, Q11§12.
57.   Lukács, "Class Consciousness," 51.
58.   Lukács, *Lenin*, 56.
59.   Rees, *The Algebra of Revolution*, 260, note 134.
60.   Lenin, "The Debate on Self-Determination Summed-Up," 355.
61.   Lenin, "What Is to Be Done?," 423 and 412–17, 421–36 more generally.
62.   Trotsky, "What Next?," 134.
63.   Marx, *The Poverty of Philosophy*, 211. The first use of the distinction between class "in itself" and class "for itself" seems to be in Bukharin, *Historical Materialism*, 292–93.
64.   Draper, "The Two Souls of Socialism," 3.
65.   Marx and Engels, *The German Ideology*, 52–53.
66.   In this context the terms "era" and "epoch" (as used, for example, by Webber) can be treated as interchangeable.

2. PRECONDITIONS FOR AN ERA OF BOURGEOIS REVOLUTION

1.   Lochhead, *The Bourgeois Revolutions*, 5.
2.   Lawrence Stone, "The Causes of the English Revolution," 57–58.
3.   Ibid., 58–117.
4.   Marx, "Preface to *A Contribution to the Critique of Political Economy*," 425–26.
5.   For an explanation that usefully synthesizes the current state of our knowledge about the Maya, see Diamond, *Collapse*, 157–77.
6.   Marx, "Preface to *A Contribution to the Critique of Political Economy*," 426.
7.   Ellen Meiksins Wood, *The Origin of Capitalism*, 118.
8.   Lukács, "The Changing Function of Historical Materialism," 242–43.
9.   I therefore disagree with Daniel Bensaïd when he rejects any comparison between bourgeois and proletarian revolutions, since this judgment is only sustainable if the Dutch or English revolutions are taken as paradigmatic of the former. See *Marx for Our Times*, 29–31.
10.   Marx, "Preface to *A Contribution to the Critique of Political Economy*," 426.
11.   Gramsci, "The Modern Prince," 178, Q13§17.
12.   Bertram, "International Competition in Historical Materialism," 122.
13.   Marx and Engels, "The Manifesto of the Communist Party," 68.
14.   Wickham, "Productive Forces and the Economic Logic of the Feudal Mode of Production," 20.
15.   Marx, "Another British Revelation," 516. This aphorism was actually made of Britain, during its disastrous performance in the Crimean War, but the point is of wider application.

16. Marx, "Preface to *A Contribution to the Critique of Political Economy*," 426.
17. Shanin, *Russia*, vol. 1, 312.
18. Lenin, "The Collapse of the Second International," 213–14.
19. Ste. Croix, *The Class Struggle in the Ancient Greek World*, 52.
20. Banaji, "Modes of Production in a Materialsit Conception of History," 93.
21. Hilton, "Feudalism in Europe," 2; Kula, *An Economic Theory of the Feudal System*, 9.
22. Duby, *The Early Growth of the European Economy*, 192–99; Kitsikopoulos, "Technological Change in Medieval England," 406–10.
23. Wickham, "Productive Forces and Economic Logic of the Feudal Mode of Production," 17.
24. Bois, *The Crisis of Feudalism*, 4056.
25. Perry Anderson, *Passages from Antiquity to Feudalism*, 197–209, 246–64; Bois, *The Crisis of Feudalism*, 263–99; Hilton, "Was There a General Crisis of Feudalism?"
26. Epstein, "The Late Medieval Crisis as an 'Integration' Crisis," 34.
27. Braudel, *Capitalism and Civilization*, vol. 2, 372.
28. Marx, *Capital*, vol. 3, 452–54.
29. Callinicos, "Bourgeois Revolutions and Historical Materialism," 134.
30. Adam Smith, *The Wealth of Nations*, vol. 1, Book I, 138–43; Book III, 420–45.
31. Postan, *The Medieval Economy and Society*, 239.
32. See, for example, Katz, *From Feudalism to Capitalism*, 88.
33. Mielants, *The Origins of Capitalism and the "Rise of the West"*, 80–81.
34. Brenner, "Agrarian Class Structure and Economic Development in Pre-Industrial Europe," 38–40; Samuel K. Cohn, *Lust for Liberty*, 42–52, 109–11; Hilton, *Bond Men Made Free*, 119–34, 186–207; Merrington, "Town and Country in the Transition to Capitalism," 177–78, 180–2, 191–92; Mollat and Wolff, *The Popular Revolutions of the Middle Ages*, 297.
35. Trotsky, "Three Conceptions of the Russian Revolution," 60.
36. Perry Anderson, *Lineages of the Absolutist State*, 301–2; Steinberg, *Why Switzerland?*, 17–26.
37. Deutsch and Weilenmann, "The Swiss City Canton," 406.
38. Engels, "[On the Decline of Feudalism the Emergence of National States]," 563. See also Luxemburg, "The National Question and Autonomy," 118–20 and the passages from Engels and Kautsky quoted there.
39. Cliff, "The Nature of Stalinist Russia," 78.
40. Braudel, *Capitalism and Civilization*, , vol. 3, 63.
41. Carling, "Analytic Marxism and Historical Materialism," 52–54. See also Carling, *Social Division*, 62–65.
42. Lukács, "Reification and the Consciousness of the Proletariat," 162–63. See also Lukács's "The Marxism of Rosa Luxemburg," 27–29.
43. One of the reasons I find Trotsky's notion of "differentiated unity" less compelling than that of "mediated totality" is because it refers solely to our method of analyzing the world rather than to the world itself. The other is that the idea of mediation implies movement, the process of becoming, and is consequently more dialectical. See Trotsky, "The Notebooks in Translation," 97.
44. Ollman, "Marxism and Political Science," 139 and 138–44 more generally.
45. Harvey, "On Countering the Marxian Myth—Chicago-Style," 75, 78.
46. Sayer, *Marx's Method*, 101.
47. I owe the notion of "entailment" to Colin Barker.
48. Marx, "Preface to *A Contribution to the Critique of Political Economy*," 425; Marx, *Grundrisse*, 108.
49. Benjamin, "Convolute K," 392.
50. Collier, *Marx*, 46.
51. Engels to Bloch, September 21, 1890.
52. Marx, *Capital*, vol. 1, 1064.

53.   Davidson, *Discovering the Scottish Revolution*, 31–34, 207–9.

54.   Commission of the C.C. of the C.P.S.U. (B.). *History of the Communist Party of the Soviet Union (Bolsheviks)*, 122.

55.   Ellen Meiksins Wood, "Marxism and the Course of History," 101–2.

56.   Rigby, *Marxism and History*, 131.

57.   Cardan, *History and Revolution*, 6; Castoriadis, "Marxism and Revolutionary Theory," 18–19. "Cardan" was the pseudonym under which Castoriadis worked as an activist in the French post-Trotskyist group Socialism or Barbarism.

58.   James D. Young, *The Rousing of the Scottish Working Class*, 46.

59.   Ferraro, *Freedom and Determination in History According to Marx and Engels*, 118, 190.

60.   Plekhanov, "The Development of the Monist View of History," 697.

61.   See, for example, Bukharin, "The Economics of the Transition Period," 121 or Lenin, *The Development of Capitalism in Russia*, 596.

62.   Eric Olin Wright, "Gidden's Critique of Marx," 27–28. See also Wright, Levine, and Sober, *Reconstructing Marxism*, 80–83.

63.   Torrance, "Reproduction and Development," 398.

64.   Alasdair MacIntyre, "Notes from the Moral Wilderness," 55.

65.   Diamond, *Guns, Germs and Steel*, 93–156, 264–92. The emergence of classes is brought out more clearly in an earlier work by the same author, *The Rise and Fall of the Third Chimpanzee*, 169–71. As two reviewers have noted, although Diamond "seems blithely unaware" of the fact, he has nevertheless made "a major contribution to historical materialist scholarship," See Carling and Nolan, "Historical Materialism, Natural Selection," 216, 259.

66.   Brenner, "The Social Basis of Economic Development," 45.

67.   [Wedderburn], *The Complaynt of Scotland*, 123. I have here translated the Middle Scots in which Wedderburn wrote into modern English.

68.   Musgrave, *The Early Modern European Economy*, 51.

69.   Whittle, *The Development of Agrarian Capitalism*, 310.

70.   Byres, *Capitalism from Above and Capitalism from Below*, 28, 66–68; Manning, "The English Revolution and the Transition from Feudalism to Capitalism," 81–83; McNally, *Political Economy and the Rise of Capitalism*, 5–7; Mooers, *The Making of Bourgeois Europe*, 36–37.

71.   Byres, "Differentiation of the Peasantry under Feudalism and the Transition to Capitalism," 55, 57, 64.

72.   Whittle, *The Development of Agrarian Capitalism*, 309–10.

73.   Hilton, *Bond Men Made Free*, 169.

74.   Hilton, "Peasant Movements in England before 1381," 61.

75.   Hoyle, "Tenure and the Land Market in Early Modern England," 5.

76.   Torras, "Class Struggle in Catalonia," 261.

77.   Outhwaite, "Progress and Backwardness in English Agriculture," 9, 12.

78.   Woodward, "Wage Rates and Living Standards in Pre-Industrial England," 178–79.

79.   Croot and Parker, "Agrarian Class Structure and the Development of Capitalism," 88.

80.   Wordie, "The Chronology of English Enclosure," 484.

81.   Ibid., 494–95, 502.

82.   Duplessis, *Transitions to Capitalism in Early Modern Europe*, 67. See also McNally, *Political Economy and the Rise of Capitalism*, 6.

83.   Kitsikopoulos, "Technological Change in Medieval England," 443.

84.   Overton, *Agricultural Revolution in England*, 205.

85.   Whittle, *The Development of Agrarian Capitalism*, 308.

86.   Hipkin, "Property, Economic Interest and the Configuration of Rural Conflict in Sixteenth and Seventeenth-Century England," 71, 77.

87.   Teschke, "Bourgeois Revolution, State Formation and the Absence of the International," 19.

88. Hoffman, *Growth in a Traditional Society*, 201.

89. Ibid., 23.

90. Braudel, *Capitalism and Civilization*, vol. 2, 282–83.

91. Heller, *Labor, Science and Technology in France*, 28–36.

92. Kriedte, *Peasants, Landlords and Merchant Capitalists*, 107–8, 111.

93. David Parker, *Class and State in Ancien Regime France*, 53, 54, 237, 272. On the last point see also Heller, *Labor, Science and Technology in France*, 36: "Historically, expropriation and dependence on wages are quite distinct phases. The loss of land through expropriation is not automatically followed by the offer or the acceptance of wage employment."

94. Hoyle, "Tenure and the Land Market in Early Modern England," 18.

95. Marx, *Grundrisse*, 540.

96. Chibber, "What Is Living and What is Dead in the Marxist Theory of History," 76, 77 and 73–78 more generally. Christopher Bertram also invokes "emulation or conquest" as the means of diffusion. See "International Competition in Historical Materialism," 120.

97. Bukharin, "The Economics of the Transition Period," 71.

98. Schoenberger, "The Origins of the Market Economy," 689, 690.

99. Spufford, *Power and Profit*, 260, 265 and 258–66 more generally.

100. Duffy, *The Military Experience in the Age of Reason*, 231.

101. Coleman, *Industry in Tudor and Stuart England*, 35.

102. Marx, *Capital*, vol. 1, 511.

103. Ogilvie, "Social Institutions and Proto-Industrialization," 35.

104. Geoffrey Parker, *The Military Revolution*, 24, 148, 151.

105. Heller, *The Bourgeois Revolution in France*, 96, 103, 119, 129.

106. Cipolla, "Guns and Sails," 52 and 52–55 more generally.

107. Treblicock, *The Industrialization of the Continental Powers*, 208.

108. Gatrell, *Government, Industry and Rearmament in Russia*, 15.

109. Unger, *The Ship in the Medieval Economy*, 275.

110. Geoffrey Parker, *The Military Revolution*, 102–3.

111. Rediker, *Between the Devil and the Deep Blue Sea*, 78, 114.

112. Lenman, *Britain's Colonial Wars*, 167.

113. Adam Smith, *The Wealth of Nations*, vol. 2, Book IV, 230–31.

114. Blaut, *The Colonizer's View of the World*, 152–53, 206.

115. Blackburn, *The Making of New World Slavery*, 527–28.

116. Braudel, *The Mediterranean and the Mediterranean World in the Age of Phillip II*, vol. 2, 739–43.

117. Vilar, "The Age of Don Quixote," 65.

118. Banaji, "Modes of Production in a Materialist Conception of History," 93.

119. Newitt, "Plunder and the Rewards of Office in the Portuguese Empire," 27 and 24–27 more generally.

120. Davis, *Late Victorian Holocausts*, 296.

121. Dobb, *Studies in the Development of Capitalism*, 218; Sweezy, "A Critique," 39–40.

122. Marx, *Capital*, vol. 1, 450.

123. Ibid., 556.

124. Duplessis, *Transitions to Capitalism in Early Modern Europe*, 241; Hobsbawm, "The Crisis of the Seventeenth Century," 50–53; Kriedte, *Peasants, Landlords and Merchant Capitalists*, 123–27.

125. Stern, *Peru's Indian Peoples and the Challenge of Spanish Conquest*, 85–86.

126. Blackburn, *The Making of New World Slavery*, 332–35.

127. C. L. R. James, *The Black Jacobins*, 85–86.

128. Blackburn, *The Making of New World Slavery*, 300–301.

129. Bois, *The Crisis of Feudalism*, 389.

130. Coveney, "An Early Modern European Crisis?," 22.

131.   Goldstone, "East and West in the Seventeenth Century," 133.
132.   Brenner and Isett, "England's Divergence from China's Yangzi Delta," 613.
133.   Mielants, *The Origins of Capitalism and "the Rise of the West"*, 159.
134.   Epstein, "Late Medieval Crisis as an 'Integration' Crisis," 45.
135.   The following discussion of absolutism derives, in broad outline, from Perry Anderson, *Lineages of the Absolutist State*, 16–24 [taking into account the critical comments in Miliband, "Political Power and Historical Materialism," 56–62] and Brenner, "The Agrarian Roots of European Capitalism," 288–90. Anderson refers to Western Europe in general and Brenner to France in particular. The similarity of their positions is not in this case because Anderson has taken France as a normative model for developments elsewhere but because Brenner fails to see the extent to which the development of absolutism in France was simply the most advanced case of a general process. As we shall see below, this leads him to treat France as if it was dominated by an "absolute" mode of production.
136.   Whittle, *The Development of Agrarian Capitalism*, 311
137.   Bois, *The Crisis of Feudalism*, 407.
138.   Brenner, "Agrarian Class Structure and Economic Development in Pre-Industrial Europe," 55.
139.   Ellen Meiksins Wood, *The Pristine Culture of Capitalism*, 159.
140.   Ellen Meiksins Wood, *The Origin of Capitalism*, 184.
141.   Teschke, *The Myth of 1648*, 191.
142.   Marx, *Grundrisse*, 443.
143.   Amin, *Unequal Development*, 15–16.
144.   Wickham, "The Uniqueness of the East," 48–50.
145.   Ibid., 72.
146.   Wolf, *Europe and the Peoples without History*, 247. See also Engels to Danielson, June 10, 1890.
147.   Marx, *Capital*, vol. 3, 925–27.
148.   Berktay, "The Feudalism Debate," 301–10; Haldon, "The Feudalism Debate Once More," 9–15.
149.   Haldon, *The State and the Tributary Mode of Production*, 67, 84 and 63–69, 75–109 more generally. See also Wolf, *Europe and the Peoples without History*, 79–88. Wickham has now accepted this, writing that "it now seems to me that both [feudalism and the tributary mode] are sub-types of the same mode of production, in that both are based on agrarian surplus extracted, by force if necessary, from the peasant majority." See *Framing the Early Middle Ages*, 60.
150.   Perry Anderson, *Lineages of the Absolutist State*, 404.
151.   Hirst, "The Uniqueness of the West," 110 and 106–19 more generally. See also Wickham, "The Uniqueness of the East," 47.
152.   Wickham, "Uniqueness of the East," 75 ["Additional note to Chapter 2" of *Land and Power*].
153.   Banaji, "Introduction: Themes in Historical Materialism," 24, 25, and 23–40 more generally. See also "Modes of Production: A Synthesis," 354–56.
154.   Abu-Lughod, *Before European Hegemony*, 367.
155.   Ibid., 18–19, 359–66.
156.   Haldon, *The State and the Tributary Mode of Production*, 257, 260.
157.   Mielants, *The Origins of Capitalism*, 80.
158.   Wickham, *Framing the Early Middle Ages*, 145.
159.   Callinicos, *Theories and Narratives*, 171–76. This argument does not involve the—clearly unsustainable—claim that these conditions are in themselves sufficient to produce capitalism: the European feudal societies in which the central state was weakest—Scotland in the West and Poland in the East—experienced even less capitalist development than China.

160. Crone, *Pre-industrial Societies*, 156.
161. Ogilvie, "Social Institutions and Proto-Industrialization," 25.
162. Kermode, *Medieval Merchants*, 203.
163. Christopher Hill, *The World Turned Upside Down*, 46.
164. Bois, "Against the Neo-Malthusian Orthodoxy," 114.
165. Hobson, *The Eastern Origins of Western Civilization*, 313.
166. Wickham, "Historical Materialism, Historical Sociology," 73–74.
167. Pomeranz, *The Great Divergence*, 70.
168. Elvin, *The Pattern of Chinese History*, 69.
169. John A. Hall, "States and Societies," 37–38.
170. Arrighi, *Adam Smith in Beijing*, 314; Callinicos, *Imperialism and Global Political Economy*, 120–23.
171. Gernet, *A History of Chinese Civilization*, 475.
172. Needham, *The Shorter Science and Civilization in China*, vol. 1, 253–254.
173. Adam Smith, *The Wealth of Nations*, Book I, 80, 81.
174. Adam Ferguson, *An Essay on the History of Civil Society*, 111.
175. Marx, "Chinese Affairs," 216. This article is one of the very few occasions where Marx actually uses the base (or "substructure") and superstructure metaphor outside of the 1859 "Preface."
176. Barkey and Batzell, "Comparisons across Empires," 230–33.
177. Rodinson, *Islam and Capitalism*, 11–19.
178. Ashtor, *A Social and Economic History of the Near East in the Middle Ages*, 180.
179. Ibid., 247.
180. Mielants, *The Origins of Capitalism*, 143.
181. Hoodbhoy, *Islam and Science*, 132.
182. Khaldun, *The Muqaddimah*, 137, 142–42.
183. Habib, "Potentialities of Capitalist Development in the Economy of Mughal India," 231.
184. Bayly, *Indian Society and the Making of the British Empire*, 47.
185. Ibid., 48.
186. Chandra, "Some Aspects of the Growth of a Money Economy in India during the Seventeenth Century," 244, 246.
187. Darwin, *After Tamerlane*, 224.
188. Davis, *Late Victorian Holocausts*, 285, 287 and 280–88 more generally. It is possible to exaggerate the degree to which these precolonial states or communities other than the Chinese could withstand vast climatic changes. Michael Watts, a friendly critic of Davis, has noted that, although the Qing state was capable of protecting the Chinese population from starvation, this was not necessarily true of his other main examples: "Faced with the sorts of shortfall induced by severe El Niño events—half to three-quarters of the harvest wiped out over wide areas, near-total decimation of livestock—it seems implausible that either the Mughal state or the lineaments of a moral economy in the [Brazilian] *sertao* could have held off disaster." See "Black Acts," 132.
189. Darwin, *After Tamerlane*, 275–76.
190. Kiernan, *State and Society in Europe*, 270.
191. Perry Anderson, *Lineages of the Absolutist State*, 221–35; Barkey and Batzell, "Comparisons across Empires," 229–30.
192. Amin, *Class and Nation Historically and in the Current Crisis*, 88.
193. Christopher Hill, "The Bourgeois Revolution in Soviet Scholarship," 11–12.
194. Norman Cohn, *The Pursuit of the Millennium*, 61–70; Runciman, *A History of the Crusades*, vol. 1, 134–41.
195. Samuel K. Cohn, *Lust for Liberty*, 102–3, 214–17.
196. Marx and Engels, "The Manifesto of the Communist Party," 71.
197. Chesneaux, *Peasant Revolts in China*, 21.

198. Trotsky, "Three Conceptions of the Russian Revolution," 60.

199. Wolf, *Peasant Wars of the Twentieth Century*, 37.

200. Gilly, *The Mexican Revolution*, 147 and 147–81 more generally.

201. For Engels's acknowledgement of Haxthausen's supposed discovery of the *mir*, see Engels to Danielson, June 10, 1890.

202. Dennison and Carus, "The Invention of the Russian Rural Commune," 580.

203. Maza, "Luxury, Morality, and Social Change," 212.

204. Bookchin, *The Third Revolution*, vol. 1, 13.

205. Indeed, even in the texts where Marx is most insistent on the virtues of the English and French bourgeoisies compared to the German, he does not suggest that they consciously prepared for their revolutions. Marx is often represented as holding a more positive view of the bourgeoisie than he in fact did through the way in which his words are rendered in translation. A famous passage from 1848 is now usually given as: "In both revolutions, the bourgeoisie was the class which was *genuinely* to be found at the head the movement." The original German reads: "In beiden Revolutionen war die Bourgeoisie die Klasse, die sich *wirklich* an der Spitze der Bewegung befand." This can be translated as: "In both revolutions the bourgeoisie was the class which *effectively* found itself located at the head [or forefront] of the movement." The former implies that the bourgeoisie consciously sought this position; the latter that it was at least partly unintended. Compare Marx, "The Bourgeoisie and the Counter-Revolution," in *The Revolutions of 1848*, 192 and "Die Bourgeoisie und die Kontrerevolution," 107. I owe this point to Kevin Wooten.

206. Corcoran, "The Bourgeoisie and Other Villains," 479.

207. Perry Anderson, "Socialism and Pseudo-Empiricism," 8.

208. Ellen Meiksins Wood, *The Origin of Capitalism*, 14.

209. Corcoran, "The Bourgeoisie and Other Villains," 479.

210. Maza, "Luxury, Morality, and Social Change," 210–11.

211. Bell, "Class Consciousness, and the Fall of the Bourgeois Revolution," 333.

212. Maza, "Luxury, Morality, and Social Change," 201–2.

213. Ellen Meiksins Wood, *The Origin of Capitalism*, 14.

214. Neal Wood, *John Locke and Agrarian Capitalism*, 20.

215. Teschke, "Bourgeois Revolution, State Formation and the Absence of the International," 11, 12.

216. Greenfeld, *The Spirit of Capitalism*, 147–48.

217. Fox Genovese and Genovese, "On the Social History of the French Revolution," 225–26.

218. Edward P. Thompson, "The Patricians and the Plebs," 83–84.

219. Draper, *Karl Marx's Theory of Revolution*, vol. 2, 169.

220. Ibid., 289.

221. Perry Anderson, "The Notion of a Bourgeois Revolution," 112.

222. Marx, *Capital*, vol. 3, 1025–27.

223. Althusser, "The Underground Current of the Materialism of the Encounter," 202.

224. Braudel, *The Mediterranean and the Mediterranean World*, vol. 2, 725, 729 and 725–34 more generally.

225. Kamen, *European Society*, 144.

226. John H. Elliott, *Imperial Spain*, 198.

227. Bennassar, "Consommation, Investissements, Mouvements de Capitaux"; Jago, "The 'Crisis of the Aristocracy,'" 60–63, 89–90; Maravall, *La Cultura del Barroco*, 71–74.

228. John H. Elliott, *Imperial Spain*, 311. See also "A Non-Revolutionary Society," which concludes: "The price of revolution may have been high, but the price of non-revolution was perhaps even higher." Ibid., 91.

229. Berger, *Success and Failure of Picasso*, 20.

230. Hans Baron, "A Sociological Interpretation of the Early Renaissance," 431, 432, 433.

231. Habermas, *The Structural Transformation of the Public Sphere*, 23.
232. King James VI and I, "Basilicon Doron," 29, 30. Raising the blue blanket was the signal for a riot by the Scottish craft guilds.
233. Manning, *The English People and the English Revolution*, 235.
234. Eric Olin Wright, "Exploitation, Identity, and Class Structure," 203.
235. Harvey, *The Enigma of Capital*, 135.
236. Edward P. Thompson, "The Peculiarities of the English," 325, 326.
237. For Lenin's actual position, see Draper, "The Myth of Lenin's 'Concept of the Party'," 188–94, 198–201 and. Lih, *Lenin Rediscovered*, 644–67.
238. Goldmann, *The Hidden God*, 117.
239. Mann, *The Sources of Social Power*, vol. 2, 229, 230.
240. Gramsci, "The Intellectuals," 5–6, Q12§3.
241. Perry Anderson, *Lineages of the Absolutist State*, 154–62; P. J. Jones, "Communes and Despots," 82–85, 92–94.
242. Arrighi, *The Long Twentieth Century*, 227.
243. Breuilly, *Nationalism and the State*, 3–4.
244. Gramsci, "The Renaissance," 226; Gramsci, *Prison Notebooks*, vol. 2, 366, Q5§123.
245. Gramsci, "The Question of the Language and the Italian Intellectual Classes," 169; Gramsci, *Prison Notebooks*, vol. 2, 74, Q3§76; Larner, *Italy in the Age of Dante*, 1–9.
246. Mielants, *The Origins of Capitalism and "the Rise of the West,"* 157.
247. Perry Anderson, "The Notion of a Bourgeois Revolution," 112.
248. Gareth Stedman Jones, "Society and Politics at the Beginning of the World Economy," 87.
249. Teich, "Afterword," 216.
250. Koenigsberger, "Republics and Courts in Italian and European Culture in the Sixteenth and Seventeenth Centuries," 36–39, 54; Nauert, *Humanism and the Culture of the Renaissance*, 93–94.
251. Gramsci, "The Renaissance," 229–230; Gramsci, *Prison Notebooks*, vol. 2, 369, Q5§123.
252. Leff, *Heresy in the Later Middle Ages*, 606–707.
253. Betts, "Social and Constitutional Development," 38–45; Norman Cohn, *The Pursuit of the Millennium*, 205–22; Klassen, "The Disadvantaged and the Hussite Revolution," 264–67. For a brief but useful discussion of the Hussite movement with the wider context of European peasant revolt, see Graus, "From Resistance to Revolt," 5, 7.
254. Marshall, *Presbyters and Profits*, 250.
255. Marx, *Capital*, vol. 1, 881–83.
256. Israel, *The Dutch Republic*, 176.
257. Marx, *Capital*, vol. 1, 172.
258. Interestingly, Michael Mann, a sociologist who—the rhetoric of transcendence aside—owes far more to Weber than Marx, has claimed that Christianity in general, as an "ideological power network," began to play this role in Western Europe during the feudal epoch through a program of "normative pacification": "Without this ecumenical reorganization, neither markets, nor property ownership, nor 'rational restlessness' would have flowed so within these territories." See *The Sources of Social Power*, vol. 1, 506. See also the more extended discussion on 381–85. One of the problems with this claim, as Perry Anderson has remarked, is that Christianity was not coterminous with Western Europe: the Byzantine Church was also engaged in "normative pacification," yet it did not oversee a level of economic development comparable to the Roman Catholic Church. See "Michael Mann's Sociology of Power," 84–85.
259. Marx, *Grundrisse*, 232.
260. According to Karl Löwith, he did not engage directly with what Marx wrote (unsurprisingly, given the absence of such writing) but rather with the work of Rudolf Stammler, who had attempted to apply a Marxist analysis to the history of religion. See *Max Weber and Karl Marx*, 101.

261. Max Weber, *The Protestant Ethic and the Spirit of Capitalism*, 172, 180, 91.

262. Hans Baron, "A Sociological Interpretation of the Early Renaissance in Florence," 437.

263. Marshall is quite right to insist, however, that in terms of their methodology, Marx and Weber cannot be reconciled. See *Presbyters and Profits*, 247–51. Interestingly, Weber goes out of his way to praise the work of the arch-revisionist, Eduard Bernstein, particularly in comparison with the "schematicism of [Karl] Kautsky." See *The Protestant Ethic and the Spirit of Capitalism*, 219, 258, 278.

264. The position that holds that Protestantism was a justification for capitalism was introduced into the debate, not by a Marxist, but by the Christian Socialist Tawney in *Religion and the Rise of Capitalism*, first published in 1926. According to Tawney, "whatever its theological merits or defects, [Protestantism] was admirably designed to liberate economic energies, and to weld into a disciplined social force the rising bourgeoisie, conscious of the contrast between its own standards and those of a laxer world, proud of its vocation as the standard bearer of the economic virtues, and determined to indicate an open road for its own way of life by the use of every weapon, including political revolution and war, because the issue at stake was not merely convenience or self-interest, but the will of God." Tawney concludes his discussion with an aphorism that excellently summarizes his position: "Calvin did for the bourgeoisie of the sixteenth century what Marx did for the proletariat of the nineteenth." See *Religion and the Rise of Capitalism*, 119–20. It was this position, superimposed on Engels's claims for Calvinism as a revolutionary ideology, which became almost by default accepted as the Marxist interpretation of the Reformation. And not only by opponents of Marxism (who can usually be relied on to denounce it for "economic determinism"), but many who considered themselves to be Marxists, or at least influenced by Marxist theory. This was relatively easy in Britain, where Marxism remained theoretically underdeveloped until after 1956, and where Tawney's powerful interpretation filled the gap in this area of intellectual history for decades.

265. The sources cited by Marshall regarding "Marx's and Engels' account of the relationship between Reformation and the rise of capitalism" are in fact both by Engels: *Socialism: Utopian and Scientific* and *Ludwig Feuerbach and the End of Classical German Philosophy*. See *Presbyters and Profits*, 367, note 55.

266. Engels, "On the Peasant War," 554.

267. Engels, *Ludwig Feuerbach and the End of Classical German Philosophy*, 396. Engels rightly takes the period of the English Revolution to span the events of both 1640–1660 and 1688–89. The notion that the latter ended in a "compromise" is, however, to assume that the nobility were still in some sense a feudal class, rather than one whose members were already largely engaged in capitalist landownership.

268. Mann, *The Sources of Social Power*, vol. 1, 465.

269. Cameron, *The European Reformation*, 199.

270. See the two classic accounts produced by Marxists of the Second International: Mehring, "The German Reformation and Its Consequences," 8, 23–24 and Kautsky, *Thomas More and His Utopia*, 59–60.

271. Trevor-Roper, "Religion, the Reformation and Social Change," 33.

272. Chadwick, *The Reformation*, 137.

273. Nischan, "Confessionalism and Absolutism," 181. The occasion for this outburst was the public declaration by Elector John Sigismund of Brandenburg on Christmas Day, 1613, of his conversion to Calvinism. Brandenburg was virtually the only German state where the ruler moved from Lutheranism to Calvinism, a transition that seems to have been inspired by his alliance with the Dutch and Palatine Calvinists, whose support he needed in the Julich-Cleves succession dispute. Such shifts in allegiance were only possible, however, once the initial division of the European state system on the denominational basis outlined above had taken place. See ibid., 181–85.

274. Skinner, "The Origins of the Calvinist Theory of Revolution," 314–26.

275. Heller, *The Conquest of Poverty*, 240, 247. It is in any case by no means certain that the Huguenot cause in France was the only one supported by "capitalist" elements in French society. Indeed, there is a good case for arguing that the Catholic Holy League, which seized power in Paris during 1584, had a more plebeian base and radical agenda than the Huguenots ever did. One analysis of the leadership of the Catholic League, "the Sixteen," shows them "to have been widely representative of the middle classes, with particular strength among the middle and lower ranks of the legal profession." See Salmon, "The Paris Sixteen," 549–50. For examples of their radicalism, see ibid., 552–53.

276. Gramsci, "Problems of Marxism," 394–95, Q16§9.

277. Trevor-Roper, "The Religious Origins of the Enlightenment," 233–35.

278. Spinoza, *Tractatus Theologicus-Politicus*, 53.

279. Pellicani, "Weber and the Myth of Calvinism," 72, 73, note 77. It is indicative that, during the latter half of the eighteenth century, when Scottish capitalism did begin its remarkable ascent, local Enlightenment thinkers were forced to reject the Calvinist legacy as much as the absolutist obscurantism of the Jacobites. See Davidson, "The Scottish Path to Capitalist Agriculture 3," 17–21.

280. Marshall, *Presbyteries and Profits*, 276.

281. Bertram, "International Competition in Historical Materialism," 119–20.

282. Ibid., 122.

283. Brenner, *Merchants and Revolution*, 708–9.

284. Paulin, "Introduction," 32.

285. Milton, *Paradise Lost*, Book XII, lines 506–24, 529–42. Christopher Hill argues that, taken in conjunction with Milton's other writings, these passages must be understood as referring to the emergence of apostasy at some—never exactly specified—point between the death and resurrection of Christ and the reign of the Emperor Constantine. But given that Milton had expected the English Revolution to produce the Rule of the Saints, there is no reason why the notion of betrayal could not embrace both the original apostasy and the subsequent failure of the English Revolution to reestablish the pristine purity of the church at the time of the Apostles. See *The Experience of Defeat*, 292–95.

3. PATTERNS OF CONSUMMATION

1.   Hobsbawm, "Revolution," 23–24.

2.   Perry Anderson, "Civil War, Global Distemper," 251.

3.   Chistozvonov, "The Concept and Criteria of Reversibility and Irreversibility of an Historical Process," 9–10.

4.   Marx, *Grundrisse*, 106–7.

5.   Rudra, "Pre-Capitalist Modes of Production in Non-European Societies," 366.

6.   Ste. Croix, *The Class Struggle in Ancient Greek World*, 52.

7.   Marx, *Capital*, vol. 1, 645–46, 1019–38.

8.   Preobrazhensky, *The New Economics*, 185–86.

9.   Lenin, "The Economic Content of Narodism and the Criticism of It in Mr. Struve's Book (The Reflection of Marxism in Bourgeois Literature)," 466.

10.   Lenin, "New Data on the Laws Governing the Development of Capitalism in Agriculture," 22.

11.   Banaji, "Modes of Production in a Materialist Conception of History," 50–52, 92–94; Marx, *Grundrisse*, 463. For a helpful summary of Banaji's occasionally opaque position, see Bakan, "Plantation Slavery and the Capitalist Mode of Production," 75–77. For a related analysis, but which emphasizes the benefits for capital of retaining precapitalist rural social relations of production, rather than the assimilation by the former of the latter, see Bernstein, *Class Dynamics of Agrarian Change*, 92–95.

12. Callinicos, "Trotsky's Theory of 'Permanent Revolution' and Its Relevance to the Third World Today," 110.
13. Gerstenberger, *Impersonal Power*, 7.
14. Barker, "The State as Capital," 20–23.
15. Ollman, "Why Does the Emperor Need the Yakuza?," 200.
16. Waswo, *Japanese Landlords*, 13.
17. Hobsbawm, "Revolution," 27.
18. Ellen Meiksins Wood, "The Separation of the Economic and Political in Capitalism," 81–82.
19. Draper, *Karl Marx's Theory of Revolution*, vol. 1, 321–24.
20. Adam Smith, *The Wealth of Nations*, Book I, 278.
21. Schmitt, "The Concept of the Political," 63 and 62–65, 71–72 more generally.
22. Bernard Porter, *Empire and Superempire*, 49.
23. Wallerstein, *Historical Capitalism*, 42.
24. Wilson, *Europe's Tragedy*, 347–61; Polisensky, *The Thirty Years' War*, 137–50, 244–53.
25. Kiernan, *State and Society in Europe*, 273,
26. Linden, "Marx and Engels, Dutch Marxism and the "Model Capitalist Nation of the Seventeenth Century'," 187.
27. Brenner, "The Agrarian Roots of European Capitalism," 325–26; Brenner, "The Low Countries and the Transition to Capitalism," 330–34; Hobsbawm, "The Crisis of the Seventeenth Century," 41–43; Kreidte, *Peasants, Landlords and Merchant Capitalists*, 87–91.
28. Gramsci, "The Renaissance," 223; Gramsci, *Prison Notebooks*, vol. 2, 363, Q5§123.
29. Daalder, "Consociationalism, Center and Periphery in the Netherlands," 182.
30. Greenfeld, *The Spirit of Capitalism*, 91.
31. Israel, *The Dutch Republic*, 276–84.
32. Brandon, "Marxism and the 'Dutch Miracle,'" 141 and 135–41 more generally.
33. James R. Jones, *The Anglo-Dutch Wars of the Seventeenth Century*, 7, 12.
34. Hobsbawm, "The Crisis of the Seventeenth Century," 43.
35. Adam Smith, *Lectures on Jurisprudence*, 265.
36. Coveney, "An Early Modern European Crisis?," 21.
37. Marx, *Capital*, vol. 1, 884. For a typical reaffirmation of this position, see Saville, *The Consolidation of the Capitalist State*, 6.
38. Pinkus, 1688, 483, 484, 485.
39. Roy Porter, *Enlightenment*, 27.
40. Halliday, *Revolution and World Politics*, 185.
41. Teschke, *The Myth of 1648*, 263.
42. McLynn, *The Jacobites*, 29.
43. Brewer, *The Sinews of Power*, 24 and 27–217 more generally. For an example of how Brewer's analysis of the British fiscal-military state has now entered mainstream historiography, see Hoppit, *A Land of Liberty?*, 124–31.
44. Mooers, *The Making of Bourgeois Europe*, 161–62.
45. McLynn, *1759*, 1, 391 and passim. For a more sober but essentially concurrent account, see Simms, *Three Victories and a Defeat*, chapter 16.
46. Wallerstein, *The Modern World-System II*, 257.
47. Lenman, *Britain's Colonial Wars*, 3.
48. In fact, as Alex Callinicos argues, Britain was the first truly hegemonic capitalist power. See *Imperialism and Global Political Economy*, 142–44.
49. Perry Anderson, "The Notion of a Bourgeois Revolution," 118.
50. Armitage and Subrahmanyam, "Introduction: The Age of Revolutions," xiii and xii–xvi more generally. For a critique of earlier refusals to differentiate between revolutions, in this case those of the 1640s, see Lublinskaya, *French Absolutism*, 101.
51. Israel, *Radical Enlightenment*, 515–27; David Parker, *Class and State in Ancien Regime*

France, 208; Roy Porter, *Enlightenment*, 6–12.

52.   Lenman, *Britain's Colonial Wars*, 258–59.
53.   Mooers, *Making of Bourgeois Europe*, 93–94.
54.   Heller, *The Bourgeois Revolution in France*, 67–69, 70, 147.
55.   Mooers, *The Making of Bourgeois Europe*, 95.
56.   Fox-Genovese and Genovese, "The Political Crisis of Social History," 229.
57.   Heller, *The Bourgeois Revolution in France*, 54–60.
58.   Sewell, *A Rhetoric of Bourgeois Revolution*, 64.
59.   Foucault, "Truth and Power," 133.
60.   Chatterjee, *Nationalist Thought and the Colonial World*, 168.
61.   Ellen Meiksins Wood, *The Origin of Capitalism*, 190.
62.   Teich, "Afterword," 217.
63.   Israel, *Radical Enlightenment*, 71–72.
64.   Ibid., 11.
65.   Venturi, *Utopia and Reform in the Enlightenment*, 133.
66.   Robertson, *The Case for Enlightenment*, 391, 405.
67.   Pilbeam, *The Middle Classes in Europe*, 233.
68.   Gareth Stedman Jones, "Society and Politics at the Beginning of the World Economy," 87.
69.   Maza, *The Myth of the French Bourgeoisie*, 6, 7.
70.   Colin Jones, "Bourgeois Revolution Revivified."
71.   Greenfeld, *The Spirit of Capitalism*, 148.
72.   Shafer, "Bourgeois Nationalism in the Pamphlets on the Eve of the French Revolution," 47–48.
73.   Miliband, "Barnave," 46.
74.   Lucas, "Nobles, Bourgeois and the Origins of the French Revolution," 124–26.
75.   Robespierre, "Extracts from 'Answer to Louvet's Accusation,'" 43.
76.   Sewell, *A Rhetoric of Bourgeois Revolution*, 189; Marx, "The Eighteenth Brumaire of Louis Bonaparte," 146–50.
77.   Israel, *A Revolution of the Mind*, 232–33.
78.   Hoffman, *Growth in a Traditional Society*, 194.
79.   Heller, *The Bourgeois Revolution in France*, 88, 89.
80.   David Parker, *Class and State in Ancien Régime France*, 217.
81.   Friedrichs, "The War and German Society," 208–15.
82.   Hoffman, *Growth in a Traditional Society*, 198.
83.   Charles Post argues that capitalist plantation-agriculture was only established in the South by the end of the nineteenth century. See "Social Property Relations, Class Conflict and the Origins of the US Civil War," 275–77.
84.   McPherson, "The Second American Revolution," 10–11, 16.
85.   Heller, *The Bourgeois Revolution in France*, 94, 101, 102, 113, 137. See also Ado, *Paysans en révolution*, 433–34, 437; and Livesey, *Making Democracy in the French Revolution*, 101–2, 130.
86.   Nesbitt, *Universal Emancipation*, 172.
87.   Blanning, *The Pursuit of Glory*, 351.
88.   Schama, *Patriots and Liberators*, 12–15.
89.   Crouzet, "Western Europe and Great Britain," 342–43.
90.   Chateaubriand, *Memoires D'outre-Tombe*, vol. 3, 647.
91.   Marx to Nieuwenhuis, February 22, 1881.
92.   O'Brien, "The Impact of the Revolutionary and Napoleonic Wars," 383; O'Rourke, "The Worldwide Economic Impact of the French Revolutionary and Napoleonic Wars," 148–49.
93.   Darwin, *After Tamerlane*, 237 and 237–45 more generally.
94.   Davidson, "The Scottish Path to Capitalist Agriculture 2;" Davidson, "The Scottish Path

to Capitalist Agriculture 3;" Davidson, "Scotland: Birthplace of Passive Revolution?"

95.   Blum, *The End of the Old Order in Rural Europe*, 372, 373, 376.
96.   Hobsbawm, *The Age of Capital*, 188.
97.   Bayly, *The Birth of the Modern World*, 298.
98.   Norman Stone, *Europe Transformed*, 17–18.
99.   Mann, *The Sources of Social Power*, vol. 2, 354.
100. Hobsbawm, *Echoes of the Marseillaise*, 46.
101. Beales, "Social Forces and Enlightened Policies," 9–10; Outram, *The Enlightenment*, 122–23.
102. Marx, "The Eighteenth Brumaire of Louis Bonaparte," 241.
103. Torras, "Peasant Counter-Revolution?," 74, 75.
104. Fraser, *Napoleon's Cursed War*, 480.
105. Duggan, *The Force of Destiny*, 121, 123.
106. Hobsbawm, *The Age of Empire*, 21.
107. Crouzet, "Western Europe and Great Britain," 344–45.
108. Woolf, "The Construction of a European World-View in the Revolutionary-Napoleonic Years," 101.
109. Mann, *Sources of Social Power*, vol. 2, 311.
110. Bayly, *Birth of the Modern World*, 426–30.
111. Nairn, "The Twilight of the British State," 49.
112. Cannadine, "The Context, Performance and Meaning of Ritual," 120–50.
113. Bukharin, *Imperialism and World Economy*, 128. These remarks were probably made in response to the Austrian attempts to explain imperialism as an effect of aristocratic influence on international politics. See, for an example, which postdates Bukharin's work, Schumpeter, "The Sociology of Imperialisms," 84–97.
114. Mann, "Ruling Class Strategies and Citizenship," 200.
115. Shillory, "The Meiji Restoration," 20.
116. Marx, *Theories of Surplus Value*, vol. 2, 302.
117. Marx, *Capital*, vol. 1, 935 and see 931–40 more generally.
118. Marx, *Theories of Surplus Value*, vol. 2, 303.
119. Amin, *Class and Nation Historically and in the Current Crisis*, 21.
120. Luxemburg, *The Accumulation of Capital*, 369.
121. Dalziel, "Southern Islands," 589. The situation in South Africa was different from North America and Australasia in that the native population was not economically marginalized but became enmeshed in capitalist social relations, again during the last third of the nineteenth century. Some Marxists have claimed that the Zulu Kingdom in South Africa had become fully dominated by capitalist laws of motion by the end of the 1880s. See, for example, Guy, "The Destruction and Reconstruction of Zulu Society," 189–90.
122. Lynch, *The Spanish American Revolutions*, 340, 341.
123. Tapia, "Constitution and Constitutional Reform in Bolivia," 160.
124. Choonara, "The Relevance of Permanent Revolution," 181.
125. Knight, "The Mexican Revolution," 26.
126. Semo, *Historia Mexicana*, 299–315; Semo, "Reflexiones Sobre la Revolución Mexicana," 147, 148.
127. One of the problems with Semo's analysis is that he regards the Mexican experience as distinct from the rest of the continent, writing, "The difference between the Mexican bourgeoisie and that of other Latin American countries is that the former lost its revolutionary faculties after making ample use of them, while the others have never led and will never lead a bourgeois revolution." See *Historia Mexicana*, 305.
128. Gilly, *The Mexican Revolution*, 13, 15 and 11–17 more generally.
129. Dabat and Lorenzano, *Argentina*, 12 and 10–12 more generally.
130. Moore, *The Social Origins of Dictatorship and Democracy*, 112.

131. Post, "Social Property Relations, Class Conflict and the Origins of the US Civil War," 249. For similar arguments about the conformity of the Civil War to the orthodox model of bourgeois revolution, see Kulikoff, "Was the American Revolution a Bourgeois Revolution?," 64.
132. Novack, "Introduction," 15–17.
133. Kolchin, *American Slavery*, 99–105.
134. Fields, "Slavery, Race and Ideology in the United States of America," 108.
135. Allen, *The Invention of the White Race*, vol. 2, 249.
136. "The whole thing in Germany will depend on whether it is possible to back the proletarian revolution by some second edition of the Peasants' war. In which case the affair should go swimmingly." Marx to Engels, April 16, 1856.
137. Bowman, "Antebellum Planters and Vormarz Junkers in Comparative Perspective," 783, 785–86, 795, 806–7.
138. Tchakerian, "Productivity, Extent of Markets, and Manufacturing in the Late Antebellum South and Midwest," 519–20.
139. Kolchin, *American Slavery*, 153.
140. Bakan, "Plantation Slavery and the Capitalist Mode of Production," 86–91; Gavin Wright, "Capitalism and Slavery on the Islands," 865–73.
141. Turley, "Slave Emancipations in Modern History," 187–89.
142. Blackburn, *The Overthrow of Colonial Slavery*, 492–93.
143. Ransom and Sutch, "Capitalists without Capital," 138–39.
144. Berman, *Why America Failed*, 132.
145. Fogel, *Without Consent or Contract*, 414–15.
146. Gavin Wright, "Capitalism and Slavery on the Islands," 863.
147. Beard, *The Rise of American Civilization*, vol. 2, 115.
148. McPherson, *Battle Cry of Freedom*, 861.
149. Davidson, *Discovering the Scottish Revolution*, 272–75.
150. Ashworth, *Capitalism, and Politics in the Antebellum Republic*, vol. 2, 639, 640.
151. Creighton, *The Commercial Empire of the St. Lawrence*, 222.
152. Bernier and Sallee, *The Shaping of Quebec Politics and Society*, 100.
153. Creighton, *The Commercial Empire of the St. Lawrence*, 273.
154. Martin, *Britain and the Origins of Canadian Confederation*, 294.
155. Creighton, *The Road to Confederation*, 110.
156. Whitelaw, "Reconstructing the Quebec Conference," 134.
157. Creighton, *The Road to Confederation*, 145.
158. Reed, *Ten Days That Shook the World*, 129; Trotsky, *The History of the Russian Revolution*, 1168.
159. Fanon, *The Wretched of the Earth*, 143–44.
160. Cabral, "A Brief Analysis of the Social Structure in Guinea," 52.
161. Davidson, "China: Unevenness, Combination, Revolution?," 216–22; Harvey, *A Brief History of Neoliberalism*, 120–35.
162. D'Amato, "The Necessity of Permanent Revolution."
163. Marx and Engels, *The German Ideology*, 48–54.
164. Dadoo, "Introduction," xvii–xviii.
165. Vanaik, "Subcontinental Strategies," 113.
166. Slovo, "South Africa—No Middle Road," 142–43.
167. See, for example, Johnson, "False Start in South Africa," and the response by Patrick Bond, "In Power in Pretoria?"
168. Kingsnorth, *One No, Many Yeses*, 119.
169. Ibid., 118.
170. Webber, *From Rebellion to Reform in Bolivia*, 153–236.
171. García Linera, "The MAS is of the Center-Left."

172. Choonara, "The Relevance of Permanent Revolution," 174–75.
173. In an article published in English around the time of his appointment to the Bolivian vice-presidency, García Linera set out alternative outcomes of a "revolutionary epoch": one "a restoration of the old regime (coup d'etat)," the other, "a negotiated and peaceful modification of the political system through the partial or substantial incorporation of the insurgents and their proposals for change into the power bloc." The relevance of the second outcome to his situation scarcely needs emphasis. See "State Crisis, Popular Power," 82.
174. Choonara, "The Relevance of Permanent Revolution," 182.
175. Goodwin, *No Other Way Out*, 298, 302, and 293–306 more generally.
176. Klooster, *Revolutions in the Atlantic World*, 158.
177. Harman, "The Prophet and the Proletariat," 344.
178. Binns, "Revolution and State Capitalism in the Third World," 42–43.
179. McDaniel, *Autocracy, Capitalism and Revolution in Russia*, 41–47.
180. Ibid., 407.
181. Davis, "Sand, Fear and Money in Dubai," 53–54. Indeed, in the case of China, it might be said that the neoliberal turn after 1978 actually resumed the process of uneven and combined development originally detected by Trotsky in the 1920s, which had been consciously halted by a Maoist leadership only too conscious of the explosive effects of uncontrolled urban expansion. See Davidson, "China: Unevenness, Combination, Revolution?" 214–16.
182. Silver, *Forces of Labor*, 164.
183. Ginsborg, *A History of Contemporary Italy*, 47–53, 223–29; Hardt and Negri, *Empire*, 287–89.
184. Luttwak, *Turbo-capitalism*, 25–26.
185. Halliday, *Revolution and World Politics*, 320–21.
186. Milton, *Paradise Lost*, Book XII, line 646.
187. Auden, "Spain," 136.

EPILOGUE: REFLECTIONS IN A SCOTTISH CEMETERY

1. Campbell, *Standing Witnesses*, 90, 91.
2. Davidson, *Discovering the Scottish Revolution*, 131–56.
3. Horne, *The Great Museum*, 74.
4. Ibid., 80–81.
5. For Edinburgh, see Youngson, *The Making of Classical Edinburgh*, 59–65; for Paris, see Benjamin, "Convolute E," and Harvey, *Paris*, 125–40, 142–44.
6. Robin, "The First Counter-revolutionary," 67–73.
7. Hume, *A Treatise of Human Nature*, 156. See also ibid., 193.
8. Max Weber, *Economy and Society*, vol. 1, 24–26.
9. Hume, *A Treatise of Human Nature*, Books 2 and 3, 159.
10. Horkheimer, "The End of Reason," 30. This is not the only aspect of Hume's work that depends on assuming a community of interest; so too does his moral philosophy and it is consequently open to the same critique. Alasdair MacIntyre writes: "We have moral rules because we have common interests. Should someone succeed in showing us that the facts are different from what we conceive them to be so that we have no common interests, then our moral rules would lose their justification. Indeed, the initial move of Marx's moral theory can perhaps be understood as a denial that there are common interests shared by the whole of society in respect of, for instance, the distribution of property meets Hume on his own ground." See "Hume on 'Is' and 'Ought,'" 116.
11. Ritzer, *The McDonaldization of Society*, 121–42. This was a venerable theme of the Frank-

furt School. See, for example, Marcuse, "Industrialization and Capitalism," 207.

12. Trotsky, "Fragments from the First Seven Months of the War," 879.
13. Gamble, *Hayek*, 32–33.
14. Hayek, *The Fatal Conceit*, 136.
15. Spinoza, *Tractatus Theologicus-Politicus*, 297.
16. Ibid., 56.
17. Voltaire to D'Alembert, September 2, 1768, 112.
18. Siegel, *The Meek and the Militant*, 22.
19. Hume, *A Treatise of Human Nature*, chapter 10.
20. Hume, "Of Interest," 130–31.
21. Hirschman, *The Passions and the Interests*, 66.
22. Ibid., 130, 131.
23. Ibid., 132–35.
24. Peck, *Constructions of Neoliberal Reason*, 7–8.
25. Lukács, "The Changing Function of Historical Materialism," 225. For a more recent judgment along similar lines, see Gerstenberger, *Impersonal Power*, 686.
26. Robertson, "The Enlightenment above National Context," 697; Rothschild, *Economic Sentiments*, 16.
27. McPherson, *Battle Cry of Freedom*, 326.
28. Douglass, "The Future of the Colored Race," 196. See also, Douglass, "Why Should a Colored Man Enlist?," 341. For the original poem, see Burns, "A Man's a Man," 512–16.
29. Twain, *Life on the Mississippi*, 46.
30. Hook, "Scott and America," 103–10; Hook, "The South, Scotland, and William Faulkner," 193–201.
31. McPherson, *For Cause and Comrades*, 27.
32. Schurz, "Report on the Condition of the South," 354.
33. See, for example, Foner, *Reconstruction* ("unfinished revolution") and Camejo, *Racism, Revolution, Reaction* ("Republican betrayal").
34. McPherson, *The Struggle for Equality*, 430–31.
35. Luraghi, "The Civil War and the Modernization of American Society," 233–34, 242.
36. Lowe, *Immigrant Acts*, 27–28.
37. Milner II, "National Initiatives," 179–80.
38. Furet, "Terror," 458–59; Soboul, *The French Revolution*, 342.
39. Corish, "The Cromwellian Conquest," 339–42; Ohlmeyer, "The Civil Wars in Ireland," 98–99.
40. Raymond Williams, *The Country and the City*, 50–51.
41. Wallerstein, *Historical Capitalism*, 40.
42. Griffiths, *Pip Pip*, 185, 193–95.
43. Burbach, *Globalization and Postmodern Politics*, 85, 86–87.
44. Bookchin, *Remaking Society*, 89.
45. Wallerstein, *Historical Capitalism*, 40.
46. Wallerstein, "Eurocentrism and Its Avatars," 104–5.
47. Armstrong, "Back to the Future—Part Two," 35.
48. Bookchin, *The Ecology of Freedom*, 87.
49. Bookchin, *The Third Revolution*, vol. 1, ix.
50. Linebaugh and Rediker, *The Many-Headed Hydra*, 26.
51. McMurtry, *The Cancer Stage of Capitalism*, 204–5, 213.
52. Blackburn, *The Making of New World Slavery*, 15.
53. Patterson, *Inventing Western Civilization*, 132.
54. Neil Young with Crazy Horse, "Cortez the Killer."
55. Patterson, *The Inca Empire*, 157–65.
56. Perry Anderson, *Passages from Antiquity to Feudalism*, 148–50; Graus, "From Resistance

to Revolt," 3; Marx, *Capital*, vol. 1, 885.

57.   Christopher Hill, *The World Turned Upside Down*, 15.

58.   Holstun, *Ehud's Dagger*, 24–25.

59.   Ibid., ix.

60.   Ibid., 89.

61.   Holstun, "Utopia Pre-empted," 40. In this text Holstun is more circumspect about the ability of what he calls "monarcho-populism" to "graft a progressive small production onto a benevolent despotism that would help check capitalist forces." See ibid., 41.

62.   Linebaugh, "Review of *The Making of New World Slavery*," 192.

63.   Holstun, "Communism, George Hill and the *Mir*," 137.

64.   Manning, *1649*, 109–34.

65.   Armstrong, "Back to the Future—Part Two," 36.

66.   Gareth Stedman Jones, "Society and Politics at the Beginning of the World Economy," 87.

67.   Ennew, Hirst, and Tribe, "'Peasantry' as an Economic Category," 309–10.

68.   Luxemburg, *The Accumulation of Capital*, 368–71, 402, 416.

69.   Marx and Engels, "The Manifesto of the Communist Party,"68.

70.   Marx, *Capital*, vol. 1, 915, 918.

71.   Marx, *The Poverty of Philosophy*, 174–78.

72.   Jameson, "The Cultural Logic of Late Capitalism," 47.

73.   Linebaugh and Rediker, *The Many-Headed Hydra*, 352–53.

74.   Edward P. Thompson, *The Making of the English Working Class*, 12.

75.   Bookchin, *The Third Revolution*, vol. 1, 12–13. As a example of Bookchin's rather uncertain grasp of the Marxist attitude to these revolutions, it is worth noting that, in relation to the German Peasant War, Lukács certainly highlighted the tactical inadequacy of the peasants, which he ascribed to problems in forming a fully revolutionary consciousness, but which scarcely suggests that he regarded them as "reactionaries." See Lukács, "Class Consciousness," 53 and "Tailism and the Dialectic," 86–94.

76.   Bensaïd, *Marx for Our Times*, 54.

77.   Davidson, *Discovering the Scottish Revolution*, 290–94.

78.   Marx, *Capital*, vol. 1, 926.

79.   Israel, *Democratic Enlightenment*, 951. Unfortunately this final volume appeared in print too late for me to make full use of it here.

80.   Gramsci to Carlo, December 19, 1929. See also, Gramsci, "The Modern Prince," 175 and Gramsci, *Prison Notebooks*, vol. 3, 73, Q6§86. It should be noted that this was a personal credo, not the voluntaristic slogan—"pessimism of the intellect, optimism of the will"—it has subsequently become.

81.   Gordon, "On the Supposed Obsolescence of the French Enlightenment," 204.

82.   Callinicos, *Social Theory*, 56.

83.   Marx and Engels, "The Manifesto of the Communist Party," 85, 73.

84.   Jefferson, "The Unanimous Declaration of the Thirteen United States of America," 4.

85.   Bérubé, "It's Renaissance Time," 205.

86.   Eagleton, *The Illusions of Postmodernism*, 113.

87.   Douglass, "The Meaning of July Fourth for the Negro," 192, 200, 201.

88.   Douglass, "The Constitution of the United States," 477.

89.   Buck-Morss, "Hegel and Haiti," 865.

90.   Morris, "A Dream of John Ball," 31. A. C. Bradley, a very different Victorian thinker than Morris, saw the inevitability of people to accomplish their intended goals as the very essence of tragedy: "The tragic world is a world of action, and action is the translation of thought into reality. We see men and women confidently attempt it. They strike into the existing order of things in pursuance of their ideas. But what they achieve is not what they intend; it is terribly unlike it. . . . They fight blindly in the dark, and the power that works through them makes them the instrument of a design which is not

BIBLIOGRAPHY

Works are listed chronologically by date of original publication. Where this differs from the edition cited, it is shown after the author's first name in square brackets, except in the case of Gramsci's prison notebooks, where precise dating is not always possible. Where the date of composition significantly differs from the date of publication, as in the cases of Smith's *Lectures on Jurisprudence* or Marx's *Grundrisse*, I have used the former, but not where only a few years are involved. Author's names have been given in the style that was in use at the time a work was published, even if this has subsequently changed. In the case of unsigned newspaper or magazine articles, state documents, or records of meetings, the publication is listed as the author. URLs have been listed here only where an item exists solely in electronic format, otherwise the published version has been given. In keeping with tradition, I have not included specific editions of works by William Shakespeare or John Milton.

Abbott, Andrew [1997]. "On the Concept of Turning Point." In *Time Matters: On Theory and Method*, 240–60. Chicago: Chicago University Press, 2001.

Abu-Loghod, Janet L. *Before European Hegemony: The World System, 1250–1350*. New York: Oxford University Press, 1989.

Ado, Anatoli [1971]. *Paysans en révolution: terre, pouvoir et jacquerie, 1789–1794*. Paris: Société des Etudes Robespierristes, 1996.

Albert, Michael. *Parecon: Life after Capitalism*. London: Verso, 2003.

Allen, Theodore. *The Invention of the White Race*, vol. 2, *The Origin of Racial Oppression in Anglo-America*. London: Verso, 1997.

Althusser, Louis [1976]. *Machiavelli and Us*. London: Verso, 1999.

——— [1982–83]. "The Underground Current of the Materialism of the Encounter." In *Philosophy of the Encounter: Later Writings, 1978–1987*, edited by Francois Matheron and Olivier Corpet, 163–207. London: Verso, 2006.

Amin, Samir [1973]. *Unequal Development: An Essay on the Social Formations of Peripheral Capitalism*. Hassocks: Harvester Press, 1976.

———. *Class and Nation Historically and in the Current Crisis*. New York: Monthly Review Press, 1980.

Anderson, Perry. "Socialism and Pseudo-Empiricism," *New Left Review* 1, no. 35 (January–February 1966): 2–42.

————. *Passages from Antiquity to Feudalism*. London: New Left Books, 1974.

————. *Lineages of the Absolutist State*. London: New Left Books, 1974.

———— [1976]. "The Notion of a Bourgeois Revolution." In *English Questions*, 105–18. London: Verso, 1992.

————. *Arguments within English Marxism*. London: Verso, 1980.

———— [1983]. "Geoffrey de Ste Croix and the Ancient World." In *A Zone of Engagement*, 1–24. London: Verso, 1992.

———— [1986]. "Michael Mann's Sociology of Power." In *A Zone of Engagement*, 76–86. London: Verso, 1992

————. "Foreword." In *English Questions*. London: Verso, 1992.

Armitage, David and Sanjay Subrahmanyam. "Introduction: The Age of Revolutions, c. 1760–1840—Global Causation, Connection and Comparisons." In *The Age of Revolutions in Global Context, c. 1760–1840*, xii–xxxii. London: Palgrave Macmillan, 2010.

Armstrong, Alan. "Back to the Future—Part Two: 1492 and 1992—Redemption, Improvement and Progress," *Cencrastus* 51 (Spring 1995): 35–40.

Arrighi, Giovanni. *The Long Twentieth Century: Money, Power and the Origins of Our Times*, London: Verso, 1994.

————. *Adam Smith in Beijing*. London: Verso, 2007.

Ashtor, Eliyahu. *A Social and Economic History of the Near East in the Middle Ages*. London: Collins, 1976.

Ashworth, John. *Slavery, Capitalism, and Politics in the Antebellum Republic*, vol. 1, *Commerce and Compromise, 1820–1850*. Cambridge: Cambridge University Press, 1995.

Auden, W. H. [1937]. "Spain." In *Poetry of the Thirties*, edited by Robin Skelton, 133–36. Harmondsworth: Penguin, 1964.

Bakan, Abigail. "Plantation Slavery and the Capitalist Mode of Production: An Analysis of the Development of the Jamaican Labour Force," *Studies in Political Economy* 22 (1987): 73–99.

Banaji, Jairus [1977]. "Modes of Production in a Materialist Conception of History." In *Theory as History: Essays on Modes of Production and Exploitation*, 45–102. Leiden: E. J. Brill, 2010.

————. "Introduction: Themes in Historical Materialism." In *Theory as History: Essays on Modes of Production and Exploitation*, 1–44. Leiden: E. J. Brill, 2010.

————. "Modes of Production: A Synthesis." In *Theory as History: Essays on Modes of Production and Exploitation*, 349–60. Leiden: E. J. Brill, 2010.

Barker, Colin. "The State as Capital," *International Socialism*, second series, 1 (July 1978): 16–42.

Barkey, Karen and Rudi Batzell. "Comparisons across Empires: The Critical Social Structures of the Ottomans, Russians and Habsburgs during the Seventeenth Century." In *Tributary Empires in Global History*, edited by Peter Fibiger Bang and Christopher A. Bayly, 227–61. Houndmills: Palgrave Macmillan, 2011.

Baron, Hans. "A Sociological Interpretation of the Early Renaissance in Florence," *South Atlantic Quarterly* 38, no. 4 (October 1939): 427–48.

Bayly, Christopher A. *Indian Society and the Making of the British Empire*, vol. 2.1 of *The New Cambridge History of India*. Cambridge: Cambridge University Press, 1988.

————. *The Birth of the Modern World, 1780–1914: Global Connections and Comparisons*. Oxford: Blackwell, 2004.

Beales, Derek E. D [1987]. "Social Forces and Enlightened Policies." In *Enlightenment and Reform in Eighteenth-Century Europe*, 7–27. London: I. B. Tauris, 2005.

Beard, Charles and Mary Beard [1927]. *The Rise of American Civilization*. 2 volumes in 1, new edition, revised and enlarged, New York: Macmillan, 1935.

Bell, David. "Class Consciousness, and the Fall of the Bourgeois Revolution," *Critical Review* 16, nos 2/3 (2004): 323–51.

Bennassar, Bartolomé. "Consommation, Investissements, Mouvements de Capitaux en Castille aux XVI' et XVII' Siècles." In *Conjoncture Economique, Structures Socials: Hommage a Ernest Labrousse*, edited by Fernand Braudel et al., 139–55. Paris, Mouton, 1974.

Benjamin, Walter [1927–40]. "Convolute E: [Haussmannization, Barricade Fighting]." In *The Arcades Project*, edited by Rolf Tiedemann, 120–49. Cambridge, MA: Belknap Press of Harvard University Press, 1999.

——— [1927–40]. "Convolute K: [Dream City and Dream House, Dreams of the Future, Anthropological Nihilism, Jung]." In *The Arcades Project*, edited by Rolf Tiedemann, 388–415. Cambridge, MA: Belknap Press of Harvard University Press, 1999.

Bensaïd, Daniel. *Marx for Our Times: Adventures and Misadventures of a Critique*. London: Verso, 2002.

Berger, John. *Success and Failure of Picasso*. Harmondsworth: Penguin, 1965.

Berktay, Halil. "The Feudalism Debate: The Turkish End—Is 'Tax-versus-Rent' Necessarily the Product and Sign of a Modal Difference?" *Journal of Peasant Studies* 14, no. 3 (April 1987): 291–333.

Berman, Morris. *Why America Failed: The Roots of Imperial Decline*. Hoboken, NJ: John Wiley and Sons, 2012.

Bernier, Gerald and Daniel Sallee. *The Shaping of Quebec Politics and Society: Colonialism, Power, and the Transition to Capitalism in the 19th Century*. Washington DC: Taylor and Francis, 1999.

Bernstein, Henry. *Class Dynamics of Agrarian Change*. Halifax, Nova Scotia and Sterling, Virginia: Fernwood Publishing and Kumarian Press, 2010.

Bertram, Christopher. "International Competition in Historical Materialism," *New Left Review* 1, no. 183 (September/October 1980): 116–28.

Bérubé, Michael. "Its Renaissance Time: New Historicism, American Studies, and American Identity." In *Public Access: Literary Theory and American Cultural Politics*, 203–24. New York: Verso, 1994.

Betts, R. R. "Social and Constitutional Development in Bohemia in the Hussite Period," *Past and Present* 7 (April 1955): 37–54.

Binns, Peter. "Revolution and State Capitalism in the Third World," *International Socialism*, second series, 25 (Autumn 1984): 37–68.

Blackburn, Robin. *The Overthrow of Colonial Slavery, 1776–1848*. London: Verso, 1988.

———. *The Making of New World Slavery: From the Baroque to the Modern*. London: Verso, 1997.

Blanning, Tim C. W. *The Pursuit of Glory: Europe, 1649–1815*. Harmondsworth: Penguin, 2008.

Blanqui, Jérôme-Adolphe. *Histoire de l'Economie Politique en Europe depuis les anciens jusqu'à nos jours*. Paris: Guillaumin, 1837.

Blaut, James M. *The Colonizer's View of the World: Geographical Diffusion and Eurocentric History*. New York: Guilford Press, 1993.

Blum, Jerome. *The End of the Old Order in Rural Europe*. Princeton, NJ: Princeton University Press, 1978.

Bois, Guy [1976]. *The Crisis of Feudalism: Economy and Society in Eastern Normandy, c. 1300–1550*. Cambridge and Paris: Cambridge University Press and Editions de la Maison des Sciences de L'Homme, 1991.

——— [1978]. "Against the Neo-Malthusian Orthodoxy." In *The Brenner Debate: Agrarian Class Structure and Economic Development in Pre-Industrial Europe*, edited by T. H. Aston and C. H. E. Philpin, 107–18. Cambridge: Cambridge University Press, 1985.

——— [1992]. *The Transformation of the Year One Thousand: The Village of Lournand from Antiquity to Feudalism*. Manchester: Manchester University Press, 1992.

Bond, Patrick. "In Power in Pretoria? Reply to Johnson," *New Left Review* 2, no. 58 (July/August 2009): 77–88.

Bonnassie, Pierre [1984]. "The Survival and Extinction of the Slave System in the Early Medieval West (Fourth to Eleventh Centuries)." In *From Slavery to Feudalism in Southeast*

Europe, 1–59. Cambridge and Paris: Cambridge University Press and Editions de la Maison des Sciences de L'Homme, 1991.

Bookchin, Murray. *Remaking Society: Pathways to a Green Future*. Montreal: Black Rose Books, 1989.

———. *The Ecology of Freedom: The Emergence and Dissolution of Hierarchy*. Revised edition, Montreal: Black Rose Books, 1991.

———. *The Third Revolution*, vol. 1, *Popular Movements in the Revolutionary Era*. London: Cassell, 1996.

Bowman, Shearer Davis. "Antebellum Planters and Vormarz Junkers in Comparative Perspective," *American Historical Review* 85, no. 3 (1980): 779–808.

Bradley, Andrew C. *Shakespearean Tragedy: Lectures on Hamlet, Othello, King Lear [and] Macbeth*. London: Macmillan, 1904.

Brandon, Pepijn. "Marxism and the 'Dutch Miracle': The Dutch Republic and the Transition Debate," *Historical Materialism* 19, no. 3 (2011): 106–46.

Braudel, Fernand [1949]. *The Mediterranean and the Mediterranean World in the Age of Phillip II*, volume 2. London: Fontana, 1973.

———. *Capitalism and Civilization, 15th–18th Centuries*, vol. 2, *The Wheels of Commerce*. London: Fontana, 1982.

———. *Capitalism and Civilization, 15th–18th Centuries*, vol. 3, *The Perspective of the World*. London: Fontana, 1985.

Brenner, Robert [1976]. "Agrarian Class Structure and Economic Development in Pre-Industrial Europe." In *The Brenner Debate: Agrarian Class Structure and Economic Development in Pre-Industrial Europe*, edited by T. H. Aston and C. H. E. Philpin, 10–63. Cambridge: Cambridge University Press, 1985.

——— [1982]. "The Agrarian Roots of European Capitalism." In *The Brenner Debate: Agrarian Class Structure and Economic Development in Pre-Industrial Europe*, edited by T. H. Aston and C. H. E. Philpin, 213–327. Cambridge: Cambridge University Press, 1985.

———. "The Social Basis of Economic Development." In *Analytical Marxism*, edited by John Roemer, 23–53. Cambridge: Cambridge University Press, 1986.

———. *Merchants and Revolution: Commercial Change, Political Conflict, and London's Overseas Traders, 1550–1653*. Princeton, NJ: Princeton University Press, 1993.

———. "The Low Countries and the Transition to Capitalism." In *Peasants into Farmers? The Transformation of Rural Economy and Society in the Low Countries (Middle Ages–19th Century) in Light of the Brenner Debate*, edited by Peter Hoppenbrouwers and Jan Luiten van Zanden, 275–338. Turnhout: Brepols, 2001.

——— [2007]. "Civil War, Global Distemper." In *Spectrum: From Right to Left in the World of Ideas*, edited by Perry Anderson, 232–276. London: Verso, 2007.

Brenner, Robert and Christopher Isett, "England's Divergence from China's Yangtze Delta: Property Relations, Microeconomics, and Patterns of Development," *Journal of Asian Studies* 61, no. 2 (May 2002): 609–62.

Breuilly, John [1982]. *Nationalism and the State*. Second edition, Manchester: Manchester University Press, 1993.

Brewer, John. *The Sinews of Power: War, Money and the English State, 1688–1783*. London: Unwin Hyman, 1989.

Buck-Morss, Susan. "Hegel and Haiti," *Critical Inquiry* 26, no. 4 (Summer 2000): 821–65.

Bukharin, Nikolai I [1915]. *Imperialism and World Economy*. London: Merlin, 1972.

——— [1920]. "The Economics of the Transition Period." In *The Politics and Economics of the Transition Period*, edited by Kenneth J. Tarbuck, 53–175. London: Routledge and Kegan Paul, 1979.

———. *Historical Materialism: A System of Sociology*. New York: International Publishers, 1925.

Burbach, Roger. *Globalization and Postmodern Politics: From Zapatistas to High-Tech Robber*

Barons. London: Pluto Press, 2001.

Burns, Robert [1795]. "A Man's a Man for a' That." In *The Canongate Burns: The Complete Poems and Songs of Robert Burns*, edited by Andrew Noble and Patrick Scott Hogg, 512–16. Edinburgh: Canongate, 2001.

Byres, Terence J. *Capitalism from Above and Capitalism from Below*. Basingstoke: Macmillan, 1996.

———. "Differentiation of the Peasantry under Feudalism and the Transition to Capitalism: In Defence of Rodney Hilton," *Journal of Agrarian Change* 6, no. 1 (January 2006): 17–68.

Cabral, Amilcar [1964]. "Brief Analysis of the Social Structure in Guinea." In *Revolution in Guinea: An African People's Struggle*, 46–61. London: Stage 1, 1969.

Callinicos, Alex. "Trotsky's Theory of 'Permanent Revolution' and Its Relevance to the Third World Today," *International Socialism*, second series, 16 (Spring 1982): 98–112.

———. *Making History: Agency, Structure, and Change in Social Theory*, Cambridge: Polity, 1987.

———. "Bourgeois Revolutions and Historical Materialism," *International Socialism*, second series, 43 (Summer 1989): 113–71.

———. *Theories and Narratives: Reflections on the Philosophy of History*, Cambridge: Polity, 1995.

———. *Social Theory: A Historical Introduction*. Cambridge: Polity, 1999.

———. *An Anti-Capitalist Manifesto*. Cambridge: Polity, 2003.

———. *Imperialism and Global Political Economy*. Cambridge: Polity, 2009.

Campbell, Thorbjorn. *Standing Witnesses: An Illustrated Guide to the Scottish Covenanters and Their Memorials with a Historical Introduction*. Edinburgh: Saltire Society, 1996.

Cameron, Ewan. *The European Reformation*. Oxford: Clarendon Press, 1991.

Camejo, Peter. *Racism, Revolution, Reaction, 1861–1877: The Rise and Fall of Radical Reconstruction*. New York: Monad Press, 1976.

Cannadine, David. "The Context, Performance and Meaning of Ritual: The British Monarchy and the 'Invention of Tradition,' c. 1820–1977," in *The Invention of Tradition*, edited by Eric J. Hobsbawm and Terence Ranger, 101–64. Cambridge: Cambridge University Press, 1983.

Cardan, Paul (Carlos Castoriadis) [1964]. *History and Revolution: A Revolutionary Critique of Historical Materialism*. London: Solidarity pamphlet no. 38, 1971.

Carling, Alan H. *Social Division*. London: Verso, 1991.

———. "Analytic Marxism and Historical Materialism: The Debate on Social Evolution," *Science and Society* 57, no. 1 (Spring 1993): 31–65.

Carling, Alan H. and Paul Nolan, "Historical Materialism Natural Selection and World History," *Historical Materialism* 6 (Summer 2000): 215–64.

Castoriadis, Cornelius [1964–65]. "Marxism and Revolutionary Theory." In *The Imaginary Institution of Society*, 113–230. Cambridge: Polity, 1987.

Chadwick, Owen. *The Reformation*, vol. 3 of *The Pelican History of the Church*. Revised edition, Harmondsworth: Penguin, 1968.

Chandra, Satish [1966]. "Some Aspects of the Growth of a Money Economy in India during the Seventeenth Century." In *Essays on Medieval Indian History*. New Delhi: Oxford University Press, 2003.

Chateaubriand, François-René de [1848]. *Memoires D'outre-Tombe*, Tome 3. Paris: Flammarion, 1950.

Chatterjee, Partha. *Nationalist Thought and the Colonial World: A Derivative Discourse?* London: Zed, 1986.

Chesneaux, Jean. *Peasant Revolts in China, 1840–1949*. London: Thames and Hudson, 1973.

Chibber, Vivek. "What Is Living and What Is Dead in the Marxist Theory of History," *Historical Materialism* 19, no. 2 (2011): 60–91.

Chistozvonov, Alexander. "The Concept and Criteria of Reversibility and Irreversibility of an Historical Process", *Our History* 63 (Summer 1975).

Choonara, Joseph. "The Relevance of Permanent Revolution: A Reply to Neil Davidson," *International Socialism*, second series, 131 (Summer 2011): 173–87.

Christianson, Paul. "The Causes of the English Revolution: A Reappraisal," *Journal of British Studies* 15, no. 2 (Spring 1976): 40–75.

Cipolla, Carlo M. [1965]. "Guns and Sails." In *European Culture and Overseas Expansion, 1400–1700.* Harmondsworth: Penguin, 1970.

Cliff, Tony [1948]. "The Nature of Stalinist Russia." In *Marxist Theory after Trotsky*, vol. 3 of *Selected Writings*, 1–138. London: Bookmarks, 2003.

——— [1950]. "The Class Nature of the People's Democracies." In *Neither Washington nor Moscow: Essays on Revolutionary Socialism*, 40–85. London: Bookmarks, 1984.

Cohn, Norman [1957]. *The Pursuit of the Millennium: Revolutionary Millenarians and Mystical Anarchists of the Middle Ages.* Second edition, London: Paladin, 1970.

Cohn, Samuel K. *Lust for Liberty: The Politics of Social Revolt in Medieval Europe, 1200–1425.* Cambridge, MA: Harvard University Press, 2006.

Coleman, Donald C. *Industry in Tudor and Stuart England.* London: Macmillan, 1975.

Collier, Andrew. *Marx.* Oxford: Oneworld, 2004.

Commission of the C.C. of the C.P.S.U. (B.). [1938]. *History of the Communist Party of the Soviet Union (Bolsheviks): Short Course.* Moscow: Foreign Languages Publishing House, 1943.

Corcoran, Paul E. "The Bourgeoisie and Other Villains," *Journal of the History of Ideas* 38, no. 3 (July 1977): 477–85.

Corish, Patrick. J. "The Cromwellian Conquest, 1649–53." In *A New History of Ireland*, vol. 3, *Early Modern Ireland, 1534–1691*, edited by T. W. Moody, F. X. Martin, and F. J. Byrne, 336–52. Oxford: Oxford University Press, 1976.

Coveney, Peter J. "An Early Modern European Crisis?" *Renaissance and Modern Studies* 26 (1982): 1–26.

Creighton, Donald G. *The Commercial Empire of the St. Lawrence, 1760–1850.* New Haven, CT: Yale University Press, 1937.

———. *The Road to Confederation: The Emergence of Canada, 1863–1867.* Toronto: Macmillan, 1964.

Crone, Patricia. *Pre-industrial Societies.* Oxford: Basil Blackwell, 1989.

Croot, Patricia and David Parker [1978]. "Agrarian Class Structure and the Development of Capitalism: France and England Compared." In *The Brenner Debate: Agrarian Class Structure and Economic Development in Pre-Industrial Europe*, edited by T. H. Aston and C. H. E. Philpin, 79–90. Cambridge: Cambridge University Press, 1985.

Crouzet, François. "Western Europe and Great Britain: 'Catching Up' in the First Half of the Nineteenth Century," in *Britain Ascendant: Comparative Studies in Franco-British History*, 341–84. Cambridge and Paris: Cambridge University Press and Editions de la Maison des Sciences de L'Homme, 1990.

D'Amato, Paul. "The Necessity of Permanent Revolution," *International Socialist Review* 48 (August 2006).

Daalder, Hans. "Consociationalism, Center and Periphery in the Netherlands." In *Mobilization, Center-Periphery Structures and Nation-Building: A Volume in Commemoration of Stein Rokkan*, edited by Per Torsvick, 181–240. Bergen: Universitetsforlaget, 1981.

Dabat, Alejandro and Luis Lorenzano [1982]. *Argentina: The Malvinas and the End of Military Rule.* Expanded and revised edition, London: Verso, 1984.

Dadoo, Yusuf M. "Introduction." In *South African Communists Speak: Documents from the History of the South African Communist Party, 1915–1980*, edited by Brian Bunting, xv–xix. London: Inkululenko Publications, 1981.

Dalziel, Raewyn. "Southern Islands: New Zealand and Polynesia." In *The Nineteenth Century*, vol. 3 of *The Oxford History of the British Empire*, edited by Andrew Porter, 573–96. Oxford: University of Oxford Press, 1999.

Darwin, John. *After Tamerlane: The Global History of Empire since 1405.* London: Allen Lane,

2007.

Davidson, Neil. *Discovering the Scottish Revolution, 1692–1746*. London: Pluto, 2003.

———. "The Scottish Path to Capitalist Agriculture 2: The Capitalist Offensive (1747–1815)," *Journal of Agrarian Change* 4, no. 4 (October 2004): 411–60.

———. "The Scottish Path to Capitalist Agriculture 3: The Enlightenment as the Theory and Practice of Improvement," *Journal of Agrarian Change* 5, no. 1 (2005): 1–72.

———. "China: Unevenness, Combination, Revolution?" In *100 Years of Permanent Revolution: Results and Prospects*, edited by Bill Dunn and Hugo Radice, 211–229. London: Pluto Press, 2006.

———. "Scotland: Birthplace of Passive Revolution?" *Capital and Class* 34, no. 3, special issue on *Approaching Passive Revolutions*, edited by Adam David Morton (October 2010): 343–59.

Davis, Mike. *Late Victorian Holocausts: El Niño Famines and the Making of the Third World*. London: Verso, 2001.

———. "Sand, Fear and Money in Dubai." In *Evil Paradises: Dreamworlds of Neoliberalism*, ed. Mike Davis and Daniel Bertrand Monk, 48–68. London: Verso, 2007.

Dennison, Tracy K. and A. W. Carus, "The Invention of the Russian Rural Commune: Haxthausen and the Evidence," *Historical Journal* 46, no. 3 (September 2003): 561–82.

Deutsch, Karl W. and Hermann Weilenmann, "The Swiss City Canton: A Political Invention," *Contemporary Studies in Society and History* 7 (1964/5): 393–408.

Devine, Pat. *Democracy and Economic Planning*. Cambridge: Polity, 1988.

Diamond, Jared. *The Rise and Fall of the Third Chimpanzee*. New York: Radius, 1991.

———. *Guns, Germs and Steel: A Short History of Everybody for the Last 13,000 Years*. London: Vintage, 1998.

———. *Collapse: How Societies Choose to Fail or Survive*. Harmondsworth: Penguin, 2006.

Dockes, Pierre. *Medieval Slavery and Liberation*. London: Methuen, 1982.

Dobb, Maurice [1946]. *Studies in the Development of Capitalism*. Revised edition, London: Macmillan, 1963.

Douglass, Frederick [1852], "The Meaning of July Fourth for the Negro." In *The Life and Writings of Frederick Douglass*, vol. 2, *Pre-Civil War Decade, 1850–1860*, 181–206, edited by Phillip S. Foner. New York: International Publishers, 1950.

——— [1860]. "The Constitution of the United States: Is It Pro-Slavery or Anti-Slavery." In *The Life and Writings of Frederick Douglass*, vol. 2, *Pre-Civil War Decade, 1850–1860*, 467–480, edited by Phillip S. Foner. New York: International Publishers, 1950.

——— [1863]. "Why Should a Colored Man Enlist?" In *The Life and Writings of Frederick Douglass*, vol. 3, *The Civil War, 1861–1865*, 340–44, edited by Phillip S. Foner. New York: International Publishers, 1952.

——— [1866]. "The Future of the Colored Race." In *The Life and Writings of Frederick Douglass*, vol. 4, *Reconstruction and After*, 193–96, edited by Phillip S. Foner. New York: International Publishers, 1955.

Draper, Hal [1963–4]. "The Myth of Lenin's 'Concept of the Party': Or What They Did to *What Is to Be Done?*" *Historical Materialism* 4 (Summer 1999): 187–214.

——— [1966]. "The Two Souls of Socialism." In *Socialism from Below*, edited E. Haberkern, 1–33. Atlantic Highlands, NJ: Humanities Press, 1992.

———. *Karl Marx's Theory of Revolution*, vol. 1, *State and Bureaucracy*. New York: Monthly Review Press, 1977.

———. *Karl Marx's Theory of Revolution*, vol. 2, *The Politics of Social Classes*. New York: Monthly Review Press, 1978.

Duby, Georges. *The Early Growth of the European Economy: Warriors and Peasants from the Seventh to the Twelfth Century*. London: Weidenfeld and Nicolson, 1974.

——— [1978]. *The Three Orders: Feudal Society Imagined*. Chicago: Chicago University Press, 1980.

——— [1987]. *France in the Middle Ages, 987–1460: From Hugh Capet to Joan of Arc*. Oxford:

Oxford University Press, 1991.

Duffy, Christopher. *The Military Experience in the Age of Reason*. London: Routledge, 1987.

Duggan, Christopher. *The Force of Destiny: A History of Italy since 1796*. London: Allen Lane, 2007.

Duplessis, Robert S. *Transitions to Capitalism in Early Modern Europe*. Cambridge: Cambridge University Press, 1997.

Eagleton, Terry. *The Illusions of Postmodernism*. Cambridge, MA: Blackwell, 1994.

Eley, Geoff. "The British Model and the German Road: Rethinking the Course of German History before 1914." In David Blackbourn and Geoff Eley, *The Peculiarities of German History: Bourgeois Society and Politics in Nineteenth-Century Germany*, 37–155. Oxford: Oxford University Press, 1984.

Elliott, John H. [1963]. *Imperial Spain, 1469–1716*. Harmondsworth: Penguin, 1970.

——— [1990]. "A Non-Revolutionary Society: Castille in the 1640s." In *Spain, Europe and the Wider World, 1500–1800*, 74–91. New Haven, CT: Yale University Press, 2009.

Elvin, Mark. *The Pattern of Chinese History*. Stanford: Stanford University Press, 1973.

Engels, Frederick [1880]. *Socialism: Utopian and Scientific*. New York: International Publishers, 1972.

——— [1884]. "On the Peasant War." In *Collected Works*, vol. 26, 554–55. London: Lawrence and Wishart, 1990.

——— [1884]. "On the Decline of Feudalism and the Emergence of National States." In *Collected Works*, vol. 26, 556–65. London: Lawrence and Wishart, 1990.

——— [1885]. "Preface to the Third German Edition of *The Eighteenth Brumaire of Louis Bonaparte* by Marx." In *Collected Works*, vol. 26, 302–3. London: Lawrence and Wishart, 1990.

——— [1886]. *Ludwig Feuerbach and the End of Classical German Philosophy*. In *Collected Works*, vol. 26, 357–98. London: Lawrence and Wishart, 1990.

——— [1890]. Engels to Danielson, June 10, 1890, in *Collected Works*, vol. 48, 506–7. London: Lawrence and Wishart, 2001.

——— [1890]. Engels to Bloch, September 21, 1890. In *Collected Works*, vol. 49, 33–36. London: Lawrence and Wishart, 2001.

Ennew, Judith, Paul Q. Hirst, and Keith Tribe. "'Peasantry' as an Economic Category," *Journal of Peasant Studies* 4, no. 4 (July 1977): 295–322.

Epstein, Stephen R. "The Late Medieval Crisis as an 'Integration' Crisis." In *Early Modern Capitalism: Economic and Social Change in Europe, 1400–1800*, edited by Maarten Pak, 25–50. London: Routledge, 2001.

Fanon, Frantz [1961]. *The Wretched of the Earth*. Harmondsworth: Penguin, 1967.

Ferguson, Adam [1767]. *An Essay on the History of Civil Society*, edited by Duncan Forbes. Edinburgh: Edinburgh University Press, 1966.

Ferraro, Joseph. *Freedom and Determination in History According to Marx and Engels*. New York: Monthly Review Press, 1992.

Fields, Barbara J. "Slavery, Race and Ideology in the United States of America," *New Left Review* 1, no. 181 (May/June 1990): 95–118.

Finley, Moses [1973]. *The Ancient Economy*. Second edition, Harmondsworth: Penguin, 1985.

——— [1980]. *Ancient Slavery and Modern Ideology*. Harmondsworth: Penguin, 1983.

Fogel, Robert. *Without Consent or Contract: The Rise and Fall of American Slavery*. New York: W. W. Norton, 1989.

Foner, Eric. *Reconstruction: America's Unfinished Revolution, 1863–1877*. New York: Harper and Row, 1988.

Foucault, Michel [1977]. "Truth and Power." In *Power/Knowledge: Selected Interviews and Other Writings, 1972–1977*, edited by Colin Gordon, 109–133. Brighton: Harvester, 1980.

Fraser, Ronald. *Napoleon's Cursed War: Popular Resistance in the Spanish Peninsular War, 1808–1814*. London: Verso, 2008.

Friedrichs, Christopher R. "The War and German Society." In *The Thirty Years' War*, ed. Geoffrey

Parker, 208–15. London: Routledge, 1984.

Furet, François. "Terror." In *The French Revolution in Social and Political Perspective*, edited by Peter Jones, 450–65. London: Arnold, 1996.

Gamble, Andrew. *Hayek: The Iron Cage of Liberty*. Boulder, CO: Westview Press, 1996.

García Linera, Álvaro. "State Crisis, Popular Power," *New Left Review* 2, no. 37 (January/February 2006): 73–85.

———. "The MAS Is of the Center-Left," *International Viewpoint* 373 (December 2005), http://www.internationalviewpoint.org/spip.php?article938.

Gatrell, Peter. *Government, Industry and Rearmament in Russia, 1900–1914*. Cambridge: Cambridge University Press, 1994.

Genovese, Elizabeth Fox and Eugene D. Genovese, "On the Social History of the French Revolution: New Methods, Old Ideologies." In *Fruits of Merchant Capital: Slavery and Bourgeois Property in the Rise and Expansion of Capitalism*, 213–48. Oxford: Oxford University Press, 1983.

Gernet, Jacques [1972]. *A History of Chinese Civilisation*. Second edition, Cambridge: Cambridge University Press, 1982.

Gerstenberger, Heide [1990]. *Impersonal Power: History and Theory of the Bourgeois State*. Leiden: E. J. Brill, 2007.

Giddens, Anthony. *The Class Structure of the Advanced Societies*. London: Hutchison University Library, 1973.

Gilly, Adolfo [1971]. *The Mexican Revolution*. Expanded and revised edition, London: Verso, 1983.

Ginsborg, Paul. *A History of Contemporary Italy: Society and Politics, 1943–1988*. Harmondsworth: Penguin, 1990.

Godelier, Maurice [1964/1968]. "The Concept of the 'Asiatic Mode of Production' and Marxist Models of Social Evolution." In *Relations of Production: Marxist Approaches to Economic Anthropology*, edited by David D. Seddon, 209–57. London: Frank Cass, 1978.

Goldmann, Lucien. *The Hidden God: A Study of Tragic Vision in the Pensees of Pascal and the Tragedies of Racine*. London: Routledge and Kegan Paul, 1964.

Goldstone, Jack A. "East and West in the Seventeenth Century: Political Crises in Stuart England, Ottoman Turkey, and Ming China," *Comparative Studies in Society and History* 30, no. 1 (January 1988): 103–42.

Goodwin, Jeff. *No Other Way Out: States and Revolutionary Movements, 1945–1991*. Cambridge: Cambridge University Press, 2001.

Gordon, Daniel [1999]. "On the Supposed Obsolescence of the French Enlightenment." In *Postmodernism and the Enlightenment: New Perspectives on Eighteenth-Century French Intellectual History*, edited by Daniel Gordon, 201–21. London: Routledge, 2001.

Gouldner, Alvin W. *The Future of Intellectuals and the Rise of the New Class: A Frame of Reference, Theses, Conjectures, Arguments and an Historical Perspective on the Role of Intellectuals and Intelligentsia in the International Class Contest of the Modern Era*. New York: Continuum Books, 1979.

Gramsci, Antonio [1929]. Gramsci to Carlo, December 19, 1929, in *Letters from Prison*, vol. 1, ed. Frank Rosengarten, 297–300. New York: Columbia University Press, 1994.

——— [1927–34]. "The Intellectuals." In *Selections from the Prison Notebooks*, edited by Quintin Hoare and Geoffrey Nowell-Smith, 5–23. London: Lawrence and Wishart, 1971.

——— [1927–34]. "The Modern Prince." In *Selections from the Prison Notebooks*, edited by Quintin Hoare and Geoffrey Nowell-Smith, 124–205. London: Lawrence and Wishart, 1971.

——— [1927–34]. "Problems of Marxism: Some Problems in the Study of the Philosophy of Praxis." In *Selections from the Prison Notebooks*, edited by Quintin Hoare and Geoffrey Nowell-Smith, 381–472. London: Lawrence and Wishart, 1971.

——— [1927–34]. "The Question of the Language and the Italian Intellectual Classes." In

Selections from the Cultural Writings, edited by David Forgacs and Geoffrey Nowell-Smith, 167–71. London: Lawrence and Wishart, 1985.

———— [1927–34]. "The Renaissance." In *Selections from the Cultural Writings*, edited by David Forgacs and Geoffrey Nowell-Smith, 220–22. London: Lawrence and Wishart, 1985.

————. *Prison Notebooks*, vol. 2, edited by Joseph A. Buttigieg. New York: Columbia University Press, 1996.

————. *Prison Notebooks*, vol. 3, edited by Joseph A. Buttigieg. New York: Columbia University Press, 2007.

Graus, Frantisek. "From Resistance to Revolt: The Late Medieval Peasant Wars in the Context of Social Crisis," *Journal of Peasant Studies* 3, no. 1 (October 1975): 1–9.

Green, Peter. "The First Sicilian Slave War," *Past and Present* 20 (November 1961): 10–29.

Greenfield, Liah. *The Spirit of Capitalism: Nationalism and Economic Growth*. Cambridge, MA: Harvard University Press, 2001.

Griffin, Roger. "Revolution from the Right: Fascism." In *Revolutions and the Revolutionary Tradition in the West, 1560–1991*, edited by David Parker, 185–201. London: Routledge, 2000.

Griffiths, Jay. *Pip Pip: A Sideways Look at Time*. London: Flamingo, 2000.

Grossman, Henryk. "The Evolutionist Revolt against Classical Economics: II. In England—James Steuart, Richard Jones, Karl Marx," *Journal of Political Economy* 51, no. 6 (December 1943): 506–22.

Guy, Jeff. "The Destruction and Reconstruction of Zulu Society." In *Industrialization and Social Change in South Africa: African Class Formation, Culture and Consciousness 1870–1930*, edited by Shula Marks and Richard Rathbone, 167–94. London: Longman,1982.

Habermas, Jürgen [1962]. *The Structural Transformation of the Public Sphere: An Inquiry into a Category of Bourgeois Society*. London: Polity, 1989.

Habib, Irfan [1968]. "Potentialities of Capitalist Development in the Economy of Mughal India." In *Essays in Indian History: Towards a Marxist Perception*, 180–232. London: Anthem Press, 2002.

Haldon, John. "The Feudalism Debate Once More: The Case of Byzantium," *Journal of Peasant Studies* 17, no. 1 (October 1989): 5–40.

————. *The State and the Tributary Mode of Production*. London: Verso, 1993.

Hall, John A. "States and Societies: The Miracle in Comparative Perspective." In *Europe and the Rise of Capitalism*, edited by Jean Baechler, John A. Hall, and Michael Mann, 20–38. Oxford: Basil Blackwell, 1988.

Halliday, Fred. *Revolution and World Politics: The Rise and Fall of the Sixth Great Power*. London: Macmillan, 1999.

Hardt, Michael and Antonio Negri. *Empire*. Cambridge, MA: Harvard University Press, 2000.

Harman, Chris [1994]. "The Prophet and the Proletariat." In *Selected Writings*, 301–61. London: Bookmarks, 2010.

Hartz, Louis. *The Liberal Tradition in America*. New York: Harcourt, Brace, 1955.

Harvey, David [1978]. "On Countering the Marxian Myth—Chicago Style." In *Spaces of Capital: Towards a Critical Geography*, 68–89. Edinburgh: Edinburgh University Press, 2001.

————. *Paris, Capital of Modernity*. New York: Routledge, 2003.

————. *A Brief History of Neoliberalism*. Oxford: Oxford University Press, 2005.

————. *The Enigma of Capital and the Crises of Capitalism*. London: Profile Books, 2010.

Hayek, Frederick A. "History and Politics." In *Capitalism and the Historians*, edited by Frederick A. Hayek, 3–29. Chicago: University of Chicago Press, 1954.

————. *The Fatal Conceit: The Errors of Socialism*, vol. 1 of *Collected Works*, edited by W. W. Bartley. London: Routledge 1988.

Heller, Henry. *The Conquest of Poverty: The Calvinist Revolt in Sixteenth-Century France*. Leiden: E. J. Brill, 1986.

————. *Labor, Science and Technology in France, 1500–1620*. Cambridge: Cambridge University

Press, 1996.

———. *The Bourgeois Revolution in France, 1789–1815*. New York: Berghahn Books, 2006.

Hill, Christopher [1972]. *The World Turned Upside Down: Radical Ideas in the English Revolution*. Harmondsworth: Penguin, 1975.

——— [1984]. *The Experience of Defeat: Milton and Some Contemporaries*. London: Bookmarks, 1994.

———. "The Bourgeois Revolution in Soviet Scholarship," *New Left Review* 1, no. 155 (January–February, 1986): 107–13.

Hilton, Rodney H. [1949]. "Peasant Movements in England before 1381." In *Class Conflict and the Crisis of Feudalism: Essays in Medieval Social History*, 49–65. Revised second edition, London: Verso, 1990.

——— [1951]. "Was There a General Crisis of Feudalism?" In *Class Conflict and the Crisis of Feudalism: Essays in Medieval Social History*, 166–72. Revised second edition, London: Verso, 1990.

———. *Bond Men Made Free: Medieval Peasant Movements and the English Rising of 1381*. London: Methuen, 1973.

——— [1984]. "Feudalism in Europe: Problems for Historical Materialists." In *Class Conflict and the Crisis of Feudalism: Essays in Medieval Social History*, 1–11. Revised second edition, London: Verso, 1990.

Hipkin, Stephen. "Property, Economic Interest and the Configuration of Rural Conflict in Sixteenth and Seventeenth-Century England," *Socialist History* 23 (2003): 67–88.

Hirschman, Albert O. [1977]. *The Passions and the Interests: Political Arguments for Capitalism before Its Triumph*. Twentieth anniversary edition, Princeton, NJ: Princeton University Press, 1997.

Hirst, Paul Q. [1975]. "The Uniqueness of the West—Perry Anderson's Analysis of Absolutism and Its Problems." *Marxism and Historical Writing*. London: Routledge and Kegan Paul, 1985.

Hobsbawm, Eric J. [1954]. "The Crisis of the Seventeenth Century." In *Crisis in Europe, 1560–1660: Essays from* Past and Present, edited by Trevor Aston, 5–58. London: Routledge and Kegan Paul, 1965.

——— [1962]. *The Age of Revolution: Europe, 1789–1848*. London: Weidenfeld and Nicolson, 1995.

——— [1975]. *The Age of Capital, 1848–1875*. London: Weidenfeld and Nicolson, 1995.

———. "Revolution." In *Revolution in History*, edited by Roy Porter and Milukas Teich, 5–46. Cambridge: Cambridge University Press, 1986.

———. [1987]. *The Age of Empire, 1875–1914*. London: Weidenfeld and Nicolson, 1995.

———. *Echoes of the Marseillaise: Two Centuries Look Back on the French Revolution*. London: Verso, 1990.

Hobson, John M. *The Eastern Origins of Western Civilization*. New York: Cambridge University Press, 2004.

Hoffman, Phillip. *Growth in a Traditional Society: The French Countryside, 1450–1815*. Princeton, NJ: Princeton University Press, 1996.

Holstun, James. *Ehud's Dagger: Class Struggle in the English Revolution*. London: Verso, 2000.

———. "Communism, George Hill and the *Mir*: Was Marx a Nineteenth-century Winstanleyan?" In *Winstanley and the Diggers, 1649–1999*, edited by Andrew Bradstock, 121–48. London: Frank Cass, 2000.

———. "Utopia Pre-empted : Kett's Rebellion, Commoning, and the Hysterical Sublime," *Historical Materialism* 16, no. 3 (2008): 3–53.

Hoodbhoy, Pervez A. *Islam and Science: Religious Orthodoxy and the Battle for Rationality*. London: Zed Books, 1991.

Hook, Andrew. "Scott and America." In *From Goosecreek to Gandercleugh: Studies in Scottish-American*

Literary and Cultural History, 94–115. East Linton, Scotland: Tuckwell Press, 1999.

Hook, Andrew. "The South, Scotland, and William Faulkner." In *From Goosecreek to Gandercleugh: Studies in Scottish-American Literary and Cultural History*, 193–212. East Linton, Scotland: Tuckwell Press, 1999.

Hoppit, Julian. *A Land of Liberty? England, 1689–1727*. Oxford: Clarendon Press, 2000.

Horkheimer, Max [1941]. "The End of Reason." In *The Essential Frankfurt School Reader*, edited by Anthony Arato and Eike Gebhardt, 26–48. Oxford: Basil Blackwell, 1978.

Horne, Donald. *The Great Museum: The Re-presentation of History*. London: Pluto Press, 1984.

Hoston, Germaine. "Conceptualizing Bourgeois Revolution: The Prewar Japanese Left and the Meiji Restoration," *Comparative Studies in Society and History* 33, no. 3 (July 1991): 539–87.

Hoyle, Richard. "Tenure and the Land Market in Early Modern England: Or, a Late Contribution to the Brenner Debate," *Economic History Review*, second series, vol. 43, no. 1 (January 1990): 1–20.

Hume, David [1739]. *A Treatise of Human Nature: Being an Attempt to Introduce the Experimental Method of Reasoning into Moral Subjects*, Book 1, *Of the Understanding*, edited by Donald G. C Macnabb. London: Fontana, 1962.

——— [1739–40]. *A Treatise of Human Nature: Being an Attempt to Introduce the Experimental Method of Reasoning into Moral Subjects*, Book 2, *Of the Passions* and Book 3, *Of Morals*, edited by Pall S. Ardal. London: Fontana, 1972.

——— [1752]. "Of Interest." In *Political Essays*, edited by Knud Haakonsen, 126–35. Cambridge, Cambridge University Press, 1994.

Israel, Jonathan I. *The Dutch Republic: Its Rise, Greatness, and Fall, 1477–1806*. Oxford: Clarendon Press, 1998.

———. *Radical Enlightenment: Philosophy and the Making of Modernity, 1650–1750*. Oxford: Oxford University Press, 2001.

———. *A Revolution of the Mind: Radical Enlightenment and the Intellectual Origins of Modern Democracy*. Princeton, NJ: Princeton University Press, 2010.

———. *Democratic Enlightenment: Philosophy, Revolution, and Human Rights, 1750–1790*. Oxford: Oxford University Press, 2010.

Jago, Charles. "The 'Crisis of the Aristocracy' in Seventeenth-Century Castile," *Past and Present* 84 (August 1979): 60–90.

James, C. L. R. [1938]. *The Black Jacobins: Toussaint L'Overture and the San Domingo Revolution*. New edition, London: Alison and Busby, 1980.

Jameson, Fredric [1984]. 'The Cultural Logic of Late Capitalism,' in *Postmodernism, or, the Cultural Logic of Late Capitalism*, 1–54. London: Verso, 1991.

Jefferson, Thomas et al. [1776]. "The Unanimous Declaration of the Thirteen United States of America, July 4, 1776." In *Revolution from 1789 to 1906*, edited by Raymond Postgate, 4. London: Grant Richards, 1920.

Jones, Colin [1990]. "Bourgeois Revolution Revivified: 1789 and Social Change." In *The French Revolution: Recent Debates and New Controversies*, edited by Gary Kates, 87–112. Second edition, London: Routledge, 2006.

Jones, Gareth Stedman. "Society and Politics at the Beginning of the World Economy," *Cambridge Journal of Economics* 1 (1977): 77–92.

Jones, James R. *The Anglo-Dutch Wars of the Seventeenth Century*. London: Longman, 1996.

Johnson, R. W. "False Start in South Africa," *New Left Review* 2, no. 58 (July/August 2009): 61–74.

Jones, P. J. "Communes and Despots: the City-State in Late-Medieval Italy," *Transactions of the Royal Historical Society*, fifth series, 15 (1964): 71–96.

Kamen, Henry [1971]. *European Society, 1500–1700*. London: Hutchison, 1984.

Katz, Claudio J. *From Feudalism to Capitalism: Marxian Theories of Class Struggle and Social Change*. New York: Greenwood Press, 1989.

Kautsky, Karl [1888]. *Thomas More and His Utopia*. London: A. C. Black, 1927.

Kermode, Jenny. *Medieval Merchants: York, Beverley and Hull in the Later Middle Ages*. Cambridge: Cambridge University Press, 1998.

Khaldun, Ibn el. *The Muqaddimah: An Introduction to History*, edited by N. J. Dawood. London: Routledge and Kegan Paul, 1967.

Kiernan, Victor G. *State and Society in Europe, 1550–1650*. Oxford: Basil Blackwell, 1980.

King James VI and I [1599]. "Basilicon Doron." In *Political Writings*, edited by Johann P. Sommerville, 1–61. Cambridge: Cambridge University Press, 1994.

Kingsnorth, Paul. *One No, Many Yeses: A Journey to the Heart of the Global Resistance Movement*. London: Free Press, 2003.

Kitsikopoulos, Harry. "Technological Change in Medieval England: A Critique of the Neo-Malthusian Argument," *Proceedings of the American Philosophical Society* 144, no. 4 (December 2000): 397–449.

Klassen, John. "The Disadvantaged and the Hussite Revolution," *International Review of Social History* 35 (1990): 249–72.

Klooster, Wim. *Revolutions in the Atlantic World: A Comparative History*. New York: New York University Press, 2009.

Knight, Alan. "The Mexican Revolution: Bourgeois? Nationalist? Or Just a 'Great Rebellion'? *Bulletin of Latin American Research* 4, no. 2 (1985): 1–37.

Koenigsberger, Hans G. "Republics and Courts in Italian and European Culture in the Sixteenth and Seventeenth Centuries," *Past and Present* 83 (May 1979): 32–56.

Kolchin, Peter. *American Slavery, 1619–1877*. Harmondsworth: Penguin, 1993.

Kreidte, Peter. *Peasants, Landlords and Merchant Capitalists: Europe and the World Economy, 1500–1800*. Leamington Spa: Berg Publishers, 1983.

Kulikoff, Allen. "Was the American Revolution a Bourgeois Revolution?" In *Transforming Hand of Revolution: Reconsidering the American Revolution as a Social Movement*, edited by Ronald Hoffman and Peter J. Albert, 59–89. Charlottesville: University of Virginia Press, 1996.

Lakatos, Imre. "Falsification and the Methodology of Scientific Research Programmes." In *Criticism and the Growth of Knowledge*, edited by Imre Lakatos and Alan Musgrave, 91–196. Cambridge: Cambridge at the University Press, 1970.

Larner, John. *Italy in the Age of Dante and Petrarch, 1216–1380*. London: Longman, 1980.

Leff, Gordon [1967]. *Heresy in the Later Middle Ages: The Relation of Heterodoxy to Dissent, c. 1250–c. 1450*. Manchester: Manchester University Press, 1999.

Lenin, Vladimir I. [1895]. "The Economic Content of Narodism and the Criticism of It in Mr. Struve's Book (*The Reflection of Marxism in Bourgeois Literature*)." In *Collected Works*, vol. 1, *1893–1894*, 333–507. Moscow: Foreign Languages Publishing House, 1960.

————— [1899]. *The Development of Capitalism in Russia: The Process of the Formation of Home Market for Large Scale Industry*. In *Collected Works*, vol. 3, *1899*, 23–607. Moscow: Foreign Languages Publishing House, 1960.

————— [1899]. "What Is to Be Done? Burning Questions of Our Movement." In *Collected Works*, vol. 5, *May 1901–February 1902*, 347–529. Moscow: Foreign Languages Publishing House, 1961.

————— [1915]. "The Collapse of the Second International." In *Collected Works*, vol. 21, *August 1914–December 1915*, 205–59. Moscow: Foreign Languages Publishing House, 1964.

————— [1915]. "New Data on the Laws Governing the Development of Capitalism in Agriculture, Part One: Capitalism and Agriculture in the United States of America," in *Collected Works*, vol. 22, *December 1915–July 1916*, 13–102. Moscow: Foreign Languages Publishing House. 1964.

————— [1916]. "The Discussion on Self-determination Summed-Up." In *Collected Works*, vol. 22, *December 1915–July 1916*, 320–60. Moscow: Foreign Languages Publishing House, 1964.

Lenman, Bruce J. *Britain's Colonial Wars, 1688–1783*. Harlow: Longman, 2001.

Lih, Lars T. *Lenin Rediscovered:* What Is to Be Done? *in Context*. Leiden: Brill Academic Publishing, 2005.

Linden, Marcel van der. "Marx and Engels, Dutch Marxism and the 'Model Capitalist Nation of the Seventeenth Century,'" *Science and Society* 61, no. 2 (Summer 1997): 161–92.

Linebaugh, Peter. "Review of *The Making of New World Slavery*," *Historical Materialism* 1 (Autumn 1997): 185–95.

Linebaugh, Peter and Marcus Rediker. *The Many-Headed Hydra: The Hidden History of the Revolutionary Atlantic*. London: Verso, 2000.

Livesey, James. *Making Democracy in the French Revolution*. Cambridge, MA: Harvard University Press, 2001.

Lochhead, Robert. *The Bourgeois Revolutions*. International Institute for Research and Education, Notebooks for Research and Study, no. 11/12 (1989).

Losurdo, Domenico [2006]. *Liberalism: A Counter-history*. London: Verso, 2011.

Lowe, Lisa. *Immigrant Acts: On Asian American Cultural Politics*. Durham, NC: Duke University Press, 1996.

Löwith, Karl [1960]. *Max Weber and Karl Marx*, edited by Tom Bottomore and William Outhwaite. London: George Allen and Unwin, 1982.

Lublinskaya, A. D. [1965]. *French Absolutism: The Crucial Phase, 1620–1629*. New York, Cambridge University Press, 1968.

Lucas, Colin. "Nobles, Bourgeois and the Origins of the French Revolution," *Past and Present* 60 (August 1973): 84–126.

Lukács, Georg [1923]. "The Marxism of Rosa Luxemburg." In *History and Class Consciousness: Studies in Marxist Dialectics*, 27–45. London: Merlin, 1971.

—— [1923]. "Class Consciousness." In *History and Class Consciousness: Studies in Marxist Dialectics*, 46–82. London: Merlin, 1971.

—— [1923]. "Reification and the Consciousness of the Proletariat." In *History and Class Consciousness: Studies in Marxist Dialectics*, 83–222. London: Merlin, 1971.

—— [1923]. "The Changing Function of Historical Materialism." In *History and Class Consciousness: Studies in Marxist Dialectics*, 223–55. London: Merlin, 1971.

—— [1923]. "Legality and Illegality." In *History and Class Consciousness: Studies in Marxist Dialectics*, 256–71. London: Merlin, 1971.

—— [1923]. "Critical Observations on Rosa Luxemburg's 'Critique of the Russian Revolution.'" In *History and Class Consciousness: Studies in Marxist Dialectics*, 272–94. London: Merlin, 1971.

—— [1924]. *Lenin: A Study in the Unity of His Thought*. London: New Left Books, 1970.

—— [1925–6]. "Tailism and the Dialectic." In *A Defence of* History and Class Consciousness, 45–149. London: Verso, 2000.

Luraghi, Raimondo. "The Civil War and the Modernization of American Society: Social Structure and Industrial Revolution in the Old South Before and During the War," *Civil War History* 18 (September 1972): 230–50.

Luttwak, Edward. *Turbo-capitalism: Winners and Losers in the Global Economy*. London: Weidenfeld and Nicolson, 1998.

Luxemburg, Rosa [1908–9]. "The National Question and Autonomy." In *The National Question: Selected Writings*, edited by Howard B. Davis, 101–287. New York: Monthly Review Press, 1976.

—— [1913]. *The Accumulation of Capital*. London: Routledge and Kegan Paul, 1963.

Lynch, John. *The Spanish American Revolutions, 1808–1826*. London: Weidenfeld and Nicolson, 1973.

MacIntyre, Alasdair [1958–59]. "Notes from the Moral Wilderness." In *Alasdair MacIntyre's Engagement with Marxism: Selected Writings, 1953–1974*, edited by Paul Blackledge and

Neil Davidson, 45–68. Leiden: E. J. Brill, 2008.

—— [1959]. "Hume on 'Is' and 'Ought.'" In *Against the Self-Images of the Age: Essays on Ideology and Philosophy*, 109–124. London: Duckworth, 1971.

—— [1960]. "Breaking the Chains of Reason." In *Alasdair MacIntyre's Engagement with Marxism: Selected Writings, 1953–1974*, edited by Paul Blackledge and Neil Davidson, 135–66. Leiden: E. J. Brill, 2008.

—— [1965]. "Marxist Mask and Romantic Face: Lukács on Thomas Mann." In *Alasdair MacIntyre's Engagement with Marxism: Selected Writings, 1953–1974*, edited by Paul Blackledge and Neil Davidson, 317–27. Leiden: E. J. Brill, 2008.

MacLeod, Ken. *The Restoration Game*. London: Orbit, 2010.

Mann, Michael. *The Sources of Social Power*, vol. 1, *A History of Power from the Beginning to 1760 AD*. Cambridge: Cambridge University Press, 1986.

——. "Ruling Class Strategies and Citizenship." In *States, Wars and Capitalism: Studies in Political Sociology*, 188–210. Oxford: Oxford University Press, 1988.

——. *The Sources of Social Power*, vol. 2, *The Rise of Classes and Nation-States, 1760–1914*. Cambridge: Cambridge University Press, 1993.

Manning, Brian [1976]. *The English People and the English Revolution, 1640–1649*. Second edition, London: Bookmarks, 1991.

——. *1649: The Crisis of the English Revolution*. London: Bookmarks, 1992.

Maravall, José Antonio. *La Cultura del Barroco: Análisis de una Estructura Histórica*. Barcelona: Ariel, 1975.

Marcuse, Herbert [1964]. "Industrialization and Capitalism in Max Weber." In *Negations: Essays in Critical Theory*, 201–26. Harmondsworth: Penguin, 1972.

Marshall, Gordon. *Presbyteries and Profits: Calvinism and the Development of Capitalism in Scotland, 1560–1707*. Oxford: Clarendon Press, 1980.

Martin, Ged. *Britain and the Origins of Canadian Confederation, 1837–67*. Houndmills: Macmillan, 1995.

Marx, Karl [1847]. *The Poverty of Philosophy: Answer to the* Philosophy of Poverty *by M. Proudhon*. In *Collected Works*, vol. 6, 105–212. London: Lawrence and Wishart, 1976.

—— [1848]. "Die Bourgeoisie und die Kontrerevolution," in *Werke*, Band 6, S, 102–24. Berlin: Dietz Verlag, 1959.

—— [1848]. "The Bourgeoisie and the Counter-Revolution." In *The Revolutions of 1848*, vol. 1 of *Political Writings*, edited by David Fernbach, 186–212. Harmondsworth: Penguin/New Left Review, 1973.

—— [1852]. "The Eighteenth Brumaire of Louis Bonaparte." In *Surveys from Exile*, vol. 2 of *Political Writings*, edited by David Fernbach, 143–249. Harmondsworth: Penguin/New Left Review, 1973.

—— [1855]. "Another British Revelation." In *Collected Works*, vol. 14, 513–18. London: Lawrence and Wishart, 1980.

—— [1856]. Marx to Engels, April 16, 1856. In *Collected Works*, vol. 40, 37–41. London: Lawrence and Wishart, 1983.

—— [1857–58]. *Grundrisse: Foundations of the Critique of Political Economy (Rough Draft)*. Harmondsworth: Penguin/New Left Review, 1973.

—— [1859]. "Preface to *A Contribution to the Critique of Political Economy*." In *Early Writings*, 424–28. Harmondsworth: Penguin/New Left Review, 1975.

—— [1862]. "Chinese Affairs." In *Collected Works*, vol. 19, 216–18. London: Lawrence and Wishart, 1984.

—— [1862–3]. *Theories of Surplus Value*, part 2, edited by S. Ryazanskaya. Moscow: Progress Publishers, 1969.

—— [1867]. *Capital: A Critique of Political Economy*, vol. 1, Harmondsworth: Penguin/New Left Review, 1976.

———— [1881]. Marx to Nieuwenhuis, February 22, 1881, in *Collected Works*, vol. 46, 65–66. London: Lawrence and Wishart, 1992.

———— [1894]. *Capital: A Critique of Political Economy*, vol. 3. Harmondsworth: Penguin/New Left Review, 1981.

Marx, Karl and Frederick Engels [1845–46]. *The German Ideology: Critique of Modern German Philosophy According to Its Representatives Feuerbach, B. Bauer and Stirner, and of German Socialism According to Its Various Prophets*. In *Collected Works*, vol. 5, 19–539. London: Lawrence and Wishart, 1975.

———— [1848]. "The Manifesto of the Communist Party." In *The Revolutions of 1848*, vol. 1 of *Political Writings*, edited by David Fernbach, 67–98. Harmondsworth: Penguin/New Left Review, 1973.

Maza, Sarah. "Luxury, Morality, and Social Change: Why There Was No Middle-Class Consciousness in Prerevolutionary France," *Journal of Modern History* 69, no. 2 (June 1997): 199–229.

————. *The Myth of the French Bourgeoisie: An Essay on the Social Imaginary, 1750–1850*. Cambridge, MA: Harvard University Press, 2003.

McDaniel, Tim. *Autocracy, Capitalism, and Revolution in Russia*. Berkeley and Los Angeles: University of California Press, 1988.

McLynn, Frank J. *The Jacobites*. London: Routledge and Kegan Paul, 1985.

————. *1759: The Year Britain Became Master of the World*. London: BCA, 2004.

McMurty, John. *The Cancer Stage of Capitalism*. London: Pluto Press, 1999.

McNally, David. *Political Economy and the Rise of Capitalism*. Berkeley and Los Angeles: University of California Press, 1988.

McPherson, James [1964]. *The Struggle for Equality: Abolitionist and the Negro in the Civil War and Reconstruction*. Princeton, NJ: Princeton University Press, 1995.

McPherson, James M. [1982]. "The Second American Revolution." In *Abraham Lincoln and the Second American Revolution*, 3–22. New York: Oxford University Press, 1991.

————. *Battle Cry of Freedom: The Civil War Era*. New York: Oxford University, 1988.

————. *For Cause and Comrades*. New York: Oxford University, 1997.

Mehring, Franz [1897]. "The German Reformation and Its Consequences." In *Absolutism and Revolution in Germany, 1525–1848*, 1–32. London: New Park, 1975.

Merrington, John. "Town and Country in the Transition to Capitalism." In *The Transition from Feudalism to Capitalism*, edited by Rodney H. Hilton, 170–195. London: New Left Books, 1976.

Mielants, Eric H. *The Origins of Capitalism and the "Rise of the West."* Philadelphia: Temple University Press.

Miliband, Ralph. "Barnave: A Case of Bourgeois Class Consciousness." In *Aspects of History and Class Consciousness*, edited by Istvan Meszaros, 22–48. London: Routledge and Kegan Paul, 1971.

———— [1075]. "Political Power and Historical Materialism." In *Class Power and State Power*, 50–62. London: Verso, 1983.

Milner, Clyde A. "National Initiatives." In *The Oxford Book of the American West*, edited by Clyde A. Milner, Carol A. O'Connor and Martha A. Sandweiss, 155–93. New York: Oxford University Press, 1994.

Mollat, Michael and Phillipe Wolff. *The Popular Revolutions of the Middle Ages*. London: George Allen and Unwin, 1973.

Mooers, Colin. *The Making of Bourgeois Europe: Absolutism, Revolution and the Rise of Capitalism in England, France and Germany*. London: Verso, 1991.

Moore, Barrington [1966]. *The Social Origins of Dictatorship and Democracy: Lord and Peasant in the Making of the Modern World*. Harmondsworth: Penguin, 1973.

Morris, William. "A Dream of John Ball." In *A Dream of John Ball* and *A King's Lesson*, London:

Reeves and Turner, 1888.

Musgrave, Peter. *The Early Modern European Economy*, Houndmills: Macmillan, 1999.

Nairn, Tom. "The Twilight of the British State," *New Left Review* 1, no. 101–2 (February–April 1977): 3–61.

Nauert, Charles G. *Humanism and the Culture of Renaissance Europe*. Cambridge: Cambridge University Press, 1995.

Needham, Joseph [1956]. *The Shorter Science and Civilisation in China*, vol. 1, abridged by Colin A. Ronan. Cambridge: Cambridge University Press, 1978.

Neocleous, Mark. *Administering Civil Society: Towards a Theory of State Power*. Houndmills: Macmillan, 1996.

Nesbitt, Nick. *Universal Emancipation: The Haitian Revolution and the Radical Enlightenment*. Charlottesville: University of Virginia, 2008.

Newitt, Malyn D. D. "Plunder and the Rewards of Office in the Portuguese Empire." In *The Military Revolution and the State, 1500–1800*, edited by Michael Duffy, 10–28. Exeter: University of Exeter Press, 1980.

Nischan, Bodo. "Confessionalism and Absolutism: The Case of Brandenburg." In *Calvinism in Europe, 1540–1620*, edited by Andrew Pettigree, Alastair Duke, and Gillian Lewis, 181–204. Cambridge: Cambridge University Press, 1994.

Novack, George. "Introduction." In *America's Revolutionary Heritage*, edited by George Novak, 9–20. New York: Pathfinder, 1976.

O'Brien, Patrick K. "The Impact of the Revolutionary and Napoleonic wars, 1793–1815, on the Long-run Growth of the British Economy," *Review* 12 (1989): 335–95.

Ogilvie, Sheilagh C. "Social Institutions and Proto-Industrialisation.," In *European Proto-Industrialization*, edited by Sheilagh C. Ogilvie and Markus Cerman, 23–37. Cambridge: Cambridge University Press, 1996.

[Ogilvie, William]. *An Essay on the Right of Property in Land, with Respect to Its Foundation in the Laws of Nature; Its Present Establishment by the Municipal Laws of Europe; and the Regulation by Which It Might be Rendered More Beneficial to the Lower Ranks of Mankind*. London: J. Walter, 1782.

Ohlmeyer, Jane. "The Civil Wars in Ireland." In *The Civil Wars: A Military History of England, Scotland and Ireland, 1638–1660*, edited by John Kenyon and Jane Ohlmeyer, 73–102. Oxford: Oxford University Press, 1998.

Ollman, Bertell [1979]. "Marxism and Political Science: Prolegomenon to a Debate on Marx's Method." In *Dance of the Dialectic: Steps in Marx's Method*, 135–54. Urbana: University of Illinois Press, 2003.

———— [2001]. "Why Does the Emperor Need the Yakuza? Prolegomenon to a Marxist Theory of the Japanese State." In *Dance of the Dialectic: Steps Marx's Method*, 193–216. Urbana: University of Illinois, 2003.

O'Rourke, Kevin H. "The Worldwide Economic Impact of the French Revolutionary and Napoleonic Wars, 1793–1815," *Journal of Global History* 1 (2006): 123–49.

Ossowski, Stanislaw [1957]. *Class Structure in the Social Consciousness*. London: Routledge and Kegan Paul, 1963.

Outhwaite, R. B. "Progress and Backwardness in English Agriculture, 1500–1650," *Economic History Review*, second series, vol. 39, no. 1 (February 1986): 1–18.

Outram, Dorinda. *The Enlightenment*. Cambridge: Cambridge University Press, 1995.

Overton, Mark, *Agricultural Revolution in England: The Transformation of Agrarian Economy, 1500–1800*. Cambridge: Cambridge University Press, 1996.

Parker, David. *Class and State in Ancien Regime France: The Road to Modernity?* London: Routledge, 1996.

Parker, Geoffrey. *The Military Revolution: Military Innovation and the Rise of the West, 1500–1800*. Cambridge: Cambridge University Press, 1988.

Patterson, Thomas C. *The Inca Empire*. Providence: Berg, 1991.

―――. *Inventing Western Civilisation*. New York: Monthly Review Press, 1997.

Paulin, Tom. "Introduction." In *The Faber Book of Political Verse*, 15–52. London: Faber and Faber, 1986.

Peck, Jamie. *Constructions of Neoliberal Reason*. Oxford: Oxford University Press, 2010.

Pellicani, Luciano. "Weber and the Myth of Calvinism," *Telos* 75 (Spring 1988): 57–85.

Pilbeam. Pamela M. *The Middle Classes in Europe, 1789–1914: France, Germany, Italy and Russia*. London: Macmillan, 1990.

Pinkus, Steve. *1688: The First Modern Revolution*. New Haven, CT: Yale University Press, 2009.

Plekhanov, Georgy V. [1895]. "The Development of the Monist View of History." In *Selected Philosophical Works*, vol. 1, 542–782. Moscow: Foreign Languages Publishing House, 1961.

Polisensky, Josef V [1970]. *The Thirty Years' War*. London: New English Library, 1974.

Poly, Jean-Pierre and Eric Bournazel [1984]. *The Feudal Transformation: 900–1200*. New York: Holmes and Meier, 1991.

Pomeranz, Kenneth. *The Great Divergence: China, Europe and the Making of the Modern World Economy*. Princeton, NJ: Princeton University Press, 2000.

Popper, Karl. *The Poverty of Historicism*. London: Routledge and Kegan Paul, 1957.

Porter, Bernard. *Empire and Superempire: Britain, America and the World*. New Haven, CT: Yale University Press, 2006.

Porter, Roy. *Enlightenment: Britain and the Creation of the Modern World*. London: Allen Lane, 2000.

Post, Charles. "Social Property Relations, Class Conflict and the Origins of the US Civil War: Toward a New Social Interpretation." In *The American Road to Capitalism: Studies in Class-Structure, Economic Development and Political Conflict, 1620–1877*, 195–251. Leiden: E. J. Brill, 2011.

Postan, Michael M. [1972]. *The Medieval Economy and Society*. Harmondsworth: Penguin, 1975.

Poulantzas, Nicos [1968]. *Political Power and Social Classes*. London: New Left Books, 1973.

Preobrazhensky, Evgeny A. [1924/1926]. *The New Economics*. Oxford: Clarendon Press, 1965.

Ransom, Richard and Richard Sutch. "Capitalists without Capital: The Burden of Slavery and the Impact of Emancipation," *Agricultural History* 62, no. 3 (1988): 133–60.

Rediker, Marcus. *Between the Devil and the Deep Blue Sea: Merchant Seaman, Pirates and the Anglo-American Maritime World, 1700–1750*. Cambridge: Cambridge University Press, 1987.

Reed, John [1919]. *Ten Days That Shook the World*. Harmondsworth: Penguin, 1977.

Rees, John. *The Algebra of Revolution: The Dialectic and the Classical Marxist Tradition*. London: Macmillan, 1998.

Rigby, Stephen H. *Marxism and History: A Critical Introduction*. Second edition, Manchester: Manchester University Press, 1998.

Ritzer, George [1993]. *The McDonaldization of Society: An Investigation into the Changing Character of Social Life*. Revised edition, Thousand Oaks, CA: Pine Forge Press, 1996.

Robertson, John. "The Enlightenment above National Context: Political Economy in Eighteenth-Century Scotland and Naples," *Historical Journal* 40, no. 3 (July 1997): 667–97.

―――. *The Case for Enlightenment: Scotland and Naples, 1680–1760*. Cambridge: Cambridge University Press, 2005.

Robespierre, Maximilien [1792]. "Extracts from 'Answer to Louvet's Accusation.'" In *Virtue and Terror*, 39–48. London: Verso, 2007.

Robin, Corey [2008]. "The First Counter-revolutionary." In *The Reactionary Mind: Conservatism from Edmund Burke to Sarah Palin*, 61–75. New York: Oxford University Press, 2011.

Rodinson, Maxime [1966]. *Islam and Capitalism*. Harmondsworth: Penguin, 1977.

Rothschild, Emma. *Economic Sentiments: Adam Smith, Condorcet, and the Enlightenment*. Cambridge, MA: Harvard University Press, 2001.

Rudra, Ashok. "Pre-Capitalist Modes of Production in Non-European Societies," *Journal of Peasant Studies* 15, no. 3 (April 1988): 373–94.

Runciman, Steven [1951]. *A History of the Crusades*, vol. 1, *The First Crusade and the Foundation of the Kingdom of Jerusalem*. Harmondsworth: Penguin, 1965.

Salmon, J. H. M. "The Paris Sixteen, 1584–94: The Social Analysis of a Revolutionary Movement," *Journal of Modern History* 44, no. 4 (December 1972): 540–76.

Saville, John. *The Consolidation of the Capitalist State, 1800–1850*. London: Pluto, 1994.

Sayer, Derek. *Marx's Method: Ideology, Science and Critique in* Capital. Brighton: Harvester, 1979.

Schama, Simon [1977]. *Patriots and Liberators: Revolution in the Netherlands, 1780–1813*. Second edition, London: Fontana, 1992.

Schmitt, Carl [1932]. "The Concept of the Political." In *The Concept of the Political*, 19–79. Expanded edition, Chicago: University of Chicago Press, 2007.

Schoenberger, Erica. "The Origins of the Market Economy: State Power, Territorial Control, and Modes of War Fighting," *Comparative Studies in Society and History* 50, no. 3 (2008): 663–91.

Schumpeter, Joseph A. [1919]. "The Sociology of Imperialisms." In *Imperialism and Social Classes*, edited by Paul M. Sweezy, 3–98. Oxford: Blackwell, 1951.

Schurz, Carl [1865]. "Report on the Condition of the South." In *Speeches, Correspondence, and Political Papers* Volume 1, *October 20, 1852 to November 26, 1870*, edited by Frederic Bancroft, New York: G. P. Putnam's Sons, 1913.

Semo, Enrique. *Historia Mexicana: Economía y Lucha de Clases*. México DF: Serie Popular Era, 1978.

———. "Reflexiones sobre la Revolución Mexicana." In Adolfo Gilly, Arnaldo Córdova, Armando Bartra, Manuel Aguilar Mora, and Enrique Semo, 135–50. *Interpretaciones de la Revolución Mexicana*. Mexico City: Nueva Imagen, 1979.

Sewell, William, *A Rhetoric of Bourgeois Revolution: The Abbé Sieyès and* What Is the Third Estate? Durham, NC: Duke University Press, 1994.

Shafer, Boyd C. "Bourgeois Nationalism in the Pamphlets on the Eve of the French Revolution," *Journal of Modern History* 10, no. 1 (March 1938): 31–50.

Shanin, Teodor. *Russia, 1905–07: Revolution as a Moment of Truth*, vol. 2 of *The Roots of Otherness: Russia's Turn of the Century*. Houndmills: Macmillan, 1986.

Shillory, Ben-Ami. "The Meiji Restoration: Japan's Attempt to Inherit China." In *War, Revolution and Japan*, edited by Ian Neary, Folkestone: Curzon Press, 1993.

Siegel, Paul M. *The Meek and the Militant: Religion and Power across the World*. London: Zed, 1986.

Silver, Beverley. *Forces of Labor: Workers' Movements and Globalization since 1870*. Cambridge: Cambridge University Press, 2003.

Simms, Brendan. *Three Victories and a Defeat: The Rise and Fall of the First British Empire, 1714–1783*. Harmondsworth: Penguin, 2008.

Skinner, Quentin. "The Origins of the Calvinist Theory of Revolution." In *After the Reformation: Essays in Honor of J. H. Hexter*, edited by Barbara C. Malament, 309–30. Manchester, Manchester University Press, 1980.

Skocpol, Theda. *States and Social Revolutions: A Comparative Analysis of France, Russia and China*. Cambridge: Cambridge University Press, 1979.

Slovo, Joe. "South Africa—No Middle Road." In Basil Davidson, Joe Slovo, and Anthony R. Wilkinson, *Southern Africa: The New Politics of Revolution*, 103–210. Harmondsworth: Penguin, 1976.

Smith, Adam [1762–63, 1766]. *Lectures on Jurisprudence*, edited by Ronald L. Meek, David D. Raphael, and Peter G. Stein, Oxford: Oxford University Press, 1978.

——— [1776]. *An Inquiry into the Nature and Causes of the Wealth of Nations*, edited by Edwin

Cannan. Chicago: University of Chicago Press, 1976.

Soboul, Albert [1962]. *The French Revolution, 1787–1799: From the Storming of the Bastille to Napoleon.* London: Unwin Hyman, 1989.

Spinoza, Baruch [1670]. *Tractatus Theologicus-Politicus.* Leiden: E. J. Brill, 1989.

Spufford, Peter. *Power and Profit: The Merchant in Medieval Europe.* London: Thames and Hudson, 2002.

Ste. Croix, Geoffrey de. *The Class Struggle in the Ancient Greek World: From the Archaic Age to the Arab Conquests.* London: Duckworth, 1981.

Stern, Steve J. *Peru's Indian Peoples and the Challenge of Spanish Conquest: Huamanga to 1640.* Madison: University of Wisconsin Press, 1982.

Stone, Lawrence [1970/1972]. "The Causes of the English Revolution." In *The Causes of the English Revolution, 1529–1642,* 47–164. London: Routledge and Kegan Paul, 1972.

Stone, Norman. *Europe Transformed, 1878–1919.* London: Fontana, 1983.

Tapia, Luis. "Constitution and Constitutional Reform in Bolivia." In *Unresolved Tensions: Bolivia Past and Present,* edited by John Crabtree and Lawrence Whitehead, 160–76. Pittsburgh: University of Pittsburg, 2008.

Tawney, R. H. [1922/1926]. "Preface to the 1937 Edition." In *Religion and the Rise of Capitalism,* vi–xiii. Harmondsworth: Penguin, 1961.

Tchakerian, Viken. "Productivity, Extent of Markets, and Manufacturing in the Late Antebellum South and Midwest," *Journal of Economic History* 54, no. 3 (1994): 497–525.

Teich, Mikulas. "Afterword." In *The Enlightenment in National Context,* edited by Roy Porter and Mikulas Teich, 215–217. Cambridge: Cambridge University Press, 1981.

Teschke, Benno. *The Myth of 1648: Class, Geopolitics and the Making of Modern International Relations.* London: Verso, 2003.

———. "Bourgeois Revolution, State Formation and the Absence of the International," *Historical Materialism* 13, no. 2 (2005): 3–26.

Thompson, Edward P. [1963]. *The Making of the English Working Class.* Second edition, Harmondsworth: Penguin, 1980.

———. "The Peculiarities of the English." In *The Socialist Register.* Edited by Ralph Miliband and John Saville, 311–62. London: Merlin Press, 1965.

———. "The Patricians and the Plebs." In *Customs in Common,* 16–96. London: Merlin, 1991.

Torrance, John. "Reproduction and Development: A Case for a 'Darwinian' Mechanism in Marx's Theory of History," *Political Studies* 33, no. 3 (1985): 382–98.

Torras, Jaime. "Class Struggle in Catalonia: A Note on Brenner," *Review* 4, no. 2 (Fall 1980): 253–65.

Torras, Jaume. "Peasant Counter-Revolution?" *Journal of Peasant Studies* 5, no. 1 (October 1977): 66–78.

Treblicock, Clive. *The Industrialization of the Continental Powers.* Harlow: Longman, 1981.

Trevor-Roper, Hugh R. [1961/1963]. "Religion, the Reformation and Social Change." In *Religion, the Reformation and Social Change and Other Essays,* 1–45. London: Macmillan, 1967.

———. "The Religious Origins of the Enlightenment." In *Religion, the Reformation and Social Change and Other Essays,* London: Macmillan, 1967.

Trotsky, Leon D. [1930–32]. *The History of the Russian Revolution.* London: Pluto, 1977.

——— [1932]. "What Next? Vital Questions for the German Proletariat." In *The Struggle against Fascism in Germany,* 110–244. Harmondsworth: Penguin, 1975.

——— [1933–5]. "The Notebooks in Translation." In *Trotsky's Notebooks, 1933–1935: Writings on Lenin, Dialectics, and Evolutionism,* 75–116. New York: Columbia University Press, 1986.

——— [1939]. "Three Conceptions of the Russian Revolution." In *Writings of Leon Trotsky [1939–40],* edited by Naomi Allen and George Breitman, 55–73. Second edition, New York: Pathfinder, 1973.

————[1940]. "Fragments from the First Seven Months of the War," in *Writings of Leon Trotsky: Supplement (1934–40)*, edited by George Breitman, 872–79. New York: Pathfinder Press, 1979.

Turley, David. "Slave Emancipations in Modern History." In *Serfdom and Slavery: Studies in Legal Bondage*, edited by Michael Bush, 181–96. London: Longman, 1996.

Twain, Mark [1883]. *Life on the Mississippi*. Teddington: Echo Press, 2006.

Unger, Richard W. *The Ship in the Medieval Economy, 600–1600*. London and Montreal: Croom Helm and McGill Queen's University Press, 1980.

Vanaik, Achin. "Subcontinental Strategies," *New Left Review* 2, no. 70 (July/August 2011): 101–14.

Venturi, Franco. *Utopia and Reform in the Enlightenment*. Cambridge: Cambridge University Press, 1971.

Vilar, Pierre [1956]. "The Age of Don Quixote," *New Left Review* 1, no. 68 (July–August 1971): 59–71.

Voltaire [1768]. Voltaire to D'Alembert, September 2, 1768. In *Oeuvres Complètes*, vol. 46. Paris: Bernier Frères, 1880.

Wallerstein, Immanuel. *The Modern World System II: Mercantilism and the Consolidation of the European World-Economy, 1600–1750*. New York: Academic Press, 1980.

————. *Historical Capitalism*. London: Verso, 1983.

————. "Eurocentrism and Its Avatars: The Dilemmas of Social Science," *New Left Review* 1, no. 226 (November/December 1997): 83–107.

Waswo, Ann. *Japanese Landlords: The Decline of a Rural Elite*, Berkeley and Los Angeles: University of California Press, 1977.

Watts, Michael. "Black Acts," *New Left Review* 2, no. 9 (May/June 2001): 125–39.

Weber, Max [1904–5]. *The Protestant Ethic and the Spirit of Capitalism*. London: George Allen and Unwin, 1976.

————[1921]. *Economy and Society: An Outline of Interpretative Sociology*, vol. 1, edited by Guenther Roth and Claus Wittich. Berkeley and Los Angeles: University of California Press, 1978.

Webber, Jeffery R. "Rebellion to Reform in Bolivia. Part II: Revolutionary Epoch, Combined Liberation and the December 2005 Elections," *Historical Materialism* 16, no. 3 (2008): 55–76.

————. *From Rebellion to Reform in Bolivia: Class Struggle, Indigenous Liberation, and the Politics of Evo Morales*. Chicago: Haymarket, 2011.

[Wedderburn, Robert]. [1549]. *The Complaynt of Scotland wyth ane Exortatione to the Three Estaits to Be Vigilante in the Deffens of their Public Veil*. 1549. With an appendix of contemporary English tracts, re-edited from the originals by J. A. H. Murray. London: Scottish Text Society, 1822.

Whitelaw, W. Menzies. "Reconstructing the Quebec Conference," *Canadian Historical Review* 19, no. 2 (June 1938): 123–37.

Whittle, Jane. *The Development of Agrarian Capitalism: Land and Labour in Norfolk, 1450–1550*. Oxford: Clarendon Press, 2000.

Wickham, Chris [1984]. "The Other Transition: From the Ancient World to Feudalism." In *Land and Power: Studies in Italian and European Social History, 400–1200*, 7–42. London: British School at Rome, 1994.

———— [1985]. "The Uniqueness of the East." In *Land and Power: Studies in Italian and European Social History, 400–1200*, 43–75. London: British School at Rome, 1994.

————. "Historical Materialism, Historical Sociology," *New Left Review* 1, no. 171 (September/October 1988): 63–78.

————. *Framing the Early Middle Ages, Europe and the Mediterranean, 400–800*. Oxford: Oxford University Press, 2005.

————. "Productive Forces and the Economic Logic of the Feudal Mode of Production," *Historical Materialism* 16, no. 2 (2008): 3–22.

Williams, Raymond. *The Country and the City*. Oxford: Oxford University Press, 1975.

Wilson, Peter H. *Europe's Tragedy: a History of the Thirty Years War*. London: Allen Lane, 2009.

Wohlforth, Tim [1963]. "The Theory of Structural Assimilation." In *"Communists" against Revolution: Two Essays on Post-war Stalinism*, 1–91. London, Folrose Books, 1978.

Wolf, Eric R. [1969]. *Peasant Wars of the Twentieth Century*. London: Faber and Faber, 1973.

————. *Europe and the Peoples without History*. Berkeley and Los Angeles: University of California Press, 1982.

Wood, Ellen Meiksins. "The Separation of the Economic and Political in Capitalism," *New Left Review* 1, no. 127 (May/June 1981): 66–95.

————. "Marxism and the Course of History," *New Left Review* 1, no. 147 (September–October 1984): 95–108.

————. *The Pristine Culture of Capitalism: An Essay on Old Regimes and Modern States*. London: Verso, 1991.

————[1999]. *The Origin of Capitalism: A Longer View*. London: Verso, 2002.

Wood, Neal. *John Locke and Agrarian Capitalism*. Berkeley and Los Angeles: University of California Press, 1984.

Woodward, Donald, "Wage Rates and Living Standards in Pre-Industrial England," *Past and Present* 91, (May 1981): 28–46.

Woolf, Stuart. "The Construction of a European World-View in the Revolutionary-Napoleonic Years," *Past and Present* 137 (November 1992): 72–101.

Wordie, J. R. "The Chronology of English Enclosure, 1500–1914," *Economic History Review*, second series, vol. 36, no. 4 (November, 1983): 483–505.

Wright, Eric Olin. "Gidden's Critique of Marx," *New Left Review* 1, no. 138 (March–April 1983): 11–35.

————. "Exploitation, Identity, and Class Structure: A Reply to My Critics." In *The Debate on Classes*, 191–211. Verso: London, 1989.

Wright, Eric Olin, Andrew Levine, and Elliot Sober. *Reconstructing Marxism: Essays on Explanation and the Theory of History*. London: Verso, 1992.

Wright, Gavin. "Capitalism and Slavery on the Islands: A Lesson from the Mainland," *Journal of Interdisciplinary History* 17, no. 4 (1987): 851–70.

Young, James D. *The Rousing of the Scottish Working Class*. London: Croom Helm, 1979.

Youngson, A. J. *The Making of Classical Edinburgh, 1750–1840*. Edinburgh: Edinburgh at the University Press, 1966.

Zagorin, Perez. *Rebels and Rulers, 1500–1660*, vol. 1, *Society, States and Early Modern Revolutions: Agrarian and Urban Rebellions*. Cambridge: Cambridge University Press, 1982.

INDEX

Abbott, Andrew, 5
absolutist states, 55–56
    characteristics of, 55
    See also precapitalist states
Abu-Loghod, Janet L., 59
Africa, 134–135, 138–139, 161
ahistorical anticapitalism, 158, 159
alternativity, 26
Althusser, Louis, 11, 73
American Civil War, 126–131, 154
American Constitution, 171
American War of Independence, 102–104
Amin, Samir, 56, 66, 122
ancien régime, 97, 103, 113, 118, 132
Anderson, Perry, 4
    on bourgeoisie, 70, 72, 79
    on capitalism in one country, 90
    on capitalist mode of production, 101
    on modes of production, 9
    on precapitalist modes of production, 58
Anglo-Chinese Opium War of 1839, 101
Anglo-Dutch Wars, 97
Argentina, 125
Armstrong, Alan, 160, 164, 165
Arrighi, Giovanni, 78
Ashworth, John, 131
Asiatic mode of production, 12
Auden, W. H., 144–145

Banaji, Jairus, 27, 49–50, 58–59, 92
Barg, Mikhail, 66–67
Baron, Hans, 75, 83
Bayly, Christopher, 64, 116, 120
Beard, Charles, 131
Beard, Mary, 131

Bell, David, 71
Benjamin, Walter
    on production, 34
Bensaïd, Daniel, 168
Berger, John, 74
Berktay, Halil, 57
Berman, Morris, 128
Bertram, Christopher, 24, 88
Binns, Peter, 141–142
Bismarck, Otto von, 4
Blackburn, Robin, 49, 163–164
Blanning, Tim C. W., 112
Blaut, James M., 49
Blum, Jerome, 116
Bohemia, Kingdom of, 81
Bois, Guy, 28, 52–53, 61
Bolivia, 124, 139, 140
Bookchin, Murray, 159–161, 168
bourgeois revolution(s)
    end of, 68–69, 133–136
    preconditions for, 21–89
    See also social revolution(s): eras of
    meanings and scope of the term, xvi, 4
    past, present, and future "projects" in,
        66–67
    reasons for studying, xii–xxv
    that did not take place (*see* revisionism)
    types of, xv
    See also specific topics
bourgeoisie
    reasons for the centrality of the non-
        economic, 79
    as a revolutionary leadership, 66–80
    See also specific topics
Brandon, Pepijn, 96, 97

Braudel, Fernand, 29, 32, 44, 73
Brenner, Robert, 38–42
    England and, 53
    France and, 56
Breuilly, John, 78
Brewer, John, 99
Britain. *See* England
Buck-Morss, Susan, 171
Bukharin, Nikolai I, 45–46, 121
Byres, Terence J., 39–40

Callinicos, Alex, 10, 29–30, 60, 92
Calvinism, 82–88
Calvinist International, 85
Calvinist Reformation. *See* Protestant
    Reformation
Canada, 131–133
    capital accumulation, establishing an
        independent center of, 92
capitalism, 158–160, 165–166
    bourgeois revolution and, xiii
    from capitalism to socialism, 12–20
    transition from feudalism to, 80
    See also under Anderson, Perry; Wood,
        Ellen Meiksins
capitalist alternative, possibility of a, 32–54
capitalist class, 93–94
capitalist states
    activities that they must perform, 93
    nature of, 109
capitalist world economy, 166–167
capitals, types of competition between, 78
Carling, Alan H., 33
Catholic Church, 77, 80–82, 84–86
Chadwick, Owen, 85–86
Chandra, Satish, 65
Chateaubriand, François-René de, 113
Chesneaux, Jean, 68
Chevington, John M., 156
Chibber, Vivek, 45
China, 136
Chinese Empire, 61–66
Chinese Revolution, 134
Choonara, Joseph, 124, 140
Christianity, 80–88. *See also* religion
Cipolla, Carlo M., 47
class struggle
    political and social revolutions
        varieties of, 5–12
class systems, struggle within vs. between,
    11–12
Cliff, Tony

on deflected permanent revolution, 141
on feudalism, 32
on French Revolution, 4
socialism and, 141
Coleman, Donald C., 46
Collier, Andrew, 34
commercial republicanism, 111
commercial society, 30
Communist Manifesto, The
    (Marx and Engels), 3, 11, 166, 170
competition between capitals, types of, 78
Constitution, U.S., 171
consummation, 20
    patterns of, 90
    the moment of systemic irreversibility,
        90, 95–101, 109
    necessary outcomes, 90–95
Corcoran, Paul E., 70–71
Coveney, Peter J., 53, 97
Crouzet, François, 113, 119
Cuba, 20, 135

D'Amato, Paul, 137
Dante Alighieri, 78, 79
Darwin, John, 65, 66
Davis, Mike, 50, 65, 66
Declaration of Independence, 169, 171
deflected permanent revolution, 137, 141–
    142
democracy
    See also "bourgeois-democratic" revolu-
        tion; "national-democratic" phase;
        Social Democracy
Deutscher, Isaac xi–xiii
Deutscher Memorial Prize, xi
Discovering the Scottish Revolution (David-
    son), xvii, 169
Dobb, Maurice, 50
Douglass, Frederick, xvii, 170–171
Draper, Hal, 7–8, 72, 94
Duby, Georges, 12
Duffy, Christopher, 46
Duplessis, Robert S., 42
Dutch Republic. *See* United Provinces
Dutch Revolt, 96, 141

Eagleton, Terry, xvi, 170
Eley, Geoff, 4, 8
emancipation
    See also slavery
Engels, Frederick

See also Communist Manifesto; specific topics
England, xviii
    lack of peasant revolt in, 17
    threats to, 98–99
    English Peasants Revolt of 1381, 171
    revolution of 1640 and, 10, 97–98, 117
    Scotland and, 9
    Steve Pinkus on, 98
    English revolutions, 98–99
    Calvinism and, 86
    origins of, 21–22
Enlightenment, 104–105, 151, 169
Epstein, Stephen R., 29
evolutionary rationalism, 150–151

Fanon, Frantz, 134–135
Ferguson, Adam, 62, 172
Ferraro, Joseph, 36
feudal crisis
    actuality of the, 27–32
    in France, 101–102
feudal fission (thesis), 33, 45
feudal vs. tributary mode, 56–57
feudalism, 54–55
    crisis of, 84
    Hobsbawm on, 97
    from slavery to, 8, 12–20
    Spanish imperialism as highest stage of, 49–50
    See also under Smith, Adam
Foucault, Michel, 104
France
    crisis of, 101–102
    See also Third Estate; *specific topics*
French Canadians, 132
French Physiocrats. See Physiocrats
French Revolution (1789–1799)
    Hobsbawm on, 3, 117
    lessons from, 117
    Lukács on, 6
    Theda Skocpol on, 7
    Tony Cliff on, 4
    uniqueness of, 101–114

García Linera, Álvaro, 139
Gatrell, Peter, 48
Genovese, Elizabeth Fox, 72, 103
Genovese, Eugene D., 72, 103
German Empire contrasted with Austro-Hungarian Empire, 119–120
German Unification, 4, 126, 132

Germany, 110, 160
Gerstenberger, Heide, 92–93
Giddens, Anthony, 11
Gilly, Adolfo, 69, 125
Global South, xix–xx, 41, 140, 142, 143
Goldmann, Lucien, 77
Goldstone, Jack A., 53
Goodwin, Jeff, 140
Gordon, Daniel, 169–170
Gouldner, Alvin W., 11
Gramsci, Antonio, 18
    on Christianity, 86–87
    Italy and, 78, 96
    on Netherlands, 96
    on organic crises, 23
    on organic intellectuals, 77
    prison letters and notebooks, 169
    on "two currents" in the Renaissance, 80
Great Reform (Bill/Great Reform Act), 9
Greenfield, Liah, 72, 96, 106
Griffiths, Jay, 158–159

Habermas, Jürgen, 75
Habib, Irfan, 64
Haldon, John, 57, 59
Hall, John A., 62
Halliday, Fred, 98
Harman, Chris, 141
Harrington, James
    on nobility governing Scotland, xii
Harvey, David, 33–34, 76
Haxthausen, August von, 69
Hayek, Friedrich A., 150–151, 153
Heller, Henry, 44, 86, 102, 103, 111–112
Hill, Christopher
    on English Revolution of 1640–60, 162–163
    on "projects" of the past, present, and future, 66–67
Hilton, Rodney H., 40
Hirschman, Albert O., 152
Hirst, Paul Q., 58
Historical Materialism (journal), xi
Hitchens, Christopher, xx, 151–152
Hobbes, Thomas
    on reason and passions, 149
Hobsbawm, Eric
    on Bohemia, 116
    on bringing revolutions to an end, 90
    on England, 94
    on feudalism, 97
    on French Revolution, 3, 117

on Hungary, 116
on revolutionaries, vii
on revolutions of 1848, 119
on United Provinces, 97
Hobson, John M., 61
Hoffman, Phillip, 43, 110
Holland. *See* Dutch Revolt
Holstun, James, 163, 164
Horkheimer, Max, 149
Hoyle, Richard, 45
Hume, David, 149, 151–153
Hundred Years' War (1337–1360), 54, 78
Hussite Revolt, 81

Intellectuals
bourgeois, 142, 153
"organic," 77–80
international structural adaptation, toward
from revolution to reform, 114–133
uniqueness of French Revolution, 101–
114
Iran, 141
Ireland, 19
irreversibility, moment of systemic, 90, 95–
101, 109
Isett, Christopher, 53
Israel, Jonathan I., 105
Italian Mezzogiorno, 129, 143, 155
Italian unification (il Risorgimento), 4, 126,
132, 143, 155
Italy, 80
defection of bourgeoisie in, 73

Jacobin methods, 125
Jacobins and Jacobinism, , 108–109, 111
Jamaica, 128
James, C. L. R., 52
James VI and I, 75–76
Japan. *See* Meiji Restoration
Jews and Judaism, 68
Jones, Gareth Stedman. *See* Stedman Jones,
Gareth

Kamen, Henry, 73–74
Katz, Claudio J., 10
Khaldun, Ibn El, 64
Kiernan, Victor G., 66
Kingsnorth, Paul, 139
Klooster, Wim, 141
Knight, Alan, 124

Latin America, 123–125, 128, 139, 161–

162
colonization of, 49–50
Lenman, Bruce J., 100
Lepore, Jill, xvii
Linebaugh, Peter, 160–161, 167
Livesey, James, 111
Lochhead, Robert, 21
Losurdo, Domenico, 2
Lowe, Lisa, 155
Lucas, Colin, 107
Lukács, Georg, 13, 18, 153
on French Revolution, 6
History and Class Consciousness, 6
on mediated totality, 33
on revisionism, 18
on transition from feudalism to capital-
ism, 22
Lutheran Reformation. *See* Protestant Ref-
ormation
Luttwak, Edward, 143
Luxemburg, Rosa, 122, 165–166
Lynch, John, 123

Machiavelli, Niccolò, 79, 80
MacIntyre, Alasdair, 2, 38
Mann, Michael, 77, 84
Mannerism, 80
market compulsion, 57
Marshall, Gordon, 82, 87–88
Maza, Sarah, 70, 71
McDaniel, Tim, 142
McLynn, Frank J., 99, 100
McMurtry, John, 161
McPherson, James, 131, 155
Meiji Restoration, 5, 6, 27, 93–94
Mexican Revolution, 68–69, 124–125
Mielants, Eric H., 30, 54, 59–60, 63–64
Miliband, Ralph, 107
Milton, John, 89
Mooers, Colin, 99
Morris, William, 171
Musgrave, Peter, 39

Nairn, Tom, 120
Naples, Kingdom of, 118
Napoleonic Wars, 112–116, 118, 119
"national-democratic" phase, 137–138
nationalism, 93
Native Americans, 126
Neocleous, Mark, 9
neoliberalism, 139
Netherlands, *See also* United Provinces

Netherlands Revolution,
  See also Dutch Revolt
New Model Army, 88, 112, 157
Nicaraguan Revolution, 141–142
Novack, George, 126

O'Connell, Daniel, xx
Ogilvie, Sheilagh C., 47, 60, 171–172
Old Calton Cemetery
  reflections in, 147–172
Ollman, Bertell, 33
"organic" crises, 10, 23, 24. *See also* feudal
  crisis
Orwell, George, xvii
Outhwaite, R. B., 41
Overton, Mark, 42–43

Paine, Thomas
  American Revolution and, xx
Paris, Treaty of, 100
Parker, David, 109–110
Patterson, Thomas C., 161
Paulin, Tom, 89
peasantry
  obstacles to becoming revolutionary
    force in the transition to capitalism,
    67–69
  opposing interests among, 69
Pellicani, Luciano, 87
performative contradiction, 169–170
permanent revolution
  deflected. (*see* deflected permanent revo-
    lution)
  future for, 136–144
  in United States, 130
Pilbeam. Pamela M., 105–106
Pinkus, Steve, 5, 98
Poland, xix–xxx
political economy. *See also* commercial soci-
  ety
Pomeranz, Kenneth, 62
Porter, Bernard, 95
Porter, Roy, 98
Portugal, 49–50
Post, Charles, 5, 126
Postan, Michael M., 30
Poulantzas, Nicos, 4
precapitalist states, structural capacities of,
  54–66
Preobrazhensky, Evgeny A., 91–92
production
  capitalist relations of (*see* capitalist social

property relations)
  establishing general conditions of, 93
  the forces and relations of, 34
  modes of, 92, 121
  productive force determinism, critique
    of, 36–37
Protestant Reformation, 148
  Enlightenment compared with, 104–
    105
  and the first ideology of transformation,
    82–86
Protestantism, 85

Qing Dynasty, 65
Quebec, 132, 133

racism, 154. *See also* slavery
rationality, 150
Rediker, Marcus, 48, 160–161, 167
Reform Act 1832. *See* Great Reform
  Bill/Great Reform Act
religion,151. *See also* Christianity
Renaissance, 80
revolutionary epoch, 10
revolutionary situations, 26
Revolutionary War. *See* American War of
  Independence
revolutions
  from below, 6, 24, 101, 107, 135, 156–
    157
Rigby, Stephen H., 36
Risorgimento. *See* Italian unification
Robertson, John, 105
Robespierre, Maximilien, 108
Roman Empire, 12, 15
Rosas, José Manuel de, 125
Rudra, Ashok, 91

Sachs, Michael, 139
Sayer, Derek, 34
Schmitt, Carl, 95
Schoenberger, Erica, 46
Schurz, Carl, 154–155
Scott, Walter, 154
Scottish Cemetery, reflections in a. *See* Old
  Calton Cemetery
Semo, Enrique, 124–125
Seven Years' War, 100
Sewell, William, 103–104, 108
Shafer, Boyd C., 106–107
Shanin, Teodor, 26
Shillory, Ben-Ami, 121

Siegel, Paul M., 151
Silver, Beverley, 143
Skinner, Quentin, 86
Skocpol, Theda, 6–7
slavery, 121
    in Portuguese Empire, 52
    in United States, 126–131, 154, 155
    See also American Civil War; feudalism
Slovo, Joe, 138–139
Smith, Adam
    on China, 62
    on colonialism, 49
    on commercial society, 30
    feudal absolutism and, 97, 153
    feudalism and, 30
    Hume and, 153
    legacy, 147–148
    on merchants and manufacturers, 94–95
    on war, 49
    The Wealth of Nations, 148
social crises, "organic," 10, 23, 24. See also
    feudal crisis
Social Democracy, 20
social revolution(s)
    eras of, 22
    between two, 1–5 (see also class struggle;
        socialism)
socialism
    from below, 20
    from capitalism to, 12–20
    in one country, 90, 137
Socialism in One Country, 137
South Africa, 138–139
Spain
    defection of bourgeoisie in, 73–74
Spanish Empire. See Dutch Revolt
Spanish imperialism as highest stage of
    feudalism, 49–50
Spinoza, Baruch, 87, 151
Stalin, Joseph V., 137
Ste. Croix, Geoffrey de, 91
Stedman Jones, Gareth, 79
Stone, Lawrence, 21
Stone, Norman, xix
Sweezy, Paul M., 50
Switzerland, 31–32

Tafur, King, 67
Tapia, Luis, 123–124
taxation, 60
Tea Party, xiv
Teich, Mikulas, 80

Teschke, Benno, xi, 56, 71, 98–99
Thatcher, Margaret, xix
Third Estate (France), 107
Thirty Years' War, 74, 75, 95, 110
Thompson, Edward P., 76, 167–168
Tibet, Chinese occupation of, 159
Torrance, John, 37–38
Torras, Jaime, 41
transformation
    the first ideology of, 80–89
Treblicock, Clive, 47
Trevor-Roper, Hugh R.
    on Calvinism, 85, 87
tributary empire, 66
tributary mode, 54, 56–58, 66
tributary states, , 5, 14, 62, 64, 66, 92, 94, 95
Trotsky, Leon D., 144
    capitalism and, 142
    on China, 1,820, 68
    on classes, 19
    on conceptions of Russian Revolution, 715
    democracy and, 139–140
    on international extension of Russian
        Revolution, 137
    on peasants and peasant uprisings, 31, 68
    permanent revolution and, 137, 139–140
    on reason, 150
    "turning point" analysis, 5
    uneven and combined development, 104

United Provinces (Dutch Republic), 23–25,
    80, 82, 84, 95–97
United States. See American Civil War;
    American War of Independence
Urban II, Pope, 67

van der Linden, Marcel, 96
Vanaik, Achin, 138
Venturi, Franco, 105
Villar, Pierre, 49
Voltaire, François Marie Arouet de, 151

Wallerstein, Immanuel, 95, 100–101, 158,
    159
Wang Fu-Chih, 62
Waswo, Ann, 93–94
Webber, Jeffery R., 10
Weber, Max, 81–83, 149
Wedderburn, Robert, 38–39
Whittle, Jane, 39, 40, 55–56
Wickham, Chris, 17, 24, 56–58, 60, 61
William II, Kaiser, 120

Williams, Raymond, 157
Wolf, Eric R., 68–69
Wood, Ellen Meiksins, 36, 38, 70
    on absolutism as a mode of production,
      56
    on capitalism, 22, 71, 94, 104
    on Enlightenment, 104
    Robert Brenner, Brenner thesis, and, 56
Wood, Neal, 71
Woodward, Donald, 41
Wordie, J. R., 42
Wright, Eric Olin, 37, 76
Wright, Gavin, 129

Young, James D., 36
Young, Neil, 161–162

ABOUT THE AUTHOR

© Cathy Watkins

Neil Davidson currently lectures in sociology with the School of Social and Political Science at the University of Glasgow. He is the author of *The Origins of Scottish Nationhood* (2000), *Discovering the Scottish Revolution* (2003), for which he was awarded the Deutscher Memorial Prize, *How Revolutionary Were the Bourgeois Revolutions?* (2012), *Holding Fast to an Image of the Past* (2014), *We Cannot Escape History* (2015), and *Nation-States* (2016).

ABOUT HAYMARKET BOOKS

Haymarket Books is a nonprofit, progressive book distributor and publisher, a project of the Center for Economic Research and Social Change. We believe that activists need to take ideas, history, and politics into the many struggles for social justice today. Learning the lessons of past victories, as well as defeats, can arm a new generation of fighters for a better world. As Karl Marx said, "The philosophers have merely interpreted the world; the point however is to change it."

We take inspiration and courage from our namesakes, the Haymarket Martyrs, who gave their lives fighting for a better world. Their 1886 struggle for the eight-hour day reminds workers around the world that ordinary people can organize and struggle for their own liberation.

For more information and to shop our complete catalog of titles, visit us online at www.haymarketbooks.org.

ALSO BY NEIL DAVIDSON

HOW REVOLUTIONARY WERE THE BOURGEOIS REVOLUTIONS?

HOLDING FAST TO AN IMAGE OF THE PAST
Explorations in the Marxist Tradition

NATION-STATES
Consciousness and Competition

WE CANNOT ESCAPE HISTORY
Nations, States and Revolutions

AS RADICAL AS REALITY ITSELF
Marxism and Tradition